Also by Sarah Schlesinger

500 Fat-Free Recipes

The Garden Variety Cookbook

The Pointe Book
(with Janice Barringer)

The Low-Cholesterol Olive Oil Cookbook
(with Barbara Earnest)

The Low-Cholesterol Oat Plan
(with Barbara Earnest)

500 Low-Fat Fruit and Vegetable Recipes

500 Low-Fat and Fat-Free Appetizers, Snacks, and Hors d'Oeuvres

500
(Practically)
Fat-Free
Pasta Recipes

500
(PRACTICALLY)
FAT-FREE
PASTA RECIPES

SARAH SCHLESINGER

Villard   New York

Library of Congress Cataloging-in-Publication Data
Schlesinger, Sarah.
500 (practically) fat-free pasta recipes / Sarah
Schlesinger.
p.   cm.
Includes index.
ISBN 0-679-45664-3
1. Cookery (Pasta)   2. Cookery (Rice)   3. Cookery (Cereals)
4. Low-fat diet—Recipes.   I. Title.
TX809.M17S248   1997
641.8′22—dc20   96-19384

To Sam Gossage, the co-creator of this book,
whose heart is the source and center of my happiness

Special thanks to Robert Cornfield, David Rosenthal, Annik La Farge, Ruth Fecych, Benjamin Dreyer, Brian McLendon, and the enthusiastic cooks and tasters who shared in the process of creating this book.

Diet and health are matters that vary greatly from individual to individual. Be sure to consult your physician about your personal needs before beginning any diet program. Consultation with a medical professional is particularly important if you are under medical care for any illness or are taking medication.

FOREWORD

During the past fifteen years our family has taken a diet and nutrition journey shared by millions of other Americans. When my husband, Sam Gossage, had his first heart attack, we began a self-education process that has brought us to a whole new way of thinking about food and has been the inspiration for six cookbooks related to the connection between eating and better health.

After multiple coronary bypass surgery and many changes in his lifestyle, exercise, and diet, Sam was told five years ago that although his heart was strong, his coronary arteries were blocked once again. However, this time surgery could not be safely undertaken. Rather than allowing this grim prognosis to be the final word, we decided to fight back with more dramatic dietary changes. Encouraged by Dr. Dean Ornish's book *Dr. Ornish's Program for Reversing Heart Disease Without Drugs or Surgery* (Random House, 1990) we began a drastic reduction in our daily fat and cholesterol consumption.

While our earlier dietary revisions made this new regimen easier to accept, we found that eating such a reduced-fat diet was incredibly inconvenient. At that point, there were very few fat-free foods on supermarket shelves, and restaurants had not acknowledged the possibility that some of their patrons were interested in fat-free or reduced-fat offerings. Our new diet required us to prepare almost everything we consumed, and we soon learned that few cookbooks addressed our specific needs. This led us to develop the collection of accessible recipes that became the basis of *500 Fat-Free Recipes*.

In communicating with readers about that book, we have discovered that reduced-fat and fat-free cooking is now a vital part of the mainstream American diet. The tremendous increase in new products on supermarket shelves and in low-fat and nonfat items on restaurant menus attests to this steadily growing concern with lower-fat eating. The doubters who expressed the opinion that Americans would not stick to lower-fat diets have been proven wrong.

After five years of eating an extremely low-fat and low-cholesterol diet, we consider it an eating plan for life. Sam has been thankfully free of new coronary events, and we have flourished on a largely vegetarian diet supplemented occasionally by small quantities of seafood and poultry.

The fact that we have spent these years eating food we genuinely enjoy has made it easy for us to adhere to this diet. Lower-fat and fat-free eating is not a fad or a craze for most people, who commit to it for either curative or preventive reasons. To be truly effective, it has to be a lifetime proposition. But a diet sharply reduced in fat can't work for anyone over an extended period of time if severe deprivation is a major part of the scenario.

We have learned that it is entirely possible to eat low-fat and fat-free and still eat a full spectrum of delectable foods. Our first years on the diet were about survival, but our emphasis now is on finding ways to savor good food in the framework of a specific ingredient list. Since manufacturers continue to emphasize snack foods and salad dressings as the primary area for developing low-fat and fat-free products, the best way to enjoy exciting soups, main dishes, side dishes, and salads is to create them in your own kitchens. We invite you to share our 500 low-fat recipes for pastas, rice, and grains with the hope that they will make your own journey to more healthful eating as pleasant and rewarding as ours has been.

CONTENTS

❋

RICE

GRAINS

INTRODUCTION

✦

500 (Practically) Fat-Free Pasta Recipes is a collection of 500 more ways to reduce the fat in your diet while enjoying great food. Each recipe contains 3 grams of fat or less per serving. Ranging from soup to dessert, these dishes are also limited in cholesterol and sodium and high in nutrients and fiber.

This book is a one-stop resource for creating easy, elegant soups, main dishes, side dishes, salads, and desserts in which pasta, rice, or grain is a main ingredient. The recipes are up-to-date, contemporary, nutritionally sound, and ethnically diverse. They'll guide you through low-fat strategies for creating simple, delicious, and versatile pasta, rice, and grain dishes for every occasion from a formal dinner to a quick snack. As we move toward a diet that is lower in fat and calories and higher in fiber and complex carbohydrates, pasta, rice, and grains have gained new importance. Some of our oldest foods are being rediscovered by contemporary cooks who are placing them in starring roles at mealtime. These convenient, versatile, and inexpensive foods are at the heart of this collection of recipes with roots in our past and the promise of a healthier future.

500 (Practically) Fat-Free Pasta Recipes is organized into three sections. The first, "Low-Fat Pasta Recipes," features a guide to cooking with pasta and recipes for pasta soups, pastas with vegetables and fruit, pastas with beans, pastas with seafood, and pastas with poultry. The second section, "Low-Fat Rice Recipes," starts with helpful hints on cooking with rice and includes rice dishes that range from soup to dessert. The third section, "Low-Fat Grain Recipes," introduces cooking techniques and dishes that are created from barley, bulgur, cornmeal, millet, hominy, buckwheat, couscous, and wheat berries.

Since each recipe focuses on lower-fat cooking, the cooking techniques and ingredients used have been selected to keep calorie, fat, and cholesterol counts low.

▪ LOW-FAT COOKING TECHNIQUES ▪

▪ A variety of liquids is used to replace the fat in cooking. Water, defatted chicken stock, vegetable stock, wine, and fruit or vegetable juices are often used to sauté ingredients. To sauté without fat, use a nonstick pan over a medium-high flame. Add liquid. Bring to a sizzle. Add food and stir quickly, making sure all the ingredients are cooked evenly.

▪ Foods are often steamed to avoid cooking with fat. To steam, fill a heavy saucepan with an inch or two of water, add the food in a steamer basket, cover with a snugly fitting lid, and steam over medium heat. Most vegetables that have been cut in serving-size pieces will steam in less than five minutes. Denser foods such as small new potatoes or large green beans may take ten or fifteen minutes. Foods that are steamed keep more of their water-soluble-vitamin content intact. When steaming, try using wine in place of water, or adding lemon juice or flavored vinegars to the water. Steaming liquids can be seasoned with garlic, onions, leeks, whole peppercorns, bay leaves, and fresh and dried herbs such as rosemary, basil, oregano, thyme, or dill.

▪ The only fat used is monounsaturated olive oil or canola oil in extremely small quantities. Butter and margarine are not used.

▪ Nonstick cookware is used for pan-sautéing and baking. Olive oil sprays are also used.

▪ INGREDIENTS ▪

The following foods are used in *500 (Practically) Fat-Free Pasta Recipes:*

Anchovies Anchovies are dark blue-and-silver fish found in warm waters. They average between 2½ to 3 inches and are sold fresh and preserved in either water or oil. A jar of salted anchovies should keep indefinitely if the fish are covered by liquid and taken out with a clean spoon. The canned, oiled variety will also keep well as long as the fish are covered in oil.

Artichoke Hearts Canned artichoke hearts are baby artichokes with tender leaves and bottom in which the bristly choke is undeveloped and therefore edible. Buy only artichoke hearts packed in water. They can be stored unopened on a cool, dry pantry shelf for a year.

Bamboo shoots The tender-crisp ivory-colored shoots of a particular, edible species of bamboo. They are cut as soon as they appear aboveground. Canned shoots are available in most supermarkets.

A nutritional analysis is given for each recipe per serving. This analysis includes calories; fat (in grams); cholesterol (in milligrams); protein (in grams); carbohydrates (in grams); dietary fiber (in grams); and sodium (in milligrams). Numbers in the analyses are rounded off to the nearest whole digit.

When the ingredient listing gives more than one choice, the first ingredient listed is the one analyzed. Optional ingredients are not included in the analyses.

Because of inevitable variations in the ingredients you may select, nutritional analyses should be considered approximate.

Be aware that some recipes are considerably higher in sodium than others because certain fat-free products, such as fat-free mayonnaise and fat-free cheeses, have very high sodium contents. If you are particularly concerned about controlling sodium intake, be sure to check the sodium counts in individual recipes.

▪ USEFUL EQUIPMENT FOR COOKING ▪ LOW-FAT PASTA, RICE, AND GRAINS

- Good stainless steel colander, large enough to hold 2 pounds of pasta
- Glass container marked for measuring in both ounces and cups
- Nest of measuring spoons from ¼ teaspoon to 1 tablespoon
- Wire whisk for mixing and blending
- Small cylindrical cheese grater
- Garlic press
- Parsley mincer
- Paring knife
- Big chef's knife
- Plastic gravy strainer or fat-separator cup with a long spout, to remove fat from soups, stocks, and sauces.
- Wooden forks of several sizes are good for stirring different lengths of pasta; spoons and flat wooden paddles are also useful for stirring sauces.
- Heavy commercial-gauge aluminum pans with nonstick interiors are good choices; buy these with removable handles so they can be popped into the oven or under the broiler.
- Baking pans with nonstick interiors
- Heavy skillets, medium and large, with nonstick surfaces
- Heavy saucepan with a snugly fitting lid and a stainless steel basket steamer insert
- Uncovered shallow rectangular roasting pans with racks in various sizes
- Large, shallow, flat-bottomed bowl for serving a large quantity of pasta
- Plastic and glass storage containers for pasta, rice, and grains
- Pots: Use a large stockpot or saucepan. Pots are available with built-in steamers or strainers that will allow you to lift cooked pasta out of the pot, leaving the hot water. Pasta strainers that will fit inside a large pot are also available. Enameled cast-iron pots from France and Belgium are excellent choices for cooking pasta and other grains. Copper pots are good for cooking sauces.
- Spaghetti forks: Forks that are designed to lift stranded pasta easily from boiling water and hold it firmly while the water is shaken off

▪ NUTRITIONAL CONTENT ANALYSIS ▪

The recipes in this book have been nutritionally analyzed using *Nutritionist IV* software. The primary sources for this database are USDA Handbooks No. 8, No. 16, and No. 81.

Barley   A hearty grain with a chewy texture and nutty taste. It looks like rice and puffs up when cooked. The soluble fiber in barley is believed to be just as effective as that in oats in lowering cholesterol levels. Barley is commercially hulled to shorten the cooking time. Pearled barley is the most common variety.

Bean Sprouts   Sprouts are infant plants that grow out of beans in a moist, warm environment. Look for moist and crisp-looking sprouts with a fresh scent. The shorter the tendrils, the younger and tenderer the sprout. Fresh sprouts will keep for 7 to 10 days in a plastic bag in the refrigerator. They should be kept moist but don't allow a lot of free water to build up on the inside of the bag. Canned bean sprouts are also available.

Beans   Cannellini beans, pinto beans, kidney beans, Great Northern beans, navy beans, black beans, chickpeas, black-eyed peas, and lentils are used in the recipes. Read labels on canned beans carefully. Most beans contain some natural fat, which will be indicated on the label. However, avoid those that have meats like bacon or pork added. Look for low-sodium products and/or drain them and rinse well before adding to a recipe. Rinsing can reduce the sodium in canned beans by half. If you begin with dry beans, 1 cup of dried beans (8 ounces) is equal to 2 to 2½ cups of cooked beans. Before cooking, wash and pick over beans, discarding cracked or shriveled ones.

Buckwheat   Buckwheat has a rich and earthy flavor. It can be used in cereals, pilafs, or salads, and also ground into flour for use in pancakes and baked goods.

Bulgur   Bulgur is made from whole wheat kernels. The wheat kernels are parboiled, dried, and partially debranned, then cracked into coarse fragments to make bulgur.

Canola Oil   Canola oil is lower in saturated fat than any other oil. It also contains more cholesterol-balancing monounsaturated fat *than any oil except olive oil,* and omega-3 fatty acids. It is a bland-tasting oil that can be used for both cooking and salad dressing.

Capers   Capers are the flower bud of a bush native to the Mediterranean and parts of Asia. They are picked, sun-dried, and packed in a vinegar brine. Capers should be rinsed before using. In your supermarket, look for capers near olives or in the gourmet food section.

Cayenne Pepper   Cayenne is a small, thin, hot red pepper usually found in a ground version on supermarket spice racks.

Cellophane Noodles Noodles made from powdered mung beans. These noodles have to be soaked, after which they are gelatinous and springy. They don't need to be cooked at all after soaking, but can be briefly stir-fried. Soak wiry bundles of cellophane noodles in warm water for 25 to 30 minutes, then cut with kitchen scissors to desired lengths.

Cheeses There are many fat-free cheeses on the market. Be sure to check the labels for their cholesterol content as well as fat content, since some of these products are also cholesterol free. Parmesan cheese, mozzarella cheese, cheddar cheese, Swiss cheese, American cheese, cream cheese, ricotta cheese, and cottage cheese are all available in fat-free form. Most of these cheeses are made from skim milk. Both fat-free cheese slices and grated products can also be found. These cheeses require special handling:

- Bake casseroles completely and sprinkle with shredded or grated nonfat cheeses when they come out of the oven. The heat from the food will melt the cheese.
- When broiling with nonfat cheeses, add the cheeses during the last 3 minutes.
- When adding cheese to soups or stews, stir in during the last 5 minutes of cooking.
- When baking layered dishes, such as lasagna, that include nonfat cheeses, cover with foil before baking.

Chicken All the recipes call for skinless chicken breast cutlets.

Chicken Broth Look for fat-free, low-sodium canned chicken broth. If you cannot find fat-free broth, refrigerate in a glass or plastic container without lid overnight (or place in freezer for 30 minutes) until fat congeals and rises to the top. Skim fat off before using. You can also make your own broth and skim the fat off before using. If you make a large quantity, you can freeze it in cubes for easy access. Homemade broth will have maximum flavor and quality if it is reduced by a third.

Chutney Chutney is a spicy condiment that contains fruit, vinegar, sugar, and spices. It can range in texture from chunky to smooth and can range in degree of spiciness from mild to hot. Mango chutney, which is readily available in most supermarkets, is suggested in some of the recipes.

Clams When buying hard-shell clams in the shell, be sure the shells are tightly closed. Tap any slightly open shells. If they don't snap closed, the clam is dead and should be discarded. Store live clams for up to 2 days in a 40-degree refrigerator.

Shucked clams should be plump and packaged in clear clam liquor. Store shucked clams in the refrigerator in their liquor for up to 4 days. Clams can also be purchased canned in the canned-fish section of your supermarket. Before steaming clams, scrub them thoroughly with a brush. Rinse several times. To steam clams, place ½ inch of water in the bottom of a steamer. Place clams on a steamer rack. Cover the pot and steam the clams over medium heat for 5 to 10 minutes or until they open, but no longer. Discard any unopened clams.

Cod   A popular white, lean, firm saltwater fish with a mild flavor. It is available year-round.

Cornmeal   Cornmeal is ground yellow or white corn kernels. Yellow cornmeal has more vitamin A. Cornmeal can be used to make polenta, an Italian pudding or mush that can be eaten hot or cold with sauce and other ingredients sprinkled over it.

Couscous   A precooked cracked-wheat product that is an alternative to rice, couscous is made from white durum wheat from which the bran and germ have been removed. Once cooked, it has a very light, airy quality and a silky texture. Couscous can be found with other grains such as rice, or in the imported-food aisle.

Crabmeat   Crabmeat is sold fresh, frozen, and canned. It may be in the form of cooked lump meat (whole pieces of the white body meat) or flaked meat (small bits of light and dark meat from the body and claws).

Curry Powder   Curry powder is a blend of herbs and spices, varying according to the country of origin. Curry powders can differ in intensity of flavor, so use them carefully. Curry flavor strengthens in a dish that is refrigerated and then reheated.

Dijon Mustard   Dijon is a strong French mustard that is easy to find in supermarkets. Avoid varieties with added oil or eggs. Store in the refrigerator.

Dressings   There are now many fat-free commercially prepared dressings on the market. Many are also packaged in dried form to be mixed as needed. Fat-free Italian dressing is used in recipes that might otherwise require large amounts of oil.

Eggs and Egg Substitute   Our recipes call for egg whites, but not for egg yolks, which are extremely high in cholesterol. Egg whites contain half the protein found in an egg, but no fat or cholesterol. Two egg whites can be substituted for a whole egg. When buying commercial egg substitutes, be sure to check the labels for fat content. Buy brands with 1 gram fat (or less) per serving. Eight ounces (1 cup) of a commercial egg substitute replaces 4 whole eggs and 8 egg whites. Two ounces (¼ cup) egg substitute is equivalent to 1 medium egg.

Fruit   Fresh fruits such as strawberries, cantaloupe, honeydew, peaches, nectarines, grapes, lemons, limes, raspberries, apples, and pears are often called for in the recipes. When fresh fruit is not available, consider substituting frozen or canned fruit. When using canned fruit, buy fruit packed in juice or water. Canned fruits used in the recipes include pineapples (crushed and chunk), mandarin oranges, pears, peaches, and apricots.

Dried Fruit: Keep raisins, dried apricots, peaches, pears, dates, pineapple slices, and prunes on hand. Dried fruit can be plumped in your microwave by combining ½ cup dried fruit with 2 tablespoons orange juice and microwaving for 2 minutes on HIGH until juice is absorbed. Let stand 5 minutes.

Flounder   Flounder is a large flatfish with a fine texture and delicate flavor. Flounder is available whole or in fillets.

Fruit Juice   Shop for natural juices without added sugar or syrup.

Garlic   Buy fresh garlic, chopped garlic packed without oil, and minced dried garlic. When buying fresh garlic, look for bulbs with large cloves. They are easier to handle and more flavorful than small cloves. Store garlic in a cool, dry place. Instead of sautéing fresh garlic, roast it in its skin to bring the flavor out before adding it to a dish. Before adding minced garlic to a dish, try microwaving it with a bit of lemon juice for 30 seconds.

Gingerroot   Fresh gingerroot, which adds a distinctive, spicy flavor to many dishes, can be found in the produce department of many supermarkets. To use, peel the tan skin and thinly slice the root. You can freeze leftover gingerroot wrapped in plastic freezer wrap until ready to use.

Grape Leaves   Buy unstuffed leaves in the international foods section of your supermarket or in Greek or Middle Eastern markets.

Haddock   Haddock, a lower-fat relative of cod, has a firm texture and a mild flavor.

Herbs   Herbs used in these recipes include basil, oregano, dill, rosemary, and sage. Dried herbs are called for because fresh herbs are not always available. However, be sure to substitute fresh herbs anytime you have access to them. Half a teaspoon of dried herbs equals 1 tablespoon of fresh herbs. Dried herbs should be replaced once a year. You can intensify their flavor by crushing or rubbing them between your fingers. Store dried herbs in airtight containers in a dark and cool place.

Hominy   Hominy is dried corn that has had its hull and germ removed with lye or soda. Hominy grits—ground hominy grains—are white and about the size of toast crumbs. They have a thick, chewy texture when cooked.

Honey   Honey is sweeter than granulated sugar and easier to digest. Its flavor and sweetness vary, depending on what kind of nectar the bees were eating when they made the honey.

Leeks   Leeks should have crisp, brightly colored stalks and an unblemished white portion. Avoid leeks with withered or yellow-spotted stalks. The smaller the leek, the more tender it will be. Refrigerate leeks in a plastic bag for up to 5 days. Before using, trim nodes and stalk ends. Slit leeks from top to bottom and wash thoroughly to remove all the dirt trapped between the layers.

Lemon Juice and Lime Juice   Lemon and lime juices are most flavorful when freshly squeezed. Store fresh lemons and limes in the refrigerator, or if using within a few days, at room temperature.

Lemon Peel   Either grate the peel of fresh lemons or buy grated lemon peel in the spice section of your supermarket.

Milk   Buy fresh skim milk, nonfat buttermilk, and instant nonfat dry milk.
   Evaporated Skim Milk: Evaporated skim milk can give dishes much of the richness of cream with almost none of the fat. It is a heat-sterilized, concentrated skim milk with half the water removed. As a result, the consistency of evaporated skim milk resembles that of whole milk. Once a can of evaporated skim milk has been opened, the contents should be refrigerated, tightly sealed, and used within five days.

Millet   A protein-rich cereal grain that is prepared like rice.

Mushrooms   Buy young, pale, cultivated button mushrooms. Brush and wipe them with a damp cloth. If you need to wash them, be sure to dry them thoroughly. When serving them raw, sprinkle with lemon or white wine to keep them light in color.
   Shiitake Mushrooms: Shiitake mushrooms can be found in the produce departments of many supermarkets. They are parasol-shaped, brownish-black, and

have a light garlic aroma. They contain B vitamins and minerals, and are available both fresh and dried. To reconstitute the dried ones, cover with water and soak for about 30 minutes, or until they are soft. Drain. Squeeze out excess water. Remove and discard stems. Other wild mushrooms called for in recipes are porcini, which are pale brown and have a smooth, meaty texture and pungent woodsy flavor. Wild mushrooms can be substituted for cultivated mushrooms in most recipes.

Mussels   Buy mussels with tightly closed shells or those that snap shut when tapped. Avoid those that have broken shells, that feel unusually heavy, or that feel light and loose when shaken. Fresh mussels should be stored in the refrigerator and used within a day or two. Scrub to remove sand and dirt, scraping off any barnacles from the shell with a knife, and remove the beard. To get rid of grit inside the shells, place mussels in a pot and cover with salted cold water. Add 1 tablespoon flour for each gallon of water in the bottom of a steamer. Place mussels on steamer rack. Cover the pot, and steam over medium heat for 5 to 10 minutes or until they open, but no longer. Discard any unopened mussels.

Nuts   Buy dry-roasted, unsalted nuts. Most nuts will keep for 1 month at room temperature and for 3 months in the refrigerator. They can also be frozen for 6 to 12 months. Frozen nuts do not need to be thawed before using.

Olive Oil   Buy mild light-flavored olive oil for all-purpose use, and extra-virgin olive oil to use as a dressing for cold dishes.
   Olive Oil Spray: Buy nonstick olive oil spray for spraying baking pans or other utensil surfaces while cooking. You can also buy an inexpensive plastic spray bottle and fill it with olive oil or canola oil.

Olives   Buy pitted green and black olives, and pimento-stuffed olives. Be sure to rinse them well to get rid of salty brine before using.

Orange Peel   Either grate the peel of fresh oranges, or buy grated orange peel in the spice section of your supermarket.

Orange Roughy   A low-fat fish with firm white flesh and a mild flavor.

Orzo   Orzo is a tiny pasta that resembles elongated rice or barley.

Parsley   Since fresh parsley is now widely available, we have specified its use in the recipes. Parsley may be either curly-leaf or flat-leaf. Flat-leaf parsley is often called Italian parsley; many cooks feel it is superior in taste.

pepper, crushed red pepper, allspice, caraway seeds, celery seeds, dry mustard, mustard seeds, poppy seeds, ground and stick cinnamon, ground coriander, ground cumin, ground ginger, nutmeg, paprika, saffron, and turmeric.

Tomatoes   It is important to use the right tomato for pasta dishes. When using canned tomatoes, choose Italian plum tomatoes if possible. Do not keep unopened canned tomato products for more than 6 months. Store them on a cool, dry shelf. After opening, canned tomato products should be stored in clean, covered glass containers. They tend to take on a metallic flavor if left in their cans. You can safely keep opened canned tomatoes in the refrigerator for a week. Leftover tomato paste and tomato sauce can be frozen for up to 2 months in airtight containers. Drop leftover tomato paste by the tablespoon on a sheet of wax paper and freeze. When frozen, place in a plastic freezer bag and store in freezer until needed. When using fresh tomatoes, choose firm, ripe ones. Ripen fresh tomatoes in a brown paper bag and leave the bag in indirect sunlight. To remove tomato skins, dunk the tomatoes in boiling water for 10 seconds, then dip them in cold water for 10 seconds. With a paring knife, remove the stem and peel the skin off.

Sun-Dried Tomatoes: Buy dry-packed sun-dried tomatoes if possible. If you can only find them packed in oil, rinse them in boiling water before using.

Tuna

Canned Tuna: Buy white albacore tuna that is packed in water, not in oil. Cans labeled "solid" or "fancy" contain large pieces of fish; those marked "chunk" contain smaller pieces.

Fresh Tuna: Fresh tuna is available from late spring into early fall. Frozen tuna is available year-round and is usually sold as steaks.

Turkey

Ground Turkey: Buy low-fat ground turkey breast with a fat content under 7 percent.

Smoked or Roast Turkey: When buying smoked and roast turkey at your deli counter, look for products that are at least 97 percent fat-free. Buy sliced, fresh roast turkey breast whenever available.

Vegetable Broth   Commercially prepared nonfat vegetable broth can be found at your supermarket. You can also make vegetable broth from leftover raw and cooked vegetables. Freeze it in cubes for easy access.

Vegetables   Fresh vegetables are used in the recipes whenever possible. Vegetables used include broccoli, green beans, lima beans, cabbage, carrots, cauliflower, celery, corn, cucumbers, eggplant, escarole, kale, okra, green peas, snow peas, potatoes, bell peppers, parsnips, spinach, summer and winter squash, and turnips. When using canned vegetables, look for those without added salt. When using frozen vegetables, look for frozen vegetables with no added salt or fat. Some frozen vegetables frequently called for in the recipes include corn, green peas, lima beans, and spinach.

Vinegars   Vinegars are very sour liquids fermented from a distilled alcohol, often wine or apple cider. Tightly capped vinegar keeps up to a year at room temperature, or until sediment appears at the bottom of the bottle.

Wine Vinegar: Buy red and white wine vinegars.

Balsamic Vinegar: Balsamic vinegar adds an elegant, complex, sweet-and-sour taste to food. It is aged in Italy in wooden casks for about four years with the skins from red wine grapes, which gives it a wine sweetness.

Cider Vinegar: Cider vinegar is made from apple cider.

Rice Wine Vinegar: Japanese and Chinese vinegars made from fermented rice are milder than most Western vinegars. They can be found in many supermarkets and in Asian markets.

Water Chestnuts   The canned variety of water chestnut, which is round and woody and about the size of a cherry tomato, can be refrigerated, covered in liquid, for 1 week after opening.

Watercress   Watercress has small dark-green leaves. Their flavor is pungent and slightly bitter, with a peppery snap. Choose crisp leaves that have a deep color and show no sign of yellowing or wilting. Refrigerate in a plastic bag for up to 5 days. Wash and shake dry before using. Watercress can be substituted for parsley in many recipes, and can be used as a garnish.

Wine   Dry white wine, red wine, and sherry are used as flavoring in some of the recipes. Nonalcoholic wines can be substituted if desired.

Wheat Berries   A chewy grain made from whole wheat kernels with only the outer layer removed. They have a nutlike taste and are bursting with nutrients.

Worcestershire Sauce   A thin, dark, piquant sauce that is usually a blend of garlic, soy sauce, tamarind, onion, molasses, lime, anchovies, vinegar, and various seasonings.

Yogurt   Buy only nonfat, plain yogurt with less than 1 gram of fat per serving.

PASTA

LOW-FAT PASTA RECIPES

❖

▪ ABOUT PASTA ▪

In today's nutrition-conscious world, pasta is one of our most popular health foods. Each year Americans eat more than 4 billion pounds of pasta, an average of 17 pounds per person. Pasta is high in energy-sustaining carbohydrates but low in calories.

Although pasta was long perceived as a "fattening food," in fact 2 ounces of uncooked spaghetti or macaroni provides only 210 calories. Pasta's image as a high-fat food comes from calorie-laden sauces and cooking methods and not from pasta itself. Pasta is low in fat and sodium; it's a good source of complex carbohydrates, and enriched pastas provide B vitamins, essential amino acids, and iron. The durum wheat from which most pasta is made is high in protein.

Pasta making has a long history. The Etruscans, who lived in Italy, had special pasta-shaping implements in the 4th century B.C. By 100 B.C. broad noodles were a regular part of the Greek diet, and rice and wheat noodles were being used throughout Asia in more complex dishes. To be assured of a constant supply of wheat, the ancient Romans kept granaries throughout their empire.

Noodles were commonplace in China and Japan by the 7th century A.D. By the 13th century, when Marco Polo left for his journey, noodles were a staple food in Italy, Asia, the Middle East, and part of North Africa. The Mongols, who, led by the Khans, swept across the Old World from western Asia may have introduced noodles to the Middle East and eastern Europe. Russia had been invaded by the Tartars, and as a result noodle-dough dumplings became an integral part of the Russian diet. Flat noodles were served in England at the court of Richard II in the 14th century.

Pasta making was considered an art in Italy by the 15th century. Thanks to the influence of the Arab invaders, Spaniards were also eating noodles. They brought them to the New World.

Noodle eating became common throughout Europe in the 18th century. Thomas Jefferson introduced pasta to the United States in 1786 after he returned from serving as ambassador to France. He brought home a spaghetti die (a pierced metal disc) and used it to make small quantities of pasta for his family and friends. But pasta did not appear commercially in the United States until 1848, when an Italian immigrant opened the first American pasta factory in Brooklyn, New York. After professional noodle-making machines became more sophisticated and technologically advanced, factories were opened in Italy and the United States in the 20th century, and the industry expanded.

▪ HOW PASTA IS MADE ▪

In Italian, *pasta* means "paste." And that's what pasta is: a pasty mixture of ground grain and liquid. "Pasta" is the general name for many variously shaped flour, water, and dough products ranging from broad lasagna noodles to tiny pastini for soup. Available in more than 150 different sizes and shapes, pasta can be classified as long goods (spaghetti), short goods (macaroni), specialty products (shells and bow ties), or egg noodles.

Pasta is made from durum and other hard wheats. These wheats give it a yellow-amber color, a nutty flavor, and the ability to retain its shape and firmness when cooked. Ingredients are sometimes added to give pastas a variety of colors. Beets and tomatoes impart a reddish hue, carrots an orange tint, spinach a green tone, and squid ink, a shade of black.

Pasta and noodles can be served hot or cold, spicy or mild, as main courses or side dishes. You can buy domestic or imported dried pasta (pasta secca), or commercially made or homemade fresh pasta (pasta fresca). The recipes in this book are based on dried pasta and typically call for 2 ounces of dried pasta per serving.

When dried pasta is manufactured, flour and water are combined and kneaded into a smooth dough, which is pressed through dies to produce solid rods. If a steel pin is placed in the center of each die, the dough emerges as hollow rods, macaroni. To produce short elbow styles, a notched pin is used, allowing the dough to move through more quickly on one side. Long strands of spaghetti and macaroni are placed on racks and put in drying ovens. The shorter varieties are placed on drying trays, then into drying cabinets. Pasta is dried slowly while filtered air constantly passes over it.

When shopping for dried pastas, look for brands that feature pasta made of the fine flour obtained from the cleaned endosperm or heart of the durum (hard) wheat grain, which is high in protein. This flour is called semolina. When ground it is yellow and has a coarse consistency similar to granulated sugar. Semolina gives structure and elasticity to pasta dough.

Fresh pastas can be bought in gourmet specialty shops, and many supermarkets now offer a variety of refrigerated and frozen packaged fresh pasta products. Fresh homemade pasta can either be rolled out by hand or made with a manual or electric pasta maker. Pasta-making attachments are also available for food processors and electric mixers. Electric pasta makers produce a pasta that has a roughened surface and allows easier absorption of liquids in sauces. Homemade pastas can be made from semolina flour or all-purpose flour. Making your own pasta offers the opportunity to experiment with different flours and to customize flavors and colors with vegetable juices, spices, and herbs.

Homemade pastas can be made from semolina flour or all-purpose flour. Many homemade pasta recipes include eggs and olive oil and are too high in cholesterol and fat for eaters concerned about watching their fat intake. However, you can create delicious pastas without using oil or eggs. Most homemade pasta recipe collections include one or two eggless choices, and you can experiment with decreasing the amount of oil used or dropping the oil altogether.

▪ PASTA COOKING TIME ▪

Fresh pasta is much moister than the dry product, so you need a greater weight for each serving—3½ ounces of fresh pasta, as opposed to 2 ounces of dry. You can substitute fresh pasta for dried pasta in the recipes in this book. When substituting fresh pasta for pasta in these recipes, be sure to follow cooking instructions on the fresh pasta package or in the guidebook that accompanies your pasta machine.

While cooking times for commercial pastas are suggested on the package, it is a good idea to test pastas beginning 1 or 2 minutes before the suggested cooking time is up. Do not cook pasta until it becomes mushy. It should be "al dente," or firm to the bite. If pasta breaks easily against the side of the pan when prodded with a spoon, it has probably been cooked too long.

Cooking time will vary between dried and fresh pastas; fresh pasta rarely requires more than 1 minute of cooking to become al dente. Cooking times also vary from manufacturer to manufacturer and with the pasta's size and shape. The thinner and moister the pasta, the shorter the cooking time. If the pasta is going to be used in a baked casserole, shorten the cooking time by a few minutes. Remember that pasta is still cooking even when the pot is removed from the stove and while you are tossing it with hot sauce.

Sample Dried-Pasta Cooking Times

Elbow Macaroni: 8 to 10 minutes
Farfalle: 11 to 12 minutes
Fettuccine: 10 to 12 minutes
Lasagne: 10 to 12 minutes
Linguine: 8 to 10 minutes
Manicotti: 10 to 12 minutes
Mostaccioli: 6 to 8 minutes
Rigatoni: 14 to 16 minutes
Rotini: 10 to 12 minutes
Spaghetti: 8 to 10 minutes
Vermicelli: 4 to 6 minutes
Ziti: 12 to 14 minutes

Tips for Cooking Pasta

- Always use enough water to allow pasta to swirl around to prevent sticking. For a pound of pasta, bring 4 to 6 quarts of water to a rapid boil in a large pot.
- Stir pasta immediately after adding it to the pot to prevent sticking.
- If you are cooking more than 2 pounds of pasta, use more than 1 pot. This will make draining easier.
- Adding salt to the cooking water is optional; if you are watching your sodium intake, don't add salt.
- Don't add oil to cooking water or sauce. It adds fat grams to the recipe and makes the pasta more slippery to handle.
- Have all ingredients ready before starting to cook pasta. When serving pasta with a sauce you are making from scratch, have the sauce components measured and arranged close by. If you are using previously prepared sauce, place it in a pot over low heat before you stir the pasta into boiling water.
- Protect your hands with two oven mitts when you are pouring pasta and water into a colander in the sink. Keep your head up to avoid the steam.
- Don't let drained pasta sit in the colander. If it is going into a sauce, toss it as soon as it is drained. Return pasta to the pot in which it was cooked after draining and toss with half of your topping or sauce, using two wooden forks or spoons. Dish pasta out onto individual serving plates. Add remaining sauce, cheese, and other garnishes, and serve. If pasta is going into a casserole or baked dish, assemble the dish as soon as the pasta is drained. If it is going into a salad, rinse it and assemble the salad ingredients as soon as possible.
- To eat pasta, put a fork into a few strands of spaghetti. Let the tines of the fork rest against the curve of the bowl or the curved indentation of the plate.

Pasta   See pages 3–9 for a full discussion of the pastas used in the recipes.

Peanut Butter   Buy reduced-fat peanut butter, which is available at supermarkets and health food stores.

Peppers

Bell Peppers: Sweet thick-fleshed peppers come in several colors. The flavor of red peppers is slightly sweeter than that of green peppers. Yellow peppers are even sweeter and more mellow.

Fresh Chile Peppers: Jalapeño peppers, frequently used in these recipes, are usually found green, but are sometimes red when ripe. They are small and blunt-tipped and range from hot to fiery. They will contribute less heat to a recipe if the seeds are removed. Be sure to wear protective gloves when handling pepper seeds and be careful to wash your hands immediately after handling them. Be especially careful not to touch your eyes.

Crushed Red Pepper: Crushed red pepper contains the seeds and flesh of the long red New Mexican chile. It's mildly hot and is often packaged as flakes, in shaker-top jars.

Canned Chile Peppers: Canned green chiles can be found in the international foods section of your supermarket with other ingredients used in Mexican cooking.

Pepper Sauce: Tabasco-type sauces are very hot purees of red chiles, vinegar, and numerous seasonings. They are bright red when fresh. They will last up to a year at room temperature. When pepper sauce turns brown, throw it out.

Red Snapper   Red snapper is a saltwater fish with reddish-pink skin and red eyes; it has firm flesh and very little fat.

Rice   See pages 185–188 for a full discussion of the various kinds of rice used in the recipes.

Saffron   Saffron is the most expensive spice in the world, but a tiny amount goes a long way. It can be purchased in threads, which can be steeped in water to release their full flavor, or in powdered form.

Salmon   Canned salmon, fresh salmon, and smoked salmon are called for in recipes in this book. Smoked salmon is fresh, uncooked salmon that has undergone a smoking process.

Salsas   Salsas, relishes made from chopped vegetables, can be found in your supermarket's condiments or chips aisle, or with the international foods. Some fresh-vegetable salsas are also kept in the refrigerator case alongside fresh tortillas.

Scallions   Choose those with crisp, bright green tops and a firm white base. Store, wrapped in a plastic bag, in the vegetable crisper of your refrigerator for up to 3 days.

Scallops   Scallops should have a sweet smell and a fresh, moist sheen. Because they perish quickly out of water, they're usually sold shucked. They should be refrigerated immediately after purchase and used within a day or two. Bay scallops average about 100 to a pound, and their meat is sweeter and more succulent than that of the sea scallop. Sea scallops average 1½ inches in diameter, and there are about 30 to a pound. Though slightly chewier, the meat of sea scallops is still sweet and moist.

Seeds   Buy raw, unsalted sesame and sunflower seeds.

Sesame Oil   This oil, made from sesame seeds, can be found in the international foods section of your supermarket or at Asian markets. Light sesame oil is milder than dark sesame oil.

Shrimp   Raw shrimp should smell of the sea, with no hint of ammonia. Cooked, shelled shrimp should look plump and succulent. Whether or not you devein shrimp is a matter of personal preference. Deveining small and medium shrimp is primarily cosmetic. However, in large shrimp, the intestinal vein may contain grit. There are usually 31 to 35 medium shrimp to a pound and 21 to 30 large shrimp to a pound. To cook fresh shrimp, drop them, unshelled, into boiling water, reduce the heat at once, and simmer for 3 to 4 minutes.

Snow Peas   Choose bright, crisp-colored pods with small seeds. Refrigerate in a plastic bag for up to 3 days. To prepare snow peas, trim ends and remove strings. Blanch for 15 seconds in boiling water. Remove with a slotted spoon, plunge into ice water, drain, and pat dry with paper towels.

Soy Sauce   Light soy sauce contains from 33 to 46 percent less sodium than regular soy sauce, with little to no difference in flavor. Store in refrigerator.

Sour Cream   Buy nonfat sour cream.

Spices   Keep dried spices tightly covered in an airtight container. Don't expose them to extremely high heat or intense light. Dried spices are best if used within 6 months to a year, so it is wise to date containers when you purchase or store them. During the summer months, store ground cayenne pepper, paprika, chili powder, and crushed red pepper in the refrigerator. Spices used in these recipes include black and white pepper, chili powder, cloves, ground cayenne

Twirl the fork, giving it brief, quick lifts to prevent too much pasta from accumulating.

▪ GUIDE TO THE DRIED PASTAS ▪ USED IN THE RECIPES

Angel's Hair—Sometimes called capelli d'angelo; very thin pasta. Often sold in clusters as well as in straight rods.

Bucatini—A long, round, thin spaghetti with a pierced hollow down the center.

Capellini—Very fine, delicate pasta. Like angel hair, but slightly thicker. Often sold in clusters as well as in straight rods.

Cavatelli—Short, curled noodles; dried cavatelli are shell-shaped, with a rippled surface and a slightly ruffled edge.

Conchiglie—Pasta "shells," in sizes from tiny to jumbo.

Conchiglie Rigati—Ridged pasta shells.

Conchigliette Piccole—Very tiny shells.

Cravatte—Bow-tie pasta.

Ditalini—"Little thimbles"; short lengths of very small macaroni.

Elbows—Pastas cut in small semicircles; elbow pasta may be ridged.

Farfalle—Often called bows or butterflies because of their shape.

Fedelini—Thin spaghetti cut into short curved lengths.

Fettuccelle—Narrow fettuccine.

Fettuccine—Fettuccine noodles are ¼ inch wide. The word *fettuccine* means "small ribbons."

Fusilli—A long, fat, solid spiral spaghetti, or a short fat screwlike pasta similar to rotelle.

Gemelli—Called twins because they look like two short, fat pieces of spaghetti twisted together like a rope.

Lasagne—Very wide, flat pasta usually used in baked dishes.

Linguine—Narrow, flat noodles. The word *linguine* means "little tongue."

Macaroni—Term used to describe hollow or pierced pasta products.

Mafalda—Broad, flat noodles rippled on both edges.

Manicotti—Tube pasta, 4 inches long and 1 inch in diameter, with the ends cut on the diagonal. Manicotti are often ridged.

Maruzze—Pasta shells, available from tiny to jumbo.

Mezzani—Tubular pasta 1 to 2 inches long, with a smooth exterior.

Mezzani Rigati—Tubular pasta 1 to 2 inches long, with a ridged exterior.

Mostaccioli—Their name means "small moustaches," but they look like penne: medium-sized pasta tubes, 2 inches long, with diagonally cut ends.

Orecchiette—"Little ears," which are round, fat, half-inch saucerlike disks.

Orzo—Small pasta that looks like rice and is cooked much the same way. Orzo is a staple in Greek cooking.

Penne—Tubular pasta, about 1½ inches long; the ends are cut diagonally. Penne have a smooth surface.

Penne Rigate—Penne with a ridged surface.

Perciatelli—Long, round, hollow spaghetti; a fatter version of bucatini.

Radiatore—Short, fat pasta, rippled and ringed like a radiator.

Rigatoni—Very large grooved tubular pasta.

Rotelle—Short (1½- to 2-inch), fat, wheel-like pasta, similar to fusilli. *Rotelle* means "small wheels."

Rotini—Rotini are a smaller version of rotelle.

Spaghetti—Long, thin, solid, round pasta, as distinguished from macaroni, which is round, but hollow; linguine, which is solid, but flatter; and noodles generally, which are flat.

Spaghettini—Long, thin, solid, round pasta, thinner than spaghetti.

Stivaletti—Small elbow macaroni.

Tagliatelle—Fettuccine-like noodles (the verb *tagliare* means "to cut"). Tagliatelle can be ¼ inch to ¾ inch wide.

Tortellini—Small, stuffed pasta.

Tubetti Lunghi—1-inch lengths of slim macaroni.

Vermicelli—Very thin strands of pasta, often sold in clusters as well as straight rods.

Ziti—Large tubular macaroni.

Ziti Rigati—Ziti with ridges.

You can use pasta other than that specified for each recipe by looking for a counterpart or an approximation of the specified pasta. Asian pastas, such as Japanese soba noodles, cellophane noodles, and rice sticks, can also be substituted in cold dishes.

■ USING LEFTOVER PASTA ■

- Cooked leftover pasta can be reheated in boiling water in a saucepan for 1 to 2 minutes. Drain.
- Leftover pasta can be reheated in a colander in the sink. Place pasta in colander. Pour boiling water over pasta until heated through. Drain.
- Heat leftover pasta in the microwave on HIGH for 2 to 3 minutes or until heated through.

▪ STORING PASTA ▪

Commercially dried pasta lasts indefinitely when stored in a cool, dry place. Once a package has been opened, transfer any unused contents to an airtight container.

Commercially prepared fresh pasta can be frozen according to package directions. Be alert to "sell" dates on these products. If they are held too long in the refrigerator case at your supermarket, they dry out.

Homemade pasta should be used within a week of making it if you intend to eat it undried. Place it loosely in an airtight container in the refrigerator for up to a week, or in the freezer for up to a month. Pasta can be dried completely for later use by placing it over a clothesline or towel rack or on the back of a chair for 4 hours. Or dry it in a loose heap on a towel. You can also wrap bunches of noodles around your hands to form loose nests and set them on a clean cloth to dry. When dried, placed in a metal, plastic, or glass container with a tight-fitting top, and stored in a cool, dry pantry or cabinet, homemade pasta will keep indefinitely.

PASTA SOUPS

Broccoli-Orzo Soup ▪ Orzo-Lentil Soup ▪ Tomato-Carrot Soup ▪
Leek and Angel Hair Pasta Soup ▪ Zucchini-Tomato-Fettuccine
Soup ▪ Black Bean–Fusilli Soup ▪ Elbow Macaroni–Pinto Bean
Soup ▪ Shiitake-Vegetable-Vermicelli Soup ▪ Quick White
Bean–Cavatelli Soup ▪ Chickpea-and-Stivaletti Soup ▪ Old World
Minestrone ▪ Radiatore-Shrimp Soup ▪ Conchiglie-Seafood
Chowder ▪ Conchigliette Piccole Soup ▪ Yellow Squash Soup with
Turkey Meatballs ▪ Zucchini-Orzo Soup

Broccoli-Orzo Soup

Orzo and broccoli are combined with yellow bell pepper, garlic, and chicken broth.

YIELD: 6 servings • PREPARATION TIME: 20 minutes •
COOKING TIME: 28 minutes

6¼ cups nonfat chicken broth
1 cup orzo
1 yellow bell pepper, cut into thin strips
1 clove garlic, minced

½ cup minced fresh parsley
1 teaspoon grated orange peel
3 cups diced broccoli stems
3 cups chopped broccoli florets

1. Bring 6 cups of chicken broth to a boil. Add orzo. Cook for 15 minutes.
2. Put remaining ¼ cup chicken broth in a skillet. Sauté yellow pepper for 5 minutes. Add garlic, parsley, and orange peel. Cook for 1 minute.
3. Add broccoli stems to orzo and cook for 5 more minutes.
4. Add broccoli florets. Simmer for 2 minutes.
5. Stir sautéed yellow bell pepper mixture into soup.

Calories Per Serving: 165
Fat: 2 g
Cholesterol: 0 mg
Protein: 12 g

Carbohydrates: 27 g
Dietary Fiber: 4 g
Sodium: 376 mg

Orzo-Lentil Soup

Lentils augment orzo in this simple, tasty soup.

YIELD: 5 servings • PREPARATION TIME: 15 minutes •
COOKING TIME: 45 minutes

1½ cups lentils, rinsed well
6¼ cups nonfat chicken broth
¼ teaspoon ground cumin

¼ teaspoon ground black pepper
¾ cup orzo
1 medium onion, chopped

1. Combine lentils, 6 cups broth, cumin, and black pepper in a large pot. Bring to a boil; reduce heat, cover, and simmer for 25 minutes.
2. Stir in orzo and continue to simmer until orzo and lentils are tender, about 20 more minutes. Stir in the onion and serve immediately.

Calories Per Serving: 125
Fat: 2 g
Cholesterol: 0 mg
Protein: 10 g

Carbohydrates: 21 g
Dietary Fiber: 2 g
Sodium: 424 mg

Tomato-Carrot Soup

Pasta shells are added to a hearty soup made with carrots, tomatoes, celery, onion, and basil.

*YIELD: 4 servings • PREPARATION TIME: 20 minutes •
COOKING TIME: 35 minutes*

¼ cup nonfat chicken broth
1 clove garlic
1 celery stalk, chopped
⅔ medium onion, chopped
2 cups shredded carrot

3½ cups low-sodium canned plum
  tomatoes
2 cups water
½ teaspoon dried basil
4 ounces ditalini
¼ teaspoon ground black pepper

1. Heat chicken broth in skillet over medium heat. Sauté garlic, celery, and onion for 3 minutes.
2. Stir in carrot, tomatoes, water, and basil and bring to a boil.
3. Reduce heat and simmer for 20 minutes.
4. Stir in the ditalini and cook for 8 more minutes.
5. Season with black pepper.

Calories Per Serving: 97
Fat: 1 g
Cholesterol: 0 mg
Protein: 4 g

Carbohydrates: 21 g
Dietary Fiber: 3 g
Sodium: 71 mg

Leek and Angel Hair Pasta Soup

Leeks and angel hair pasta are simmered in chicken stock.

*YIELD: 4 servings • PREPARATION TIME: 15 minutes •
COOKING TIME: 20 minutes*

5¼ cups nonfat chicken broth
4 leeks, sliced crosswise
2 tablespoons chopped green bell pepper
1 clove garlic, minced

½ cup angel hair pasta broken into 1- or
   2-inch lengths
¼ teaspoon ground black pepper

1. Heat ¼ cup chicken broth in a skillet over medium heat. Add leeks and sauté over low heat for 3 minutes, not allowing them to brown.
2. Add green bell pepper and garlic and sauté briefly.
3. Add remaining 5 cups chicken broth, pasta, and black pepper. Simmer for 10 minutes.

Calories Per Serving: 215
Fat: 2 g
Cholesterol: 0 mg
Protein: 12 g

Carbohydrates: 41 g
Dietary Fiber: 3 g
Sodium: 488 mg

Zucchini-Tomato-Fettuccine Soup

Zucchini, fettuccine, garlic, and onion are featured in this robust tomato soup.

YIELD: *8 servings* • PREPARATION TIME: *20 minutes* •
COOKING TIME: *40 minutes plus pasta cooking time*

3 pounds zucchini, diced
4 quarts plus ¼ cup water
6¼ cups nonfat chicken broth
4 cups chopped onion

8 cups chopped low-sodium canned
   tomatoes, with juice
3 cloves garlic, chopped
¼ teaspoon ground black pepper
8 ounces fettuccine

1. Combine zucchini and ¾ cup water in large soup pot. Cook over medium heat for 10 minutes.
2. Heat ¼ cup broth in large skillet over medium heat. Add onion and cook, stirring, until tender.
3. Add tomatoes, remaining broth, garlic, and black pepper to soup pot.
4. Bring 4 quarts water to a rapid boil in a second large, covered pot. Add pasta by holding it in a bundle at one end and slowly bending it inside the pot as the pasta softens. Keep water boiling; stir pasta with a long-handled wooden fork to prevent it from sticking together. Follow cooking time recommendation on package. Pasta should be cooked through but still firm. Check for

doneness by biting into a piece of pasta rinsed in cold water. Drain cooked pasta into a colander in the sink.

5. Add fettuccine to soup. Heat through.

Calories Per Serving: 332
Fat: 3 g
Cholesterol: 0 mg
Protein: 16 g

Carbohydrates: 66 g
Dietary Fiber: 5 g
Sodium: 305 mg

Black Bean—Fusilli Soup

Black beans and fusilli are combined with plum tomatoes.

YIELD: *8 servings* • PREPARATION TIME: *15 minutes* •
COOKING TIME: *18 minutes plus pasta cooking time*

5¼ cups nonfat chicken broth
1 medium onion, sliced
2 cloves garlic, minced
2 quarts water
4 ounces fusilli
3 large ripe tomatoes, diced

3½ cups low-sodium canned plum
   tomatoes, chopped, with juice
4 cups cooked or low-sodium canned
   black beans, rinsed and drained
¼ teaspoon ground black pepper

1. Heat ¼ cup chicken broth in a large soup pot over medium heat. Add onion and garlic. Sauté for 5 minutes.
2. Bring water to a rapid boil in a large, covered pot. Slowly stir in pasta. Return water to boil. Stir pasta with a long-handled wooden fork to prevent it from sticking together. Follow cooking time recommendation on package. Pasta should be cooked through but still firm. Check for doneness by biting into a piece of pasta rinsed in cold water. Drain cooked pasta into a colander in the sink.
3. Add remaining broth, ripe tomatoes, canned tomatoes, beans, and black pepper. Bring to boil. Reduce heat and simmer for 5 minutes.
4. Add cooked fusilli to soup. Heat through.

Calories Per Serving: 190
Fat: 2 g
Cholesterol: 0 mg
Protein: 13 g

Carbohydrates: 34 g
Dietary Fiber: 8 g
Sodium: 244 mg

Elbow Macaroni–Pinto Bean Soup

Elbow macaroni, pinto beans, tomatoes, green bell pepper, and onion are joined in this flavorful soup.

YIELD: 8 servings • *PREPARATION TIME: 20 minutes* •
COOKING TIME: 35 minutes plus pasta cooking time

4 cups low-sodium canned plum toma-
    toes, chopped, with juice
1 cup nonfat chicken broth
2½ quarts water
1 tablespoon lemon juice
5 cloves garlic, minced
½ cup chopped onion

½ teaspoon ground cumin
½ teaspoon hot pepper sauce
½ teaspoon dried basil
1 cup elbow macaroni
3 cups cooked or low-sodium canned
    pinto beans, rinsed and drained
1 cup chopped green bell pepper

1. Combine tomatoes, broth, 2 cups water, lemon juice, garlic, onion, cumin, hot pepper sauce, and basil in a large soup pot. Heat to boiling; reduce heat and simmer for 25 minutes.
2. Bring remaining 2 quarts water to a rapid boil in a large, covered pot. Slowly stir in pasta. Return water to a boil. Stir pasta with a long-handled wooden fork to prevent it from sticking together. Follow cooking time recommendation on package. Pasta should be cooked through but still firm. Check for doneness by biting into a piece of pasta rinsed in cold water. Drain cooked pasta into a colander in the sink.
3. Stir in pinto beans and green bell pepper. Simmer for 10 minutes.
4. Add pasta and heat through.

Calories Per Serving: 172
Fat: 1 g
Cholesterol: 0 mg
Protein: 9 g

Carbohydrates: 33 g
Dietary Fiber: 6 g
Sodium: 65 mg

Shiitake-Vegetable-Vermicelli Soup

This tangy soup combines shiitake mushrooms, Chinese cabbage, snow peas, and green bell pepper.

YIELD: 6 servings • *PREPARATION TIME: 25 minutes* •
COOKING TIME: 15 minutes plus pasta cooking time

2 quarts water
2 ounces vermicelli
6 cups nonfat chicken broth
½ teaspoon minced fresh gingerroot
2 cups chopped Chinese cabbage
1 cup snow peas
½ cup sliced carrots

½ cup sliced celery
½ cup chopped green bell pepper
6 fresh shiitake mushrooms, sliced
1 tablespoon rice vinegar
1 teaspoon reduced-sodium soy sauce
⅛ teaspoon cayenne pepper
4 scallions, chopped

1. Bring water to a rapid boil in a large, covered pot. Add pasta by holding it in a bundle at one end and slowly bending it inside the pot as the pasta softens. Keep water boiling; stir pasta with a long-handled wooden fork to prevent it from sticking together. Follow cooking time recommendation on package. Pasta should be cooked through but still firm. Check for doneness by biting into a piece of pasta rinsed in cold water. Drain cooked pasta into a colander in the sink.
2. Heat broth in a large soup pot and add gingerroot. Simmer for 10 minutes.
3. Add cabbage, snow peas, carrots, celery, and green bell pepper. Simmer for 3 minutes.
4. Add mushrooms, cooked vermicelli, rice vinegar, soy sauce, cayenne pepper, and scallions to soup pot. Heat through.

Calories Per Serving: 118
Fat: 2 g
Cholesterol: 0 mg
Protein: 8 g

Carbohydrates: 21 g
Dietary Fiber: 1 g
Sodium: 382 mg

Quick White Bean–Cavatelli Soup

Great Northern beans, cavatelli, onion, and garlic are simmered in chicken broth.

YIELD: 6 servings · PREPARATION TIME: 20 minutes ·
COOKING TIME: 20 minutes

½ cup cavatelli
¼ cup chopped red bell pepper
1 teaspoon dried basil
1 large tomato, chopped
1 medium onion, chopped

1 clove garlic, minced
3 cups cooked or low-sodium canned Great Northern beans, rinsed and drained
4 cups nonfat chicken broth

1. Combine all ingredients in a large soup pot. Bring to a boil.
2. Cover and simmer for 15 minutes, or until cavatelli are tender.

Calories Per Serving: 187

Fat: 2 g

Cholesterol: 0 mg

Protein: 14 g

Carbohydrates: 32 g

Dietary Fiber: 7 g

Sodium: 344 mg

Chickpea-and-Stivaletti Soup

Chickpeas and small elbow macaroni are the featured ingredients in this tomato soup.

*YIELD: 4 servings • PREPARATION TIME: 15 minutes •
COOKING TIME: 15 minutes plus pasta cooking time*

2 quarts water

4 ounces stivaletti

4 cups nonfat chicken broth

1 cup minced onion

2 garlic cloves, minced

1 cup low-sodium canned plum
    tomatoes, chopped, with juice

2 cups cooked or low-sodium canned
    chickpeas, rinsed and drained

1 teaspoon dried oregano

⅛ teaspoon ground black pepper

1. Bring water to a rapid boil in a large, covered pot. Slowly stir in pasta. Return water to a boil. Stir pasta with a long-handled wooden fork to prevent it from sticking together. Follow cooking time recommendation on package. Pasta should be cooked through but still firm. Check for doneness by biting into a piece of pasta rinsed in cold water. Drain cooked pasta into a colander in the sink.
2. Heat ¼ cup of chicken broth in a large soup pot over medium heat. Add onion and garlic. Sauté for 3 minutes.
3. Add remaining broth and tomatoes and bring to a boil. Reduce heat and simmer for 5 minutes.
4. Add chickpeas, pasta, oregano, and black pepper. Heat through.

Calories Per Serving: 106

Fat: 1 g

Cholesterol: 0 mg

Protein: 7 g

Carbohydrates: 19 g

Dietary Fiber: 4 g

Sodium: 127 mg

Old World Minestrone

This classic Italian soup is full of winter vegetables, two kinds of beans, and ditalini.

YIELD: 8 servings ▪ PREPARATION TIME: 25 minutes ▪
COOKING TIME: 40 minutes plus pasta cooking time

3½ quarts water
2 ounces ditalini
¼ cup nonfat chicken broth
1 large onion, chopped
1 carrot, chopped
4 cups chopped cabbage
2 cups low-sodium plum tomatoes,
   chopped

2 cups low-sodium canned dark red
   kidney beans, rinsed and drained
2 cups low-sodium cannellini beans,
   rinsed and drained
1 10-ounce package frozen chopped
   spinach, thawed
½ teaspoon dried thyme
⅛ teaspoon ground black pepper

1. Bring 2 quarts water to a rapid boil in a large, covered pot. Slowly stir in pasta. Return water to a boil. Stir pasta with a long-handled wooden fork to prevent it from sticking together. Follow cooking time recommendation on package. Pasta should be cooked through but still firm. Check for doneness by biting into a piece of pasta rinsed in cold water. Drain cooked pasta into a colander in the sink.
2. Heat chicken broth in a large soup pot over medium heat. Sauté onion and carrot for five minutes.
3. Add cabbage, tomatoes, and remaining 1½ quarts of water. Heat to boiling. Reduce heat to low. Simmer for 30 minutes.
4. Add kidney and cannellini beans, spinach, thyme, black pepper, and cooked ditalini. Simmer until heated through.

Calories Per Serving: 147
Fat: 1 g
Cholesterol: 0 mg
Protein: 11 g

Carbohydrates: 33 g
Dietary Fiber: 8 g
Sodium: 194 mg

Radiatore-Shrimp Soup

Radiatore and shrimp soup is flavored with the fresh citrus taste of lime and zesty cilantro.

Yield: 4 servings ▪ *Preparation Time: 10 minutes* ▪
Cooking Time: 9 minutes plus pasta cooking time

2 quarts plus 1 cup water
4 ounces radiatore pasta
4 cups nonfat chicken broth

¾ pound medium shrimp, shelled and
  deveined
¼ cup lime juice
1 teaspoon dried cilantro

1. Bring 2 quarts water to a rapid boil in a large, covered pot. Slowly stir in pasta. Return water to a boil. Stir pasta with a long-handled wooden fork to prevent it from sticking together. Follow cooking time recommendation on the package. Pasta should be cooked through but still firm. Check for doneness by biting into a piece of pasta rinsed in cold water. Drain cooked pasta into a colander in the sink.
2. Bring remaining water and broth to a boil over medium-high heat in a medium saucepan. Add the shrimp and cook for 5 minutes, or until the shrimp are pink.
3. Add pasta and heat through. Remove from heat.
4. Stir in lime juice and cilantro and serve.

Calories Per Serving: 192
Fat: 3 g
Cholesterol: 129 mg
Protein: 24 g

Carbohydrates: 18 g
Dietary Fiber: 1 g
Sodium: 123 mg

Conchiglie-Seafood Chowder

Scallops and fish are combined with conchiglie and vegetables in this delectable chowder.

Yield: 8 servings ▪ *Preparation Time: 25 minutes* ▪
Cooking Time: 33 minutes plus pasta cooking time

2 quarts water
4 ounces conchiglie
1½ cups low-sodium plum tomatoes,
   crushed
¾ cup white wine
6 cups nonfat chicken broth
2 carrots, diced
1 bay leaf
⅛ teaspoon red pepper

½ teaspoon dried basil
2 medium onions, chopped
4 cloves garlic, minced
1 large red bell pepper, chopped
1 lemon, sliced
½ pound bay scallops
1 pound haddock, cut into 1-inch cubes
¼ cup chopped fresh parsley

1. Bring water to a rapid boil in a large, covered pot. Slowly stir in pasta. Return water to a boil. Stir pasta with a long-handled wooden fork to prevent it from sticking together. Follow cooking time recommendation on package. Pasta should be cooked through but still firm. Check for doneness by biting into a piece of pasta rinsed in cold water. Drain cooked pasta into a colander in the sink.
2. Combine tomatoes, wine, 5¾ cups chicken broth, carrots, bay leaf, red pepper, and basil in large soup pot. Bring to a boil and simmer for 10 minutes.
3. Heat remaining ¼ cup chicken broth and sauté onions and garlic for 3 minutes. Add bell pepper and sauté for 3 more minutes. Add onion–bell pepper mixture to soup pot.
4. Add lemon slices, scallops, and haddock. Cover and simmer 8 minutes or until the fish is cooked.
5. Add cooked conchiglie and heat through.
6. Garnish with parsley.

Calories Per Serving: 243
Fat: 2 g
Cholesterol: 44 mg
Protein: 23 g

Carbohydrates: 31 g
Dietary Fiber: 2 g
Sodium: 327 mg

Conchigliette Piccole Soup

This easy pasta soup is made with carrot and celery.

YIELD: 4 servings ▪ PREPARATION TIME: 15 minutes ▪
COOKING TIME: 15 minutes

3 cups nonfat chicken broth
2 cups water
2 carrots, thinly sliced

2 stalks celery, thinly sliced
8 ounces conchigliette piccole

1. Bring broth, water, and carrot slices to boil.
2. Add the celery and conchigliette piccole. Reduce heat and simmer for 5 minutes, or until pasta is done.

Calories Per Serving: 141
Fat: 1 g
Cholesterol: 0 mg
Protein: 8 g

Carbohydrates: 26
Dietary Fiber: 1 g
Sodium: 284 mg

Yellow Squash Soup with Turkey Meatballs

Yellow squash, carrots, and conchiglie plus turkey meatballs make this a meal in a bowl.

YIELD: 7 servings • PREPARATION TIME: 25 minutes •
COOKING TIME: 27 minutes

¾ pound ground turkey breast
½ cup soft whole-grain bread crumbs
¼ cup chopped fresh parsley
⅛ teaspoon ground black pepper
5½ cups nonfat chicken broth

1½ cups chopped carrot
4 cups diced yellow summer squash
1 teaspoon dried oregano
8 ounces conchiglie

1. Combine ground turkey, bread crumbs, parsley, and black pepper in a bowl and blend thoroughly. Shape into 1-inch meatballs.
2. Heat ¼ cup chicken broth in a large soup pot over medium heat. Add meatballs and carrot. Cover and reduce heat. Cook 10 minutes or until turkey is no longer pink. Add more chicken broth as needed.
3. Add summer squash, remaining chicken broth, and oregano. Bring to a boil. Add conchiglie; cover, reduce heat, and simmer for 5 minutes.
4. Cover and simmer for 7 minutes.

Calories Per Serving: 206
Fat: 2 g
Cholesterol: 31 mg
Protein: 19 g

Carbohydrates: 30 g
Dietary Fiber: 2 g
Sodium: 314 mg

Zucchini-Orzo Soup

Zucchini and orzo are simmered with tomatoes, onion, and garlic.

YIELD: 6 servings • PREPARATION TIME: 20 minutes •
COOKING TIME: 20 minutes

6¼ cups nonfat chicken broth
1 medium onion, finely chopped
1 clove garlic, minced
1 stalk celery, chopped
2 medium zucchini, chopped
¼ teaspoon ground black pepper

2 cups fresh or low-sodium canned
    tomatoes, chopped
1 teaspoon dried basil leaves
1 teaspoon dried oregano
½ cup orzo
2 tablespoons chopped fresh parsley

1. Heat ¼ cup chicken broth in a large, heavy soup pot. Add the onion and garlic. Sauté, stirring often, until tender, about 3 minutes. Add the celery and
   zucchini and cook for 3 minutes. Add more liquid during this process if
   needed.
2. Add remaining broth, pepper, tomatoes, basil, oregano, and orzo. Bring to a
   boil, cover, and simmer for 8 minutes, or until orzo is tender.
3. Sprinkle with parsley before serving.

Calories Per Serving: 103
Fat: 2 g
Cholesterol: 0 mg
Protein: 8 g

Carbohydrates: 17 g
Dietary Fiber: 2 g
Sodium: 356 mg

PASTA WITH VEGETABLES

❖

Angel Hair Pasta with Asparagus in Mushroom-Wine Sauce · Fusilli with Asparagus-Ricotta Sauce · Bucatini with Asparagus and Sugar Snap Peas · Mafalda with Asparagus Sauce · Maruzze with Green Beans · Fedelini with Bok Choy · Garlic-Saffron Orzo · Ziti with Broccoli and Sliced Carrot · Tricolor Fusilli with Broccoli and Tomatoes · Ziti Rigati with Lemon Broccoli · Mostaccioli with Broccoli Sauce · Conchiglie with Broccoli and Red Onion · Rigatoni with Broccoli and Red Bell Pepper · Cravatte with Broccoli · Orzo-Stuffed Zucchini · Orzo with Cabbage and Tomato Puree · Green Pea–Raisin Orzo Pilaf · Fettuccine with Red Cabbage and Chickpeas · Baked Macaroni and Vegetables · Vermicelli with Cabbage and Carrot in Peanut Sauce · Fettuccelle with Carrot Sauce · Rotelle with Carrots · Radiatore with Cauliflower · Tortellini with Corn, Plum Tomatoes, and Thyme · Raisin-Almond Orzo · Eggplant-Mushroom Lasagna · Ziti Rigati with Eggplant Sauce · Spaghettini with Eggplant and Zucchini · Penne Rigate, Eggplant, and Ricotta Casserole · Cavatelli with Eggplant and Red Wine · Gemelli with Endive and Great Northern Beans · Orecchiette with Escarole · Capellini with Mushroom-Wine Sauce · Mezzani with Lemon-Mushroom Sauce · Perciatelli with Mushrooms and Peas · Spinach Fettuccine with Shiitake Mushrooms

in White Wine Sauce ▪ Fedelini with Red Onions and Roast Garlic ▪
Spaghettini with Green Bell Pepper Sauce ▪ Green Bell Pepper, Corn,
and Orzo ▪ Mezzani Rigati with Roasted Bell Peppers ▪ Farfalle
with Yellow-Pepper Topping ▪ Tricolor Fusilli with Tricolor Peppers
▪ Spinach Orzo ▪ Baked Orzo, Chickpeas, and Spinach ▪ Orzo-
Spinach Pie ▪ Spinach-Stuffed Lasagna Rolls ▪ Cavatelli with
Spinach-Anchovy Sauce ▪ Vermicelli with Spinach, Yellow Squash,
and White Beans ▪ Linguine with Spinach and Ricotta ▪ Shiitake-
Spinach Lasagna ▪ Angel Hair Pasta with Scallions ▪ Summer
Squash–Carrot Orzo ▪ Orzo with Black Olives and Sun-Dried
Tomatoes ▪ Tomatoes Stuffed with Orzo ▪ Rotelle with Fresh
Tomato Sauce ▪ Fettuccine with Cilantro-Tomato Sauce ▪
Spaghettini for Two with Red Onion–Tomato Sauce ▪ Radiatore
with Red Wine–Tomato Sauce ▪ Penne Arrabbiata ▪ Tagliatelle with
Jalapeño-Tomato Sauce ▪ Cavatelli for Two with Easy Coriander-
Cumin-Tomato Sauce ▪ Farfalle for Two with Tomato-Yogurt Sauce ▪
Angel Hair Pasta with Orange-Tomato Sauce ▪ Fedelini Puttanesca ▪
Cravatte with Mushroom-Tomato Sauce ▪ Bucatini with Tomato-
Curry Sauce ▪ Fusilli for Two with Arugula-Tomato Sauce ▪ Inside-
out Lasagna ▪ Mostaccioli with Zucchini ▪ Rigatoni with
Tomato-Zucchini Sauce ▪ Linguine with Gingered Zucchini ▪
Saffron Orzo with Vegetables ▪ Maruzze with Vegetable Sauce ▪
Vegetable-Stuffed Manicotti ▪ Garden Harvest Spaghetti ▪ Tricolor
Fusilli–Vegetable Salad ▪ Radiatore-Vegetable Salad ▪ Penne Rigate
Salad ▪ Farfalle-Fruit Salad ▪ Orange-Tomato Linguine ▪
Cravatte-Cucumber Salad

Angel Hair Pasta with Asparagus in Mushroom-Wine Sauce

Delicate angel hair pasta is served with asparagus, mushrooms, and white wine.

YIELD: 6 servings • *PREPARATION TIME: 20 minutes* •
COOKING TIME: 10 minutes plus pasta cooking time

1¼ cups nonfat chicken broth
¾ pound asparagus, cut into 1-inch
    lengths
4 scallions, sliced
4 cloves garlic, minced
2 cups sliced fresh mushrooms
1 large ripe tomato, diced
1 teaspoon dried basil

¼ teaspoon dried oregano
½ cup dry white wine
6 pitted black olives, sliced
½ teaspoon ground black pepper
6 quarts water
12 ounces angel hair pasta
¼ cup grated nonfat Parmesan

1. Heat ¼ cup broth in a large skillet. Add asparagus, scallions, and garlic. Sauté for 2 minutes. Add mushrooms; sauté for 2 additional minutes. Add tomato, basil, and oregano and sauté for 2 more minutes. Stir in wine, remaining broth, olives, and black pepper. Simmer for 4 minutes.
2. Bring water to a rapid boil in a large, covered pot. Add pasta by holding it in a bundle at one end and slowly bending it inside the pot as the pasta softens. Keep water boiling; stir pasta with a long-handled wooden fork to prevent it from sticking together. Follow cooking time recommendation on package. Pasta should be cooked through but still firm. Check for doneness by biting into a piece of pasta rinsed in cold water. Drain cooked pasta into a colander in the sink.
3. Serve sauce over pasta, topped with Parmesan.

Calories Per Serving: 281
Fat: 2 g
Cholesterol: 3 mg
Protein: 12 g

Carbohydrates: 50 g
Dietary Fiber: 2 g
Sodium: 157 mg

Fusilli with Asparagus-Ricotta Sauce

Fusilli are combined with asparagus, gingerroot, ricotta, and yogurt.

*YIELD: 4 servings ▪ PREPARATION TIME: 20 minutes ▪
COOKING TIME: 12 minutes plus pasta cooking time*

¼ cup nonfat chicken broth
1 pound asparagus, cut diagonally into
    half-inch pieces
3 scallions, minced
2 tablespoons minced fresh gingerroot
¾ cup nonfat ricotta, at room tempera-
    ture

¾ cup nonfat plain yogurt, at room
    temperature
4 quarts water
8 ounces fusilli
¼ teaspoon ground black pepper
¼ cup grated nonfat Parmesan

1. Heat broth in a large skillet. Add asparagus, scallions, and gingerroot. Sauté until asparagus is just tender, about 10 minutes.
2. Combine ricotta and yogurt in a blender or food processor and blend until smooth.
3. Bring water to a rapid boil in a large, covered pot. Slowly stir in pasta. Return water to a boil. Stir pasta with a long-handled wooden fork to prevent it from sticking together. Follow recommended cooking time on the package. Pasta should be cooked through but still firm. Check for doneness by biting into a piece of pasta rinsed in cold water. Drain cooked pasta into a colander in the sink.
4. Stir ricotta mixture into asparagus mixture.
5. Combine fusilli and asparagus-ricotta sauce. Season with black pepper.
6. Serve topped with Parmesan.

Calories Per Serving: 323
Fat: 2 g
Cholesterol: 9 mg
Protein: 21 g

Carbohydrates: 55 g
Dietary Fiber: 1 g
Sodium: 205 mg

Bucatini with Asparagus and Sugar Snap Peas

Bucatini are served with fresh asparagus, sugar snaps, and Parmesan.

*YIELD: 4 servings ▪ PREPARATION TIME: 15 minutes ▪
COOKING TIME: 4 minutes plus pasta cooking time*

4½ quarts water
8 ounces bucatini
1 pound fresh asparagus, cut into 1½-
inch pieces

½ pound sugar snap peas, strings re-
moved
1 teaspoon olive oil
2 tablespoons grated nonfat Parmesan
¼ teaspoon ground black pepper

1. Bring 4 quarts water to a rapid boil in a large, covered pot. Add pasta by holding it in a bundle at one end and slowly bending it inside the pot as the pasta softens. Keep water boiling; stir pasta with a long-handled wooden fork to prevent it from sticking together. Follow cooking time recommendation on package. Pasta should be cooked through but still firm. Check for doneness by biting into a piece of pasta rinsed in cold water. Drain cooked pasta into a colander in the sink.
2. Bring remaining 2 cups water to a boil. Add asparagus and boil 2 minutes. Add peas and boil until vegetables are just tender-crisp, about 2 minutes. Plunge asparagus and peas into cold water. Drain well.
3. Combine pasta with vegetable mixture in a large serving bowl. Drizzle with olive oil, sprinkle with Parmesan and pepper, and serve.

Calories Per Serving: 285
Fat: 3 g
Cholesterol: 5 mg
Protein: 14 g

Carbohydrates: 51 g
Dietary Fiber: 3 g
Sodium: 66 mg

Mafalda with Asparagus Sauce

Mafalda noodles are served with an asparagus and wine-leek sauce.

YIELD: 6 servings ▪ *PREPARATION TIME: 15 minutes plus 1 hour asparagus soaking time* ▪ *COOKING TIME: 16 minutes plus pasta cooking time*

1¼ cups nonfat chicken broth
2 cloves garlic, minced
1 leek, thinly sliced
½ cup dry white wine
½ teaspoon ground black pepper

1½ pounds fresh asparagus
6 quarts water
12 ounces mafalda
¼ cup grated nonfat Parmesan

1. Heat ¼ cup chicken broth in a large skillet. Stir in garlic and leek. Cover and simmer for 8 minutes. Stir in remaining broth, wine, black pepper, and asparagus. Bring to a boil, reduce heat, cover, and simmer for 8 minutes.

2. Cut tips from asparagus stalks and set aside. Transfer remaining asparagus mixture to a blender or food processor and process until smooth.
3. Bring water to a rapid boil in a large, covered pot. Add pasta by holding it in a bundle at one end and slowly bending it inside the pot as the pasta softens. Keep water boiling; stir pasta with a long-handled wooden fork to prevent it from sticking together. Follow cooking time recommendation on package. Pasta should be cooked through but still firm. Check for doneness by biting into a piece of pasta rinsed in cold water. Drain cooked pasta into a colander in the sink.
4. Pour asparagus sauce over pasta; top with asparagus tips and Parmesan.

Calories Per Serving: 336
Fat: 2 g
Cholesterol: 3 mg
Protein: 14 g

Carbohydrates: 63 g
Dietary Fiber: 1 g
Sodium: 118 mg

Maruzze with Green Beans

Maruzze are served with garlic-flavored green beans.

YIELD: 4 servings • PREPARATION TIME: 10 minutes •
COOKING TIME: 3 minutes plus pasta cooking time

3 cups fresh green beans, cut into 1-inch
    lengths
2 cloves garlic, crushed
4 quarts water

8 ounces small maruzze
1 teaspoon olive oil
3 tablespoons grated nonfat Parmesan

1. Combine beans, garlic, and 2 tablespoons water in a microwave-safe bowl and cover with vented plastic wrap.
2. Microwave on 100% HIGH for 3 minutes.
3. Bring water to a rapid boil in a large, covered pot. Slowly stir in pasta. Return water to a boil. Stir pasta with a long-handled wooden fork to prevent it from sticking together. Follow cooking time recommendation on the package. Pasta should be cooked through but still firm. Check for doneness by biting into a piece of pasta rinsed in cold water. Drain cooked pasta into a colander in the sink.
4. Combine pasta and beans in a large serving bowl. Toss with the olive oil and Parmesan.

Calories Per Serving: 204
Fat: 2 g
Cholesterol: 4 mg
Protein: 8 g

Carbohydrates: 39 g
Dietary Fiber: 3 g
Sodium: 38 mg

Fedelini with Bok Choy

Fedelini are served with bok choy, onion, and carrots.

YIELD: 6 servings ▪ *PREPARATION TIME: 15 minutes* ▪
COOKING TIME: 15 minutes plus pasta cooking time

1¾ cups nonfat chicken broth
1 medium onion, chopped
3 carrots, sliced
1½ teaspoons paprika
½ teaspoon ground black pepper
3 tablespoons reduced-sodium soy sauce

1 small head bok choy (about 1
pound), stems cut into 1-inch slices,
leaves cut into bite-size pieces
6 quarts water
12 ounces fedelini

1. Heat ¼ cup broth in a large saucepan. Add onion and carrots. Sauté until onion is lightly golden, about 3 minutes.
2. Stir in paprika and pepper; add remaining broth and soy sauce. Bring to a boil, reduce heat, cover, and simmer for 5 minutes. Stir in bok choy, and simmer for 3 minutes more. Increase heat and cook until most of the liquid is absorbed, about 3 minutes.
3. Bring water to a rapid boil in a large, covered pot. Add pasta by holding it in a bundle at one end and slowly bending it inside the pot as the pasta softens. Keep water boiling; stir pasta with a long-handled wooden fork to prevent it from sticking together. Follow cooking time recommendation on package. Pasta should be cooked through but still firm. Check for doneness by biting into a piece of pasta rinsed in cold water. Drain cooked pasta into a colander in the sink.
4. Top pasta with sauce and serve.

Calories Per Serving: 200
Fat: 1 g
Cholesterol: 0 mg
Protein: 9 g

Carbohydrates: 40 g
Dietary Fiber: 3 g
Sodium: 395 mg

Garlic-Saffron Orzo

Orzo is simmered in chicken broth and garlic, then tossed with saffron.

YIELD: 6 servings ▪ *PREPARATION TIME: 5 minutes* ▪ *COOKING TIME: 10 minutes*

4 cups nonfat chicken broth
10 cups water
2 cups orzo

3 cloves garlic, minced
¼ teaspoon powdered saffron

1. In a saucepan, bring chicken broth and water to a boil. Stir in orzo and garlic. Simmer until orzo is just tender, about 10 minutes.
2. Drain orzo. Transfer to a large serving bowl, toss with saffron, and serve immediately.

Calories Per Serving: 311
Fat: 2 g
Cholesterol: 0 mg
Protein: 15 g

Carbohydrates: 55 g
Dietary Fiber: 3 g
Sodium: 236 mg

Ziti with Broccoli and Sliced Carrot

Ziti is combined with steamed-sautéed broccoli and carrots, then sprinkled with Parmesan.

YIELD: 6 servings ▪ *PREPARATION TIME: 15 minutes plus vegetable steaming time* ▪ *COOKING TIME: 7 minutes plus pasta cooking time*

2¼ cups nonfat chicken broth
1 small white onion, finely chopped
2 cloves garlic, minced
4 cups broccoli florets, steamed tender-
   crisp

2 cups sliced carrots, steamed tender-
   crisp
6 quarts water
12 ounces ziti
¼ cup grated nonfat Parmesan
¼ teaspoon ground black pepper

1. Heat ¼ cup broth in a large skillet. Add onion and garlic and sauté until onion is light gold, about 3 minutes.
2. Add remaining chicken broth to onion; bring to boil. Reduce heat, stir in broccoli and carrots, and simmer for 2 minutes.

3. Bring water to a rapid boil in a large, covered pot. Slowly stir in pasta. Return water to a boil. Stir pasta with a long-handled wooden fork to prevent it from sticking together. Follow cooking time recommendation on the package. Pasta should be cooked through but still firm. Check for doneness by biting into a piece of pasta rinsed in cold water. Drain cooked pasta into a colander in the sink.
4. Combine pasta with broccoli-carrot mixture. Sprinkle with Parmesan and black pepper.

Calories Per Serving: 250
Fat: 2 g
Cholesterol: 3 mg
Protein: 12 g

Carbohydrates: 48 g
Dietary Fiber: 2 g
Sodium: 176 mg

Tricolor Fusilli with Broccoli and Tomatoes

A colorful combination of tricolor fusilli and a sauce of steamed broccoli, fresh tomatoes, and black olives.

YIELD: 5 servings • *PREPARATION TIME: 15 minutes* •
COOKING TIME: 11 minutes plus pasta cooking time

4 quarts water
8 ounces tricolor fusilli
¼ cup nonfat chicken broth
2 cloves garlic, minced
1 teaspoon cayenne pepper
8 pitted black olives, sliced

3 ripe tomatoes, chopped
1 tablespoon dried oregano
2½ cups broccoli, cut into bite-size
  pieces and steamed tender-crisp
¼ cup chopped fresh parsley

1. Bring water to a rapid boil in a large, covered pot. Slowly stir in pasta. Return water to a boil. Stir pasta with a long-handled wooden fork to prevent it from sticking together. Follow cooking time recommendation on the package. Pasta should be cooked through but still firm. Check for doneness by biting into a piece of pasta rinsed in cold water. Drain cooked pasta into a colander in the sink.
2. Heat broth in a large skillet over medium heat. Add garlic, cayenne, olives, and tomatoes. Sauté for 3 minutes. Add oregano; cover and simmer for 5 minutes.
3. Add steamed broccoli to sauce and heat through.
4. Mix together fusilli and sauce. Garnish with parsley and serve.

Calories Per Serving: 204

Carbohydrates: 39 g

Fat: 2 g

Dietary Fiber: 2 g

Cholesterol: 0 mg

Sodium: 101 mg

Protein: 8 g

Ziti Rigati with Lemon Broccoli

Ziti rigati is topped with broccoli in a lemon-caper sauce.

YIELD: 4 servings • *PREPARATION TIME: 10 minutes* •
COOKING TIME: 8 minutes plus pasta cooking time and broccoli steaming time

4 quarts water
8 ounces ziti rigati
¼ cup nonfat chicken broth
1 medium onion, finely chopped
3 cloves garlic, minced

3 cups broccoli florets, steamed tender-crisp
2 tablespoons lemon juice
1 tablespoon capers
⅛ teaspoon cayenne pepper

1. Bring water to a rapid boil in a large, covered pot. Slowly stir in pasta. Return water to a boil. Stir pasta with a long-handled wooden fork to prevent it from sticking together. Follow cooking time recommendation on the package. Pasta should be cooked through but still firm. Check for doneness by biting into a piece of pasta rinsed in cold water. Drain cooked pasta into a colander in the sink.
2. Heat broth in a large skillet. Add onion and garlic and sauté until onion is tender, about 3 minutes.
3. Add the ziti and broccoli and cook for 2 minutes.
4. Stir in the lemon juice, capers, and cayenne.

Calories Per Serving: 151

Carbohydrates: 31 g

Fat: 1 g

Dietary Fiber: 4 g

Cholesterol: 0 mg

Sodium: 31 mg

Protein: 7 g

Mostaccioli with Broccoli Sauce

This broccoli topping is made in the microwave in 3 minutes.

YIELD: *4 servings* • PREPARATION TIME: *10 minutes* •
COOKING TIME: *3 minutes plus pasta cooking time*

4 quarts water	2 tomatoes, chopped
8 ounces mostaccioli	3 cups chopped broccoli
2 cloves garlic, minced	1 tablespoon dried basil
½ cup nonfat chicken broth	1 tablespoon grated nonfat Parmesan

1. Bring water to a rapid boil in a large, covered pot. Slowly stir in pasta. Return water to a boil. Stir pasta with a long-handled wooden fork to prevent it from sticking together. Follow cooking time recommendation on the package. Pasta should be cooked through but still firm. Check for doneness by biting into a piece of pasta rinsed in cold water. Drain cooked pasta into a colander in the sink.
2. Combine the garlic, broth, tomatoes, and broccoli in a microwave-safe casserole dish. Cover and microwave on HIGH until the broccoli is bright green and just tender, about 3 minutes.
3. Toss the vegetables with the cooked pasta, basil, and Parmesan.

Calories Per Serving: 246
Fat: 2 g
Cholesterol: 1 mg
Protein: 11 g

Carbohydrates: 49 g
Dietary Fiber: 5 g
Sodium: 82 mg

Conchiglie with Broccoli and Red Onion

Broccoli, red onion, garlic, cayenne pepper, and Parmesan make a robust sauce for this dish.

YIELD: *4 servings* • PREPARATION TIME: *15 minutes* •
COOKING TIME: *15 minutes plus pasta cooking time and broccoli steaming time*

4 quarts plus 2 cups water	1 carrot, grated
8 ounces conchiglie	¼ teaspoon cayenne pepper
1 cup nonfat chicken broth	3 cups fresh broccoli cut into 1-inch
1 medium red onion, chopped	pieces
1 clove garlic, minced	3 tablespoons grated nonfat Parmesan

1. Bring 4 quarts water to a rapid boil in a large, covered pot. Slowly stir in pasta. Return water to a boil. Stir pasta with a long-handled wooden fork to prevent it from sticking together. Follow cooking time recommendation on the package. Pasta should be cooked through but still firm. Check for doneness by biting into a piece of pasta rinsed in cold water. Drain cooked pasta into a colander in the sink.

2. Heat ¼ cup broth in a skillet. Add onion and garlic and sauté until onion is lightly golden, about 3 minutes. Add carrot and sauté for 1 additional minute.

3. Add the remaining broth and the cayenne pepper. Simmer for 5 minutes. Remove from heat and set aside.

4. Bring remaining 2 cups of water to a boil in the bottom of a steamer. Add the broccoli and steam until tender-crisp.

5. Combine the broccoli with the onion mixture. Toss the conchiglie with the broccoli-onion sauce and the Parmesan.

Calories Per Serving: 274   Carbohydrates: 53 g
Fat: 2 g   Dietary Fiber: 5 g
Cholesterol: 4 mg   Sodium: 211 mg
Protein: 13 g

Rigatoni with Broccoli and Red Bell Pepper

This pasta dish can also be made with cauliflower and green bell peppers.

YIELD: 4 servings • PREPARATION TIME: 15 minutes •
COOKING TIME: 7 minutes plus pasta cooking time and broccoli steaming time

4 quarts water
8 ounces rigatoni
¼ cup nonfat chicken broth
1 red bell pepper, chopped
½ cup chopped onion
4 pitted black olives, sliced

½ teaspoon dried oregano
½ teaspoon ground black pepper
3 cups coarsely chopped broccoli,
    steamed for 3 minutes, drained
2 tablespoons grated nonfat Parmesan

1. Bring water to a rapid boil in a large, covered pot. Slowly stir in pasta. Return water to a boil. Stir pasta with a long-handled wooden fork to prevent it from sticking together. Follow cooking time recommendation on the package. Pasta should be cooked through but still firm. Check for doneness by biting into a piece of pasta rinsed in cold water. Drain cooked pasta into a colander in the sink.

2. Heat broth in a large skillet. Add red bell pepper and onion and sauté until onion softens, about 3 minutes. Add olives, oregano, and black pepper and sauté for 2 minutes.
3. Combine red pepper mixture with pasta and broccoli. Sprinkle with Parmesan.

Calories Per Serving: 259
Fat: 2 g
Cholesterol: 3 mg
Protein: 11 g

Carbohydrates: 51 g
Dietary Fiber: 5 g
Sodium: 168 mg

Cravatte with Broccoli

Bow-tie pasta is topped with a creamy broccoli-ricotta sauce.

YIELD: *4 servings* • PREPARATION TIME: *10 minutes* •
COOKING TIME: *8 minutes plus pasta cooking time*

4 quarts water
8 ounces cravatte
½ cup nonfat chicken broth
4 cups chopped broccoli

4 cloves garlic, minced
1½ cups nonfat ricotta
1 tablespoon dried basil

1. Bring water to a rapid boil in a large, covered pot. Slowly stir in pasta. Return water to a boil. Stir pasta with a long-handled wooden fork to prevent it from sticking together. Follow cooking time recommendation on the package. Pasta should be cooked through but still firm. Check for doneness by biting into a piece of pasta rinsed in cold water. Drain cooked pasta into a colander in the sink.
2. Meanwhile, heat broth in a skillet. Add broccoli and garlic, and sauté for 4 minutes. Reduce heat, cover, and simmer for 4 minutes.
3. Stir in ricotta and basil. Remove from heat.
4. Spoon sauce over hot pasta.

Calories Per Serving: 305
Fat: 1 g
Cholesterol: 6 mg
Protein: 23 g

Carbohydrates: 52 g
Dietary Fiber: 3 g
Sodium: 221 mg

Orzo-Stuffed Zucchini

Large zucchini halves are stuffed with a hearty mixture of orzo, chopped onion, and black beans.

YIELD: 4 servings • *PREPARATION TIME: 15 minutes* •
COOKING TIME: 28 minutes plus pasta cooking time

4 cups water
1 cup orzo
¼ cup nonfat chicken broth
1 medium onion, chopped
2 cloves garlic, minced

1 cup cooked or canned low-sodium
   black beans, rinsed and drained
½ teaspoon ground black pepper
2 large zucchini, halved lengthwise,
   seeds and about half of flesh
   removed

1. Bring water to a boil in a large saucepan. Stir in orzo and cook for 10 minutes.
2. In a large skillet, heat broth. Add onion and garlic and sauté for 3 minutes.
3. Preheat oven to 350 degrees.
4. Combine orzo, onions, beans, and black pepper. Arrange zucchini in a non-stick baking dish, fill with the orzo mixture, and bake until zucchini is tender and ingredients are heated through, about 25 minutes.

Calories Per Serving: 201
Fat: 1 g
Cholesterol: 0 mg
Protein: 10 g

Carbohydrates: 40 g
Dietary Fiber: 4 g
Sodium: 38 mg

Orzo with Cabbage and Tomato Puree

An unusual combination of orzo and cabbage in a tomato sauce flavored with marjoram.

YIELD: 8 servings • *PREPARATION TIME: 15 minutes* •
COOKING TIME: 20 minutes

¼ cup nonfat chicken broth
1½ cups chopped onion
3½ cups shredded cabbage
1 teaspoon dried marjoram
2 stalks celery, chopped

2 cups low-sodium tomato puree
2 cups water
¼ teaspoon ground black pepper
1 cup orzo

1. Heat chicken broth in a large skillet over medium heat. Add onion, cabbage, marjoram, and celery and sauté until cabbage is just tender.
2. Stir in tomato puree, water, black pepper, and orzo. Bring to a boil; reduce heat, cover, and simmer until orzo is just tender, about 15 minutes.

Calories Per Serving: 130
Fat: 1 g
Cholesterol: 0 mg
Protein: 6 g

Carbohydrates: 26 g
Dietary Fiber: 3 g
Sodium: 27 mg

Green Pea–Raisin Orzo Pilaf

Instead of rice, orzo is used in this tasty pilaf.

YIELD: 4 servings • *PREPARATION TIME: 15 minutes* •
COOKING TIME: 24 minutes

4¼ cups nonfat chicken broth
1 medium onion, chopped
½ cup raisins

1 cup orzo
¼ teaspoon ground black pepper
1 cup fresh or frozen green peas

1. Heat ¼ cup broth in a large skillet. Add onion and sauté for 3 minutes. Add remaining broth, raisins, orzo, and black pepper. Cover and simmer for 10 minutes.
2. Stir in peas and simmer until liquid is absorbed, about 10 minutes.

Calories Per Serving: 221
Fat: 2 g
Cholesterol: 0 mg
Protein: 11 g

Carbohydrates: 44 g
Dietary Fiber: 3 g
Sodium: 371 mg

Fettuccine with Red Cabbage and Chickpeas

Fettuccine is tossed with sautéed red cabbage, onion, garlic, and chickpeas.

YIELD: 6 servings • *PREPARATION TIME: 20 minutes* •
COOKING TIME: 12 minutes plus pasta cooking time

½ cup nonfat chicken broth
1 medium onion, thinly sliced
2 cups shredded red cabbage
2 cloves garlic, minced
3 tablespoons chopped fresh parsley

1 cup canned chickpeas, rinsed and
   drained
¼ teaspoon ground black pepper
6 quarts water
12 ounces fettuccine

1. Heat the broth in a large skillet. Add onion and sauté for 3 minutes.
2. Add the cabbage and garlic and sauté for 3 minutes. Cover and simmer for 5 minutes.
3. Add the parsley, chickpeas, and black pepper. Simmer for 4 minutes.
4. Bring water to a rapid boil in a large, covered pot. Add pasta by holding it in a bundle at one end and slowly bending it inside the pot as the pasta softens. Keep water boiling; stir pasta with a long-handled wooden fork to prevent it from sticking together. Follow cooking time recommendation on package. Pasta should be cooked through but still firm. Check for doneness by biting into a piece of pasta rinsed in cold water. Drain cooked pasta into a colander in the sink.
5. Toss sauce with pasta.

Calories Per Serving: 339
Fat: 2 g
Cholesterol: 0 mg
Protein: 13 g

Carbohydrates: 67 g
Dietary Fiber: 5 g
Sodium: 191 mg

Baked Macaroni and Vegetables

A modern variation on almost everyone's "security blanket."

YIELD: 6 servings • PREPARATION TIME: 20 minutes •
COOKING TIME: 30 minutes plus pasta cooking time

4 quarts water
8 ounces elbow macaroni
1 cup chopped broccoli
1 cup chopped carrots
1 cup chopped cauliflower
olive oil cooking spray
¼ cup nonfat chicken broth
2 scallions, sliced
3 tablespoons all-purpose flour

2 cups skim milk
¼ cup chopped fresh parsley
½ teaspoon ground black pepper
¼ teaspoon dried basil
¼ teaspoon dried thyme
1 cup nonfat cottage cheese
½ cup shredded nonfat mozzarella
¼ cup grated nonfat Parmesan
⅔ cup bread crumbs

1. Bring water to a rapid boil in a large, covered pot. Slowly stir in pasta. Return water to a boil. Stir pasta with a long-handled wooden fork to prevent it from sticking together. Follow cooking time recommendation on package. Pasta should be cooked through but still firm. Check for doneness by biting into a piece of pasta rinsed in cold water. Drain cooked pasta into a colander in the sink.
2. Pour 1 inch of water into the bottom of a steamer pot and bring to a boil. Place broccoli, carrots, and cauliflower in a colander or steamer basket over the boiling water and steam, covered, for 4 to 6 minutes, or until vegetables are just tender. Run cold water over vegetables, drain, and set aside.
3. Preheat oven to 350 degrees. Lightly spray a 2½-quart baking dish with olive oil cooking spray.
4. Heat broth in a large saucepan over medium heat. Sauté scallions for 3 minutes. Add flour and cook for several minutes, stirring constantly. Slowly add milk and continue to stir. Add parsley, pepper, basil, thyme, and cottage cheese. Cook until sauce thickens.
5. Combine macaroni, steamed vegetables, and cottage cheese sauce in a large bowl. Pour into baking dish. Bake for 15 minutes or until heated through. Top with grated mozzarella and bake for 5 more minutes.
6. Remove from oven, sprinkle with Parmesan and bread crumbs, and serve.

Calories Per Serving: 236
Fat: 1 g
Cholesterol: 7 mg
Protein: 19 g

Carbohydrates: 38 g
Dietary Fiber: 3 g
Sodium: 390 mg

Vermicelli with Cabbage and Carrot in Peanut Sauce

An Asian-style dish of vermicelli with fresh vegetables and peanut-sesame sauce.

YIELD: *4 servings* • PREPARATION TIME: *10 minutes* •
COOKING TIME: *3 minutes plus pasta cooking time*

4 quarts water
4 ounces vermicelli
1 tablespoon reduced-sodium soy sauce
2 tablespoons reduced-fat peanut butter
3 tablespoons rice vinegar

1 teaspoon sesame oil
¼ cup minced scallions
2 cups thinly sliced green cabbage
1 carrot, cut into very thin strips

1. Bring water to a rapid boil in a large, covered pot. Add pasta by holding it in a bundle at one end and slowly bending it inside the pot as the pasta softens. Keep water boiling; stir pasta with a long-handled wooden fork to prevent it from sticking together. Follow cooking time recommendation on package. Pasta should be cooked through but still firm. Check for doneness by biting into a piece of pasta rinsed in cold water. Drain cooked pasta into a colander in the sink.
2. To make the peanut-sesame sauce, combine the soy sauce, peanut butter, rice vinegar, and sesame oil.
3. Toss the scallions, cabbage, and carrot in a large bowl with the pasta. Pour the peanut-sesame sauce over the pasta-and-vegetable mixture.

Calories Per Serving: 161
Fat: 3 g
Cholesterol: 0 mg
Protein: 5 g

Carbohydrates: 28 g
Dietary Fiber: 1 g
Sodium: 210 mg

Fettuccelle with Carrot Sauce

Fettuccelle are topped with a creamy puree of carrots, ricotta, and yogurt.

YIELD: *2 servings* ▪ PREPARATION TIME: *15 minutes plus carrot steaming time* ▪
COOKING TIME: *5 minutes plus pasta cooking time*

2 quarts water
4 ounces fettuccelle
1½ cups baby carrots, cut lengthwise into quarters and steamed tender-crisp

½ cup nonfat ricotta
½ cup nonfat plain yogurt
¼ teaspoon ground nutmeg
⅛ teaspoon ground black pepper

1. Bring water to a rapid boil in a large, covered pot. Add pasta by holding it in a bundle at one end and slowly bending it inside the pot as the pasta softens. Keep water boiling; stir pasta with a long-handled wooden fork to prevent it from sticking together. Follow cooking time recommendation on package. Pasta should be cooked through but still firm. Check for doneness by biting into a piece of pasta rinsed in cold water. Drain cooked pasta into a colander in the sink.
2. Meanwhile, combine carrots, ricotta, yogurt, nutmeg, and black pepper in a blender or food processor and blend until smooth.
3. Pour the sauce over hot fettuccelle.

Calories Per Serving: 349
Fat: 1 g
Cholesterol: 8 mg
Protein: 18 g

Carbohydrates: 67 g
Dietary Fiber: 4 g
Sodium: 201 mg

Rotelle with Carrots

Wheel–shaped pasta in a wine sauce with carrots and onions.

YIELD: 6 servings • *PREPARATION TIME: 15 minutes* •
COOKING TIME: 10 minutes plus pasta cooking time

6 quarts plus ½ cup water
12 ounces rotelle
2 tablespoons white wine vinegar
¾ cup dry white wine
½ teaspoon dried thyme

2 bay leaves
¼ teaspoon ground black pepper
3 cups carrots cut into ¼-inch-by-2-inch
  pieces
2 cups onions cut into half-inch wedges

1. Bring 6 quarts water to a rapid boil in a large, covered pot. Slowly stir in pasta. Return water to a boil. Stir pasta with a long-handled wooden fork to prevent it from sticking together. Follow cooking time recommendation on package. Pasta should be cooked through but still firm. Check for doneness by biting into a piece of pasta rinsed in cold water. Drain cooked pasta into a colander in the sink.
2. Combine remaining ½ cup water, vinegar, wine, thyme, bay leaves, and black pepper in a large saucepan. Add carrots and bring to a boil; reduce heat, cover, and simmer for 5 minutes.
3. Stir in onions and simmer until carrots are just tender. Remove from heat and discard bay leaves.
4. Mix pasta with vegetables and wine sauce.

Calories Per Serving: 307
Fat: 2 g
Cholesterol: 0 mg
Protein: 10 g

Carbohydrates: 62 g
Dietary Fiber: 3 g
Sodium: 48 mg

Radiatore with Cauliflower

"Little radiators" served with a tomato–wine sauce and cauliflower.

YIELD: *4 servings* • PREPARATION TIME: *16 minutes plus cauliflower steaming time* • COOKING TIME: *23 minutes plus pasta cooking time*

¼ cup nonfat chicken broth
½ teaspoon dried basil
1 medium onion, thinly sliced
1 carrot, coarsely shredded
2 cloves garlic, minced
3 cups low-sodium canned tomatoes, chopped, liquid reserved
½ cup dry white wine

4 quarts water
8 ounces radiatore
2 cups coarsely chopped cauliflower, steamed tender-crisp
¼ teaspoon ground black pepper
¼ cup chopped fresh parsley
¼ cup grated nonfat Parmesan

1. Heat broth in a large skillet. Add basil, onion, and carrot. Sauté for 4 minutes.

2. Stir in garlic, tomatoes and their liquid, and wine. Bring to a boil, reduce heat, cover, and simmer for 10 minutes. Remove cover, increase heat, and continue to simmer for 10 additional minutes.

3. Bring water to a rapid boil in a large, covered pot. Slowly stir in pasta. Return water to a boil. Stir pasta with a long-handled wooden fork to prevent it from sticking together. Follow cooking time recommendation on package. Pasta should be cooked through but still firm. Check for doneness by biting into a piece of pasta rinsed in cold water. Drain cooked pasta into a colander in the sink.

4. Toss pasta with cauliflower and tomato sauce. Sprinkle with pepper, parsley, and Parmesan.

Calories Per Serving: 307
Fat: 2 g
Cholesterol: 5 mg
Protein: 13 g

Carbohydrates: 58 g
Dietary Fiber: 2 g
Sodium: 120 mg

Tortellini with Corn, Plum Tomatoes, and Thyme

Packaged tortellini make an easy and delicious entree when tossed with thyme, corn, and tomatoes.

YIELD: 6 servings • PREPARATION TIME: 10 minutes • COOKING TIME: 8 minutes

4 quarts water
1 9-ounce package meat-filled tortellini
1½ cups fresh, canned, or thawed frozen corn kernels
1 clove garlic, minced
2 cups chopped fresh or low-sodium canned plum tomatoes, drained

3 scallions, sliced
1 tablespoon dried thyme
2 tablespoons grated nonfat Parmesan
1 teaspoon olive oil
⅛ teaspoon ground black pepper

1. Bring water to a boil in a saucepan. Add tortellini and boil for 3 minutes. Add corn and cook for an additional 3 minutes. Drain well.
2. Add tortellini, corn, garlic, tomatoes, scallions, thyme, Parmesan, olive oil, and black pepper. Toss to coat all ingredients and serve immediately.

Calories Per Serving: 95
Fat: 2 g
Cholesterol: 4 mg
Protein: 4 g

Carbohydrates: 18 g
Dietary Fiber: 2 g
Sodium: 90 mg

Raisin-Almond Orzo

Orzo is simmered with raisins and cinnamon, then topped with almonds.

YIELD: 4 servings • PREPARATION TIME: 5 minutes • COOKING TIME: 10 minutes

2 cups nonfat chicken broth
1 cup orzo
2 tablespoons seedless raisins

1 teaspoon minced orange peel
½ teaspoon ground cinnamon
1 tablespoon chopped toasted almonds

1. Heat broth in a large saucepan. Stir in orzo, raisins, orange peel, and cinnamon. Bring to a boil; reduce heat, cover, and simmer until liquid is absorbed, about 10 minutes.

2. Transfer orzo to a serving bowl, sprinkle with almonds, and serve immediately.

Calories Per Serving: 262
Fat: 3 g
Cholesterol: 0 mg
Protein: 12 g

Carbohydrates: 45 g
Dietary Fiber: 2 g
Sodium: 188 mg

Eggplant-Mushroom Lasagna

A delicious, low-fat vegetarian lasagna.

YIELD: 5 servings • PREPARATION TIME: 15 minutes • COOKING TIME: 1 hour, 30 minutes plus pasta cooking time and 5 minutes standing time

6 tablespoons nonfat chicken broth
1 medium onion, chopped
2 cloves garlic, minced
1 medium eggplant, peeled and diced
2 cups sliced fresh mushrooms
2 cups low-sodium canned plum tomatoes, chopped and drained
1 cup low-sodium tomato sauce
½ cup dry red wine
1 carrot, shredded

¼ cup minced fresh parsley
1 teaspoon dried oregano
1 teaspoon dried basil
¼ teaspoon ground black pepper
3 quarts water
9 lasagna noodles
2 cups nonfat ricotta
8 ounces mozzarella cut into thin strips
½ cup grated nonfat Parmesan

1. Heat broth in a large skillet. Add onion, garlic, eggplant, and mushrooms and simmer, stirring frequently, for 15 minutes.
2. Preheat oven to 350 degrees.
3. Stir in tomatoes, tomato sauce, wine, carrot, parsley, oregano, basil, and black pepper. Bring to a boil, reduce heat, cover, and simmer for 30 minutes. Return to a boil until sauce is reduced to about 5 cups. Remove from heat and set aside.
4. Bring water to a rapid boil in a large, covered pot. Add pasta by holding it in a bundle at one end and slowly bending it inside the pot as the pasta softens. Keep water boiling; stir pasta with a long-handled wooden fork to prevent it from sticking together. Follow cooking time recommendation on package. Check for doneness by biting into a piece of pasta rinsed in cold water. Since pasta will cook further in the oven, it should be slightly underdone. Drain cooked pasta into a colander in the sink and rinse with cold water.

5. Lightly spray a 9-inch-by-13-inch baking dish with olive oil spray. Spread about a quarter of the sauce in the bottom of the dish. Arrange 3 lasagna noodles on the sauce. Dot noodles with a third of the ricotta. Top with a third of the mozzarella and sprinkle 2 tablespoons Parmesan over the layer. Repeat with second and third layers. Spread remaining sauce over the third layer and bake until heated through, about 45 minutes.
6. Remove from oven. Sprinkle with remaining Parmesan and allow to stand for 5 minutes before cutting into individual pieces.

Calories Per Serving: 435
Fat: 1 g
Cholesterol: 22 mg
Protein: 41 g

Carbohydrates: 63 g
Dietary Fiber: 3 g
Sodium: 610 mg

Ziti Rigati with Eggplant Sauce

Cayenne pepper adds zing to this wholesome, hearty eggplant dish.

YIELD: 6 servings • *PREPARATION TIME: 25 minutes* •
COOKING TIME: 45 minutes plus pasta cooking time

½ cup nonfat chicken broth
1 medium eggplant, peeled and diced
  (about 2 cups)
½ cup sliced fresh mushrooms
1 clove garlic, minced
4 large ripe tomatoes, diced
2 tablespoons chopped fresh parsley

1 teaspoon dried basil
¼ teaspoon ground black pepper
¼ teaspoon cayenne pepper
6 quarts water
12 ounces fusilli
6 tablespoons grated nonfat Parmesan

1. Heat ¼ cup chicken broth in a large skillet. Add the eggplant and sauté for 12 minutes. Add the mushrooms and garlic and sauté for an additional 5 minutes.
2. Add the remaining chicken broth and bring to a boil. Stir in the tomatoes, parsley, basil, black pepper, and cayenne pepper. Reduce heat. Simmer for 30 minutes.
3. Bring water to a rapid boil in a large, covered pot. Slowly stir in pasta. Return water to a boil. Stir pasta with a long-handled wooden fork to prevent it from sticking together. Follow cooking time recommendation on package. Pasta should be cooked through but still firm. Check for doneness by biting into a piece of pasta rinsed in cold water. Drain cooked pasta into a colander in the sink.
4. Pour hot sauce over ziti. Top with Parmesan.

Calories Per Serving: 261
Fat: 1 g
Cholesterol: 5 mg
Protein: 11 g

Carbohydrates: 52 g
Dietary Fiber: 3 g
Sodium: 155 mg

Spaghettini with Eggplant and Zucchini

The vegetables are simmered in a basil-tomato sauce.

*YIELD: 6 servings • PREPARATION TIME: 20 minutes •
COOKING TIME: 23 minutes plus pasta cooking time*

¼ cup nonfat chicken broth
1 medium onion, thinly sliced
2 cloves garlic, minced
1 small eggplant, about 1 pound,
    peeled and cut into half-inch cubes
2 medium zucchini, coarsely chopped
    (about 4 cups)

4 cups low-sodium canned tomatoes,
    coarsely chopped, juice reserved
½ teaspoon dried basil
½ teaspoon dried oregano
¼ teaspoon ground black pepper
6 quarts water
12 ounces spaghettini
¼ cup grated nonfat Parmesan

1. Heat broth in a large skillet. Add onion and garlic and sauté until just tender, about 3 minutes.
2. Stir in eggplant, zucchini, tomatoes with their juice, basil, oregano, and black pepper. Cover and simmer for 20 minutes, stirring occasionally.
3. Bring water to a rapid boil in a large, covered pot. Add pasta by holding it in a bundle at one end and slowly bending it inside the pot as the pasta softens. Keep water boiling; stir pasta with a long-handled wooden fork to prevent it from sticking together. Follow cooking time recommendation on package. Pasta should be cooked through but still firm. Check for doneness by biting into a piece of pasta rinsed in cold water. Drain cooked pasta into a colander in the sink.
4. Combine pasta and sauce. Sprinkle with Parmesan.

Calories Per Serving: 292
Fat: 2 g
Cholesterol: 3 mg
Protein: 12 g

Carbohydrates: 59 g
Dietary Fiber: 2 g
Sodium: 74 mg

Penne Rigate, Eggplant, and Ricotta Casserole

Ridged penne in a baked casserole with a sauce of eggplant, tomatoes, and ricotta.

YIELD: 6 servings • *PREPARATION TIME: 15 minutes* •
COOKING TIME: 50 minutes plus pasta cooking time

4 quarts plus ½ cup water
8 ounces penne rigate
¼ cup nonfat chicken broth
1 cup chopped onion

4 cups eggplant, peeled and cut into
   ¾-inch cubes
2 cups low-sodium tomato sauce
1½ cups nonfat ricotta
¼ cup grated nonfat Parmesan

1. Preheat oven to 375 degrees.
2. Bring 4 quarts water to a rapid boil in a large, covered pot. Slowly stir in pasta. Return water to a boil. Stir pasta with a long-handled wooden fork to prevent it from sticking together. Follow cooking time recommendation on package. Pasta should be cooked through but still firm. Check for doneness by biting into a piece of pasta rinsed in cold water. Drain cooked pasta into a colander in the sink.
3. Heat broth in a large pot. Add onion and sauté until light gold, about 3 minutes.
4. Add the eggplant and simmer until it is just tender, about 8 minutes.
5. Stir in the tomato sauce and the ½ cup water; bring to a boil. Reduce heat and simmer for 10 minutes.
6. Remove pot from heat, add the pasta, and toss.
7. Spread half the pasta-and-sauce mixture into a shallow baking dish. Top with ricotta. Add another layer of pasta.
8. Cover the dish with foil and bake for 30 minutes. Remove foil and sprinkle the Parmesan over the pasta. Serve immediately.

Calories Per Serving: 246
Fat: 1 g
Cholesterol: 7 mg
Protein: 17 g

Carbohydrates: 43 g
Dietary Fiber: 1 g
Sodium: 409 mg

Cavatelli with Eggplant and Red Wine

A savory pasta dish, with eggplant, mushrooms, olives, and fresh tomato in a wine sauce.

YIELD: 4 servings　•　PREPARATION TIME: 15 minutes　•
COOKING TIME: 12 minutes plus pasta cooking time

6 quarts water
12 ounces cavatelli
¼ cup nonfat chicken broth
1 medium eggplant, peeled and cut into
　½-inch cubes (about 3 cups)
6 cloves garlic, minced
1 green bell pepper, cut into narrow
　strips

6 large fresh mushrooms, sliced
1 teaspoon dried oregano
⅛ teaspoon cayenne pepper
⅓ cup dry red wine
1 large ripe tomato, chopped
6 large pitted black olives
2 tablespoons grated nonfat Parmesan

1. Bring water to a rapid boil in a large, covered pot. Slowly stir in pasta. Return water to a boil. Stir pasta with a long-handled wooden fork to prevent it from sticking together. Follow cooking time recommendation on package. Pasta should be cooked through but still firm. Check for doneness by biting into a piece of pasta rinsed in cold water. Drain cooked pasta into a colander in the sink.
2. Meanwhile, heat broth in a large skillet. Add eggplant and garlic. Cover and simmer, stirring occasionally, until eggplant is just tender, about 5 minutes.
3. Stir in green bell pepper, mushrooms, oregano, and cayenne, and sauté for 4 minutes.
4. Add wine and cook another 2 minutes. Stir in tomato and olives; cook 1 additional minute.
5. Combine pasta and sauce. Top with Parmesan.

Calories Per Serving: 167
Fat: 3 g
Cholesterol: 3 mg
Protein: 10 g

Carbohydrates: 26 g
Dietary Fiber: 2 g
Sodium: 472 mg

Gemelli with Endive and Great Northern Beans

Spaghetti "twists" in a protein-rich, garlicky sauce of Great Northern beans, endive, and tomatoes.

YIELD: *6 servings* • PREPARATION TIME: *15 minutes* •
COOKING TIME: *12 minutes plus pasta cooking time*

6 quarts water
12 ounces gemelli
¼ cup nonfat chicken broth
2 medium onions, chopped
5 cloves garlic, minced
6 cups endive torn into bite-size pieces

3½ cups canned low-sodium tomatoes
  with their juice
2 cups cooked or canned low-sodium
  Great Northern beans, rinsed and
  drained

1. Bring water to a rapid boil in a large, covered pot. Add pasta by holding it in a bundle at one end and slowly bending it inside the pot as the pasta softens. Keep water boiling; stir pasta with a long-handled wooden fork to prevent it from sticking together. Follow cooking time recommendation on package. Pasta should be cooked through but still firm. Check for doneness by biting into a piece of pasta rinsed in cold water. Drain cooked pasta into a colander in the sink.
2. Heat broth in a large skillet. Add onions and garlic and sauté until onions are light gold.
3. Stir in endive and cook for 3 minutes.
4. Add tomatoes with juice and cook for an additional 3 minutes.
5. Stir in beans and simmer until mixture begins to thicken, about 3 minutes.
6. Pour hot sauce over pasta.

Calories Per Serving: 299
Fat: 1 g
Cholesterol: 0 mg
Protein: 14 g

Carbohydrates: 59 g
Dietary Fiber: 3 g
Sodium: 48 mg

Orecchiette with Escarole

Pasta "ears" tossed with sautéed escarole and garlic.

YIELD: *4 servings* • PREPARATION TIME: *10 minutes* •
COOKING TIME: *7 minutes plus pasta cooking time*

4 quarts water
8 ounces orecchiette
2 tablespoons nonfat chicken broth

4 cloves garlic, minced
¼ teaspoon cayenne pepper
4 cups escarole cut into 3-inch strips

1. Bring water to a rapid boil in a large, covered pot. Slowly stir in pasta. Return water to a boil. Stir pasta with a long-handled wooden fork to prevent it from sticking together. Follow cooking time recommendation on package. Pasta should be cooked through but still firm. Check for doneness by biting into a piece of pasta rinsed in cold water. Drain cooked pasta into a colander in the sink.
2. Heat broth in a large skillet. Add garlic and cayenne pepper. Sauté for 1 minute. Add the escarole and sauté until most of the liquid has evaporated, about 12 minutes.
3. Mix together orecchiette and cooked escarole. Serve immediately.

Calories Per Serving: 94
Fat: 2 g
Cholesterol: 0 mg
Protein: 3 g

Carbohydrates: 17 g
Dietary Fiber: 2 g
Sodium: 14 mg

Capellini with Mushroom-Wine Sauce

Angel hair pasta in a sauce flavored with capers, garlic, and parsley.

YIELD: *6 servings* • PREPARATION TIME: *20 minutes* •
COOKING TIME: *30 minutes plus pasta cooking time*

¼ cup nonfat chicken broth
2 cups chopped onions
6 cloves garlic, minced
1 cup chopped fresh parsley
4 cups sliced fresh mushrooms
½ cup dry white wine

3 tablespoons capers, drained
3½ cups canned low-sodium tomatoes,
 chopped, juice reserved
½ teaspoon cayenne pepper
6 quarts water
12 ounces capellini

1. Heat broth in a large skillet over medium heat. Sauté onions, garlic, and parsley until onions are lightly golden, about 3 minutes.
2. Add mushrooms and sauté for 5 minutes.
3. Add wine and capers and sauté until wine evaporates.
4. Stir in tomatoes and their juice. Add cayenne pepper and simmer for 15 minutes.
5. Bring water to a rapid boil in a large, covered pot. Add pasta by holding it in a bundle at one end and slowly bending it inside the pot as the pasta softens. Keep water boiling; stir pasta with a long-handled wooden fork to prevent it from sticking together. Follow cooking time recommendation on package. Pasta should be cooked through but still firm. Check for doneness by biting into a piece of pasta rinsed in cold water. Drain cooked pasta into a colander in the sink.
6. Combine pasta and sauce in a large serving bowl. Toss until capellini are well coated, and serve immediately.

Calories Per Serving: 157	Carbohydrates: 30 g
Fat: 1 g	Dietary Fiber: 3 g
Cholesterol: 0 mg	Sodium: 45 mg
Protein: 6 g	

Mezzani with Lemon-Mushroom Sauce

Long, tubular pasta tossed with mushrooms sautéed in garlic and lemon juice.

YIELD: 4 servings • *PREPARATION TIME: 15 minutes* •
COOKING TIME: 5 minutes plus pasta cooking time

4 quarts water	*6 cups thinly sliced fresh mushrooms*
8 ounces mezzani	*¼ teaspoon ground black pepper*
¼ cup nonfat chicken broth	*1 tablespoon lemon juice*
2 cloves garlic, minced	*¼ cup chopped fresh parsley*

1. Bring water to a rapid boil in a large, covered pot. Add pasta by holding it in a bundle at one end and slowly bending it inside the pot as the pasta softens. Keep water boiling; stir pasta with a long-handled wooden fork to prevent it from sticking together. Follow cooking time recommendation on package. Pasta should be cooked through but still firm. Check for doneness by biting into a piece of pasta rinsed in cold water. Drain cooked pasta into a colander in the sink.

2. Heat broth in a large skillet. Add the garlic, mushrooms, and pepper. Reduce heat, cover, and simmer for 5 minutes. Remove from heat; stir in the lemon juice and parsley.
3. Add the sauce to the pasta, toss gently to coat, and serve immediately.

Calories Per Serving: 242 Carbohydrates: 48 g
Fat: 1 g Dietary Fiber: 1 g
Cholesterol: 0 mg Sodium: 32 mg
Protein: 10 g

Perciatelli with Mushrooms and Peas

Hollow spaghetti in a cheese sauce with mushrooms and peas.

*YIELD: 4 servings ▪ PREPARATION TIME: 5 minutes ▪
COOKING TIME: 7 minutes plus pasta cooking time*

4 quarts water *1 cup frozen green peas*
8 ounces perciatelli *1 cup nonfat ricotta*
¼ cup nonfat chicken broth *¼ cup skim milk*
2½ cups sliced fresh mushrooms *2 tablespoons grated nonfat Parmesan*

1. Bring water to a rapid boil in a large, covered pot. Add pasta by holding it in a bundle at one end and slowly bending it inside the pot as the pasta softens. Keep water boiling; stir pasta with a long-handled wooden fork to prevent it from sticking together. Follow cooking time recommendation on package. Pasta should be cooked through but still firm. Check for doneness by biting into a piece of pasta rinsed in cold water. Drain cooked pasta into a colander in the sink.
2. Heat broth in a skillet over medium heat. Add mushrooms and sauté for 4 minutes. Add peas, cover, and simmer for 3 additional minutes. Remove from heat and set aside.
3. Mix the ricotta, milk, and Parmesan in a small bowl. Combine with the mushrooms and peas.
4. Drain the pasta thoroughly. Toss with mushroom-pea sauce.

Calories Per Serving: 228 Carbohydrates: 29 g
Fat: 3 g Dietary Fiber: 3 g
Cholesterol: 32 mg Sodium: 314 mg
Protein: 25 g

Spinach Fettuccine with Shiitake Mushrooms in White Wine Sauce

Green fettuccine in a sauce of both shiitake and white mushrooms, wine, and tomatoes.

YIELD: 4 servings • *PREPARATION TIME: 10 minutes* •
COOKING TIME: 11 minutes plus pasta cooking time

4 quarts water
8 ounces spinach fettuccine
6 tablespoons nonfat chicken broth
1½ cups quartered fresh shiitake
   mushrooms
1½ cups quartered fresh white
   mushrooms

1 clove garlic, minced
½ cup dry white wine
2 tomatoes, diced
¼ cup chopped fresh parsley
¼ teaspoon ground black pepper

1. Bring water to a rapid boil in a large, covered pot. Add pasta by holding it in a bundle at one end and slowly bending it inside the pot as the pasta softens. Keep water boiling; stir pasta with a long-handled wooden fork to prevent it from sticking together. Follow cooking time recommendation on package. Pasta should be cooked through but still firm. Check for doneness by biting into a piece of pasta rinsed in cold water. Drain cooked pasta into a colander in the sink.
2. Heat broth in a large skillet. Add mushrooms and sauté until they begin to brown, about 6 minutes. Stir in garlic and wine. Bring to a boil; reduce heat and simmer until liquid is reduced by about half, about 4 minutes.
3. Stir in tomatoes, parsley, and black pepper. Simmer for 1 minute.
4. Pour sauce over fettuccine and toss to coat.

Calories Per Serving: 149
Fat: 1 g
Cholesterol: 19 mg
Protein: 5 g

Carbohydrates: 27 g
Dietary Fiber: 3 g
Sodium: 47 mg

Fedelini with Red Onions and Roast Garlic

Short, thin spaghetti and sweet, roasted garlic.

YIELD: *6 servings* • PREPARATION TIME: *20 minutes* •
COOKING TIME: *50 minutes plus pasta cooking time*

2 large red onions
1 whole garlic bulb, unpeeled, top cut off
6 quarts water
12 ounces fedelini
¼ cup nonfat chicken broth

2 teaspoons red wine vinegar
1½ tablespoons minced fresh parsley
¼ teaspoon ground black pepper
2 teaspoons olive oil
3 tablespoons grated nonfat Parmesan

1. Preheat oven to 400 degrees. Tightly wrap the onions and the garlic bulb together in aluminum foil. Roast for 45 minutes. Remove from the oven, unwrap, and allow to cool; then pop the softened individual garlic cloves out of their skins. Coarsely chop onions.
2. Bring water to a rapid boil in a large, covered pot. Add pasta by holding it in a bundle at one end and slowly bending it inside the pot as the pasta softens. Keep water boiling; stir pasta with a long-handled wooden fork to prevent it from sticking together. Follow cooking time recommendation on package. Pasta should be cooked through but still firm. Check for doneness by biting into a piece of pasta rinsed in cold water. Drain cooked pasta into a colander in the sink.
3. Heat the chicken broth in a saucepan over medium heat. Add the onions, garlic, vinegar, parsley, and black pepper. Cover and simmer for 3 minutes.
4. Toss pasta with sauce and olive oil. Sprinkle with Parmesan.

Calories Per Serving: 342
Fat: 3 g
Cholesterol: 2 mg
Protein: 12 g

Carbohydrates: 67 g
Dietary Fiber: 2 g
Sodium: 39 mg

Spaghettini with Green Bell Pepper Sauce

Crisp bell peppers and diced onion are simmered in a tomato sauce flavored with mellow sherry, tangy citrus, and a trio of pungent spices.

YIELD: *4 servings* • PREPARATION TIME: *15 minutes* •
COOKING TIME: *12 minutes plus pasta cooking time*

1 small onion, finely diced
2 green bell peppers, diced
¼ cup dry sherry
¾ cup fresh orange juice
1 tablespoon minced orange peel
½ teaspoon ground cinnamon

1 teaspoon ground cumin
¼ teaspoon cayenne pepper
⅓ cup low-sodium tomato puree
4 quarts water
8 ounces spaghettini

1. Combine onion, green bell peppers, sherry, orange juice, orange peel, cinnamon, and cumin in a saucepan. Cover and simmer for 8 minutes.
2. Stir in the cayenne pepper and simmer for 4 more minutes.
3. Stir in the tomato puree and simmer for 2 minutes more.
4. Bring water to a rapid boil in a large, covered pot. Add pasta by holding it in a bundle at one end and slowly bending it inside the pot as the pasta softens. Keep water boiling; stir pasta with a long-handled wooden fork to prevent it from sticking together. Follow cooking time recommendation on package. Pasta should be cooked through but still firm. Check for doneness by biting into a piece of pasta rinsed in cold water. Drain cooked pasta into a colander in the sink.
5. Toss pasta with sauce, and serve immediately.

Calories Per Serving: 285
Fat: 1 g
Cholesterol: 0 mg
Protein: 9 g

Carbohydrates: 56 g
Dietary Fiber: 2 g
Sodium: 12 mg

Green Bell Pepper, Corn, and Orzo

Orzo is cooked with corn kernels and minced green bell peppers, then sauced with orange juice.

YIELD: 4 servings • *PREPARATION TIME: 15 minutes* • *COOKING TIME: 15 minutes*

2 quarts water
1½ cups orzo
2 cups fresh, canned, or thawed frozen
    corn kernels

1 green bell pepper, minced
6 tablespoons orange juice concentrate,
    thawed
1 teaspoon minced orange peel

1. Bring water to a boil in a large saucepan. Stir in orzo. Return to a boil, reduce heat, and simmer until orzo is not quite tender, about 10 minutes.

2. Add corn kernels and green pepper to orzo and cook for 2 more minutes.
3. Drain; stir in orange juice concentrate and orange peel. Serve immediately.

Calories Per Serving: 357	Carbohydrates: 72 g
Fat: 1 g	Dietary Fiber: 4 g
Cholesterol: 0 mg	Sodium: 5 mg
Protein: 13 g	

Mezzani Rigati with Roasted Bell Peppers

Ridged mezzani in a tomato sauce with colorful, roasted red and green bell peppers.

YIELD: 6 servings ▪ PREPARATION TIME: 20 minutes ▪
COOKING TIME: 25 minutes plus standing time for peppers and pasta cooking time

4 red bell peppers
4 green bell peppers
½ cup nonfat chicken broth
1 small onion, thinly sliced
4 cloves garlic, minced

2 cups canned low-sodium tomatoes,
    chopped
½ teaspoon dried basil
¼ teaspoon ground black pepper
6 quarts water
12 ounces mezzani rigati

1. Preheat broiler. Meanwhile, cut the peppers in half and place them cut side down on a nonstick baking sheet. Broil until skin blackens, about 5 minutes. Put peppers in a paper bag. Close the bag tightly and allow to stand 10 minutes to make them easier to peel. Peel and core the peppers, then cut them into thin strips and set aside.
2. Heat ¼ cup of broth in a large skillet over medium heat. Add the onion and garlic, and sauté until onions are light gold, about 3 minutes.
3. Add peppers, tomatoes, basil, black pepper, and remaining broth; simmer, stirring occasionally, for 15 minutes.
4. Meanwhile, bring water to a rapid boil in a large, covered pot. Slowly stir in pasta. Return water to a boil. Stir pasta with a long-handled wooden fork to prevent it from sticking together. Follow cooking time recommendation on package. Pasta should be cooked through but still firm. Check for doneness by biting into a piece of pasta rinsed in cold water. Drain cooked pasta into a colander in the sink.
5. Top pasta with sauce and serve.

4 quarts water
8 ounces radiatore
¼ cup nonfat chicken broth
1 scallion, thinly sliced
1 clove garlic, minced

8 ounces medium shrimp, peeled and
   deveined
1 large ripe tomato, diced
¼ teaspoon dried oregano
1 cup sliced zucchini
¼ teaspoon ground black pepper

1. Bring water to a rapid boil in a large, covered pot. Slowly stir in pasta. Return water to a boil. Stir pasta with a long-handled wooden fork to prevent it from sticking together. Follow cooking time recommendation on package. Pasta should be cooked through but still firm. Check for doneness by biting into a piece of pasta rinsed in cold water. Drain cooked pasta into a colander in the sink.
2. Heat broth in a large skillet. Stir in scallion and garlic and sauté for 3 minutes. Add shrimp and sauté until pink, about 2 minutes. Add tomato and oregano; cover, remove from heat, and set aside.
3. Heat 2 inches of water in the bottom of a steamer. Steam zucchini until just tender. Sprinkle with black pepper.
4. Toss pasta with shrimp and zucchini.

Calories Per Serving: 311
Fat: 2 g
Cholesterol: 86 mg
Protein: 21 g

Carbohydrates: 51 g
Dietary Fiber: 2 g
Sodium: 147 mg

Cavatelli with Albacore Tuna

Crinkle-edged shells are served with a garlic–plum tomato sauce and albacore tuna.

YIELD: *4 servings* • PREPARATION TIME: *10 minutes* •
COOKING TIME: *38 minutes plus pasta cooking time*

¼ cup nonfat chicken broth
3 cloves garlic, minced
¼ cup chopped fresh parsley
1½ cups low-sodium canned plum
   tomatoes, chopped, with juice

1 6½-ounce can water-packed albacore
   tuna, drained and flaked
¼ teaspoon ground black pepper
4 quarts water
8 ounces cavatelli

1. Heat broth in a large skillet. Add garlic and sauté for 2 minutes. Add parsley and sauté for 1 additional minute.

2. Add tomatoes with their juice, and simmer, stirring frequently, for 30 minutes.
3. Add tuna and black pepper and simmer slowly for 5 additional minutes.
4. Bring water to a rapid boil in a large, covered pot. Slowly stir in pasta. Return water to a boil. Stir pasta with a long-handled wooden fork to prevent it from sticking together. Follow cooking time recommendation on package. Pasta should be cooked through but still firm. Check for doneness by biting into a piece of pasta rinsed in cold water. Drain cooked pasta into a colander in the sink.
5. Toss pasta with sauce.

Calories Per Serving: 287	Carbohydrates: 48 g
Fat: 2 g	Dietary Fiber: 1 g
Cholesterol: 8 mg	Sodium: 68 mg
Protein: 20 g	

Ziti Rigati with Flounder and Clams

Ridged ziti is topped with chunks of flounder fillet, canned clams, and a savory tomato sauce.

YIELD: 6 servings • *PREPARATION TIME: 15 minutes* •
COOKING TIME: 32 minutes plus pasta cooking time

4 quarts water	½ cup chopped fresh parsley
8 ounces ziti rigati	1 teaspoon lemon peel, minced
¼ cup nonfat chicken broth	½ teaspoon dried basil
1 cup chopped onion	¼ teaspoon cayenne pepper
1 clove garlic, minced	1 cup canned clams, liquid reserved
3½ cups low-sodium canned tomatoes, chopped, with juice reserved	½ pound flounder fillet, cut into ¾-inch cubes
2 cups low-sodium tomato juice	

1. Bring water to a rapid boil in a large, covered pot. Slowly stir in pasta. Return water to a boil. Stir pasta with a long-handled wooden fork to prevent it from sticking together. Follow cooking time recommendation on package. Pasta should be cooked through but still firm. Check for doneness by biting into a piece of pasta rinsed in cold water. Drain cooked pasta into a colander in the sink.
2. Heat broth in a large saucepan. Add onion and garlic, and sauté until just tender, about 3 minutes. Stir in tomatoes with their juice, tomato juice, parsley,

Calories Per Serving: 267
Fat: 1 g
Cholesterol: 0 mg
Protein: 10 g

Carbohydrates: 55 g
Dietary Fiber: 3 g
Sodium: 32 mg

Farfalle with Yellow-Pepper Topping

Butterfly pasta tossed in a sauce of yellow bell peppers, garlic, tomatoes, and onion.

YIELD: 4 servings • PREPARATION TIME: 15 minutes •
COOKING TIME: 10 minutes plus pasta cooking time

4 quarts water
8 ounces farfalle
¼ cup water, nonfat chicken broth, nonfat vegetable broth, or wine
1 small red onion, chopped
2 cloves garlic, minced

1 jalapeño pepper, seeded and minced
3 yellow bell peppers, coarsely chopped
2 large ripe tomatoes, chopped
⅛ teaspoon ground black pepper
⅛ teaspoon cayenne pepper

1. Bring water to a rapid boil in a large, covered pot. Slowly stir in pasta. Return water to a boil. Stir pasta with a long-handled wooden fork to prevent it from sticking together. Follow cooking time recommendation on package. Pasta should be cooked through but still firm. Check for doneness by biting into a piece of pasta rinsed in cold water. Drain cooked pasta into a colander in the sink.
2. Heat water, broth, or wine in a large skillet over medium heat. Add onion and garlic and sauté until onion is lightly golden, about 3 minutes.
3. Add jalapeño, yellow bell peppers, tomatoes, black pepper, and cayenne; sauté for 6 more minutes.
4. Serve pasta topped with the sauce.

Calories Per Serving: 257
Fat: 1 g
Cholesterol: 0 mg
Protein: 9 g

Carbohydrates: 53 g
Dietary Fiber: 3 g
Sodium: 117 mg

Tricolor Fusilli with Tricolor Peppers

Tricolor fusilli and a color-coordinated sauce of yellow, red, and green peppers.

YIELD: 6 servings • *PREPARATION TIME: 20 minutes* •
COOKING TIME: 11 minutes plus 10 minutes standing time and pasta cooking time

2 red bell peppers
1 yellow bell pepper
2 green bell peppers
½ cup nonfat chicken broth
4 cloves garlic, minced
1 teaspoon dried basil

¼ teaspoon ground black pepper
4 tablespoons red wine
6 quarts water
12 ounces tricolor fusilli
¼ cup grated nonfat Parmesan
2 tablespoons minced fresh parsley

1. Preheat broiler. Meanwhile, cut the peppers in half and place them cut side down on a nonstick baking sheet. Broil peppers until skin blackens, about 5 minutes. Place peppers in a paper bag. Close the bag tightly and allow to stand for 10 minutes to make them easier to peel. Peel and core the peppers; then cut them into thin strips and set aside.
2. Heat broth in a large skillet. Add minced garlic and simmer for 4 minutes. Stir in basil, black pepper, and wine. Set aside.
3. Bring water to a rapid boil in a large, covered pot. Slowly stir in pasta. Return water to a boil. Stir pasta with a long-handled wooden fork to prevent it from sticking together. Follow cooking time recommendation on package. Pasta should be cooked through but still firm. Check for doneness by biting into a piece of pasta rinsed in cold water. Drain cooked pasta into a colander in the sink.
4. Add the bell peppers to the garlic mixture and simmer for 3 minutes.
5. Top fusilli with sauce. Sprinkle with parsley and Parmesan and serve.

Calories Per Serving: 240
Fat: 1 g
Cholesterol: 0 mg
Protein: 8 g

Carbohydrates: 48 g
Dietary Fiber: 1 g
Sodium: 42 mg

Spinach Orzo

Orzo is simmered in chicken broth and garlic and blended with fresh spinach.

YIELD: 4 servings • *PREPARATION TIME: 10 minutes* • *COOKING TIME: 15 minutes*

¼ cup nonfat chicken broth
2 cloves garlic, minced
3½ cups water

1½ cups orzo
2 cups chopped fresh spinach
2 tablespoons grated nonfat Parmesan

1. Heat chicken broth in a large saucepan over medium heat. Add garlic and sauté 1 minute.
2. Add water and orzo. Bring to a boil, reduce heat, and simmer until orzo is tender, about 12 minutes.
3. Stir in spinach and simmer 1 additional minute.
4. Remove from heat and sprinkle with Parmesan.

Calories Per Serving: 210
Fat: 1 g
Cholesterol: 3 mg
Protein: 10 g

Carbohydrates: 38 g
Dietary Fiber: 3 g
Sodium: 72 mg

Baked Orzo, Chickpeas, and Spinach

An easy-to-prepare one-dish meal.

YIELD: 4 servings • *PREPARATION TIME: 15 minutes* •
COOKING TIME: 30 minutes plus orzo cooking time

3 cups water
1 cup orzo
1 10-ounce package frozen chopped
   spinach, thawed and drained
1 cup canned chickpeas, rinsed and
   drained
2 tablespoons soft whole-grain bread
   crumbs

1 tablespoon grated nonfat Parmesan
1 teaspoon dried oregano
¼ teaspoon ground black pepper
1 large ripe tomato, chopped
2 cloves garlic, minced
4 egg whites, lightly beaten
olive oil spray

1. Combine water and orzo. Bring to a boil, reduce heat, and simmer until orzo is tender, about 12 minutes.
2. Meanwhile, preheat oven to 350 degrees.
3. Combine spinach, chickpeas, orzo, bread crumbs, Parmesan, oregano, black pepper, tomato, garlic, and egg whites. Mix well.
4. Transfer to 3-quart casserole that has been lightly sprayed with vegetable oil spray.
5. Bake, uncovered, until lightly browned, about 30 minutes. Serve immediately.

Calories Per Serving: 298 Carbohydrates: 52 g
Fat: 2 g Dietary Fiber: 5 g
Cholesterol: 1 mg Sodium: 216 mg
Protein: 17 g

Orzo-Spinach Pie

Cooked orzo is used as a shell for a ricotta-spinach filling.

YIELD: 6 servings • *PREPARATION TIME: 15 minutes* • *COOKING TIME: 1 hour*

2 cups water
1½ cups orzo
4 egg whites, beaten
2 cups canned low-sodium tomato sauce
3 tablespoons grated nonfat Parmesan
olive oil spray

1 10-ounce package frozen spinach
½ cup nonfat ricotta
¼ teaspoon ground nutmeg
½ cup shredded nonfat mozzarella

1. Preheat oven to 350 degrees.
2. Meanwhile, bring water to a boil in a large saucepan. Stir in orzo; return to a boil, reduce heat, and simmer until orzo is just tender, about 15 minutes.
3. Combine orzo, egg whites, ½ cup tomato sauce, and Parmesan. Spray a 9-inch pie plate with olive oil spray. Spread the orzo mixture over the bottom and sides of the pie plate to form a shell.
4. Cook spinach according to package directions. Drain well. Combine spinach, ricotta, and nutmeg. Fill the orzo shell with this mixture, spread the remaining tomato sauce over the top, and bake for 30 minutes.
5. Sprinkle with shredded mozzarella. Return to oven until cheese melts, about 3 minutes. Allow pie to cool for 5 minutes and serve.

Calories Per Serving: 268 Carbohydrates: 41 g
Fat: 1 g Dietary Fiber: 4 g
Cholesterol: 7 mg Sodium: 290 mg
Protein: 22 g

Spinach-Stuffed Lasagna Rolls

Individual lasagna rolls, filled with spinach and ricotta and enlivened with a bright tomato sauce.

YIELD: 4 servings • *PREPARATION TIME: 15 minutes* •
COOKING TIME: 35 minutes plus pasta cooking time

4 quarts water
8 lasagna noodles
1 package frozen spinach, thawed, well
   drained, and finely chopped
2 tablespoons grated nonfat Parmesan
1 cup nonfat ricotta
¼ teaspoon ground nutmeg

¼ teaspoon ground black pepper
2 cups low-sodium tomato sauce
2 cloves garlic, minced
½ cup chopped onion
½ teaspoon dried oregano
½ teaspoon cayenne pepper

1. Bring water to a rapid boil in a large, covered pot. Add pasta by holding it in a bundle at one end and slowly bending it inside the pot as the pasta softens. Keep water boiling; stir pasta with a long-handled wooden fork to prevent it from sticking together. Follow cooking time recommendation on package. Check for doneness by biting into a piece of pasta rinsed in cold water. Since pasta will cook further in the oven, it should be slightly underdone. Drain cooked pasta into a colander in the sink and rinse with cold water.
2. Preheat oven to 350 degrees.
3. Meanwhile, combine spinach, Parmesan, ricotta, nutmeg, and pepper. Spoon this mixture along the entire length of each noodle. Roll up the noodles and arrange them in a shallow baking dish.
4. Mix the tomato sauce, garlic, onion, oregano, and cayenne pepper; pour over the lasagna rolls and bake for 35 minutes.

Calories Per Serving: 346
Fat: 0 g
Cholesterol: 6 mg
Protein: 22 g

Carbohydrates: 63 g
Dietary Fiber: 5 g
Sodium: 246 mg

Cavatelli with Spinach-Anchovy Sauce

Ribbed, curled noodles are tossed with sautéed spinach, garlic, and anchovies.

YIELD: 4 servings • *PREPARATION TIME: 15 minutes* •
COOKING TIME: 6 minutes plus pasta cooking time

1 teaspoon hot pepper sauce

¼ cup nonfat chicken broth

6 anchovy fillets, drained and minced

4 cloves garlic, minced

8 cups chopped fresh spinach

4 quarts water

8 ounces cavatelli

1. Heat pepper sauce and broth in a large skillet over medium heat. Add minced anchovies and garlic and sauté for 2 minutes.
2. Stir in spinach; cover and simmer for 2 minutes.
3. Meanwhile, bring water to a rapid boil in a large, covered pot. Slowly stir in pasta. Return water to a boil. Stir pasta with a long-handled wooden fork to prevent it from sticking together. Follow cooking time recommendation on package. Pasta should be cooked through but still firm. Check for doneness by biting into a piece of pasta rinsed in cold water. Drain cooked pasta into a colander in the sink.
4. Toss pasta with spinach mixture.

Calories Per Serving: 254

Fat: 2 g

Cholesterol: 5 mg

Protein: 13 g

Carbohydrates: 48 g

Dietary Fiber: 3 g

Sodium: 357 mg

Vermicelli with Spinach, Yellow Squash, and White Beans

Very thin spaghetti is served with sautéed vegetables.

YIELD: 4 servings • PREPARATION TIME: 15 minutes •
COOKING TIME: 5 minutes plus pasta cooking time

4 quarts water

8 ounces vermicelli

2 tablespoons nonfat chicken broth

1 clove garlic, minced

3 cups finely chopped fresh spinach

2 tablespoons minced lemon peel

1½ cups thinly sliced yellow summer squash

2 cups cooked or canned Great Northern beans, rinsed and drained

1. Bring water to a rapid boil in a large, covered pot. Add pasta by holding it in a bundle at one end and slowly bending it inside the pot as the pasta softens. Keep water boiling; stir pasta with a long-handled wooden fork to prevent it from sticking together. Follow cooking time recommendation on package.

Pasta should be cooked through but still firm. Check for doneness by biting into a piece of pasta rinsed in cold water. Drain cooked pasta into a colander in the sink.

2. Heat chicken broth in a large skillet. Sauté garlic until just browned. Stir in spinach, lemon peel, squash, and beans. Cook until squash is tender-crisp, about 3 minutes.
3. Combine pasta and vegetable mixture.

Calories Per Serving: 338	Carbohydrates: 65 g
Fat: 3 g	Dietary Fiber: 8 g
Cholesterol: 0 mg	Sodium: 500 mg
Protein: 14 g	

Linguine with Spinach and Ricotta

Linguine is served with a rich green sauce of fresh spinach, parsley, basil, ricotta, and yogurt.

YIELD: 4 servings ▪ PREPARATION TIME: 10 minutes ▪
COOKING TIME: 15 minutes

4 quarts water	*1 teaspoon dried basil*
8 ounces linguine	*½ cup nonfat ricotta*
1 cup chopped fresh spinach leaves	*½ cup nonfat plain yogurt*
4 teaspoons chopped fresh parsley	*¼ teaspoon ground black pepper*

1. Bring water to a rapid boil in a large, covered pot. Add pasta by holding it in a bundle at one end and slowly bending it inside the pot as the pasta softens. Keep water boiling; stir pasta with a long-handled wooden fork to prevent it from sticking together. Follow cooking time recommendation on package. Pasta should be cooked through but still firm. Check for doneness by biting into a piece of pasta rinsed in cold water. Drain cooked pasta into a colander in the sink.
2. Blend spinach, parsley, basil, ricotta, yogurt, and pepper together in a blender or food processor.
3. Toss linguine in the sauce.

Calories Per Serving: 277	Carbohydrates: 48 g
Fat: 1 g	Dietary Fiber: 3 g
Cholesterol: 4 mg	Sodium: 133 mg
Protein: 16 g	

Shiitake-Spinach Lasagna

This classic dish is brightened with flavorful shiitake mushrooms.

YIELD: 6 servings • *PREPARATION TIME: 25 minutes* •
COOKING TIME: 1 hour plus pasta cooking time and 10 minutes standing time

4 quarts water
8 ounces lasagna noodles
1¼ cups nonfat ricotta
4 egg whites, slightly beaten
1 cup chopped fresh shiitake mushrooms
½ cup chopped onion

1 10-ounce package frozen spinach,
   thawed and drained
olive oil cooking spray
2 cups low-sodium tomato sauce
¼ cup grated nonfat Parmesan

1. Preheat oven to 350 degrees.
2. Bring water to a rapid boil in a large, covered pot. Add pasta by holding it in a bundle at one end and slowly bending it inside the pot as the pasta softens. Keep water boiling; stir pasta with a long-handled wooden fork to prevent it from sticking together. Follow cooking time recommendation on package. Check for doneness by biting into a piece of pasta rinsed in cold water. Since pasta will cook further in the oven, it should be slightly underdone. Drain cooked pasta into a colander in the sink and rinse with cold water.
3. Combine ricotta with half the egg whites and all the mushrooms and onion.
4. In a separate bowl, combine the remaining egg whites and spinach.
5. Lightly spray a baking dish with olive oil spray. Spread half the tomato sauce over the bottom of the dish. Layer with a third of the noodles, the mushroom mixture, another third of the noodles, the spinach mixture, and the remaining noodles. Top with the remaining tomato sauce.
6. Cover and bake for 50 minutes.
7. Sprinkle the Parmesan over the top and continue to bake until cheese is lightly browned, about 5 minutes. Allow to stand for 10 minutes before cutting.

Calories Per Serving: 301
Fat: 1 g
Cholesterol: 7 mg
Protein: 22 g

Carbohydrates: 53 g
Dietary Fiber: 6 g
Sodium: 265 mg

Angel Hair Pasta with Scallions

Very thin pasta is tossed in soy sauce and sesame oil, then mixed with scallions, ginger, and garlic for a taste reminiscent of Thai noodle dishes.

YIELD: 4 servings • PREPARATION TIME: 10 minutes • COOKING TIME: 8 minutes

4 quarts water	*2 tablespoons nonfat chicken broth*
8 ounces angel hair pasta	*1 tablespoon minced fresh gingerroot*
2 tablespoons reduced-sodium soy sauce	*1 garlic clove, minced*
1 teaspoon sesame oil	*16 scallions, cut into 1-inch pieces*

1. Bring water to a rapid boil in a large, covered pot. Add pasta by holding it in a bundle at one end and slowly bending it inside the pot as the pasta softens. Keep water boiling; stir pasta with a long-handled wooden fork to prevent it from sticking together. Follow cooking time recommendation on package. Pasta should be cooked through but still firm. Check for doneness by biting into a piece of pasta rinsed in cold water. Drain cooked pasta into a colander in the sink.
2. Toss pasta with soy sauce and sesame oil.
3. Heat chicken broth in a large skillet. Add gingerroot and garlic and sauté for 30 seconds. Add scallions and sauté for 2 minutes. Add pasta; heat through and serve immediately.

Calories Per Serving: 232	Carbohydrates: 44 g
Fat: 2 g	Dietary Fiber: 0 g
Cholesterol: 0 mg	Sodium: 280 mg
Protein: 9 g	

Summer Squash–Carrot Orzo

A bright dish of rice-size pasta served with carrot, thyme, and summer squash.

YIELD: 4 servings • PREPARATION TIME: 20 minutes • COOKING TIME: 20 minutes

1¼ cups nonfat chicken broth	*¼ teaspoon ground black pepper*
½ cup chopped onion	*½ cup orzo*
2 cloves garlic, minced	*½ cup shredded yellow summer squash*
½ cup diced carrot	*¼ cup shredded nonfat sharp cheddar*
1 teaspoon dried thyme	

1. Heat ¼ cup chicken broth in a large saucepan. Add onion and garlic. Sauté until onion starts to turn translucent, about 3 minutes.
2. Add remaining broth, carrot, thyme, black pepper, and orzo. Bring to a boil; reduce heat, cover, and simmer until orzo is just tender, about 15 minutes.
3. Remove from heat, stir in squash and cheese, and allow to stand for 5 minutes.

Calories Per Serving: 116
Fat: 1 g
Cholesterol: 3 mg
Protein: 7 g

Carbohydrates: 21 g
Dietary Fiber: 2 g
Sodium: 134 mg

Orzo with Black Olives and Sun-Dried Tomatoes

Cooked orzo is tossed with sun-dried tomatoes, green bell pepper, parsley, black olives, and Parmesan.

YIELD: 4 servings   •   PREPARATION TIME: 25 minutes   •
COOKING TIME: 15 minutes

3 cups water
1 cup orzo
½ ounce sun-dried tomatoes
¼ cup chopped onion
¾ cup chopped green bell pepper
2 tablespoons chopped fresh parsley

4 pitted black olives, sliced
¼ teaspoon ground black pepper
2 tablespoons red wine vinegar
1 teaspoon olive oil
¼ cup grated nonfat Parmesan

1. Bring 2 cups water to a boil in a large saucepan. Stir in orzo; return to a boil, reduce heat, and simmer until orzo is just tender, about 15 minutes.
2. Bring remaining 1 cup of water to a boil in a small saucepan and add tomatoes. Reduce heat and simmer until tomatoes are tender, about 2 minutes. Drain and chop tomatoes.
3. Combine tomatoes, orzo, onion, bell pepper, parsley, olives, black pepper, vinegar, and olive oil in a large bowl and toss well. Sprinkle with Parmesan and serve.

Calories Per Serving: 211
Fat: 2 g
Cholesterol: 5 mg
Protein: 9 g

Carbohydrates: 36 g
Dietary Fiber: 2 g
Sodium: 90 mg

Tomatoes Stuffed with Orzo

Large, ripe tomatoes are stuffed with orzo that has been simmered with orange peel and olives and mixed with sautéed celery and onion.

YIELD: *4 servings* • PREPARATION TIME: *15 minutes* •
COOKING TIME: *20 minutes*

2¼ cups nonfat chicken broth
½ cup orzo
1 tablespoon minced orange peel
8 pitted black olives, chopped
1 medium onion, chopped

1 cup chopped celery
¼ cup orange juice
4 large ripe tomatoes, tops removed and
    pulp discarded
2 tablespoons chopped fresh parsley

1. Bring 2 cups chicken broth to a boil in a large saucepan. Add orzo and orange peel; return to a boil, reduce heat, and simmer for 10 minutes. Stir in olives and simmer until orzo is tender, about 5 minutes.
2. Heat ¼ cup chicken broth in a large skillet. Add onion and celery and sauté until vegetables are just tender. Stir in orange juice.
3. Add orzo mixture to onions and celery. Remove from heat and allow to stand for 10 minutes.
4. Stuff tomatoes, garnish with parsley, and serve.

Calories Per Serving: 192
Fat: 2 g
Cholesterol: 0 mg
Protein: 8 g

Carbohydrates: 37 g
Dietary Fiber: 4 g
Sodium: 284 mg

Rotelle with Fresh Tomato Sauce

Rotelle are tossed in a classic sauce of coarsely chopped fresh tomatoes, onion, garlic, oregano, and basil.

YIELD: *4 servings* • PREPARATION TIME: *15 minutes* •
COOKING TIME: *64 minutes plus pasta cooking time*

¼ cup nonfat chicken broth	1 teaspoon dried basil
4 cloves garlic, minced	1 bay leaf
1 medium onion, chopped	2 teaspoons sugar
4 cups peeled, coarsely chopped fresh tomatoes, juice reserved	¼ teaspoon ground black pepper
¾ cup low-sodium tomato paste	⅛ teaspoon cayenne pepper
1 tablespoon dried oregano	4 quarts water
	8 ounces spaghetti

1. Heat broth in a large skillet. Add garlic and onion. Sauté until onion is lightly golden, about 3 minutes.
2. Add tomatoes with their juice, tomato paste, oregano, basil, bay leaf, sugar, black pepper, and cayenne. Bring mixture to a boil. Reduce heat and simmer, stirring occasionally, until sauce thickens, about 30 minutes. Remove bay leaf.
3. Bring water to a rapid boil in a large, covered pot. Slowly stir in pasta. Return water to a boil. Stir pasta with a long-handled wooden fork to prevent it from sticking together. Follow cooking time recommendation on package. Pasta should be cooked through but still firm. Check for doneness by biting into a piece of pasta rinsed in cold water. Drain cooked pasta into a colander in the sink.
4. Toss pasta with sauce and serve.

Calories Per Serving: 318
Fat: 2 g
Cholesterol: 0 mg
Protein: 12 g

Carbohydrates: 66 g
Dietary Fiber: 5 g
Sodium: 73 mg

Fettuccine with Cilantro-Tomato Sauce

Thin, flat pasta is topped with a tomato sauce flavored with spicy cilantro and sprinkled with Parmesan.

YIELD: 4 servings • PREPARATION TIME: 15 minutes •
COOKING TIME: 33 minutes plus pasta cooking time

¼ cup nonfat chicken broth	¾ teaspoon hot pepper sauce
2 medium onions, sliced	½ teaspoon sugar
2 cloves garlic, minced	4 quarts water
3½ cups low-sodium canned tomatoes, chopped, juice reserved	8 ounces fettuccine
1 tablespoon dried cilantro	2 tablespoons grated nonfat Parmesan

1. Heat broth in a large skillet. Add onions and garlic and sauté until onions become translucent, about 3 minutes.
2. Add tomatoes with juice, cilantro, hot pepper sauce, and sugar. Bring to a boil, reduce heat, and simmer, stirring occasionally until sauce has thickened slightly, about 30 minutes.
3. Bring water to a rapid boil in a large, covered pot. Add pasta by holding it in a bundle at one end and slowly bending it inside the pot as the pasta softens. Keep water boiling; stir pasta with a long-handled wooden fork to prevent it from sticking together. Follow cooking time recommendation on package. Pasta should be cooked through but still firm. Check for doneness by biting into a piece of pasta rinsed in cold water. Drain cooked pasta into a colander in the sink.
4. Toss pasta with sauce and sprinkle with Parmesan.

Calories Per Serving: 388   Carbohydrates: 84 g
Fat: 2 g   Dietary Fiber: 3 g
Cholesterol: 3 mg   Sodium: 82 mg
Protein: 11 g

Spaghettini for Two with Red Onion–Tomato Sauce

Thin spaghetti, prepared with a fresh tomato sauce flavored with garlic and red onion.

YIELD: 2 servings • *PREPARATION TIME: 10 minutes* •
COOKING TIME: 19 minutes plus pasta cooking time

¼ cup nonfat chicken broth   *2 quarts water*
½ cup chopped red onion   *4 ounces spaghettini*
2 cloves garlic, minced   *¼ teaspoon ground black pepper*
3 large ripe tomatoes, coarsely chopped   *2 tablespoons chopped fresh parsley*

1. Heat broth in a large skillet. Add onion and sauté 3 minutes. Add garlic and sauté for 1 additional minute.
2. Stir in tomatoes and bring to a boil. Reduce heat and simmer for 15 minutes.
3. Bring water to a rapid boil in a large, covered pot. Add pasta by holding it in a bundle at one end and slowly bending it inside the pot as the pasta softens. Keep water boiling; stir pasta with a long-handled wooden fork to prevent it

from sticking together. Follow cooking time recommendation on package. Pasta should be cooked through but still firm. Check for doneness by biting into a piece of pasta rinsed in cold water. Drain cooked pasta into a colander in the sink.

4. Toss pasta with the sauce. Sprinkle with black pepper and parsley.

Calories Per Serving: 265	Carbohydrates: 54 g
Fat: 2 g	Dietary Fiber: 3 g
Cholesterol: 0 mg	Sodium: 66 mg
Protein: 10 g	

Radiatore with Red Wine–Tomato Sauce

Little radiator shapes are tossed with a slow-cooked red wine–tomato sauce for classic Italian flavor.

YIELD: 8 servings • PREPARATION TIME: 20 minutes •
COOKING TIME: 2 hours, 40 minutes plus pasta cooking time

¼ cup nonfat chicken broth	2 tablespoons chopped fresh parsley
2 celery stalks, chopped	1 teaspoon dried oregano
2 carrots, chopped	1 teaspoon dried basil
1 large onion, chopped	2 teaspoons sugar
1 tablespoon low-sodium tomato paste	½ cup dry red wine
8 cups low-sodium canned tomatoes, juice reserved	6 quarts water
2 cloves garlic, minced	1 pound radiatore

1. Heat broth in a large saucepan over medium heat. Add celery, carrots, and onion. Sauté until vegetables begin to soften, about 8 minutes.
2. Add tomato paste, tomatoes with their juice, garlic, parsley, oregano, basil, sugar, and wine. Bring to a boil. Reduce heat and simmer slowly, uncovered, for 1 hour.
3. Bring water to a rapid boil in a large, covered pot. Slowly stir in pasta. Return water to a boil. Stir pasta with a long-handled wooden fork to prevent it from sticking together. Follow cooking time recommendation on package. Pasta should be cooked through but still firm. Check for doneness by biting into a piece of pasta rinsed in cold water. Drain cooked pasta into a colander in the sink.
4. Toss pasta with sauce.

Calories Per Serving: 290
Fat: 2 g
Cholesterol: 0 mg
Protein: 10 g

Carbohydrates: 59 g
Dietary Fiber: 3 g
Sodium: 68 mg

Penne Arrabbiata

Penne are prepared with a zesty plum tomato sauce flavored with hot red pepper flakes and garlic.

YIELD: 4 servings • PREPARATION TIME: 5 minutes •
COOKING TIME: 12 minutes plus pasta cooking time

¼ cup nonfat chicken broth
2 cloves garlic, minced
3½ cups drained, coarsely chopped
   canned plum tomatoes
1 tablespoon minced fresh parsley

½ teaspoon hot red pepper flakes
¼ teaspoon ground black pepper
4 quarts water
8 ounces penne

1. Heat broth in a large skillet over medium heat. Add garlic and sauté for 2 minutes. Add tomatoes, parsley, red pepper flakes, and black pepper. Stir well and simmer slowly for 10 minutes.
2. Bring water to a rapid boil in a large, covered pot. Slowly stir in pasta. Return water to a boil. Stir pasta with a long-handled wooden fork to prevent it from sticking together. Follow cooking time recommendation on package. Pasta should be cooked through but still firm. Check for doneness by biting into a piece of pasta rinsed in cold water. Drain cooked pasta into a colander in the sink.
3. Top pasta with the sauce.

Calories Per Serving: 257
Fat: 1 g
Cholesterol: 0 mg
Protein: 10 g

Carbohydrates: 52 g
Dietary Fiber: 2 g
Sodium: 371 mg

Tagliatelle with Jalapeño-Tomato Sauce

Tagliatelle are served with a spicy tomato sauce flavored with jalapeño, cilantro, onion, and oregano.

*YIELD: 4 servings • PREPARATION TIME: 15 minutes •
COOKING TIME: 25 minutes plus pasta cooking time*

2 tablespoons nonfat chicken broth
1 medium onion, minced
1 yellow bell pepper, diced
2 jalapeño peppers, seeded and minced
2 cloves garlic, minced
3½ cups chopped low-sodium canned
   tomatoes

1½ tablespoons minced parsley
1 teaspoon dried cilantro
½ teaspoon dried oregano
1 teaspoon sugar
¼ teaspoon ground black pepper
4 quarts water
8 ounces tagliatelle

1. Heat the broth in a large skillet over medium heat. Add the onion, bell pepper, and jalapeño peppers. Sauté for 5 minutes.
2. Add garlic, tomatoes, parsley, cilantro, oregano, sugar, and black pepper. Simmer the sauce slowly for 20 minutes.
3. Bring water to a rapid boil in a large, covered pot. Add pasta by holding it in a bundle at one end and slowly bending it inside the pot as the pasta softens. Keep water boiling; stir pasta with a long-handled wooden fork to prevent it from sticking together. Follow cooking time recommendation on package. Pasta should be cooked through but still firm. Check for doneness by biting into a piece of pasta rinsed in cold water. Drain cooked pasta into a colander in the sink.
4. Top pasta with the sauce.

Calories Per Serving: 290
Fat: 1 g
Cholesterol: 0 mg
Protein: 10 g

Carbohydrates: 60 g
Dietary Fiber: 4 g
Sodium: 205 mg

Cavatelli for Two with Easy Coriander-Cumin-Tomato Sauce

Cavatelli shells are served with a quick tomato sauce flavored with hot pepper flakes, coriander, and cumin.

YIELD: 2 servings • PREPARATION TIME: 5 minutes •
COOKING TIME: 10 minutes plus pasta cooking time

1 cup nonfat chicken broth	*¼ teaspoon ground coriander*
¾ cup low-sodium tomato paste	*¼ teaspoon ground cumin*
½ teaspoon paprika	*2 quarts water*
½ teaspoon hot red pepper flakes	*4 ounces cavatelli*
¼ teaspoon ground black pepper	*1 tablespoon grated nonfat Parmesan*

1. Combine broth, tomato paste, paprika, hot pepper flakes, black pepper, coriander, and cumin in a saucepan. Bring to a boil, reduce heat, and simmer for 10 minutes.
2. Bring water to a rapid boil in a large, covered pot. Slowly stir in pasta. Return water to a boil. Stir pasta with a long-handled wooden fork to prevent it from sticking together. Follow cooking time recommendation on package. Pasta should be cooked through but still firm. Check for doneness by biting into a piece of pasta rinsed in cold water. Drain cooked pasta into a colander in the sink.
3. Toss pasta with the sauce and sprinkle with Parmesan.

Calories Per Serving: 309	Carbohydrates: 62 g
Fat: 2 g	Dietary Fiber: 5 g
Cholesterol: 0 mg	Sodium: 243 mg
Protein: 13 g	

Farfalle for Two with Tomato-Yogurt Sauce

Pasta "butterflies," with a tomato sauce flavored with garlic and oregano.

YIELD: 2 servings • PREPARATION TIME: 10 minutes •
COOKING TIME: 6 minutes plus pasta cooking time

2 tablespoons nonfat chicken broth
2 cloves garlic, minced
¾ cup low-sodium tomato paste
1 teaspoon dried oregano
½ teaspoon ground black pepper

1 cup plain nonfat yogurt
2 quarts water
4 ounces farfalle
fresh parsley for garnish

1. Heat broth in a saucepan over medium heat. Add garlic and sauté for 1 minute. Stir in tomato paste, oregano, and black pepper; simmer for 3 minutes. Stir in yogurt and slowly warm through, about 2 minutes.
2. Bring water to a rapid boil in a large, covered pot. Slowly stir in pasta. Return water to a boil. Stir pasta with a long-handled wooden fork to prevent it from sticking together. Follow cooking time recommendation on package. Pasta should be cooked through but still firm. Check for doneness by biting into a piece of pasta rinsed in cold water. Drain cooked pasta into a colander in the sink.
3. Toss pasta with sauce. Garnish with parsley.

Calories Per Serving: 362
Fat: 2 g
Cholesterol: 3 mg
Protein: 18 g

Carbohydrates: 71 g
Dietary Fiber: 4 g
Sodium: 176 mg

Angel Hair Pasta
with Orange-Tomato Sauce

Angel hair pasta paired with a tangy, citrus- and garlic-flavored tomato sauce.

YIELD: 4 servings   •   PREPARATION TIME: 15 minutes   •
COOKING TIME: 19 minutes plus pasta cooking time

6 quarts water
12 ounces angel hair pasta
2 tablespoons nonfat chicken broth
2 cloves garlic, minced
¼ cup chopped fresh parsley

1 teaspoon dried basil
3½ cups coarsely chopped low-sodium
    canned tomatoes, juice reserved
¼ cup orange juice

1. Bring water to a rapid boil in a large, covered pot. Add pasta by holding it in a bundle at one end and slowly bending it inside the pot as the pasta softens. Keep water boiling; stir pasta with a long-handled wooden fork to prevent it from sticking together. Follow cooking time recommendation on package.

Pasta should be cooked through but still firm. Check for doneness by biting into a piece of pasta rinsed in cold water. Drain cooked pasta into a colander in the sink.

2. Heat broth in a large skillet. Add garlic, parsley, and basil. Sauté for 30 seconds. Stir in tomatoes with their juice. Simmer for 15 minutes, stirring frequently.

3. Add the orange juice and simmer for 3 additional minutes. Remove from heat.

4. Combine the pasta and the sauce. Toss gently and serve at once.

Calories Per Serving: 369
Fat: 2 g
Cholesterol: 0 mg
Protein: 13 g

Carbohydrates: 75 g
Dietary Fiber: 2 g
Sodium: 61 mg

Fedelini Puttanesca

Fedelini accompanied by a hearty sauce of tomatoes, anchovies, capers, olives, and parsley.

YIELD: *4 servings* • PREPARATION TIME: *20 minutes* •
COOKING TIME: *10 minutes plus pasta cooking time*

4 quarts water
8 ounces fedelini
5 tablespoons nonfat chicken broth
2 cloves garlic, minced
4 anchovy fillets, minced
3½ cups drained, chopped low-sodium canned tomatoes

2 tablespoons low-sodium tomato paste
2 tablespoons capers, rinsed and drained
¼ teaspoon hot pepper sauce
¼ teaspoon dried oregano
4 black olives, pitted and slivered
2 tablespoons chopped fresh parsley

1. Bring water to a rapid boil in a large, covered pot. Add pasta by holding it in a bundle at one end and slowly bending it inside the pot as the pasta softens. Keep water boiling; stir pasta with a long-handled wooden fork to prevent it from sticking together. Follow cooking time recommendation on package. Pasta should be cooked through but still firm. Check for doneness by biting into a piece of pasta rinsed in cold water. Drain cooked pasta into a colander in the sink.

2. Heat broth in a large skillet. Add garlic and anchovy fillets and sauté for 3 minutes.

3. Stir in tomatoes, tomato paste, capers, hot pepper sauce, and oregano. Simmer, stirring occasionally, for 5 minutes. Add olives and parsley and simmer for 2 additional minutes.
4. Toss pasta with sauce.

Calories Per Serving: 278
Fat: 3 g
Cholesterol: 3 mg
Protein: 11 g

Carbohydrates: 54 g
Dietary Fiber: 3 g
Sodium: 239 mg

Cravatte with Mushroom-Tomato Sauce

Bow-tie pasta is topped with a classic mushroom-tomato sauce seasoned with garlic, oregano, and basil.

YIELD: 4 servings ▪ *PREPARATION TIME: 10 minutes* ▪
COOKING TIME: 33 minutes plus pasta cooking time

2 tablespoons nonfat chicken broth
6 cups sliced fresh mushrooms
2 cloves garlic
4 large ripe tomatoes, finely diced
1 teaspoon olive oil
¼ teaspoon ground black pepper

1 teaspoon dried oregano
1 teaspoon dried basil
4 quarts water
8 ounces cravatte
¼ cup grated nonfat Parmesan

1. Heat broth in a large skillet over medium heat. Add mushrooms and garlic and sauté for 3 minutes.
2. Stir in diced tomatoes, olive oil, black pepper, oregano, and basil. Cover and simmer for 30 minutes.
3. Bring water to a rapid boil in a large, covered pot. Slowly stir in pasta. Return water to a boil. Stir pasta with a long-handled wooden fork to prevent it from sticking together. Follow cooking time recommendation on package. Pasta should be cooked through but still firm. Check for doneness by biting into a piece of pasta rinsed in cold water. Drain cooked pasta into a colander in the sink.
4. Toss sauce with pasta. Sprinkle with Parmesan.

Calories Per Serving: 292
Fat: 3 g
Cholesterol: 5 mg
Protein: 13 g

Carbohydrates: 56 g
Dietary Fiber: 3 g
Sodium: 76 mg

Bucatini with Tomato-Curry Sauce

Long macaroni is served with a spicy fresh-tomato sauce flavored with onion, cumin, coriander, and curry powder.

Yield: 4 servings ▪ *Preparation Time: 10 minutes* ▪
Cooking Time: 23 minutes plus pasta cooking time

4 quarts water
8 ounces bucatini
¼ cup nonfat chicken broth
2 cloves garlic, minced
6 large ripe tomatoes, chopped

1 medium onion, chopped
1 teaspoon ground cumin
1 teaspoon ground coriander
1 teaspoon curry powder

1. Bring water to a rapid boil in a large, covered pot. Add pasta by holding it in a bundle at one end and slowly bending it inside the pot as the pasta softens. Keep water boiling; stir pasta with a long-handled wooden fork to prevent it from sticking together. Follow cooking time recommendation on package. Pasta should be cooked through but still firm. Check for doneness by biting into a piece of pasta rinsed in cold water. Drain cooked pasta into a colander in the sink.
2. Heat broth in a large skillet. Add garlic and sauté until just tender, about 3 minutes. Stir in tomatoes, onion, cumin, coriander, and curry powder. Simmer until thickened, about 20 minutes.
3. Toss pasta with sauce.

Calories Per Serving: 279
Fat: 2 g
Cholesterol: 3 mg
Protein: 11 g

Carbohydrates: 57 g
Dietary Fiber: 3 g
Sodium: 67 mg

Fusilli for Two with Arugula-Tomato Sauce

Fusilli are served with a refreshing sauce of raw fresh tomatoes and arugula.

Yield: 2 servings ▪ *Preparation Time: 15 minutes* ▪
Cooking Time: pasta cooking time

2 quarts water
4 ounces fusilli
2 large ripe tomatoes, cut into half-inch
    cubes
2 cloves garlic, minced
2 tablespoons balsamic vinegar

½ teaspoon sugar
¼ teaspoon ground black pepper
⅛ teaspoon cayenne pepper
1 teaspoon dried basil
2 cups arugula, cut into thin strips
2 tablespoons grated nonfat Parmesan

1. Bring water to a rapid boil in a large, covered pot. Slowly stir in pasta. Return water to a boil. Stir pasta with a long-handled wooden fork to prevent it from sticking together. Follow cooking time recommendation on package. Pasta should be cooked through but still firm. Check for doneness by biting into a piece of pasta rinsed in cold water. Drain cooked pasta into a colander in the sink.
2. Combine the tomatoes, garlic, vinegar, sugar, black pepper, cayenne pepper, and basil.
3. Toss pasta with sauce and arugula and sprinkle with Parmesan.

Calories Per Serving: 373
Fat: 2 g
Cholesterol: 5 mg
Protein: 15 g

Carbohydrates: 75 g
Dietary Fiber: 2 g
Sodium: 69 mg

Inside-out Lasagna

Mafalda noodles in a sauce with conventional lasagna ingredients.

YIELD: 5 servings ▪ PREPARATION TIME: 15 minutes ▪
COOKING TIME: 10 minutes plus pasta cooking time

6 quarts water
12 ounces mafalda
¼ cup nonfat chicken broth
1 medium onion, coarsely chopped
3½ cups fresh or low-sodium canned
    tomatoes, crushed, with juice

4 cloves garlic, minced
1 teaspoon dried basil
1 teaspoon dried oregano
2 tablespoons grated nonfat Parmesan
1¼ cups nonfat ricotta
½ cup shredded nonfat mozzarella

1. Bring water to a rapid boil in a large, covered pot. Add pasta by holding it in a bundle at one end and slowly bending it inside the pot as the pasta softens. Keep water boiling; stir pasta with a long-handled wooden fork to prevent it from sticking together. Follow cooking time recommendation on package.

Pasta should be cooked through but still firm. Check for doneness by biting into a piece of pasta rinsed in cold water. Drain cooked pasta into a colander in the sink.

2. Heat broth in a large skillet over medium heat. Add onion and sauté until lightly golden, about 3 minutes.

3. Stir in tomatoes with juice, garlic, basil, and oregano. Simmer for 10 minutes. Stir in Parmesan.

4. Top mafalda with sauce and the cheeses, and serve.

Calories Per Serving: 383	Carbohydrates: 66 g
Fat: 2 g	Dietary Fiber: 2 g
Cholesterol: 10 mg	Sodium: 325 mg
Protein: 27 g	

Mostaccioli with Zucchini

This simple dish features mustache-shaped pasta tossed with sautéed zucchini and mozzarella.

YIELD: 4 servings • PREPARATION TIME: 10 minutes •
COOKING TIME: 9 minutes plus pasta cooking time

4 quarts water
8 ounces mostaccioli
¼ cup nonfat chicken broth
2 cloves garlic, minced

5 cups coarsely shredded zucchini, drained
½ cup coarsely shredded nonfat mozzarella
⅛ teaspoon ground black pepper

1. Bring water to a rapid boil in a large, covered pot. Slowly stir in pasta. Return water to a boil. Stir pasta with a long-handled wooden fork to prevent it from sticking together. Follow cooking time recommendation on package. Pasta should be cooked through but still firm. Check for doneness by biting into a piece of pasta rinsed in cold water. Drain cooked pasta into a colander in the sink.

2. Heat broth in a large skillet. Add garlic and sauté for 2 minutes. Add the zucchini and sauté for 6 minutes, until just tender.

3. Transfer linguine to a large serving bowl. Pour zucchini mixture over pasta and toss to coat. Sprinkle cheese and black pepper over the pasta, toss well, and serve immediately.

Calories Per Serving: 274
Fat: 1 g
Cholesterol: 0 mg
Protein: 15 g

Carbohydrates: 51 g
Dietary Fiber: 2 g
Sodium: 355 mg

Rigatoni with Tomato-Zucchini Sauce

Tubular pasta is served with zucchini, onion, garlic, and plum tomatoes.

YIELD: 4 servings • *PREPARATION TIME: 20 minutes* •
COOKING TIME: 33 minutes plus pasta cooking time

6 tablespoons nonfat chicken broth
½ cup finely chopped onion
3 cloves garlic, minced
1 zucchini, halved lengthwise and cut
 into ¼-inch slices
2 pounds canned plum tomatoes, seeded
 and chopped, juice reserved

⅛ teaspoon cayenne pepper
½ teaspoon dried basil
¼ teaspoon ground black pepper
8 ounces rigatoni
4 quarts water
¼ cup grated nonfat Parmesan

1. Heat 2 tablespoons broth in a large skillet over medium heat. Add onion and garlic. Sauté until onion is lightly golden, about 3 minutes. Remove onion and garlic from skillet.
2. Heat 2 more tablespoons broth in skillet. Add zucchini and sauté until tender-crisp, about 6 minutes. Remove zucchini from skillet.
3. Heat remaining broth in skillet. Add tomatoes, onion-garlic mixture, and cayenne pepper. Cook over medium heat for 20 minutes. Stir in zucchini, basil, and black pepper and cook for 5 more minutes.
4. Bring water to a rapid boil in a large, covered pot. Slowly stir in pasta. Return water to a boil. Stir pasta with a long-handled wooden fork to prevent it from sticking together. Follow cooking time recommended on the package. Pasta should be cooked through but still firm. Check for doneness by biting into a piece of pasta rinsed in cold water. Drain cooked pasta into a colander in the sink.
5. Toss pasta with sauce and sprinkle with Parmesan.

Calories Per Serving: 287
Fat: 2 g
Cholesterol: 0 mg
Protein: 11 g

Carbohydrates: 59 g
Dietary Fiber: 4 g
Sodium: 62 mg

Linguine with Gingered Zucchini

Zucchini, cherry tomatoes, and bean sprouts are steamed, then combined with Asian seasonings and linguine.

YIELD: 8 servings ・ *PREPARATION TIME: 20 minutes* ・
COOKING TIME: 2 minutes plus pasta cooking time

4 quarts water	3 tablespoons reduced-sodium soy sauce
8 ounces linguine, broken into 4-inch pieces	2 tablespoons rice vinegar
2 zucchini, halved lengthwise and cut into ¼-inch slices	½ teaspoon minced fresh gingerroot
	½ teaspoon sesame oil
1 cup cherry tomatoes cut into halves	½ teaspoon hot pepper sauce
½ cup bean sprouts	2 scallions, minced
	1 teaspoon toasted sesame seeds

1. Bring water to a rapid boil in a large, covered pot. Slowly stir in pasta. Return water to a boil. Stir pasta with a long-handled wooden fork to prevent it from sticking together. Follow cooking time recommendation on package. Pasta should be cooked through but still firm. Check for doneness by biting into a piece of pasta rinsed in cold water. Drain cooked pasta into a colander in the sink.

2. Place 2 inches of water in the bottom of a steamer. Steam the zucchini and tomatoes for 2 minutes.

3. Combine the pasta, zucchini, tomatoes, and bean sprouts.

4. In another bowl, combine soy sauce, vinegar, gingerroot, sesame oil, and hot pepper sauce.

5. Pour the sauce over the pasta-vegetable mixture. Sprinkle with scallions and sesame seeds.

Calories Per Serving: 175
Fat: 1 g
Cholesterol: 0 mg
Protein: 8 g

Carbohydrates: 34 g
Dietary Fiber: 2 g
Sodium: 228 mg

Saffron Orzo with Vegetables

Orzo is simmered in saffron, then tossed with squash, broccoli, green beans, and red bell pepper.

YIELD: 8 servings ▪ *PREPARATION TIME: 25 minutes* ▪
COOKING TIME: 25 minutes plus vegetable steaming time

2½ cups water
pinch of saffron threads
1 cup orzo
1 small yellow summer squash, diced
1 cup chopped broccoli

1 cup green beans, cut into ¾-inch
  lengths
½ red bell pepper, cut into ¼-inch strips

1. Bring water to a boil in large saucepan. Remove from heat and stir in saffron. Cover and allow to stand for 10 minutes.
2. Return water to a boil; add orzo, reduce heat, and simmer, stirring occasionally, until orzo is just tender, about 15 minutes.
3. Steam squash, broccoli, and green beans until tender-crisp. Combine vegetables with orzo and red bell pepper strips.

Calories Per Serving: 64
Fat: 0 g
Cholesterol: 0 mg
Protein: 3 g

Carbohydrates: 13 g
Dietary Fiber: 1 g
Sodium: 8 mg

Maruzze with Vegetable Sauce

Medium-size pasta shells are combined with a sauce of broccoli and cauliflower.

YIELD: 6 servings ▪ *PREPARATION TIME: 10 minutes* ▪
COOKING TIME: 15 minutes plus pasta cooking time

4 large ripe tomatoes, chopped, with
  their juice
1 teaspoon olive oil
1 clove garlic, minced
1 cup chopped broccoli
1 cup chopped cauliflower
1 cup chopped yellow summer squash

1 cup chopped green bell pepper
½ teaspoon dried basil
¼ teaspoon dried thyme
¼ teaspoon ground black pepper
6 quarts water
12 ounces maruzze
3 tablespoons grated nonfat Parmesan

1. Combine tomatoes, oil, and garlic in a saucepan. Cover and simmer until tomatoes are softened, about 5 minutes.
2. Add the broccoli, cauliflower, squash, green bell pepper, basil, thyme, and black pepper. Cover and simmer until vegetables are just tender, about 10 minutes.
3. Bring water to a rapid boil in a large, covered pot. Slowly stir in pasta. Return water to a boil. Stir pasta with a long-handled wooden fork to prevent it from sticking together. Follow cooking time recommendation on package. Pasta should be cooked through but still firm. Check for doneness by biting into a piece of pasta rinsed in cold water. Drain cooked pasta into a colander in the sink.
4. Toss pasta with the sauce and sprinkle with Parmesan.

Calories Per Serving: 258
Fat: 2 g
Cholesterol: 3 mg
Protein: 10 g

Carbohydrates: 51 g
Dietary Fiber: 2 g
Sodium: 44 mg

Vegetable-Stuffed Manicotti

Manicotti are stuffed with a mixture of shredded red bell pepper, grated zucchini, onion, and ricotta cheese, then baked in tomato sauce.

YIELD: 4 servings ▪ *PREPARATION TIME: 30 minutes* ▪
COOKING TIME: 45 minutes plus pasta cooking time

4 quarts water
8 manicotti shells
¼ cup nonfat chicken or vegetable broth
½ cup shredded red bell pepper
½ cup grated zucchini
1 cup chopped fresh mushrooms
¼ cup chopped red onion

1 clove garlic, minced
2 cups nonfat ricotta
2 teaspoons dried basil
2 egg whites, slightly beaten
8 ounces low-sodium tomato sauce
½ cup shredded nonfat mozzarella

1. Preheat oven to 350 degrees.
2. Meanwhile, bring water to a rapid boil in a large, covered pot. Slowly stir in pasta. Return water to a boil. Stir pasta with a long-handled wooden fork to prevent it from sticking together. Follow cooking time recommendation on package. Check for doneness by biting into a piece of pasta rinsed in cold water. Since pasta will cook further in the oven, it should be slightly under-

done. Drain cooked pasta into a colander in the sink and rinse with cold water.

3. Heat broth in a large skillet over medium heat. Sauté red pepper, zucchini, mushrooms, onion, and garlic for 6 minutes.

4. Stir in ricotta, basil, and egg whites.

5. Stuff partially cooked manicotti shells with vegetable-cheese mixture.

6. Spread ⅓ cup of tomato sauce in bottom of shallow baking dish. Arrange stuffed manicotti in a single layer in the dish. Top with remaining tomato sauce; cover and bake for 25 minutes.

7. Top with mozzarella and bake for 5 more minutes.

Calories Per Serving: 298
Fat: 1 g
Cholesterol: 13 mg
Protein: 32 g

Carbohydrates: 40 g
Dietary Fiber: 3 g
Sodium: 390 mg

Garden Harvest Spaghetti

Spaghetti is served with a sauce of tomatoes, broccoli, cauliflower, carrot, parsley, basil, and oregano.

YIELD: 6 servings • *PREPARATION TIME: 15 minutes* •
COOKING TIME: 33 minutes plus pasta cooking time

1 teaspoon olive oil
1 medium onion, chopped
2 cloves garlic, minced
2 cups chopped canned low-sodium
　tomatoes, drained
1 cup low-sodium tomato sauce
1 cup chopped broccoli
1 cup chopped cauliflower

1 carrot, sliced diagonally
3 tablespoons chopped fresh parsley
1 teaspoon dried basil
1 teaspoon dried oregano
6 quarts water
12 ounces spaghetti
2 tablespoons grated nonfat Parmesan

1. Heat oil in a large skillet. Add onion and sauté until light gold, about 3 minutes.

2. Add garlic, tomatoes, tomato sauce, broccoli, cauliflower, carrot, parsley, basil, and oregano. Bring to a boil; reduce heat, cover, and simmer, stirring occasionally, for 30 minutes.

3. Bring water to a rapid boil in a large, covered pot. Add pasta by holding it in a bundle at one end and slowly bending it inside the pot as the pasta softens.

Keep water boiling; stir pasta with a long-handled wooden fork to prevent it from sticking together. Follow cooking time recommendation on package. Pasta should be cooked through but still firm. Check for doneness by biting into a piece of pasta rinsed in cold water. Drain cooked pasta into a colander in the sink.

4. Toss pasta with sauce. Sprinkle with Parmesan.

Calories Per Serving: 177	Carbohydrates: 35 g
Fat: 2 g	Dietary Fiber: 3 g
Cholesterol: 2 mg	Sodium: 75 mg
Protein: 7 g	

Tricolor Fusilli–Vegetable Salad

Warm red, green, and white pasta spirals are tossed with marinated scallions, celery, red bell pepper, and yellow squash.

YIELD: 8 servings   •   PREPARATION TIME: 25 minutes plus 2 hours refrigeration time   •   COOKING TIME: pasta cooking time

3 large ripe tomatoes, coarsely chopped	*3 tablespoons red wine vinegar*
1 cup thinly sliced scallions	*1 teaspoon dried basil*
1 cup finely chopped celery	*1 teaspoon dried marjoram*
1 cup finely chopped red bell pepper	*¼ teaspoon ground black pepper*
1 cup finely chopped yellow summer squash	*4 quarts water*
	8 ounces tricolor fusilli
2 cloves garlic, minced	*¼ cup grated nonfat Parmesan*

1. Combine tomatoes, scallions, celery, red bell pepper, squash, garlic, vinegar, basil, marjoram, and black pepper in a large bowl. Toss gently. Cover and refrigerate for 2 hours.
2. Bring water to a rapid boil in a large, covered pot. Slowly stir in pasta. Return water to a boil. Stir pasta with a long-handled wooden fork to prevent it from sticking together. Follow cooking time recommendation on package. Pasta should be cooked through but still firm. Check for doneness by biting into a piece of pasta rinsed in cold water. Drain cooked pasta into a colander in the sink.
3. Transfer pasta to a large serving bowl.
4. Pour tomato mixture over pasta and toss gently to coat all ingredients. Sprinkle with Parmesan.

Calories Per Serving: 135
Fat: 1 g
Cholesterol: 3 mg
Protein: 5 g

Carbohydrates: 28 g
Dietary Fiber: 2 g
Sodium: 53 mg

Radiatore-Vegetable Salad

Radiatore is combined with vegetables and a mustard-flavored dressing.

YIELD: 8 servings ▪ *PREPARATION TIME: 15 minutes plus 1 hour chilling time* ▪
COOKING TIME: pasta cooking time

4 quarts water
8 ounces radiatore
½ cup nonfat mayonnaise
2 tablespoons vinegar
1 tablespoon Dijon mustard
1 teaspoon sugar

¼ teaspoon ground black pepper
1 cup chopped celery
1 green bell pepper, chopped
1 red bell pepper, chopped
½ cup chopped onion
½ cup chopped fresh parsley

1. Bring water to a rapid boil in a large, covered pot. Slowly stir in pasta. Return
   water to a boil. Stir pasta with a long-handled wooden fork to prevent it from
   sticking together. Follow cooking time recommended on the package. Pasta
   should be cooked through but still firm. Check for doneness by biting into a
   piece of pasta rinsed in cold water. Drain cooked pasta into a colander in the sink.
2. Combine mayonnaise, vinegar, mustard, sugar, and black pepper.
3. Toss pasta, the chopped celery, green and red pepper, onion, and dressing.
   Garnish with parsley. Chill and serve.

Calories Per Serving: 127
Fat: 1 g
Cholesterol: 0 mg
Protein: 4 g

Carbohydrates: 27 g
Dietary Fiber: 1 g
Sodium: 241 mg

Penne Rigate Salad

Ridged penne are mixed with peas, carrots, pickles, and scallions and topped
with a yogurt dressing.

YIELD: 10 servings ▪ *PREPARATION TIME: 20 minutes* ▪
COOKING TIME: pasta and pea cooking time

6 quarts water
16 ounces penne rigate
2½ cups frozen green peas, cooked according to package directions
1½ cups coarsely shredded carrots
1 cup diced dill pickles
½ cup thinly sliced scallions

½ cup nonfat mayonnaise
1½ cups nonfat plain yogurt
¼ cup vinegar
1½ teaspoons sugar
½ teaspoon dry mustard
½ teaspoon ground black pepper

1. Bring water to a rapid boil in a large, covered pot. Slowly stir in pasta. Return water to a boil. Stir pasta with a long-handled wooden fork to prevent it from sticking together. Follow cooking time recommendation on package. Pasta should be cooked through but still firm. Check for doneness by biting into a piece of pasta rinsed in cold water. Drain cooked pasta into a colander in the sink.
2. Combine pasta with peas, carrots, dill pickles, and scallions. Toss well.
3. Combine mayonnaise, yogurt, vinegar, sugar, mustard, and black pepper. Toss with pasta-vegetable mixture.

Calories Per Serving: 248
Fat: 1 g
Cholesterol: 1 mg
Protein: 10 g

Carbohydrates: 47 g
Dietary Fiber: 3 g
Sodium: 284 mg

Farfalle-Fruit Salad

Farfalle are tossed with yogurt and topped with strawberries, honeydew, and mango.

YIELD: 6 servings • *PREPARATION TIME: 15 minutes, plus pasta cooking and cooling time and 3 hours refrigeration time*

2 cups fresh or frozen strawberries
1½ cups honeydew melon balls
2 cups sliced mango
1¼ cups fresh orange juice
2 tablespoons fresh lemon juice

2 tablespoons honey
4 quarts water
1 cup farfalle
2 cups nonfat plain yogurt

1. Combine berries, melon, and mangoes in a large bowl.
2. Combine orange juice, lemon juice, and honey. Pour over the fruit. Cover the bowl and refrigerate for 3 hours.
3. Bring water to a rapid boil in a large, covered pot. Slowly stir in pasta. Return water to a boil. Stir pasta with a long-handled wooden fork to prevent

it from sticking together. Follow cooking time recommendation on package. Pasta should be cooked through but still firm. Check for doneness by biting into a piece of pasta rinsed in cold water. Drain cooked pasta into a colander in the sink. Allow to cool to room temperature.

4. Toss pasta with yogurt. Top with the chilled fruit.

Calories Per Serving: 277
Fat: 1 g
Cholesterol: 2 mg
Protein: 9 g

Carbohydrates: 48 g
Dietary Fiber: 6 g
Sodium: 62 mg

Orange-Tomato Linguine

Linguine is topped with a tomato sauce that combines the zesty flavor of red onion with sweet yellow bell pepper, tangy orange juice, and pungent basil.

YIELD: 6 servings ▪ PREPARATION TIME: 10 minutes ▪ COOKING TIME: 15 minutes

1½ cups orange juice
1 tablespoon minced orange peel
½ teaspoon ground cinnamon
1 teaspoon dried basil
2 cloves garlic, minced

1 medium red onion, sliced
1 yellow bell pepper, cut into thin strips
1 cup low-sodium tomato puree
6 quarts water
12 ounces linguine

1. Combine orange juice, orange peel, cinnamon, basil, garlic, onion, and yellow bell pepper in a saucepan. Bring to a boil; reduce heat and simmer until pepper and onion are just tender, about 8 minutes.
2. Stir in tomato puree and simmer while pasta cooks.
3. Bring water to a rapid boil in a large, covered pot. Add pasta by holding it in a bundle at one end and slowly bending it inside the pot as the pasta softens. Keep water boiling; stir pasta with a long-handled wooden fork to prevent it from sticking together. Follow cooking time recommendation on package. Pasta should be cooked through but still firm. Check for doneness by biting into a piece of pasta rinsed in cold water. Drain cooked pasta into a colander in the sink.
4. Top pasta with the sauce and serve.

Calories Per Serving: 282
Fat: 2 g
Cholesterol: 0 mg
Protein: 9 g

Carbohydrates: 57 g
Dietary Fiber: 2 g
Sodium: 15 mg

Cravatte-Cucumber Salad

Bow-tie pasta is mixed with a refreshing combination of cucumber, celery, scallions, and a yogurt dressing.

YIELD: 8 servings   •   PREPARATION TIME: 15 minutes   •   COOKING TIME: pasta cooking time plus 1 hour chilling time

4 quarts water
2 cups cravatte
⅓ cup peeled, diced cucumber
2 tablespoons red wine vinegar
⅓ cup thinly sliced celery
2 scallions, finely chopped

1 red bell pepper, cored and chopped
¼ cup nonfat mayonnaise
½ cup nonfat plain yogurt
¾ teaspoon dry mustard
1 teaspoon dried dill
⅛ teaspoon ground black pepper

1. Bring water to a rapid boil in a large, covered pot. Slowly stir in pasta. Return water to a boil. Stir pasta with a long-handled wooden fork to prevent it from sticking together. Follow cooking time recommendation on package. Pasta should be cooked through but still firm. Check for doneness by biting into a piece of pasta rinsed in cold water. Drain cooked pasta into a colander in the sink. Allow to cool to room temperature.
2. Place diced cucumber in a bowl. Add vinegar and allow to marinate for 30 minutes.
3. Combine pasta, celery, scallions, marinated cucumber, and red bell pepper. Toss well.
4. Whisk together mayonnaise, yogurt, mustard, dill, and black pepper. Add dressing to salad and toss gently to coat all ingredients.
5. Cover and chill for 1 hour before serving.

Calories Per Serving: 96
Fat: 0 g
Cholesterol: 0 mg
Protein: 4 g

Carbohydrates: 19 g
Dietary Fiber: 1 g
Sodium: 117 mg

PASTA WITH BEANS

Rigatoni Fagioli ▪ Rotelle with Black Beans ▪ Penne with Pinto
Beans ▪ Ziti with Cannellini Beans ▪ Tricolor Fusilli with Spinach-
Lentil Sauce ▪ Spinach Fettuccine with Lentils ▪ Vermicelli with
Lima Beans ▪ Mostaccioli and Chili Beans ▪ Mezzani with Beans and
Mushroom-Zucchini Sauce ▪ Conchiglie with Kidney Beans

Rigatoni Fagioli

A hearty dish of rigatoni simmered with Great Northern beans, onion, tomatoes, and garlic.

YIELD: 8 servings • *PREPARATION TIME: 15 minutes* •
COOKING TIME: 32 minutes plus pasta cooking time

4 quarts water	1 teaspoon dried basil
8 ounces rigatoni	2½ cups low-sodium canned tomatoes
8 cups nonfat chicken broth	¼ teaspoon cayenne pepper
1 cup chopped onion	¼ teaspoon ground black pepper
4 cloves garlic, minced	2 cups cooked or canned Great
4 tablespoons chopped fresh parsley	Northern beans, rinsed and drained

1. Bring water to a rapid boil in a large, covered pot. Slowly stir in pasta. Return water to a boil. Stir pasta with a long-handled wooden fork to prevent it from sticking together. Follow cooking time recommendation on package. Pasta should be cooked through but still firm. Check for doneness by biting into a piece of pasta rinsed in cold water. Drain cooked pasta into a colander in the sink.
2. Heat ¼ cup broth in a large saucepan. Add onion and sauté until lightly golden, about 3 minutes. Add garlic, parsley, and basil, and simmer 1 additional minute.
3. Add tomatoes, cayenne, and black pepper and simmer for 5 minutes. Add remaining broth and beans. Simmer for 15 minutes.
4. Add pasta and heat through. Serve immediately.

Calories Per Serving: 220	Carbohydrates: 40 g
Fat: 2 g	Dietary Fiber: 1 g
Cholesterol: 0 mg	Sodium: 337 mg
Protein: 14 g	

Rotelle with Black Beans

Rotelle are prepared with carrots, red bell pepper, tomato sauce, black beans, and artichoke hearts.

YIELD: 8 servings • *PREPARATION TIME: 20 minutes* •
COOKING TIME: 9 minutes plus pasta cooking time

4 to 5 quarts water
12 ounces rotelle
¼ cup nonfat chicken broth
1 teaspoon dried basil
½ teaspoon ground black pepper
2 cups shredded carrot
1 red bell pepper, cut into thin strips

2 cups cooked or canned black beans,
   drained and rinsed
2 cups low-sodium tomato sauce
2 cups artichoke hearts, drained and
   quartered
¼ cup grated nonfat Parmesan

1. Bring water to a rapid boil in a large, covered pot. Slowly stir in pasta. Return water to a boil. Stir pasta with a long-handled wooden fork to prevent it from sticking together. Follow cooking time recommendation on package. Pasta should be cooked through but still firm. Check for doneness by biting into a piece of pasta rinsed in cold water. Drain cooked pasta into a colander in the sink.
2. Heat broth in a large skillet. Add basil, black pepper, carrot, and red bell pepper. Sauté until carrot is tender-crisp, about 4 minutes.
3. Stir in cooked pasta, beans, tomato sauce, and artichoke hearts. Simmer, stirring occasionally, until all ingredients are heated through, about 5 minutes. Sprinkle with Parmesan.

Calories Per Serving: 299
Fat: 1 g
Cholesterol: 3 mg
Protein: 14 g

Carbohydrates: 59 g
Dietary Fiber: 4 g
Sodium: 105 mg

Penne with Pinto Beans

Penne are tossed with mushrooms and tomatoes, and a pureed sauce of carrots, celery, and pinto beans.

YIELD: 4 servings • PREPARATION TIME: 20 minutes •
COOKING TIME: 16 minutes plus pasta cooking time

4 quarts water
8 ounces penne
1 cup nonfat chicken broth
1 jalapeño pepper, seeded and minced
2 carrots, diced
2 celery stalks, diced

2 cups cooked or canned pinto beans,
   drained and rinsed
20 small mushroom caps, halved
1 large ripe tomato, chopped
1 tablespoon dried cilantro
¼ teaspoon ground black pepper

1. Bring water to a rapid boil in a large, covered pot. Slowly stir in pasta. Return water to a boil. Stir pasta with a long-handled wooden fork to prevent it from sticking together. Follow cooking time recommendation on package. Pasta should be cooked through but still firm. Check for doneness by biting into a piece of pasta rinsed in cold water. Drain cooked pasta into a colander in the sink.
2. Heat ¼ cup broth in a large saucepan. Add jalapeño, carrots, and celery. Sauté for 4 minutes. Stir in the pinto beans and ½ cup broth. Cover and simmer for 10 minutes.
3. Transfer bean mixture to a blender or food processor and puree until smooth.
4. Heat remaining broth in a skillet. Add mushrooms and sauté until they begin to brown. Remove skillet from heat and stir in the tomato, cilantro, and black pepper.
5. Toss pasta with mushrooms and the bean sauce.

Calories Per Serving: 385
Fat: 2 g
Cholesterol: 0 mg
Protein: 19 g

Carbohydrates: 75 g
Dietary Fiber: 2 g
Sodium: 211 mg

Ziti with Cannellini Beans

White beans are combined with spinach, garlic, and yellow bell pepper in basil-tomato sauce, then served with ziti.

YIELD: 6 servings • PREPARATION TIME: 15 minutes •
COOKING TIME: 6 minutes plus pasta cooking time

6 quarts water
12 ounces ziti
5 cups fresh spinach leaves
¼ cup nonfat chicken broth
2 cloves garlic, minced
1 yellow bell pepper, cut into thin strips
1½ cups cooked or canned cannellini
   beans, rinsed and drained

2 cups low-sodium canned tomatoes,
   chopped, liquid reserved
½ teaspoon cayenne pepper
1 teaspoon dried basil
¼ teaspoon ground black pepper
2 tablespoons grated nonfat Parmesan

1. Bring water to a rapid boil in a large, covered pot. Slowly stir in pasta. Return water to a boil. Stir pasta with a long-handled wooden fork to prevent it from sticking together. Follow cooking time recommendation on package.

Pasta should be cooked through but still firm. Check for doneness by biting into a piece of pasta rinsed in cold water. Drain cooked pasta into a colander in the sink.

2. Steam spinach in a large covered saucepan until wilted. Drain, then squeeze out excess liquid. Chop finely.

3. Heat broth in a large skillet over medium heat. Add garlic and yellow bell pepper and sauté until garlic is lightly browned. Add beans, tomatoes, cayenne, basil, and black pepper. Bring to a gentle simmer. Stir in spinach and cook for 1 additional minute.

4. Toss pasta with sauce. Sprinkle with Parmesan.

Calories Per Serving: 349	Carbohydrates: 70 g
Fat: 2 g	Dietary Fiber: 3 g
Cholesterol: 2 mg	Sodium: 97 mg
Protein: 16	

Tricolor Fusilli with Spinach-Lentil Sauce

Fresh spinach, red lentils, and color-coordinated fusilli are tossed together.

*YIELD: 6 servings   •   PREPARATION TIME: 20 minutes   •
COOKING TIME: 38 minutes plus pasta cooking time*

4 to 5 quarts water	⅛ teaspoon dried rosemary
12 ounces tricolor fusilli	¼ teaspoon dried thyme
2¼ cups nonfat chicken broth	¼ teaspoon ground black pepper
½ cup chopped scallions	2 large ripe tomatoes, chopped
1 stalk celery, chopped	4 cups spinach leaves torn into bite-size
4 cloves garlic, minced	pieces
½ cup red lentils	¼ cup nonfat grated Parmesan

1. Bring water to a rapid boil in a large, covered pot. Slowly stir in pasta. Return water to a boil. Stir pasta with a long-handled wooden fork to prevent it from sticking together. Follow cooking time recommendation on package. Pasta should be cooked through but still firm. Check for doneness by biting into a piece of pasta rinsed in cold water. Drain cooked pasta into a colander in the sink.

2. Heat ¼ cup broth in a large skillet over medium heat. Add scallions, celery, and garlic, and sauté until celery softens, about 3 minutes.

3. Add remaining broth, lentils, rosemary, thyme, and pepper, and bring to a boil. Reduce heat; cover and simmer for 15 minutes. Add tomatoes; cover and simmer until lentils are just tender, about 15 additional minutes.
4. Stir in spinach, cover, and simmer for 5 minutes.
5. Toss pasta with sauce. Sprinkle with cheese.

Calories Per Serving: 296
Fat: 2 g
Cholesterol: 1 mg
Protein: 14 g

Carbohydrates: 57 g
Dietary Fiber: 4 g
Sodium: 179 mg

Spinach Fettucine with Lentils

Spinach fettucine is served with a spiced tomato sauce accented with carrots, lentils, and yellow bell pepper.

YIELD: 4 servings • *PREPARATION TIME: 20 minutes* •
COOKING TIME: 29 minutes plus pasta cooking time

1¾ cups nonfat chicken broth
⅔ cup chopped onion
1 clove garlic, minced
1 carrot, finely diced
½ teaspoon dried oregano
2 cups chopped low-sodium canned
   tomatoes, juice reserved

1 cup lentils
1 bay leaf
1 yellow bell pepper, finely chopped
4 quarts water
8 ounces spinach fettuccine
2 tablespoons grated nonfat Parmesan

1. Heat ¼ cup chicken broth in a large saucepan over medium heat. Add the onion, garlic, and carrot and sauté for 4 minutes.
2. Stir in the oregano, tomatoes, lentils, bay leaf, yellow bell pepper, and remaining broth. Bring to a boil; reduce heat, cover, and simmer until the lentils are soft, about 25 minutes. Remove and discard bay leaf.
3. Bring water to a rapid boil in a large, covered pot. Add pasta by holding it in a bundle at one end and slowly bending it inside the pot as the pasta softens. Keep water boiling; stir pasta with a long-handled wooden fork to prevent it from sticking together. Follow cooking time recommendation on package. Pasta should be cooked through but still firm. Check for doneness by biting into a piece of pasta rinsed in cold water. Drain cooked pasta into a colander in the sink.
4. Toss pasta with sauce. Top with Parmesan and serve immediately.

Calories Per Serving: 395
Fat: 2 g
Cholesterol: 3 mg
Protein: 22 g

Carbohydrates: 75 g
Dietary Fiber: 7 g
Sodium: 241 mg

Vermicelli with Lima Beans

This easy sauce is made with tomatoes, lima beans, scallions, and mustard.

YIELD: 4 servings ▪ *PREPARATION TIME: 15 minutes* ▪
COOKING TIME: 9 minutes plus pasta cooking time

¾ cup nonfat chicken broth
1 cup frozen baby lima beans
2 scallions, thinly sliced
1½ tablespoons Dijon mustard

2 large ripe tomatoes, chopped
4 quarts water
8 ounces vermicelli

1. Heat the broth to a simmer in a large skillet. Add the lima beans and simmer for 6 minutes. Stir in the scallions and mustard and simmer for 1 additional minute. Add the tomato and simmer for 2 minutes.
2. Bring water to a rapid boil in a large, covered pot. Add pasta by holding it in a bundle at one end and slowly bending it inside the pot as the pasta softens. Keep water boiling; stir pasta with a long-handled wooden fork to prevent it from sticking together. Follow cooking time recommendation on package. Pasta should be cooked through but still firm. Check for doneness by biting into a piece of pasta rinsed in cold water. Drain cooked pasta into a colander in the sink.
3. Toss pasta with the lima bean mixture. Serve immediately.

Calories Per Serving: 280
Fat: 2 g
Cholesterol: 0 mg
Protein: 12 g

Carbohydrates: 55 g
Dietary Fiber: 4 g
Sodium: 162 mg

Mostaccioli and Chili Beans

"Little mustache" pasta is combined with kidney beans in a chili-tomato sauce, for an effect like Tex-Mex chili with pasta instead of rice.

YIELD: 8 servings • *PREPARATION TIME: 20 minutes plus 1 hour standing time* •
COOKING TIME: 1 hour, 45 minutes plus pasta cooking time

2 quarts water
4 ounces mostaccioli
¼ cup nonfat chicken broth
1 medium onion, chopped
2 cloves garlic, minced
1 tablespoon chili powder

6 cups cooked or canned low-sodium
   kidney beans, rinsed and drained
3 cups canned low-sodium tomatoes,
   chopped
1 4-ounce can chopped hot green chiles
½ cup shredded nonfat cheddar
½ cup finely chopped scallions

1. Bring water to a rapid boil in a large, covered pot. Slowly stir in pasta. Return water to a boil. Stir pasta with a long-handled wooden fork to prevent it from sticking together. Follow cooking time recommendation on package. Pasta should be cooked through but still firm. Check for doneness by biting into a piece of pasta rinsed in cold water. Drain cooked pasta into a colander in the sink.
2. Heat chicken broth in a large pot over medium heat. Add onion, garlic, and chili powder. Simmer for 5 minutes.
3. Add beans, tomatoes, chiles, and cooked pasta. Simmer until all ingredients are heated through and flavors are blended. Sprinkle with cheese and scallions.

Calories Per Serving: 251
Fat: 1 g
Cholesterol: 0 mg
Protein: 16 g

Carbohydrates: 46 g
Dietary Fiber: 9 g
Sodium: 146 mg

Mezzani with Beans and Mushroom-Zucchini Sauce

Black beans, Great Northern beans, and zucchini are served over mezzani.

YIELD: 8 servings • *PREPARATION TIME: 15 minutes* •
COOKING TIME: 35 minutes plus pasta cooking time

¼ cup nonfat chicken broth
4 carrots, finely shredded
1 medium onion, finely chopped
2 cloves garlic, minced
2½ cups cooked or canned low-sodium
    black beans, drained and rinsed
2½ cups cooked or canned low-sodium
    Great Northern beans, drained and
    rinsed
1 teaspoon dried basil

1 teaspoon dried marjoram
3½ cups low-sodium canned tomatoes,
    chopped, with juice reserved
¼ cup low-sodium tomato paste
2 cups sliced fresh mushrooms
2 cups chopped zucchini
¼ teaspoon ground black pepper
6 quarts water
16 ounces mezzani

1. Heat broth in a large skillet. Add carrots and onion and sauté until onion is
   lightly browned, about 4 minutes. Add garlic and sauté 1 additional minute.
2. Add black beans, Great Northern beans, basil, marjoram, tomatoes, tomato
   paste, and mushrooms. Simmer, covered, for 20 minutes. Stir in zucchini and
   black pepper. Simmer, covered, until zucchini is just tender, about 5 minutes.
3. Bring water to a rapid boil in a large, covered pot. Slowly stir in pasta. Return water to a boil. Stir pasta with a long-handled wooden fork to prevent
   it from sticking together. Follow cooking time recommendation on package.
   Pasta should be cooked through but still firm. Check for doneness by biting
   into a piece of pasta rinsed in cold water. Drain cooked pasta into a colander
   in the sink.
4. Top mezzani with the sauce.

Calories Per Serving: 176
Fat: 1 g
Cholesterol: 0 mg
Protein: 11 g

Carbohydrates: 40 g
Dietary Fiber: 11 g
Sodium: 227 mg

Conchiglie with Kidney Beans

Sautéed onions, tomatoes, and garlic are combined with pasta shells, red kidney
beans, and fresh parsley.

YIELD: *6 servings*   ▪   PREPARATION TIME: *10 minutes*   ▪
COOKING TIME: *10 minutes plus pasta cooking time*

6 quarts water
12 ounces conchiglie
¼ cup nonfat chicken broth
1 cup chopped onions
3 large fresh tomatoes, chopped
2 cloves garlic, minced

2 cups cooked or canned low-sodium
    kidney beans, rinsed and drained
½ cup minced fresh parsley
1 teaspoon dried oregano
½ teaspoon dried basil
¼ teaspoon ground black pepper

1. Bring water to a rapid boil in a large, covered pot. Slowly stir in pasta. Return water to a boil. Stir pasta with a long-handled wooden fork to prevent it from sticking together. Follow cooking time recommendation on package. Pasta should be cooked through but still firm. Check for doneness by biting into a piece of pasta rinsed in cold water. Drain cooked pasta into a colander in the sink.
2. Heat broth in a large skillet. Sauté onions, tomatoes, and garlic until onions are lightly golden, about 4 minutes.
3. Add pasta, beans, parsley, oregano, and basil. Simmer until all ingredients are heated through, about 6 minutes. Season with black pepper.

Calories Per Serving: 137
Fat: 1 g
Cholesterol: 0 mg
Protein: 7 g

Carbohydrates: 33 g
Dietary Fiber: 5 g
Sodium: 204 mg

PASTA WITH SEAFOOD

Capellini with Red Clam Sauce ▪ Vermicelli with White Clam Sauce ▪ Spinach Fettuccine with Mussels ▪ Orecchiette with Green Bell Peppers and Clams ▪ Spaghettini with Spinach and Clams ▪ Cavatelli with Clams, Summer Squash, and Shiitakes ▪ Linguine with Mussels and Red Bell Peppers ▪ Gemelli with Shrimp and Mushrooms ▪ Sugar Snap–Shrimp Penne ▪ Fusilli with Shrimp and Broccoli ▪ Farfalle with Fish and Vegetables ▪ Mezzani with Shrimp and Oranges ▪ Mafalda with Scallops and Shrimp ▪ Spaghetti with Okra and Crabmeat ▪ Cavatelli with Crabmeat ▪ Spinach Fettuccine with Crabmeat and Shiitake Mushrooms ▪ Tricolor Fusilli with Shrimp, Crab, and Sugar Snap Peas ▪ Spaghettini with Scallops and Vegetables ▪ Angel Hair Pasta with Scallops ▪ Fettuccelle with Scallops and Anchovy Sauce ▪ Curried Bucatini with Bay Scallops and Spinach ▪ Fedelini with Red Snapper ▪ Ziti Rigati with Haddock Sauce ▪ Tubetti Lunghi with Tuna ▪ Linguine with Salmon ▪ Conchiglie with Scallops and Tomato-Cucumber Sauce ▪ Capellini with Tuna-Anchovy Sauce ▪ Orecchiette with Cod ▪ Mostaccioli with Albacore Tuna ▪ Farfalle with Broccoli Florets and Albacore Tuna ▪ Rotelle with Broccoflower and Albacore Tuna ▪ Radiatore with Shrimp and Zucchini ▪ Cavatelli with Albacore Tuna ▪ Ziti Rigati with Flounder and Clams ▪ Mafalda-Shrimp Salad with Cumin-Garlic Dressing ▪ Shrimp and Orzo in Tomato-Wine Sauce ▪ Oregano Shrimp, Broccoli, and Cauliflower with Orzo ▪ Maruzze with Shrimp Salad

Capellini with Red Clam Sauce

Very thin spaghetti in a version of the classic sauce of littleneck clams, red wine, tomatoes, and garlic.

YIELD: 4 servings ▪ PREPARATION TIME: 15 minutes ▪
COOKING TIME: 25 minutes plus pasta cooking time

¼ cup nonfat chicken broth
1 clove garlic, minced
¼ cup dry red wine
2 cups chopped low-sodium canned
    tomatoes
2 tablespoons low-sodium tomato paste
1 teaspoon dried basil

½ teaspoon dried oregano
2 tablespoons chopped fresh parsley
¼ teaspoon ground black pepper
2 tablespoons lemon juice
12 littleneck clams
4 quarts water
8 ounces capellini

1. Heat broth in a large skillet. Add garlic and sauté for 2 minutes.
2. Add wine, tomatoes, tomato paste, basil, oregano, parsley, black pepper, and lemon juice. Simmer, stirring occasionally, for 20 minutes.
3. Add clams. Cover and steam until shells open, about 10 minutes.
4. Bring water to a rapid boil in a large, covered pot. Add pasta by holding it in a bundle at one end and slowly bending it inside the pot as the pasta softens. Keep water boiling; stir pasta with a long-handled wooden fork to prevent it from sticking together. Follow cooking time recommendation on package. Pasta should be cooked through but still firm. Check for doneness by biting into a piece of pasta rinsed in cold water. Drain cooked pasta into a colander in the sink.
5. Remove clams from shells and return to sauce. Discard shells. Transfer pasta to a large serving bowl; add sauce and toss to combine.

Calories Per Serving: 375
Fat: 3 g
Cholesterol: 14 mg
Protein: 18 g

Carbohydrates: 71 g
Dietary Fiber: 6 g
Sodium: 143 mg

Vermicelli with White Clam Sauce

A perennial favorite: vermicelli and a sauce of clams, garlic, parsley, and white wine.

*YIELD: 8 servings   •   PREPARATION TIME: 15 minutes   •
COOKING TIME: 11 minutes plus pasta cooking time*

6 quarts water
16 ounces vermicelli
1 tablespoon olive oil
2 cloves garlic, minced

2 cups chopped canned clams, drained,
   liquid reserved
½ cup chopped fresh parsley
¼ cup dry white wine
1 teaspoon dried basil

1. Bring water to a rapid boil in a large, covered pot. Add pasta by holding it in a bundle at one end and slowly bending it inside the pot as the pasta softens. Keep water boiling; stir pasta with a long-handled wooden fork to prevent it from sticking together. Follow cooking time recommendation on package. Pasta should be cooked through but still firm. Check for doneness by biting into a piece of pasta rinsed in cold water. Drain cooked pasta into a colander in the sink.
2. Heat oil in a large skillet over medium heat. Add garlic and sauté for 1 minute. Stir in clam liquid and parsley and simmer for 5 minutes. Add clams, wine, and basil. Simmer for an additional 5 minutes.
3. Transfer pasta to a large serving bowl and toss with sauce.

Calories Per Serving: 292
Fat: 3 g
Cholesterol: 27 mg
Protein: 18 g

Carbohydrates: 45 g
Dietary Fiber: 0 g
Sodium: 52 mg

Spinach Fettuccine with Mussels

Green fettuccine is served with mussels in a spicy tomato sauce.

*YIELD: 4 servings   •   PREPARATION TIME: 15 minutes   •
COOKING TIME: 15½ minutes plus pasta cooking time*

¼ cup nonfat chicken broth

⅓ cup chopped onion

3 cloves garlic, minced

½ teaspoon cayenne pepper

3½ cups chopped low-sodium canned
  plum tomatoes

¼ teaspoon ground black pepper

1½ teaspoons dried oregano

1 pound mussels, washed, beards removed

4 quarts water

8 ounces spinach fettuccine

2 tablespoons chopped fresh parsley

1. Heat broth in a large skillet. Add onion and sauté until lightly golden, about
   3 minutes. Add garlic and sauté for 1 additional minute. Stir in cayenne pepper and sauté for another 1 minute. Add tomatoes, black pepper, and
   oregano, and simmer, stirring frequently, until sauce thickens, about 5 minutes.
2. Add mussels to sauce. Cover pot and cook until mussels open, about 5 minutes. Discard shells and transfer meat back into the sauce.
3. Bring water to a rapid boil in a large, covered pot. Add pasta by holding it in
   a bundle at one end and slowly bending it inside the pot as the pasta softens.
   Keep water boiling; stir pasta with a long-handled wooden fork to prevent it
   from sticking together. Follow cooking time recommendation on package.
   Pasta should be cooked through but still firm. Check for doneness by biting
   into a piece of pasta rinsed in cold water. Drain cooked pasta into a colander
   in the sink.
4. Transfer pasta to a large serving bowl, sprinkle with parsley, and toss with the
   sauce.

Calories Per Serving: 328

Fat: 3 g

Cholesterol: 21 mg

Protein: 19 g

Carbohydrates: 56 g

Dietary Fiber: 2 g

Sodium: 272 mg

Orecchiette with Green Bell Peppers and Clams

"Little ear"–shaped pasta is served with a quick-and-easy clam sauce.

*YIELD: 4 servings ▪ PREPARATION TIME: 10 minutes ▪
COOKING TIME: 5 minutes plus pasta cooking time*

¼ cup nonfat chicken broth
1 clove garlic, minced
⅛ teaspoon cayenne pepper
2 cups canned clams, with liquid
2 green bell peppers, diced
½ teaspoon dried marjoram

½ teaspoon ground thyme
¼ teaspoon ground black pepper
4 quarts water
8 ounces orecchiette
¼ cup chopped fresh parsley

1. Heat broth in a large skillet. Add garlic and cayenne and sauté for 1 minute. Stir in clams, green bell peppers, marjoram, thyme, and black pepper. Cover and simmer until all ingredients are heated through, about 4 minutes.
2. Bring water to a rapid boil in a large, covered pot. Slowly stir in pasta. Return water to a boil. Stir pasta with a long-handled wooden fork to prevent it from sticking together. Follow cooking time recommendation on package. Pasta should be cooked through but still firm. Check for doneness by biting into a piece of pasta rinsed in cold water. Drain cooked pasta into a colander in the sink.
3. Top pasta with sauce, sprinkle with parsley, and serve.

Calories Per Serving: 341
Fat: 3 g
Cholesterol: 54 mg
Protein: 28 g

Carbohydrates: 49 g
Dietary Fiber: 1 g
Sodium: 147 mg

Spaghettini with Spinach and Clams

Thin spaghetti is served with a marinara sauce seasoned with garlic and hot pepper.

YIELD: 6 servings • *PREPARATION TIME: 10 minutes* •
COOKING TIME: 9 minutes plus pasta cooking time

6 quarts water
12 ounces spaghettini
¼ cup nonfat chicken broth
4 cloves garlic, minced

1 10-ounce package frozen spinach,
    thawed
3 cups canned clams, with their liquid
¼ teaspoon hot pepper sauce
3 tablespoons grated nonfat Parmesan

1. Bring water to a rapid boil in a large, covered pot. Add pasta by holding it in a bundle at one end and slowly bending it inside the pot as the pasta softens. Keep water boiling; stir pasta with a long-handled wooden fork to prevent it

from sticking together. Follow cooking time recommendation on package. Pasta should be cooked through but still firm. Check for doneness by biting into a piece of pasta rinsed in cold water. Drain cooked pasta into a colander in the sink.

2. Heat broth in a large skillet. Add garlic and sauté for 1 minute. Add spinach and sauté for 5 additional minutes. Stir in clams, their liquid, and hot pepper sauce. Simmer until heated through, about 3 minutes.

3. Top pasta with sauce and sprinkle with Parmesan.

Calories Per Serving: 356
Fat: 3 g
Cholesterol: 56 mg
Protein: 31 g

Carbohydrates: 51 g
Dietary Fiber: 2 g
Sodium: 150 mg

Cavatelli with Clams, Summer Squash, and Shiitakes

Short, curled noodles are topped with an eclectic sauce of clams, summer squash, shiitake mushrooms, black olives, balsamic vinegar, Dijon mustard, and cayenne.

YIELD: 4 servings ▪ *PREPARATION TIME: 20 minutes* ▪
COOKING TIME: 14 minutes plus pasta cooking time

¼ cup nonfat chicken broth
2 cloves garlic, minced
1 medium onion, sliced
1 green bell pepper, cut into thin strips
6 fresh shiitake mushrooms, sliced
1 small yellow summer squash, cut into ¼-inch medallions
1 6-ounce jar marinated artichoke hearts, drained

1 cup drained canned clams
6 pitted black olives, sliced crosswise
2 tablespoons balsamic vinegar
2 teaspoons Dijon mustard
⅛ teaspoon cayenne pepper
4 quarts water
6 ounces cavatelli
¼ cup chopped fresh parsley for garnish

1. Heat broth in a large skillet. Add garlic, onion, and green bell pepper; sauté until onion is translucent, about 5 minutes. Add mushrooms and sauté for 2 minutes. Add squash and sauté for 2 additional minutes.

2. Stir in artichoke hearts, clams, olives, vinegar, mustard, and cayenne. Simmer, stirring occasionally, for 5 minutes.

3. Meanwhile, bring water to a rapid boil in a large, covered pot. Slowly stir in pasta. Return water to a boil. Stir pasta with a long-handled wooden fork to prevent it from sticking together. Follow cooking time recommendation on package. Pasta should be cooked through but still firm. Check for doneness by biting into a piece of pasta rinsed in cold water. Drain cooked pasta into a colander in the sink.
4. Transfer to individual serving plates; top with sauce, sprinkle with parsley, and serve immediately.

Calories Per Serving: 235
Fat: 2 g
Cholesterol: 0 mg
Protein: 9 g

Carbohydrates: 47 g
Dietary Fiber: 4 g
Sodium: 315 mg

Linguine with Mussels and Red Bell Peppers

Linguine is served with a garlic-tomato sauce of mussels and red bell peppers.

YIELD: *6 servings* • PREPARATION TIME: *15 minutes* •
COOKING TIME: *11 minutes plus pasta cooking time*

¼ cup nonfat chicken broth
2 tablespoons chopped fresh parsley
2 cloves garlic, minced
3½ cups low-sodium canned plum
   tomatoes, drained and chopped
2 red bell peppers, chopped

2 pounds fresh mussels, washed, beards
   removed
6 quarts water
12 ounces linguine
¼ teaspoon ground black pepper
1 tablespoon grated nonfat Parmesan

1. Heat broth in a large skillet. Add parsley and garlic and sauté for 1 minute. Stir in tomatoes and bell peppers. Sauté until peppers are just tender, about 5 minutes.
2. Add mussels; cover pot and cook until they open, about 5 minutes. Discard any unopened mussels. Remove meat from open mussels and return it to the sauce. Discard shells.
3. Bring water to a rapid boil in a large, covered pot. Add pasta by holding it in a bundle at one end and slowly bending it inside the pot as the pasta softens. Keep water boiling; stir pasta with a long-handled wooden fork to prevent it from sticking together. Follow cooking time recommendation on package. Pasta should be cooked through but still firm. Check for doneness by biting into a piece of pasta rinsed in cold water. Drain cooked pasta into a colander in the sink.

4. Top pasta with sauce and black pepper, and combine well. Sprinkle with Parmesan.

Calories Per Serving: 289	Carbohydrates: 52 g
Fat: 2 g	Dietary Fiber: 1 g
Cholesterol: 15 mg	Sodium: 187 mg
Protein: 15 g	

Gemelli with Shrimp and Mushrooms

Pasta "twists" are topped with an Asian combination of shrimp, green bell peppers, mushrooms, and zucchini.

YIELD: 4 servings ▪ *PREPARATION TIME: 15 minutes* ▪
COOKING TIME: 3½ minutes plus pasta cooking time

4 quarts water
8 ounces gemelli
1 teaspoon cornstarch
⅓ cup dry sherry
2 tablespoons reduced-sodium soy sauce
2 tablespoons lemon juice
¼ cup nonfat chicken broth

2 green bell peppers, cut into ¼-inch strips
½ pound medium shrimp, peeled, deveined, and quartered
3 cloves garlic, minced
2 cups sliced fresh mushrooms
1 small zucchini, chopped

1. Bring water to a rapid boil in a large, covered pot. Slowly stir in pasta. Return water to a boil. Stir pasta with a long-handled wooden fork to prevent it from sticking together. Follow cooking time recommendation on package. Pasta should be cooked through but still firm. Check for doneness by biting into a piece of pasta rinsed in cold water. Drain cooked pasta into a colander in the sink.
2. Combine the cornstarch, sherry, soy sauce, and lemon juice.
3. Heat broth in a large skillet. Add green peppers, shrimp, and garlic and sauté for about 2 minutes, until shrimp lose their translucence. Add mushrooms and zucchini and sauté for 1 additional minute. Stir in the soy sauce mixture and cook until the sauce thickens, about 30 seconds.
4. Top pasta with the shrimp mixture.

Calories Per Serving: 341	Carbohydrates: 53 g
Fat: 2 g	Dietary Fiber: 2 g
Cholesterol: 86 mg	Sodium: 379 mg
Protein: 22 g	

Sugar Snap—Shrimp Penne

Penne are topped with shrimp, sugar snap peas, and scallions simmered in wine and lemon juice.

YIELD: 8 servings • PREPARATION TIME: 10 minutes •
COOKING TIME: 8 minutes plus pasta cooking time

½ cup dry white wine
2 tablespoons lemon juice
1 tablespoon lime juice
1 pound medium shrimp, peeled and
    deveined
1 cup sugar snap peas
6 scallions, thinly sliced

1 tablespoon chopped fresh parsley
½ teaspoon dried oregano
½ teaspoon ground black pepper
1 clove garlic, minced
1 bay leaf
6 quarts water
1 pound penne

1. Combine wine, lemon juice, and lime juice in a large skillet. Bring to a boil.
2. Add shrimp, sugar snap peas, scallions, parsley, oregano, pepper, garlic, and bay leaf. Cook, stirring constantly, until peas are just tender and shrimp are pink, about 2 minutes. Remove bay leaf.
3. Bring water to a rapid boil in a large, covered pot. Slowly stir in pasta. Return water to a boil. Stir pasta with a long-handled wooden fork to prevent it from sticking together. Follow cooking time recommendation on package. Pasta should be cooked through but still firm. Check for doneness by biting into a piece of pasta rinsed in cold water. Drain cooked pasta into a colander in the sink.
4. Top pasta with shrimp sauce.

Calories Per Serving: 291
Fat: 2 g
Cholesterol: 45 mg
Protein: 19 g

Carbohydrates: 86 g
Dietary Fiber: 1 g
Sodium: 90 mg

Fusilli with Shrimp and Broccoli

Corkscrew pasta combined with shrimp, broccoli, carrot, onion, garlic, and yellow bell peppers.

YIELD: 6 servings • PREPARATION TIME: 20 minutes •
COOKING TIME: 8 minutes plus pasta cooking time

6 quarts water
12 ounces fusilli
1½ cups nonfat chicken broth
1½ cups chopped onion
1 cup carrot, sliced in thin ovals
6 cloves garlic, minced
½ teaspoon ground black pepper

1 pound medium shrimp, peeled and
    deveined
4 cups broccoli florets
1½ yellow bell peppers, diced
1 teaspoon dried basil
3 tablespoons grated nonfat Parmesan

1. Bring water to a rapid boil in a large, covered pot. Slowly stir in pasta. Return water to a boil. Stir pasta with a long-handled wooden fork to prevent it from sticking together. Follow cooking time recommendation on package. Pasta should be cooked through but still firm. Check for doneness by biting into a piece of pasta rinsed in cold water. Drain cooked pasta into a colander in the sink.

2. Bring broth to a boil in a large skillet over medium heat. Add onion, carrot, garlic, and black pepper. Reduce heat and simmer for 5 minutes. Add shrimp, broccoli, and yellow bell peppers; return to boil. Reduce heat and simmer until shrimp become pink and broccoli is tender-crisp, about 2 minutes. Stir in basil.

3. Top pasta with shrimp-broccoli mixture. Sprinkle with Parmesan.

Calories Per Serving: 355
Fat: 3 g
Cholesterol: 117 mg
Protein: 28 g

Carbohydrates: 55 g
Dietary Fiber: 4 g
Sodium: 264 mg

Farfalle with Fish and Vegetables

Chunks of white fish are mixed with asparagus and served over butterfly-shaped pasta.

YIELD: 8 servings • PREPARATION TIME: 25 minutes •
COOKING TIME: 38 minutes plus pasta cooking time

1 cup nonfat chicken broth
2 cups sliced fresh mushrooms
½ teaspoon ground black pepper
4 cloves garlic, minced
2 large ripe tomatoes, crushed and
    drained

1 tablespoon minced fresh parsley
1 teaspoon dried oregano
⅛ teaspoon cayenne pepper
½ pound fresh cod or halibut, cut into
    bite-size pieces
2 tablespoons chopped scallions

1 pound fresh asparagus, cut into 1½-
  inch lengths
6 quarts water

16 ounces farfalle
½ cup chopped fresh parsley

1. Heat ½ cup broth in a skillet. Add mushrooms and black pepper. Sauté for 1 minute. Add garlic and sauté for 1 additional minute. Add tomatoes, parsley, oregano, and cayenne. Bring to a boil; reduce heat, cover, and simmer for 20 minutes. Add fish; cover and cook until fish is done, about 6 minutes.
2. In another skillet, heat the remaining broth. Add scallions and asparagus. Cover and simmer until asparagus is tender-crisp, about 3 minutes.
3. Bring water to a rapid boil in a large, covered pot. Slowly stir in pasta. Return water to a boil. Stir pasta with a long-handled wooden fork to prevent it from sticking together. Follow cooking time recommendation on package. Pasta should be cooked through but still firm. Check for doneness by biting into a piece of pasta rinsed in cold water. Drain cooked pasta into a colander in the sink.
4. Combine the tomato-fish mixture and the asparagus and heat through.
5. Top pasta with sauce and garnish with parsley.

Calories Per Serving: 294
Fat: 2 g
Cholesterol: 55 mg
Protein: 21 g

Carbohydrates: 47 g
Dietary Fiber: 1 g
Sodium: 96 mg

Mezzani with Shrimp and Oranges

Orange flavor and cayenne pepper blend with green bell pepper to enhance this pasta-and-shrimp combination.

YIELD: 4 servings ▪ *PREPARATION TIME: 15 minutes* ▪
COOKING TIME: 8 minutes plus pasta cooking time

4 quarts water
8 ounces mezzani
½ cup nonfat chicken broth
1 green bell pepper, chopped
12 ounces medium shrimp, peeled and
  deveined

½ teaspoon minced orange peel
⅔ cup orange juice
1 tablespoon cornstarch
⅛ teaspoon cayenne pepper
2 cups snow peas
2 navel oranges, peeled and sectioned

1. Bring water to a rapid boil in a large, covered pot. Slowly stir in pasta. Return water to a boil. Stir pasta with a long-handled wooden fork to prevent it from sticking together. Follow cooking time recommendation on package. Pasta should be cooked through but still firm. Check for doneness by biting into a piece of pasta rinsed in cold water. Drain cooked pasta into a colander in the sink.
2. Heat ¼ cup broth in a large skillet. Add green bell pepper and sauté until tender-crisp, about 4 minutes. Remove pepper. Add shrimp and sauté until shrimp are pink throughout, about 3 minutes. Remove and drain shrimp.
3. Heat remaining broth in the skillet. Combine orange peel, orange juice, cornstarch, and cayenne pepper. Add to the broth. Cook, stirring, until mixture is bubbly, about 2 minutes.
4. Stir in shrimp, peppers, snow peas, and oranges. Simmer until heated through.
5. Top pasta with sauce.

Calories Per Serving: 387	Carbohydrates: 62 g
Fat: 3 g	Dietary Fiber: 3 g
Cholesterol: 129 mg	Sodium: 175 mg
Protein: 28 g	

Mafalda with Scallops and Shrimp

Ripple-edged noodles are served with a tomato-based sauce of scallops and shrimp.

YIELD: 4 servings • PREPARATION TIME: 15 minutes •
COOKING TIME: 5 minutes plus pasta cooking time

4 quarts water
8 ounces mafalda
¼ cup nonfat chicken broth
6 cloves garlic, minced
¾ teaspoon cayenne pepper

4 cups low-sodium canned plum tomatoes, chopped, with juice
½ pound sea scallops, quartered
½ pound medium shrimp, peeled and deveined
3 tablespoons chopped fresh parsley

1. Bring water to a rapid boil in a large, covered pot. Add pasta by holding it in a bundle at one end and slowly bending it inside the pot as the pasta softens. Keep water boiling; stir pasta with a long-handled wooden fork to prevent it from sticking together. Follow cooking time recommendation on package.

Pasta should be cooked through but still firm. Check for doneness by biting into a piece of pasta rinsed in cold water. Drain cooked pasta into a colander in the sink.

2. Heat broth in a large skillet. Add garlic and cayenne pepper. Stir in tomatoes and shellfish and cook until scallops and shrimp are cooked through, about 5 minutes.

3. Top pasta with sauce. Serve immediately, topped with parsley.

Calories Per Serving: 388
Fat: 3 g
Cholesterol: 110 mg
Protein: 33 g

Carbohydrates: 57 g
Dietary Fiber: 2 g
Sodium: 256 mg

Spaghetti with Okra and Crabmeat

Spaghetti is served with a sauce inspired by Louisiana gumbo.

YIELD: 6 servings • *PREPARATION TIME: 20 minutes* •
COOKING TIME: 15 minutes plus pasta cooking time

¼ cup nonfat chicken broth
1 red bell pepper, chopped
½ cup chopped onion
2 tablespoons chopped fresh parsley
⅛ teaspoon cayenne pepper
⅛ teaspoon ground black pepper
2 cloves garlic, minced

1 tablespoon all-purpose flour
2 cups low-sodium canned tomatoes, chopped
1 cup fresh okra, sliced
2 cups cooked crabmeat
6 quarts water
12 ounces spaghetti

1. Heat broth in a large skillet. Add red bell pepper, onion, parsley, cayenne pepper, black pepper, and garlic. Sauté for 3 minutes. Add flour and tomatoes, and cook until mixture thickens, about 7 minutes. Stir in okra and crabmeat. Cook, stirring occasionally, for 5 minutes.

2. Bring water to a rapid boil in a large, covered pot. Add pasta by holding it in a bundle at one end and slowly bending it inside the pot as the pasta softens. Keep water boiling; stir pasta with a long-handled wooden fork to prevent it from sticking together. Follow cooking time recommendation on package. Pasta should be cooked through but still firm. Check for doneness by biting into a piece of pasta rinsed in cold water. Drain cooked pasta into a colander in the sink.

3. Top pasta with sauce.

Calories Per Serving: 304
Fat: 2 g
Cholesterol: 66 mg
Protein: 19 g

Carbohydrates: 51 g
Dietary Fiber: 1 g
Sodium: 136 mg

Cavatelli with Crabmeat

Short, curled noodles are topped with the classic mixture of crabmeat, lemon juice, basil, and parsley.

*YIELD: 4 servings ▪ PREPARATION TIME: 15 minutes ▪
COOKING TIME: 8 minutes plus pasta cooking time*

*4 quarts water
8 ounces cavatelli
¼ cup nonfat chicken broth
1 clove garlic, minced
1 small onion, finely chopped*

*1 stalk celery, finely chopped
¼ cup chopped fresh parsley
6 ounces fresh or canned crabmeat
2 teaspoons dried basil
1 tablespoon lemon juice*

1. Bring water to a rapid boil in a large, covered pot. Slowly stir in pasta. Return water to a boil. Stir pasta with a long-handled wooden fork to prevent it from sticking together. Follow cooking time recommendation on package. Pasta should be cooked through but still firm. Check for doneness by biting into a piece of pasta rinsed in cold water. Drain cooked pasta into a colander in the sink.
2. Heat broth in a large skillet over medium heat. Add garlic, onion, and celery and sauté until vegetables are just tender, about 4 minutes. Stir in parsley, crabmeat, basil, and lemon juice. Cook, stirring, for 4 minutes.
3. Serve pasta with sauce.

Calories Per Serving: 283
Fat: 2 g
Cholesterol: 42 mg
Protein: 17 g

Carbohydrates: 49 g
Dietary Fiber: 1 g
Sodium: 153 mg

Spinach Fettuccine with Crabmeat and Shiitake Mushrooms

This quick topping of crabmeat and shiitake mushrooms is served over green fettuccine.

YIELD: 4 servings • *PREPARATION TIME: 10 minutes* •
COOKING TIME: 7 minutes plus pasta cooking time

4 quarts water
8 ounces spinach fettuccine
½ cup nonfat chicken broth
12 ounces fresh shiitake mushrooms,
  stems removed and caps sliced

¼ teaspoon ground black pepper
1 tablespoon low-sodium tomato paste
6 scallions, thinly sliced
6 ounces crabmeat
½ teaspoon dried basil

1. Bring water to a rapid boil in a large, covered pot. Add pasta by holding it in a bundle at one end and slowly bending it inside the pot as the pasta softens. Keep water boiling; stir pasta with a long-handled wooden fork to prevent it from sticking together. Follow cooking time recommendation on package. Pasta should be cooked through but still firm. Check for doneness by biting into a piece of pasta rinsed in cold water. Drain cooked pasta into a colander in the sink.
2. Heat ¼ cup of broth in a large skillet over medium heat. Add mushrooms and black pepper and cook until mushrooms begin to soften, about 3 minutes. Stir in the tomato paste; add half of the scallions and all the remaining chicken broth. Simmer for 2 minutes. Add crabmeat and basil and cook, stirring, until all ingredients are heated through, about 2 minutes.
3. Top pasta with sauce, garnish with remaining scallions, and serve immediately.

Calories Per Serving: 272
Fat: 1 g
Cholesterol: 0 mg
Protein: 10 g

Carbohydrates: 57 g
Dietary Fiber: 2 g
Sodium: 95 mg

Tricolor Fusilli with Shrimp, Crab, and Sugar Snap Peas

A creamy seafood sauce accented with sugar snap peas is served over tricolor fusilli.

YIELD: 4 servings ▪ *PREPARATION TIME: 15 minutes* ▪
COOKING TIME: 10 minutes plus pasta cooking time

4 quarts water
8 ounces tricolor fusilli
1 cup nonfat chicken broth
6 scallions, thinly sliced
1 clove garlic, minced
⅛ teaspoon ground black pepper

1 cup evaporated skim milk
3 tablespoons unbleached flour
8 ounces medium shrimp, peeled and
  deveined
½ cup cooked crabmeat
1 cup sugar snap peas

1. Bring water to a rapid boil in a large, covered pot. Slowly stir in pasta. Return water to a boil. Stir pasta with a long-handled wooden fork to prevent it from sticking together. Follow cooking time recommendation on package. Pasta should be cooked through but still firm. Check for doneness by biting into a piece of pasta rinsed in cold water. Drain cooked pasta into a colander in the sink.
2. Bring broth to a boil in a large skillet over medium heat. Stir in scallions, garlic, and black pepper in a large skillet. Bring back to a boil.
3. Whisk together the milk and flour. Stir the milk mixture into the broth. Lower heat and cook, stirring, until the mixture begins to thicken, about 5 minutes.
4. Stir in the shrimp, crab, and sugar snap peas. Cook until the shrimp are pink and all ingredients are heated through, about 3 minutes.
5. Top pasta with sauce.

Calories Per Serving: 383
Fat: 3 g
Cholesterol: 103 mg
Protein: 30 g

Carbohydrates: 59 g
Dietary Fiber: 1 g
Sodium: 304 mg

Spaghettini with Scallops and Vegetables

Spaghettini is served with a sauce of scallops, carrots, celery, and spinach.

YIELD: 8 servings • *PREPARATION TIME: 15 minutes* •
COOKING TIME: 15 minutes plus pasta cooking time

1 pound spaghettini	½ teaspoon ground black pepper
6 quarts water	1 cup sliced celery
1 cup nonfat chicken broth	2 cups sliced carrots
½ cup dry white wine	4 scallions, sliced
2 tablespoons lemon juice	1 pound bay scallops
2 cloves garlic, minced	3 cups chopped fresh spinach leaves
1 teaspoon dried dill	

1. Bring water to a rapid boil in a large, covered pot. Add pasta by holding it in a bundle at one end and slowly bending it inside the pot as the pasta softens. Keep water boiling; stir pasta with a long-handled wooden fork to prevent it from sticking together. Follow cooking time recommendation on package. Pasta should be cooked through but still firm. Check for doneness by biting into a piece of pasta rinsed in cold water. Drain cooked pasta into a colander in the sink.
2. Bring broth to a boil in a large skillet over medium heat. Add wine, lemon juice, garlic, dill, pepper, celery, carrots, and scallions. Reduce heat, cover, and simmer for 10 minutes. Add scallops and spinach and simmer for 5 additional minutes.
3. Serve pasta topped with scallop-vegetable sauce.

Calories Per Serving: 289	Carbohydrates: 48 g
Fat: 2 g	Dietary Fiber: 1 g
Cholesterol: 19 mg	Sodium: 161 mg
Protein: 18 g	

Angel Hair Pasta with Scallops

Extra-thin spaghetti is prepared with scallops in a lemon-tomato sauce.

YIELD: 4 servings • *PREPARATION TIME: 20 minutes* •
COOKING TIME: 35 minutes plus pasta cooking time

2 tablespoons chopped fresh parsley
2 tablespoons lemon juice
1 pound bay scallops
½ cup nonfat chicken broth
1 medium onion, chopped
1 clove garlic, minced
2 cups low-sodium canned plum tomatoes, with juice, chopped

1 teaspoon dried basil
¼ teaspoon dried oregano
4 quarts water
8 ounces angel hair pasta
2 tablespoons skim milk
⅛ teaspoon ground nutmeg

1. Mix parsley and lemon juice in a glass dish. Add scallops, cover, and marinate until steps 2 and 3 are completed.
2. Heat ¼ cup broth in a large skillet over medium heat. Add onion and garlic and sauté until onion is tender, about 3 minutes. Add tomatoes, basil, and oregano; reduce heat, cover, and simmer for 30 minutes.
3. Bring water to a rapid boil in a large, covered pot. Add pasta by holding it in a bundle at one end and slowly bending it inside the pot as the pasta softens. Keep water boiling; stir pasta with a long-handled wooden fork to prevent it from sticking together. Follow cooking time recommendation on package. Pasta should be cooked through but still firm. Check for doneness by biting into a piece of pasta rinsed in cold water. Drain cooked pasta into a colander in the sink.
4. Drain scallops. Discard marinade. Heat remaining broth in a skillet; add scallops and sauté until they're opaque, about 2 minutes. Add cooked scallops, milk, and nutmeg to the tomato sauce.
5. Top pasta with sauce.

Calories Per Serving: 361
Fat: 2 g
Cholesterol: 38 mg
Protein: 29 g

Carbohydrates: 56 g
Dietary Fiber: 2 g
Sodium: 252 mg

Fettuccelle with Scallops and Anchovy Sauce

Fettuccelle accompanied by scallops, green bell peppers, and anchovies.

YIELD: 4 servings • PREPARATION TIME: 10 minutes •
COOKING TIME: 10 minutes plus pasta cooking time

6 tablespoons nonfat chicken broth
2 green bell peppers, cut into thin strips
2 cloves garlic, minced
4 anchovy fillets, finely chopped

8 ounces bay scallops
4 quarts water
8 ounces fettuccelle
3 scallions, finely chopped

1. Heat broth in a skillet. Add bell pepper and sauté until pepper begins to blister, about 5 minutes. Stir in garlic and chopped anchovy fillets. Sauté for 2 minutes. Add scallops and sauté until they are just opaque, about 3 minutes.
2. Bring water to a rapid boil in a large, covered pot. Add pasta by holding it in a bundle at one end and slowly bending it inside the pot as the pasta softens. Keep water boiling; stir pasta with a long-handled wooden fork to prevent it from sticking together. Follow cooking time recommendation on package. Pasta should be cooked through but still firm. Check for doneness by biting into a piece of pasta rinsed in cold water. Drain cooked pasta into a colander in the sink.
3. Top pasta with sauce and scallions.

Calories Per Serving: 303
Fat: 2 g
Cholesterol: 31 mg
Protein: 24 g

Carbohydrates: 48 g
Dietary Fiber: 1 g
Sodium: 321 mg

Curried Bucatini with Bay Scallops and Spinach

Bucatini and scallops are prepared with spinach and plum tomatoes in a curried yogurt sauce.

YIELD: *6 servings* • PREPARATION TIME: *20 minutes* •
COOKING TIME: *5 minutes plus pasta cooking time*

6 quarts water
12 ounces bucatini
½ cup nonfat chicken broth
6 scallions, sliced diagonally into thin
    pieces
4 teaspoons minced fresh gingerroot

3 teaspoons curry powder
2 cloves garlic, minced
6 cups chopped fresh spinach
12 ounces bay scallops
8 plum tomatoes, diced
½ cup nonfat plain yogurt

1. Bring water to a rapid boil in a large, covered pot. Add pasta by holding it in a bundle at one end and slowly bending it inside the pot as the pasta softens. Keep water boiling; stir pasta with a long-handled wooden fork to prevent it from sticking together. Follow cooking time recommendation on package. Pasta should be cooked through but still firm. Check for doneness by biting into a piece of pasta rinsed in cold water. Drain cooked pasta into a colander in the sink.
2. Heat ¼ cup broth in a large skillet. Add scallions, gingerroot, curry powder, and garlic and sauté for 2 minutes.
3. Add spinach and cook 2 minutes.
4. Add scallops and cook until they're opaque, about 2 minutes.
5. Combine pasta, scallop mixture, and tomatoes in skillet. Combine yogurt and remaining chicken broth. Blend into the sauce; cover and cook until all ingredients are heated through, about 1 minute.

Calories Per Serving: 335	Carbohydrates: 55 g
Fat: 3 g	Dietary Fiber: 4 g
Cholesterol: 19 mg	Sodium: 195 mg
Protein: 21 g	

Fedelini with Red Snapper

Fedelini are served with chunks of fish, red bell pepper, and fresh tomatoes.

YIELD: 6 servings ▪ PREPARATION TIME: 15 minutes ▪
COOKING TIME: 27 minutes plus pasta cooking time

¼ cup nonfat chicken broth
1 red bell pepper, finely chopped
1 medium onion, finely chopped
2 cloves garlic, minced
6 large ripe tomatoes, chopped, with
*   juice retained*
1 bay leaf

½ teaspoon dried marjoram
¼ teaspoon cayenne pepper
1 pound red snapper or mild white fish,
*   cut into 1-inch pieces*
6 quarts water
12 ounces fedelini
¼ cup chopped fresh parsley

1. Heat broth in a large skillet over medium heat. Add red bell pepper, onion, and garlic. Sauté for 2 minutes. Add tomatoes with their juice, bay leaf, marjoram, and cayenne. Bring to a boil. Reduce heat and simmer for 15 minutes. Add fish and cook until it flakes with a fork, about 10 minutes. Remove and discard bay leaf.

2. Bring water to a rapid boil in a large, covered pot. Add pasta by holding it in a bundle at one end and slowly bending it inside the pot as the pasta softens. Keep water boiling; stir pasta with a long-handled wooden fork to prevent it from sticking together. Follow cooking time recommendation on package. Pasta should be cooked through but still firm. Check for doneness by biting into a piece of pasta rinsed in cold water. Drain cooked pasta into a colander in the sink.

3. Top pasta with sauce and garnish with parsley.

Calories Per Serving: 293	Carbohydrates: 52 g
Fat: 2 g	Dietary Fiber: 2 g
Cholesterol: 11 mg	Sodium: 76 mg
Protein: 17 g	

Ziti Rigati with Haddock Sauce

Ridged ziti is prepared with bite-size pieces of haddock in a savory anchovy-tomato sauce.

YIELD: 4 servings • *PREPARATION TIME: 20 minutes* •
COOKING TIME: 25 minutes plus pasta cooking time

¼ cup nonfat chicken broth
1 green bell pepper, cut into ½-inch squares
1 medium onion, thinly sliced
1 clove garlic, minced
4 anchovy fillets, mashed
3 cups chopped fresh plum tomatoes

¼ teaspoon ground black pepper
¾ pound haddock fillet, cut into 1-inch squares
1 teaspoon lemon juice
4 quarts water
8 ounces ziti rigati
parsley sprigs for garnish

1. Heat broth in a large saucepan. Add green bell pepper, onion, garlic, and anchovies. Sauté for 5 minutes. Add the tomatoes and black pepper and simmer for an additional 10 minutes. Add the fish and lemon juice. Simmer until fish flakes easily, about 10 minutes.

2. Bring water to a rapid boil in a large, covered pot. Slowly stir in pasta. Return water to a boil. Stir pasta with a long-handled wooden fork to prevent it from sticking together. Follow cooking time recommendation on package. Pasta should be cooked through but still firm. Check for doneness by biting into a piece of pasta rinsed in cold water. Drain cooked pasta into a colander in the sink.

3. Top pasta with sauce and garnish with parsley.

Calories Per Serving: 356

Fat: 3 g

Cholesterol: 34 mg

Protein: 28 g

Carbohydrates: 54 g

Dietary Fiber: 3 g

Sodium: 244 mg

Tubetti Lunghi with Tuna

Short, hollow pasta is combined with grilled tuna and asparagus in a garlic-lemon sauce.

*YIELD: 6 servings ▪ PREPARATION TIME: 10 minutes ▪
COOKING TIME: 8 minutes plus pasta cooking time*

1 fresh tuna steak, about 6 ounces

1 teaspoon low-sodium soy sauce

6 quarts water

12 ounces tubetti lunghi

12 ounces fresh asparagus, cut diagonally into 1-inch lengths

¼ cup nonfat chicken broth

1 clove garlic, minced

½ teaspoon minced fresh gingerroot

1 tablespoon lemon juice

1 tablespoon minced lemon peel

1. Preheat broiler.
2. Meanwhile, brush both sides of the tuna with soy sauce. Broil until almost cooked through, about 3 minutes on each side. Flake tuna into bite-size pieces.
3. Bring water to a rapid boil in a large, covered pot. Slowly stir in pasta. Return water to a boil. Stir pasta with a long-handled wooden fork to prevent it from sticking together. Follow cooking time recommendation on package. Pasta should be cooked through but still firm. Check for doneness by biting into a piece of pasta rinsed in cold water. Drain cooked pasta into a colander in the sink.
4. Heat 2 inches of water in the bottom of a steamer. Steam the asparagus until just tender-crisp, about 3 minutes.
5. Heat broth in a skillet. Add garlic and gingerroot and sauté for 30 seconds. Add lemon juice and lemon peel.
6. Top pasta with asparagus, tuna, and garlic-lemon sauce.

Calories Per Serving: 268

Fat: 3 g

Cholesterol: 11 mg

Protein: 16 g

Carbohydrates: 44 g

Dietary Fiber: 1 g

Sodium: 66 mg

Linguine with Salmon

Linguine is prepared with a basil–lemon sauce and broiled salmon.

YIELD: 6 servings • PREPARATION TIME: 15 minutes •
COOKING TIME: 11 minutes plus pasta cooking time

6 ounces salmon fillet	¼ cup minced fresh parsley
6 quarts water	½ teaspoon dried basil
12 ounces linguine	¼ teaspoon ground black pepper
¼ cup nonfat chicken broth	2 teaspoons lemon juice
2 cloves garlic, minced	2 tablespoons grated nonfat Parmesan

1. Preheat broiler.
2. Broil salmon until done through, about 4 minutes on each side. Allow salmon to cool slightly; flake into small pieces.
3. Bring water to a rapid boil in a large, covered pot. Add pasta by holding it in a bundle at one end and slowly bending it inside the pot as the pasta softens. Keep water boiling; stir pasta with a long-handled wooden fork to prevent it from sticking together. Follow cooking time recommendation on package. Pasta should be cooked through but still firm. Check for doneness by biting into a piece of pasta rinsed in cold water. Drain cooked pasta into a colander in the sink.
4. Heat broth in a large skillet. Add garlic and sauté for 1 minute. Add parsley, basil, and black pepper. Sauté for 30 seconds.
5. Add salmon and lemon juice to herb sauce. Heat for 1 minute. Top pasta with fish and sauce. Sprinkle with Parmesan.

Calories Per Serving: 282	Carbohydrates: 47 g
Fat: 3 g	Dietary Fiber: 1 g
Cholesterol: 22 mg	Sodium: 53 mg
Protein: 16 g	

Conchiglie with Scallops and Tomato-Cucumber Sauce

Little shells are topped with a gazpacholike sauce and sautéed scallops.

YIELD: 4 servings • PREPARATION TIME: 20 minutes •
COOKING TIME: 4 minutes plus pasta cooking time

3 large ripe tomatoes, chopped
1 cucumber, peeled, seeded, and
   chopped
¼ cup chopped onion
1 celery stalk, chopped
½ green bell pepper, chopped
1 tablespoon minced fresh parsley
1 teaspoon dried basil

1 teaspoon dried cilantro
1 clove garlic, minced
¼ teaspoon ground black pepper
4 quarts water
8 ounces conchiglie
¼ cup nonfat chicken broth
1 pound bay scallops

1. Combine tomatoes, cucumber, onion, celery, green bell pepper, parsley, basil, cilantro, garlic, and black pepper in a bowl and set aside at room temperature.
2. Bring water to a rapid boil in a large, covered pot. Slowly stir in pasta. Return water to a boil. Stir pasta with a long-handled wooden fork to prevent it from sticking together. Follow cooking time recommendation on package. Pasta should be cooked through but still firm. Check for doneness by biting into a piece of pasta rinsed in cold water. Drain cooked pasta into a colander in the sink.
3. Heat broth in a skillet. Add scallops and cook until done, about 4 minutes.
4. Top pasta with scallops and sauce.

Calories Per Serving: 331
Fat: 3 g
Cholesterol: 129 mg
Protein: 26 g

Carbohydrates: 50 g
Dietary Fiber: 2 g
Sodium: 170 mg

Capellini with Tuna-Anchovy Sauce

Very thin spaghetti is topped with chunks of tuna, green bell pepper, scallions, capers, olives, and anchovies.

YIELD: 4 servings • *PREPARATION TIME: 15 minutes* •
COOKING TIME: 12 minutes plus pasta cooking time

¼ cup nonfat chicken broth
¼ cup sliced scallions
1 small green bell pepper, chopped
¾ pound fresh tuna, cut into ¾-inch
   cubes
4 cloves garlic, minced
½ tablespoon low-sodium tomato paste
4 pitted black olives, quartered

3 anchovy fillets, minced
1 tablespoon capers
¼ teaspoon ground black pepper
½ teaspoon dried oregano
4 quarts water
8 ounces capellini
¼ cup chopped fresh parsley

1. Heat broth in a skillet over medium heat. Add scallions and green bell pepper and sauté until pepper just begins to soften, about 5 minutes. Add tuna and garlic. Sauté until tuna is cooked through, about 5 minutes. Stir in tomato paste, olives, anchovies, capers, black pepper, and oregano. Heat all ingredients through.
2. Bring water to a rapid boil in a large, covered pot. Add pasta by holding it in a bundle at one end and slowly bending it inside the pot as the pasta softens. Keep water boiling; stir pasta with a long-handled wooden fork to prevent it from sticking together. Follow cooking time recommendation on package. Pasta should be cooked through but still firm. Check for doneness by biting into a piece of pasta rinsed in cold water. Drain cooked pasta into a colander in the sink.
3. Top pasta with tuna sauce and garnish with parsley.

Calories Per Serving: 339
Fat: 3 g
Cholesterol: 41 mg
Protein: 29 g

Carbohydrates: 48 g
Dietary Fiber: 1 g
Sodium: 217 mg

Orecchiette with Cod

"Little ears" in a sauce of cod, plum tomatoes, parsley, onion, and garlic.

YIELD: *4 servings* • PREPARATION TIME: *10 minutes* •
COOKING TIME: *22 minutes plus pasta cooking time*

2 tablespoons nonfat chicken broth
2 tablespoons finely chopped onion
1 clove garlic, minced
2 cups low-sodium canned plum tomatoes, crushed, with their juice
1 tablespoon low-sodium tomato paste

1 tablespoon minced fresh parsley
¼ teaspoon ground black pepper
8 ounces codfish fillet, cut into ¾-inch cubes
4 quarts water
8 ounces orecchiette

1. Heat broth in a large skillet. Add onion and sauté until tender, about 3 minutes. Add garlic and sauté for 1 minute. Add tomatoes, tomato paste, parsley, and black pepper. Simmer, stirring occasionally, until sauce begins to thicken, about 10 minutes.
2. Add the fish, cover, and simmer until fish is cooked through, about 8 minutes.
3. Bring water to a rapid boil in a large, covered pot. Slowly stir in pasta. Return water to a boil. Stir pasta with a long-handled wooden fork to prevent

it from sticking together. Follow cooking time recommendation on package. Pasta should be cooked through but still firm. Check for doneness by biting into a piece of pasta rinsed in cold water. Drain cooked pasta into a colander in the sink.

4. Toss pasta with sauce.

Calories Per Serving: 317	Carbohydrates: 49 g
Fat: 2 g	Dietary Fiber: 3 g
Cholesterol: 43 mg	Sodium: 100 mg
Protein: 24 g	

Mostaccioli with Albacore Tuna

"Little mustaches" are served with a sauce made with canned tuna, capers, and plum tomatoes.

YIELD: 4 servings • PREPARATION TIME: 15 minutes •
COOKING TIME: 24 minutes plus pasta cooking time

¼ cup nonfat chicken broth	1 6½-ounce can water-packed white al-
1 medium onion, chopped	bacore tuna, flaked into small pieces
2 cloves garlic, minced	2 tablespoons chopped capers
2 cups canned low-sodium plum toma-	4 quarts water
toes, with their juice	8 ounces mostaccioli
¼ teaspoon ground black pepper	¼ cup chopped fresh parsley

1. Heat broth in a large skillet. Add onion and garlic and sauté until onion is translucent, about 3 minutes. Add tomatoes with their juice, and black pepper. Cook, stirring occasionally, for 10 minutes.
2. Transfer tomato mixture to a blender or food processor and puree. Return to the skillet. Stir in flaked tuna and capers and cook for 10 additional minutes.
3. Bring water to a rapid boil in a large, covered pot. Slowly stir in pasta. Return water to a boil. Stir pasta with a long-handled wooden fork to prevent it from sticking together. Follow cooking time recommendation on package. Pasta should be cooked through but still firm. Check for doneness by biting into a piece of pasta rinsed in cold water. Drain cooked pasta into a colander in the sink.
4. Toss pasta with sauce and garnish with parsley.

Calories Per Serving: 306
Fat: 2 g
Cholesterol: 8 mg
Protein: 21 g

Carbohydrates: 53 g
Dietary Fiber: 2 g
Sodium: 72 mg

Farfalle with Broccoli Florets and Albacore Tuna

Butterfly pasta is combined with canned tuna, broccoli, onion, and lemon juice.

YIELD: 4 servings • *PREPARATION TIME: 10 minutes* •
COOKING TIME: 12 minutes plus pasta cooking time

4 quarts water
8 ounces farfalle
¼ cup nonfat chicken broth
½ medium onion, thinly sliced
2 cloves garlic, minced
1 6½ ounce can water-packed white albacore tuna, drained

3 tablespoons lemon juice
1 tablespoon chopped fresh parsley
1 teaspoon minced lemon peel
¼ teaspoon dried oregano
¼ teaspoon ground black pepper
2 cups broccoli cut into 1-inch pieces

1. Bring water to a rapid boil in a large, covered pot. Slowly stir in pasta. Return water to a boil. Stir pasta with a long-handled wooden fork to prevent it from sticking together. Follow cooking time recommendation on package. Pasta should be cooked through but still firm. Check for doneness by biting into a piece of pasta rinsed in cold water. Drain cooked pasta into a colander in the sink.
2. Heat broth in a large skillet. Add onion and garlic and sauté for 2 minutes. Stir in tuna, lemon juice, parsley, lemon peel, oregano, and black pepper.
3. Heat 2 inches of water in the bottom of a steamer. Steam broccoli until tender-crisp.
4. Combine broccoli and tuna mixture, and toss with the pasta.

Calories Per Serving: 291
Fat: 2 g
Cholesterol: 8 mg
Protein: 21 g

Carbohydrates: 49 g
Dietary Fiber: 2 g
Sodium: 67 mg

Rotelle with Broccoflower and Albacore Tuna

Pasta wheels are prepared with broccoflower, tuna, red bell pepper, and tomatoes.

YIELD: 6 servings ▪ PREPARATION TIME: 10 minutes ▪
COOKING TIME: 15 minutes plus pasta cooking time

6 quarts water
12 ounces rotelle
4 large ripe tomatoes, chopped, with
    their juice
1 teaspoon olive oil
1 clove garlic, minced
2 cups chopped broccoflower

1 cup chopped zucchini
1 cup chopped red bell pepper
½ teaspoon dried basil
⅛ teaspoon dried oregano
¼ teaspoon ground black pepper
1 6½-ounce can water-packed white albacore tuna, drained and flaked

1. Bring water to a rapid boil in a large, covered pot. Slowly stir in pasta. Return water to a boil. Stir pasta with a long-handled wooden fork to prevent it from sticking together. Follow cooking time recommendation on package. Pasta should be cooked through but still firm. Check for doneness by biting into a piece of pasta rinsed in cold water. Drain cooked pasta into a colander in the sink.
2. Combine tomatoes, oil, and garlic in a saucepan. Cover and simmer until tomatoes are softened, about 5 minutes.
3. Add the broccoflower, zucchini, red bell pepper, basil, oregano, and black pepper. Cover and simmer until vegetables are just tender, about 10 minutes. Stir in tuna.
4. Toss pasta with sauce.

Calories Per Serving: 285
Fat: 3 g
Cholesterol: 6 mg
Protein: 17 g

Carbohydrates: 50 g
Dietary Fiber: 2 g
Sodium: 41 mg

Radiatore with Shrimp and Zucchini

Radiator-shaped pasta with a topping of shrimp, tomato, and zucchini seasoned with garlic and oregano.

YIELD: 4 servings ▪ PREPARATION TIME: 15 minutes ▪
COOKING TIME: 13 minutes plus pasta cooking time

lemon peel, basil, and cayenne pepper. Bring to a boil; reduce heat, cover, and simmer for 25 minutes.

3. Stir in clams and fish. Bring up to a boil. Immediately reduce heat; cover and simmer for 5 minutes, or until fish is done.

4. Toss pasta with fish–clam sauce.

Calories Per Serving: 214	Carbohydrates: 27 g
Fat: 3 g	Dietary Fiber: 2 g
Cholesterol: 32 mg	Sodium: 85 mg
Protein: 20 g	

Mafalda-Shrimp Salad with Cumin-Garlic Dressing

Broad, flat noodles are tossed with shrimp and a summery combination of corn, red bell peppers, and zucchini.

YIELD: *6 servings*   ▪   PREPARATION TIME: *20 minutes*   ▪
COOKING TIME: *pasta cooking time*

4 quarts water
12 ounces mafalda
3 large ripe tomatoes, seeded and
  chopped
½ pound cooked shrimp, peeled, de-
  veined, and cut in half lengthwise
1 cup fresh or canned corn kernels, or 1
  cup frozen corn kernels, thawed
1 cup chopped red bell pepper

½ cup zucchini cut into thin strips
2 tablespoons chopped fresh parsley
3 tablespoons water
1 tablespoon cider vinegar
1 tablespoon chili powder
1 teaspoon sugar
3 cloves garlic, minced
½ teaspoon ground cumin
fresh parsley for garnish

1. Bring water to a rapid boil in a large, covered pot. Add pasta by holding it in a bundle at one end and slowly bending it inside the pot as the pasta softens. Keep water boiling; stir pasta with a long-handled wooden fork to prevent it from sticking together. Follow cooking time recommendation on package. Pasta should be cooked through but still firm. Check for doneness by biting into a piece of pasta rinsed in cold water. Drain cooked pasta into a colander in the sink. Allow to cool to room temperature.

2. Combine tomatoes, mafalda, shrimp, corn, red bell pepper, zucchini, and parsley in a large bowl and toss gently.

3. Whisk together the water, vinegar, chili powder, sugar, garlic, and cumin. Pour dressing over salad and toss to coat all ingredients. Garnish with parsley before serving.

Calories Per Serving: 295
Fat: 1 g
Cholesterol: 57 mg
Protein: 17 g

Carbohydrates: 57 g
Dietary Fiber: 2 g
Sodium: 311 mg

Shrimp and Orzo in Tomato-Wine Sauce

Shrimp are simmered in a tomato-wine sauce and combined with rice-shaped pasta.

YIELD: 6 servings • *PREPARATION TIME: 20 minutes* • *COOKING TIME: 30 minutes*

2 cups water
1 cup orzo
¼ cup nonfat chicken broth
1 medium onion, chopped
4 cloves garlic, minced
¼ cup dry white wine
3½ cups fresh or low-sodium canned tomatoes, chopped

3 tablespoons chopped fresh parsley
½ teaspoon dried oregano
½ teaspoon dried basil
¼ teaspoon ground black pepper
½ teaspoon cayenne pepper
1 pound medium shrimp, peeled and deveined

1. Bring water to a boil in a large saucepan. Stir in orzo; return to a boil, reduce heat, and simmer until pasta is just tender.
2. Heat chicken broth in a large saucepan. Add onion and garlic and sauté until onion begins to soften, about 3 minutes.
3. Add wine and bring to a boil. Stir in tomatoes, 1½ tablespoons parsley, oregano, basil, black pepper, and cayenne pepper and simmer for 5 minutes.
4. Add shrimp and simmer, stirring, until shrimp turn pink, about 2 minutes.
5. Drain orzo and combine with tomato-shrimp mixture. Sprinkle with remaining parsley.

Calories Per Serving: 251
Fat: 2 g
Cholesterol: 116 mg
Protein: 25 g

Carbohydrates: 30 g
Dietary Fiber: 3 g
Sodium: 208 mg

Oregano Shrimp, Broccoli, and Cauliflower with Orzo

This quickly prepared dish partners shrimp, broccoli, cauliflower, and oregano.

YIELD: *4 servings* • PREPARATION TIME: *15 minutes* •
COOKING TIME: *12 minutes*

2½ cups nonfat chicken broth
2 cups low-sodium canned tomatoes, drained and chopped
1½ cups fresh broccoli cut into bite-size pieces
1½ cups fresh cauliflower cut into bite-size pieces

1 cup orzo
8 ounces medium shrimp, peeled and deveined
¼ teaspoon ground black pepper
2 teaspoons dried oregano

1. Combine broth, tomatoes, broccoli, and cauliflower in a large skillet. Bring to a boil; stir in orzo, reduce heat, cover, and simmer, stirring occasionally, for 8 minutes, until pasta is cooked.
2. Add shrimp and black pepper. Simmer, stirring occasionally, until shrimp become pink, about 3 minutes.
3. Remove from heat and stir in oregano. Transfer to a large serving bowl and serve immediately.

Calories Per Serving: 323
Fat: 2 g
Cholesterol: 85 mg
Protein: 26 g

Carbohydrates: 49 g
Dietary Fiber: 5 g
Sodium: 638 mg

Maruzze with Shrimp Salad

Medium-size pasta shells are united with shrimp and snow peas in a garlic-yogurt dressing.

YIELD: *4 servings* • PREPARATION TIME: *15 minutes* •
COOKING TIME: *1 minute plus pasta cooking time and snow pea steaming time*

4 quarts plus 2 cups water
8 ounces maruzze
1 cup fresh snow peas, strings removed
1 cup nonfat plain yogurt
1 tablespoon red wine vinegar
2 cloves garlic, minced
¼ teaspoon ground black pepper

¼ teaspoon dried basil
½ pound cooked medium shrimp, peeled
   and deveined
6 cherry tomatoes, halved
½ green bell pepper, cut into ¼-inch
   strips
3 scallions, thinly sliced

1. Bring 4 quarts water to a rapid boil in a large, covered pot. Slowly stir in pasta. Return water to a boil. Stir pasta with a long-handled wooden fork to prevent it from sticking together. Follow cooking time recommendation on package. Pasta should be cooked through but still firm. Check for doneness by biting into a piece of pasta rinsed in cold water. Drain cooked pasta into a colander in the sink.

2. Bring remaining 2 cups water to a boil. Add snow peas and continue to boil until peas are just tender-crisp, about 1 minute. Drain peas and plunge into ice water. Drain.

3. Combine yogurt, vinegar, garlic, black pepper, and basil. Stir well. Add shrimp, snow peas, pasta, cherry tomatoes, green bell pepper, and scallions. Toss gently to coat.

Calories Per Serving: 313
Fat: 1 g
Cholesterol: 86 mg
Protein: 24 g

Carbohydrates: 52 g
Dietary Fiber: 3 g
Sodium: 453 mg

PASTA WITH POULTRY

Fettuccine with Chicken and Mushrooms • Tagiatelle with Paprika Chicken • Fettuccelle with Orange-Fennel Chicken • Capellini with Creole Chicken Sauce • Cavatelli with Curried Chicken and Chutney • Bucatini with Chicken and Vegetables • Maruzze with Leeks and Chicken • Gemelli with Chicken and Asparagus • Vermicelli with Shiitake-Chicken Sauce • Linguine, Pinto Beans, and Chicken in Barbecue Sauce • Spicy Spinach Fettuccine with Snow Peas and Chicken • Tubetti Lunghi with Chicken and Red Bell Peppers • Spaghettini Cacciatore with Yellow Bell Peppers • Mezzani with Chicken and Vegetables • Perciatelli with Chicken and Vegetables in Wine Sauce • Farfalle with Cumin Chicken • Eggplant-Turkey Ziti • Capellini with Chicken and Mushrooms in a Sweet-and-Sour Sauce • Tagliatelle with Shiitake-Chicken Sauce • Radiatore with Curried Chicken • Fedelini with Chicken and Shrimp in Honey-Peanut Sauce • Cravatte with Lemon-Marinated Chicken and Mixed Vegetables • Green Beans, Red Bell Peppers, and Chicken with Orzo • Orecchiette with Tomato-Wine Sauce and Ground Turkey • Ziti Rigati with Mushroom–Ground Turkey Sauce • Mezzani Rigati with Easy Turkey-Tomato Sauce • Penne Rigate with Quick and Spicy Turkey-Tomato Sauce • Linguine with Turkey-Clam Sauce • Conchiglie and Vegetables in Wine Sauce • Rigatoni with Black

Bean–Ground Turkey Sauce ▪ Ziti with White Bean–Chili Sauce ▪ Penne with Kidney Bean–Ground Turkey Sauce ▪ Mostaccioli with Ground Turkey and Snow Peas ▪ Conchiglie Rigati with Curried Tomato Sauce and Ground Turkey ▪ Maruzze Stuffed with Eggplant-Tomato Sauce ▪ Turkey Manicotti in Marinara Sauce ▪ Turkey-Jalapeño Lasagna ▪ Turkey-Vegetable Lasagna ▪ Turkey Lasagna with Yogurt Sauce ▪ Cavatelli with Turkey and Artichokes ▪ Rotelle-Chicken Salad ▪ Rotini-Chicken Salad with Red Grapes and Sugar Snap Peas ▪ Farfalle with Chicken and Yellow Bell Pepper ▪ Fusilli-Chicken Salad with Tropical Fruit Dressing ▪ Penne-Chicken Salad ▪ Chicken, Fruit, and Fusilli Salad ▪ Conchiglie with Smoked Turkey–Asparagus Salad ▪ Mostaccioli with Apples and Turkey Salad ▪ Radiatore-Turkey-Cantaloupe Salad

Fettuccine with Chicken and Mushrooms

Fettuccine is topped with broiled chicken chunks in a mushroom–tomato–white wine sauce.

YIELD: 4 servings • *PREPARATION TIME: 10 minutes* •
COOKING TIME: 17 minutes plus pasta cooking time

12 ounces skinless chicken breast cutlets	3 cups sliced fresh mushrooms
¼ cup nonfat chicken broth	¼ teaspoon ground black pepper
1 medium onion, chopped	2 tablespoons dry white wine
2 cloves garlic, minced	4 quarts water
2 cups canned low-sodium tomatoes, chopped, with juice	8 ounces fettuccine
	¼ cup chopped fresh parsley

1. Preheat broiler. Broil chicken until cooked through, about 4 minutes on each side. Allow to cool sufficiently to handle. Cut into ½-inch cubes and set aside.
2. Heat broth in a large skillet. Add onion and sauté for 3 minutes. Add garlic, tomatoes with juice, and mushrooms. Bring to a boil; reduce heat and simmer, stirring frequently, for 5 minutes.
3. Add chicken, black pepper, and wine; simmer until all ingredients are heated through.
4. Bring water to a rapid boil in a large, covered pot. Add pasta by holding it in a bundle at one end and slowly bending it inside the pot as the pasta softens. Keep water boiling; stir pasta with a long-handled wooden fork to prevent it from sticking together. Follow cooking time recommendation on package. Pasta should be cooked through but still firm. Check for doneness by biting into a piece of pasta rinsed in cold water. Drain cooked pasta into a colander in the sink.
5. Toss pasta with sauce and garnish with parsley.

Calories Per Serving: 347	Carbohydrates: 53 g
Fat: 2 g	Dietary Fiber: 2 g
Cholesterol: 56 mg	Sodium: 63 mg
Protein: 30 g	

Tagliatelle with Paprika Chicken

Tagliatelle are served with sliced chicken and a wine-flavored tomato sauce.

YIELD: 4 servings   ▪   PREPARATION TIME: 10 minutes   ▪
COOKING TIME: 45 minutes plus pasta cooking time

4 skinless chicken breast cutlets, about 4
    ounces each
1½ cups nonfat chicken broth
¼ cup all-purpose flour
1 medium onion, finely chopped
1 small green bell pepper, diced
1 tablespoon paprika
½ cup dry white wine

1 cup low-sodium canned tomatoes,
    chopped, with juice
1 clove garlic, minced
½ teaspoon ground black pepper
4 quarts water
8 ounces tagliatelle
½ cup nonfat sour cream

1. Cut each chicken cutlet into six small slices. Sprinkle chicken with flour.
2. Heat ¼ cup broth in a large pot. Add chicken and sauté until no longer pink, about 2 minutes on each side. Remove chicken with a slotted spoon and set aside.
3. Add onion and green pepper to the pot. Sauté for 5 minutes. Add more broth as needed.
4. Add paprika and chicken pieces to pot. Stir in remaining broth, wine, tomatoes with their juice, garlic, and black pepper. Lower heat and simmer until chicken is cooked through, about 20 minutes.
5. Bring water to a rapid boil in a large, covered pot. Add pasta by holding it in a bundle at one end and slowly bending it inside the pot as the pasta softens. Keep water boiling; stir pasta with a long-handled wooden fork to prevent it from sticking together. Follow cooking time recommendation on package. Pasta should be cooked through but still firm. Check for doneness by biting into a piece of pasta rinsed in cold water. Drain cooked pasta into a colander in the sink.
6. Stir sour cream into sauce and warm through.
7. Transfer pasta to serving dish and top with sauce.

Calories Per Serving: 453
Fat: 3 g
Cholesterol: 81 mg
Protein: 40 g

Carbohydrates: 64 g
Dietary Fiber: 2 g
Sodium: 178 mg

Fettuccelle with Orange-Fennel Chicken

Fettuccelle are served with sautéed chicken and fennel in an orange-flavored tomato sauce.

YIELD: *6 servings* • PREPARATION TIME: *15 minutes* •
COOKING TIME: *32 minutes plus pasta cooking time*

¼ cup or more nonfat chicken broth
1½ pounds skinless chicken breast cutlets, cut into ½-inch cubes
1 medium onion, thinly sliced
1 fennel bulb, thinly sliced, about 3 cups
1 teaspoon minced orange peel
¼ cup orange juice

¼ cup white wine vinegar
2 cups low-sodium canned tomatoes, with juice, chopped
1 clove garlic, minced
¼ teaspoon ground black pepper
¼ cup white wine
6 quarts water
12 ounces fettuccelle

1. Heat broth in a large pot. Add chicken and sauté until no longer pink, about 2 minutes on each side. Remove chicken and set aside.
2. Add onion and fennel to the pot and sauté for 10 minutes. Add water or additional broth as needed.
3. Add chicken pieces, orange peel, orange juice, wine vinegar, tomatoes with their juice, garlic, and black pepper. Simmer, partially covered, until chicken is cooked through, about 20 minutes.
4. Add wine and continue to simmer.
5. Bring water to a rapid boil in a large, covered pot. Add pasta by holding it in a bundle at one end and slowly bending it inside the pot as the pasta softens. Keep water boiling; stir pasta with a long-handled wooden fork to prevent it from sticking together. Follow cooking time recommendation on package. Pasta should be cooked through but still firm. Check for doneness by biting into a piece of pasta rinsed in cold water. Drain cooked pasta into a colander in the sink.
6. Toss pasta with orange-fennel chicken and serve.

Calories Per Serving: 390
Fat: 2 g
Cholesterol: 75 mg
Protein: 37 g

Carbohydrates: 58 g
Dietary Fiber: 1 g
Sodium: 77 mg

Capellini with Creole Chicken Sauce

Very thin spaghetti is served with okra, red bell pepper, and chicken in a zesty Creole tomato sauce.

YIELD: 6 servings • PREPARATION TIME: 20 minutes •
COOKING TIME: 32 minutes plus pasta cooking time

1¾ cups nonfat chicken broth
1½ pounds skinless chicken breast cutlets, cut into ½-inch cubes
1 medium onion, chopped
2 stalks celery, diced
1 red bell pepper, chopped
½ teaspoon cayenne pepper
1 bay leaf

1 clove garlic, minced
2 cups sliced okra
2 tablespoons tomato paste
1 cup low-sodium canned plum tomatoes, drained, chopped
¼ teaspoon hot pepper sauce
6 quarts water
12 ounces capellini

1. Heat ¼ cup broth in a large casserole dish. Add chicken and sauté until meat is no longer pink, about 2 minutes. Remove chicken from dish and set aside.
2. Add onion, celery, and red bell pepper; sauté until softened, about 8 minutes. Add cayenne pepper and sauté for an additional 2 minutes.
3. Return chicken to the casserole. Add remaining broth, bay leaf, garlic, okra, tomato paste, tomatoes, and hot pepper sauce. Cover and simmer gently until chicken is cooked through, about 20 minutes. Remove bay leaf.
4. Bring water to a rapid boil in a large, covered pot. Add pasta by holding it in a bundle at one end and slowly bending it inside the pot as the pasta softens. Keep water boiling; stir pasta with a long-handled wooden fork to prevent it from sticking together. Follow cooking time recommendation on package. Pasta should be cooked through but still firm. Check for doneness by biting into a piece of pasta rinsed in cold water. Drain cooked pasta into a colander in the sink.
5. Toss pasta with sauce, transfer to a large bowl, and serve immediately.

Calories Per Serving: 369
Fat: 3 g
Cholesterol: 75 mg
Protein: 38 g

Carbohydrates: 52 g
Dietary Fiber: 2 g
Sodium: 149 mg

Cavatelli with Curried Chicken and Chutney

Sautéed chicken is served over short, curly noodles with a chutney–yogurt sauce.

YIELD: 4 servings • PREPARATION TIME: 10 minutes •
COOKING TIME: 15 minutes plus pasta cooking time

4 quarts water
8 ounces cavatelli
1 teaspoon minced fresh gingerroot
1 clove garlic, minced
1 cup nonfat plain yogurt
1 tablespoon curry powder
¼ cup nonfat chicken broth

1 medium onion, coarsely chopped
2 celery stalks, sliced into thin diagonal
  pieces
4 skinless chicken breast cutlets, about 4
  ounces each, cut into thin slices
½ cup mango chutney

1. Bring water to a rapid boil in a large, covered pot. Slowly stir in pasta. Return water to a boil. Stir pasta with a long-handled wooden fork to prevent it from sticking together. Follow cooking time recommendation on package. Pasta should be cooked through but still firm. Check for doneness by biting into a piece of pasta rinsed in cold water. Drain cooked pasta into a colander in the sink.
2. Combine gingerroot, garlic, yogurt, and curry powder in a small bowl.
3. Heat broth in a large skillet. Add onion and celery and sauté until celery is just tender, about 5 minutes.
4. Add chicken and sauté for five minutes. Stir in the yogurt mixture and chutney. Simmer until chicken is cooked through, about 5 minutes.
5. Toss pasta with sauce and serve immediately.

Calories Per Serving: 425
Fat: 2 g
Cholesterol: 56 mg
Protein: 29 g

Carbohydrates: 72 g
Dietary Fiber: 2 g
Sodium: 316 mg

Bucatini with Chicken and Vegetables

Long, hollow spaghetti is served with a creamy, thyme-flavored chicken-vegetable sauce.

YIELD: 4 servings • PREPARATION TIME: 15 minutes •
COOKING TIME: 20 minutes plus pasta cooking time

4 quarts water
8 ounces bucatini
¾ cup nonfat chicken broth
1 medium onion, minced
2 stalks celery, cut into thin diagonal
    slices

1 pound skinless chicken breast cutlets,
    cut into ½-inch cubes
1 carrot, diced, steamed until just tender
½ cup fresh peas or frozen, thawed peas
½ teaspoon dried thyme
¼ cup skim milk
⅛ teaspoon ground white pepper

1. Bring water to a rapid boil in a large, covered pot. Add pasta by holding it in a bundle at one end and slowly bending it inside the pot as the pasta softens. Keep water boiling; stir pasta with a long-handled wooden fork to prevent it from sticking together. Follow cooking time recommendation on package. Pasta should be cooked through but still firm. Check for doneness by biting into a piece of pasta rinsed in cold water. Drain cooked pasta into a colander in the sink.
2. Heat ¼ cup of the broth in a skillet. Add onion and celery and sauté until just tender, about 5 minutes. Add chicken and sauté for 3 minutes. Stir in carrot, peas, thyme, and remaining ½ cup chicken broth. Cook until chicken is done, about 6 minutes. Stir in milk and pepper.
3. Toss pasta with sauce.

Calories Per Serving: 343
Fat: 2 g
Cholesterol: 53 mg
Protein: 29 g

Carbohydrates: 55 g
Dietary Fiber: 2 g
Sodium: 153 mg

Maruzze with Leeks and Chicken

Medium-size pasta shells are combined with chicken cutlets and a leek–tomato sauce.

YIELD: 6 servings • PREPARATION TIME: 15 minutes •
COOKING TIME: 30 minutes plus pasta cooking time

6 quarts water
8 ounces maruzze
¼ cup white wine
1 teaspoon dried basil
1 teaspoon dried oregano

1 bay leaf
1 clove garlic, minced
1½ cups nonfat chicken broth
1 pound skinless chicken breast cutlets,
    cut into ½-inch cubes

4 cups julienned leek
½ teaspoon ground black pepper

3½ cups low-sodium canned tomatoes, chopped, with juice
¼ cup grated nonfat Parmesan

1. Bring water to a rapid boil in a large, covered pot. Slowly stir in pasta. Return water to a boil. Stir pasta with a long-handled wooden fork to prevent it from sticking together. Follow cooking time recommendation on package. Pasta should be cooked through but still firm. Check for doneness by biting into a piece of pasta rinsed in cold water. Drain cooked pasta into a colander in the sink.
2. Combine wine, basil, oregano, bay leaf, garlic, and 1¼ cups broth in a large saucepan. Bring to a boil; add chicken; return to a boil. Reduce heat, cover, and simmer for 12 minutes, or until chicken is cooked through. Remove chicken from pan and set aside.
3. Heat remaining ¼ cup broth in the saucepan. Add leeks and sauté for 3 minutes, or until tender.
4. Return chicken to pan with cooked pasta, black pepper, and tomatoes. Simmer until all ingredients are heated through, about 5 minutes. Serve with Parmesan.

Calories Per Serving: 288
Fat: 2 g
Cholesterol: 38 mg
Protein: 21 g

Carbohydrates: 46 g
Dietary Fiber: 4 g
Sodium: 136 mg

Gemelli with Chicken and Asparagus

Pasta "twists" are prepared with fresh asparagus pieces, chicken strips, and lemon juice.

YIELD: *4 servings* • PREPARATION TIME: *10 minutes* •
COOKING TIME: *7 minutes plus pasta cooking time*

4 quarts water
8 ounces gemelli
¼ cup nonfat chicken broth
8 ounces asparagus, cut diagonally into ½-inch pieces
1 scallion, sliced

1 pound skinless chicken breast cutlets, cut into ½-inch strips
¼ teaspoon ground black pepper
2 tablespoons lemon juice
2 tablespoons grated nonfat Parmesan

1. Bring water to a rapid boil in a large, covered pot. Slowly stir in pasta. Return water to a boil. Stir pasta with a long-handled wooden fork to prevent it from sticking together. Follow cooking time recommendation on package. Pasta should be cooked through but still firm. Check for doneness by biting into a piece of pasta rinsed in cold water. Drain cooked pasta into a colander in the sink.
2. Heat broth in a large skillet. Add asparagus and scallion and sauté for 2 minutes. Add chicken cutlets and black pepper. Cover and simmer until chicken is cooked through, about 5 minutes. Add water as needed.
3. Toss the chicken and asparagus with the gemelli and lemon juice. Sprinkle with Parmesan.

Calories Per Serving: 346
Fat: 2 g
Cholesterol: 78 mg
Protein: 37 g

Carbohydrates: 45 g
Dietary Fiber: 1 g
Sodium: 81 mg

Vermicelli with Shiitake-Chicken Sauce

Thin spaghetti is served with sautéed chicken chunks, shiitake mushrooms, and fresh tomatoes.

YIELD: 6 servings · PREPARATION TIME: 15 minutes ·
COOKING TIME: 17 minutes plus pasta cooking time

2¾ cups nonfat chicken broth
1 pound skinless chicken breast cutlets, cut into ½-inch cubes
8 quarts water
16 ounces vermicelli
4 cloves garlic, minced

2 large ripe tomatoes, chopped
1½ pounds fresh shiitake mushrooms, sliced
6 scallions, chopped
1 teaspoon cayenne pepper
½ cup chopped fresh parsley

1. Heat ½ cup of the broth in a skillet over medium heat. Sauté chicken until cooked through, about 8 minutes.
2. Bring water to a rapid boil in a large, covered pot. Add pasta by holding it in a bundle at one end and slowly bending it inside the pot as the pasta softens. Keep water boiling; stir pasta with a long-handled wooden fork to prevent it from sticking together. Follow cooking time recommendation on package. Pasta should be cooked through but still firm. Check for doneness by biting into a piece of pasta rinsed in cold water. Drain cooked pasta into a colander in the sink.

3. Heat ¼ cup broth in a large skillet. Stir in garlic and sauté for 2 minutes. Add tomatoes, mushrooms, scallions, and cayenne pepper. Bring to a boil; reduce heat and simmer for 2 minutes. Add remaining 2 cups broth and simmer for 3 additional minutes.
4. Stir in chicken and pasta. Simmer for 2 minutes. Serve topped with parsley.

Calories Per Serving: 409
Fat: 3 g
Cholesterol: 50 mg
Protein: 33 g

Carbohydrates: 65 g
Dietary Fiber: 2 g
Sodium: 178 mg

Linguine, Pinto Beans, and Chicken in Barbecue Sauce

This quick and easy recipe combines prepared barbecue sauce, chicken, corn, pinto beans, and linguine.

YIELD: 4 servings • PREPARATION TIME: 5 minutes •
COOKING TIME: 22 minutes plus pasta cooking time

¼ cup nonfat chicken broth
4 skinless chicken breast cutlets, about 4
  ounces each, thinly sliced
1 cup low-sodium barbecue sauce
1 cup low-sodium canned pinto beans,
  rinsed and drained

2 cups fresh, canned, or frozen, thawed
  corn kernels
4 quarts water
8 ounces linguine

1. Heat broth in skillet over medium heat. Sauté chicken for 2 minutes.
2. Heat barbecue sauce in a large skillet. Add chicken and simmer for 15 minutes.
3. Add beans and corn and continue to simmer for 5 more minutes.
4. Bring water to a rapid boil in a large, covered pot. Add pasta by holding it in a bundle at one end and slowly bending it inside the pot as the pasta softens. Keep water boiling; stir pasta with a long-handled wooden fork to prevent it from sticking together. Follow cooking time recommendation on package. Pasta should be cooked through but still firm. Check for doneness by biting into a piece of pasta rinsed in cold water. Drain cooked pasta into a colander in the sink.
5. Serve linguine with sauce.

Calories Per Serving: 502   Carbohydrates: 91 g
Fat: 3 g   Dietary Fiber: 6 g
Cholesterol: 55 mg   Sodium: 902 mg
Protein: 32 g

Spicy Spinach Fettuccine with Snow Peas and Chicken

Spinach fettuccine is served with chopped chicken, snow peas, sherry, soy sauce, and minced jalapeño pepper.

YIELD: 4 servings • PREPARATION TIME: 15 minutes plus chicken cooking time •
COOKING TIME: 6 minutes plus pasta cooking time

4 quarts water
8 ounces spinach fettuccine
½ cup nonfat chicken broth
1 cup snow peas
1 clove garlic, minced

1 jalapeño pepper, seeded and minced
1 cup coarsely chopped, cooked skinless
    chicken breast cutlet
2 tablespoons reduced-sodium soy sauce
3 tablespoons dry sherry

1. Bring water to a rapid boil in a large, covered pot. Add pasta by holding it in a bundle at one end and slowly bending it inside the pot as the pasta softens. Keep water boiling; stir pasta with a long-handled wooden fork to prevent it from sticking together. Follow cooking time recommendation on package. Pasta should be cooked through but still firm. Check for doneness by biting into a piece of pasta rinsed in cold water. Drain cooked pasta into a colander in the sink.

2. Heat ¼ cup broth in a large skillet. Add snow peas, garlic, and jalapeño, and stir-fry for 1 minute. Add chicken and stir-fry for 2 minutes.

3. Add pasta, remaining ¼ cup chicken broth, soy sauce, and sherry to the skillet. Cook for 3 minutes.

Calories Per Serving: 294   Carbohydrates: 49 g
Fat: 2 g   Dietary Fiber: 1 g
Cholesterol: 28 mg   Sodium: 428 mg
Protein: 19 g

Tubetti Lunghi with Chicken and Red Bell Peppers

Tube pasta is accompanied by a simple sauce of chicken and red bell peppers.

YIELD: 4 servings • *PREPARATION TIME: 15 minutes* •
COOKING TIME: 20 minutes plus pasta cooking time

½ cup nonfat chicken broth	1 clove garlic, minced
1 pound skinless chicken breast cutlets, cut into julienne strips	⅛ teaspoon cayenne pepper
1 medium onion, chopped	2 large ripe tomatoes, chopped
2 red bell peppers, cut into thin strips	4 quarts water
	8 ounces tubetti lunghi

1. Heat ¼ cup broth in a large skillet. Add chicken and sauté until tender, about 5 minutes. Remove chicken from skillet and set aside.
2. Heat remaining ¼ cup broth in skillet. Add onion and red bell peppers and sauté until tender, about 2 minutes.
3. Return chicken to skillet, add garlic and cayenne pepper, and cook, stirring constantly, for 3 minutes. Stir in tomatoes and simmer for 10 minutes.
4. Bring water to a rapid boil in a large, covered pot. Add pasta by holding it in a bundle at one end and slowly bending it inside the pot as the pasta softens. Keep water boiling; stir pasta with a long-handled wooden fork to prevent it from sticking together. Follow cooking time recommendation on package. Pasta should be cooked through but still firm. Check for doneness by biting into a piece of pasta rinsed in cold water. Drain cooked pasta into a colander in the sink.
5. Toss pasta with sauce.

Calories Per Serving: 331	Carbohydrates: 51 g
Fat: 2 g	Dietary Fiber: 2 g
Cholesterol: 55 mg	Sodium: 68 mg
Protein: 27 g	

Spaghettini Cacciatore with Yellow Bell Peppers

Chicken cutlets are simmered in a tomato–mushroom–yellow bell pepper sauce and served over thin spaghetti.

*YIELD: 6 servings ▪ PREPARATION TIME: 15 minutes ▪
COOKING TIME: 20 minutes plus pasta cooking time*

½ cup nonfat chicken broth
1½ cups sliced onion
1½ cups sliced fresh mushrooms
1½ yellow bell peppers, coarsely chopped
2 cloves garlic, minced
6 skinless chicken breast cutlets, about 4
   ounces each

6 quarts water
12 ounces spaghettini
3 cups low-sodium tomato sauce
¼ teaspoon ground black pepper
¼ cup grated nonfat Parmesan

1. Heat ¼ cup broth in a large skillet. Add onion, mushrooms, yellow bell peppers, and garlic. Sauté until onion is translucent, about 5 minutes. Remove vegetables from skillet and set aside.
2. Heat remaining broth in the skillet. Add chicken and simmer until cooked through, about 5 minutes on each side.
3. Bring water to a rapid boil in a large, covered pot. Add pasta by holding it in a bundle at one end and slowly bending it inside the pot as the pasta softens. Keep water boiling; stir pasta with a long-handled wooden fork to prevent it from sticking together. Follow cooking time recommendation on package. Pasta should be cooked through but still firm. Check for doneness by biting into a piece of pasta rinsed in cold water. Drain cooked pasta into a colander in the sink.
4. Return vegetables to the skillet with the chicken. Add tomato sauce and black pepper and cook until all ingredients are heated through, about 5 minutes.
5. Serve pasta topped with a chicken cutlet, sauce, and Parmesan.

Calories Per Serving: 372
Fat: 2 g
Cholesterol: 58 mg
Protein: 30 g

Carbohydrates: 58 g
Dietary Fiber: 3 g
Sodium: 132 mg

Mezzani with Chicken and Vegetables

Chicken, yellow summer squash, scallions, garlic, carrot, and tomatoes are combined with tubular pasta.

YIELD: 6 servings • *PREPARATION TIME: 15 minutes plus chicken cooking time* • *COOKING TIME: 16 minutes plus pasta cooking time*

¼ cup nonfat chicken broth
1 cup chopped yellow summer squash
⅓ cup chopped scallion
2 cloves garlic, minced
1 carrot, cut into thin strips
6 quarts water

12 ounces mezzani
4 cooked skinless chicken breast cutlets,
  cut into ½-inch cubes
2 large ripe tomatoes, chopped
¼ cup grated nonfat Parmesan
¼ cup chopped fresh parsley

1. Heat broth in the skillet. Add squash, scallion, garlic, and carrot; sauté until tender-crisp.
2. Bring water to a rapid boil in a large, covered pot. Add pasta by holding it in a bundle at one end and slowly bending it inside the pot as the pasta softens. Keep water boiling; stir pasta with a long-handled wooden fork to prevent it from sticking together. Follow cooking time recommendation on package. Pasta should be cooked through but still firm. Check for doneness by biting into a piece of pasta rinsed in cold water. Drain cooked pasta into a colander in the sink.
3. Add chicken to skillet with tomatoes and cooked mezzani. Simmer for 3 minutes.
4. Top pasta with Parmesan and parsley.

Calories Per Serving: 186
Fat: 1 g
Cholesterol: 40 mg
Protein: 18 g

Carbohydrates: 26 g
Dietary Fiber: 2 g
Sodium: 78 mg

Perciatelli with Chicken and Vegetables in Wine Sauce

Long, hollow pasta is served with chicken, zucchini, asparagus, and yellow bell pepper in a white wine sauce.

YIELD: 6 servings ▪ *PREPARATION TIME: 25 minutes* ▪
COOKING TIME: 14 minutes plus pasta cooking time

6 quarts water
12 ounces perciatelli
¼ cup nonfat chicken broth
1½ pounds skinless chicken breast cutlets, cut into ½-inch strips
2 cloves garlic, minced
1 medium onion, thinly sliced
2 cups zucchini, cut into ⅛-inch rounds

1 large ripe tomato, chopped
1 pound fresh asparagus, cut into 2-inch lengths
1 yellow bell pepper, cut into thin strips
½ cup dry white wine
¼ teaspoon ground black pepper
3 tablespoons grated nonfat Parmesan

1. Bring water to a rapid boil in a large, covered pot. Add pasta by holding it in a bundle at one end and slowly bending it inside the pot as the pasta softens. Keep water boiling; stir pasta with a long-handled wooden fork to prevent it from sticking together. Follow cooking time recommendation on package. Pasta should be cooked through but still firm. Check for doneness by biting into a piece of pasta rinsed in cold water. Drain cooked pasta into a colander in the sink.

2. Heat broth in a large skillet. Add chicken and garlic and sauté until chicken is no longer pink, about 4 minutes. Add onion, zucchini, tomato, asparagus, and yellow bell pepper. Simmer, stirring occasionally, until vegetables are almost tender, about 6 minutes.

3. Stir in wine and black pepper. Simmer, stirring frequently, until heated through, about 4 minutes.

4. Arrange pasta on individual plates. Top with sauce, sprinkle with Parmesan, and serve immediately.

Calories Per Serving: 358
Fat: 3 g
Cholesterol: 58 mg
Protein: 30 g

Carbohydrates: 51 g
Dietary Fiber: 2 g
Sodium: 99 mg

Farfalle with Cumin Chicken

Butterfly pasta is served with chicken in a cumin-accented tomato sauce.

YIELD: 6 servings • PREPARATION TIME: 10 minutes •
COOKING TIME: 15 minutes plus pasta cooking time

6 quarts water
12 ounces farfalle
½ cup nonfat chicken broth
8 ounces skinless chicken breast cutlets,
    cut into ½-inch cubes
1 medium onion, chopped

4 cloves garlic, minced
1 teaspoon ground cumin
1 teaspoon dried thyme
2 cups low-sodium tomato sauce
¼ teaspoon ground black pepper

1. Bring water to a rapid boil in a large, covered pot. Add pasta by holding it in a bundle at one end and slowly bending it inside the pot as the pasta softens. Keep water boiling; stir pasta with a long-handled wooden fork to prevent it from sticking together. Follow cooking time recommendation on package. Pasta should be cooked through but still firm. Check for doneness by biting into a piece of pasta rinsed in cold water. Drain cooked pasta into a colander in the sink.
2. Heat ¼ cup broth in a large skillet. Add chicken cubes and sauté until cooked through, about 8 minutes. Remove chicken and set aside.
3. Heat remaining ¼ cup broth in the skillet. Add onion and garlic and sauté until onion is translucent, about 3 minutes. Return chicken to pan; add cumin, thyme, tomato sauce, and black pepper. Simmer until all ingredients are heated through, about 4 minutes.
4. Top pasta with sauce.

Calories Per Serving: 287
Fat: 1 g
Cholesterol: 18 mg
Protein: 15 g

Carbohydrates: 53 g
Dietary Fiber: 2 g
Sodium: 103 mg

Eggplant-Turkey Ziti

This eggplant sauce is highlighted by turkey, carrots, and tomatoes.

YIELD: 4 servings • PREPARATION TIME: 20 minutes •
COOKING TIME: 25 minutes plus pasta cooking time

4 quarts water
8 ounces ziti
½ cup nonfat chicken broth
½ pound ground turkey breast
2 cups eggplant, peeled and cut into
    1-inch cubes
1 medium onion, chopped
1 green bell pepper, diced

2 carrots, chopped
2 cloves garlic, minced
1½ cups fresh or low-sodium canned
    tomatoes, with juice
½ teaspoon dried basil
½ teaspoon ground black pepper
2 tablespoons grated nonfat Parmesan
2 tablespoons chopped fresh parsley

1. Bring water to a rapid boil in a large, covered pot. Slowly stir in pasta. Return water to a boil. Stir pasta with a long-handled wooden fork to prevent it from sticking together. Follow cooking time recommendation on package. Pasta should be cooked through but still firm. Check for doneness by biting into a piece of pasta rinsed in cold water. Drain cooked pasta into a colander in the sink.
2. Heat ¼ cup broth in a large skillet over medium heat. Add turkey and sauté until it is no longer pink, about 8 minutes. Remove from skillet and set aside. Drain fat from skillet.
3. Heat remaining ¼ cup broth in the skillet over medium heat. Add eggplant and sauté for 10 minutes. Remove eggplant from skillet and set aside.
4. Add onion, green bell pepper, carrots, and garlic; sauté for 5 minutes. Return turkey and eggplant to skillet.
5. Stir in tomatoes, basil, and pepper. Simmer for 5 minutes.
6. Toss pasta and eggplant mixture in a large bowl. Garnish with Parmesan and parsley before serving.

Calories Per Serving: 330
Fat: 2 g
Cholesterol: 34 mg
Protein: 25 g

Carbohydrates: 55 g
Dietary Fiber: 3 g
Sodium: 98 mg

Capellini with Chicken and Mushrooms in a Sweet-and-Sour Sauce

Extra-thin spaghetti is partnered with chicken chunks, mushrooms, green bell pepper, and tomato accented with soy sauce, brown sugar, and vinegar.

YIELD: 4 servings • PREPARATION TIME: 15 minutes •
COOKING TIME: 13 minutes plus pasta cooking time

4 quarts water
8 ounces capellini
1¾ cups nonfat chicken broth
8 ounces skinless chicken breast cutlets,
    cut into ½-inch cubes
1 cup sliced fresh mushrooms

1 cup shredded green bell pepper
1 large ripe tomato, chopped
2 tablespoons reduced-sodium soy sauce
1½ tablespoons brown sugar
1 tablespoon white wine vinegar

1. Bring water to a rapid boil in a large, covered pot. Add pasta by holding it in a bundle at one end and slowly bending it inside the pot as the pasta softens. Keep water boiling; stir pasta with a long-handled wooden fork to prevent it from sticking together. Follow cooking time recommendation on package. Pasta should be cooked through but still firm. Check for doneness by biting into a piece of pasta rinsed in cold water. Drain cooked pasta into a colander in the sink.
2. Heat broth in a large skillet. Add chicken and simmer until opaque, about 8 minutes. Remove chicken and set aside. Add mushrooms, green bell pepper, and tomato and simmer until just tender, about 4 minutes. Remove vegetables and set aside.
3. Whisk together the soy sauce, brown sugar, and wine vinegar. Stir into the broth in the skillet. Simmer for 1 minute. Add chicken and vegetables and heat through.
4. Serve pasta tossed with sauce.

Calories Per Serving: 317
Fat: 2 g
Cholesterol: 28 mg
Protein: 20 g

Carbohydrates: 55 g
Dietary Fiber: 1 g
Sodium: 440 mg

Tagliatelle with Shiitake-Chicken Sauce

Wide noodles are topped with chicken chunks and shiitake mushrooms in a savory tomato sauce.

YIELD: *4 servings* • PREPARATION TIME: *15 minutes* •
COOKING TIME: *18 minutes plus pasta cooking time*

4 quarts water
8 ounces tagliatelle
¼ cup nonfat chicken broth
1 pound skinless chicken breast cutlets,
    cut into ½-inch cubes
2 cups fresh shiitake mushroom caps

2 cups canned low-sodium tomatoes,
    chopped, with juice
1 tablespoon fresh chopped parsley
1 teaspoon dried basil
1 clove garlic, minced
1 tablespoon lemon juice

1. Bring water to a rapid boil in a large, covered pot. Add pasta by holding it in a bundle at one end and slowly bending it inside the pot as the pasta softens. Keep water boiling; stir pasta with a long-handled wooden fork to prevent it from sticking together. Follow cooking time recommendation on package. Pasta should be cooked through but still firm. Check for doneness by biting into a piece of pasta rinsed in cold water. Drain cooked pasta into a colander in the sink.
2. Heat broth in a large skillet. Add chicken and sauté for 8 minutes. Add mushroom caps, tomatoes with juice, parsley, basil, garlic, and lemon juice. Cover and simmer for 10 minutes.
3. Top pasta with sauce.

Calories Per Serving: 340
Fat: 2 g
Cholesterol: 55 mg
Protein: 27 g

Carbohydrates: 54 g
Dietary Fiber: 2 g
Sodium: 78 mg

Radiatore with Curried Chicken

Radiator-shaped pasta is served with chicken strips and apple simmered in a tomato-curry sauce.

YIELD: 4 servings   •   PREPARATION TIME: 15 minutes   •
COOKING TIME: 26 minutes plus pasta cooking time

¼ cup nonfat chicken broth
1 medium onion, chopped
2 cloves garlic, minced
2 teaspoons curry powder
2 cups low-sodium canned tomatoes,
    chopped, with juice
1 cup low-sodium tomato sauce

1 teaspoon sugar
¾ pound skinless chicken breast cutlets,
    cut into ½-inch-wide strips
1 apple, cored and cut into chunks
4 quarts water
8 ounces radiatore
¼ cup chopped fresh parsley

1. Heat broth in a large skillet. Add onion, garlic, and curry powder. Sauté until onion is just tender, about 3 minutes. Stir in tomatoes, tomato sauce, and sugar. Bring to a boil, reduce heat, and simmer, stirring occasionally, for 15 minutes.
2. Add chicken and apple. Continue to simmer until chicken is cooked through, about 8 minutes.
3. Bring water to a rapid boil in a large, covered pot. Slowly stir in pasta. Return water to a boil. Stir pasta with a long-handled wooden fork to prevent it from sticking together. Follow cooking time recommendation on package. Pasta should be cooked through but still firm. Check for doneness by biting into a piece of pasta rinsed in cold water. Drain cooked pasta into a colander in the sink.
4. Top pasta with sauce. Garnish with parsley before serving.

Calories Per Serving: 372
Fat: 3 g
Cholesterol: 41 mg
Protein: 24 g

Carbohydrates: 63 g
Dietary Fiber: 3 g
Sodium: 95 mg

Fedelini with Chicken and Shrimp in Honey-Peanut Sauce

Fedelini combine with strips of chicken breast, small shrimp, and mushrooms, served with a honey-peanut sauce.

YIELD: 4 servings ▪ *PREPARATION TIME: 15 minutes* ▪
COOKING TIME: 6 minutes plus pasta cooking time

2¼ cups nonfat chicken broth
1 clove garlic, minced
3 skinless chicken breast cutlets, about 4 ounces each, cut into thin strips
4 scallions, cut into 1-inch pieces
¼ pound small shrimp, peeled and halved
2 cups sliced fresh mushrooms
2 green bell peppers, diced

4 quarts water
8 ounces fedelini
3 tablespoons sherry
1 tablespoon reduced-sodium soy sauce
2 teaspoons reduced-fat peanut butter
1 tablespoon honey
2 teaspoons grated fresh gingerroot
¼ teaspoon ground black pepper

1. Heat ¼ cup broth in a large skillet. Add garlic and sauté for 1 minute. Add chicken and scallions and sauté for an additional 3 minutes. Stir in shrimp,

mushrooms, and green peppers and sauté for 2 minutes, adding more broth as needed.

2. Bring water to a rapid boil in a large, covered pot. Add pasta by holding it in a bundle at one end and slowly bending it inside the pot as the pasta softens. Keep water boiling; stir pasta with a long-handled wooden fork to prevent it from sticking together. Follow cooking time recommendation on package. Pasta should be cooked through but still firm. Check for doneness by biting into a piece of pasta rinsed in cold water. Drain cooked pasta into a colander in the sink.

3. Combine remaining broth, sherry, soy sauce, peanut butter, honey, and gingerroot. Add to the chicken-shrimp mixture and heat through. Stir in black pepper.

4. Serve pasta topped with sauce.

Calories Per Serving: 366   Carbohydrates: 52 g
Fat: 3 g   Dietary Fiber: 1 g
Cholesterol: 84 mg   Sodium: 416 mg
Protein: 31 g

Cravatte with Lemon-Marinated Chicken and Mixed Vegetables

Bow ties are topped with chicken cubes marinated in lemon juice, plus a vegetable sauce of asparagus, green bell pepper, and tomatoes.

YIELD: *4 servings* · PREPARATION TIME: *15 minutes* ·
COOKING TIME: *15 minutes plus 10 minutes marinating time and pasta cooking time*

2 tablespoons lemon juice
¾ cup nonfat chicken broth
1 clove garlic, minced
1 teaspoon dried basil
½ teaspoon dried oregano
8 ounces skinless chicken breast cutlets, cut into ¾-inch cubes
12 ounces fresh asparagus, cut into ½-inch pieces

1 green bell pepper, cut into thin strips
2 stalks celery, cut into ½-inch pieces
4 quarts water
8 ounces cravatte
2 cups canned low-sodium tomatoes, with juice
2 tablespoons grated nonfat Parmesan

1. Mix lemon juice, ¼ cup broth, garlic, basil, and oregano in a bowl. Add chicken; cover and marinate for 10 minutes.

2. Heat a large skillet. Add chicken and marinade. Cook, stirring, for 5 minutes. Remove chicken and set aside.
3. Add asparagus, green bell pepper, and celery to skillet. Add broth as needed. Cook, stirring frequently, until vegetables are just tender-crisp, about 8 minutes.
4. Bring water to a rapid boil in a large, covered pot. Slowly stir in pasta. Return water to a boil. Stir pasta with a long-handled wooden fork to prevent it from sticking together. Follow cooking time recommendation on package. Pasta should be cooked through but still firm. Check for doneness by biting into a piece of pasta rinsed in cold water. Drain cooked pasta into a colander in the sink.
5. Stir tomatoes and chicken into sauce and simmer for 3 minutes.
6. Toss pasta with sauce. Sprinkle with Parmesan.

Calories Per Serving: 240	Carbohydrates: 37 g
Fat: 3 g	Dietary Fiber: 3 g
Cholesterol: 30 mg	Sodium: 338 mg
Protein: 18 g	

Green Beans, Red Bell Peppers, and Chicken with Orzo

Orzo is combined with chicken, green beans, onion, red bell peppers, and sun-dried tomatoes.

YIELD: 6 servings   ▪   PREPARATION TIME: 20 minutes   ▪   COOKING TIME: 37 minutes

12 cups water	2 red bell peppers, chopped
12 ounces orzo	½ cup sun-dried tomatoes, minced
1 pound green beans, trimmed and cut into 1-inch lengths	2 cups low-sodium canned tomatoes, crushed, with juice
¼ cup nonfat chicken broth	1½ cups low-sodium tomato juice
¾ pound skinless chicken breast cutlets, cut into 1-inch cubes	½ teaspoon ground black pepper
	1 teaspoon dried basil
2 medium onions, chopped	

1. Bring 10 cups of the water to a boil in a large saucepan. Stir in orzo and simmer for 10 minutes, until pasta is done. Drain and set aside.
2. Place beans in a saucepan with enough water to cover. Bring to a boil and simmer for 2 minutes. Reduce heat, cover, and cook for 10 minutes, or until beans become tender. Drain beans.

3. Combine beans and orzo.
4. Heat broth in a skillet. Add chicken and sauté until it begins to turn golden, about 5 minutes. Remove chicken and set aside.
5. Add onions to the skillet and sauté until they begin to soften. Add red bell peppers and sauté for 3 more minutes.
6. Bring 2 cups of water to a boil in a small saucepan. Add sun-dried tomatoes and boil until tomatoes soften, about 5 minutes.
7. In a large skillet combine the sun-dried tomatoes, the crushed tomatoes, and the chicken with the tomato juice. Simmer for 4 minutes.
8. Stir in the orzo, green beans, onions, red peppers, black pepper, and basil. Simmer until all ingredients are heated through, about 3 minutes.

Calories Per Serving: 342
Fat: 2 g
Cholesterol: 28 mg
Protein: 23 g

Carbohydrates: 56 g
Dietary Fiber: 6 g
Sodium: 165 mg

Orecchiette with Tomato-Wine Sauce and Ground Turkey

A slow-cooking variation of Bolognese sauce with ground turkey is served over orecchiette.

YIELD: 6 servings • PREPARATION TIME: 5 minutes • COOKING TIME: 1 hour plus pasta cooking time

¼ cup nonfat chicken broth
1 cup chopped onion
1 clove garlic, minced
1 pound ground turkey breast
3½ cups low-sodium canned plum tomatoes, chopped, with juice
2 cups low-sodium tomato sauce
¾ cup low-sodium tomato paste
½ cup red wine

2 tablespoons plus ½ cup chopped fresh parsley
1 teaspoon dried basil
½ teaspoon dried oregano
¼ teaspoon ground black pepper
1 bay leaf
5 quarts water
12 ounces orecchiette

1. Heat 2 tablespoons broth in a large saucepan. Add onion and sauté until translucent, about 3 minutes. Add garlic and sauté for 2 additional minutes.
2. Add turkey and sauté until turkey is cooked through, about 5 minutes, adding broth if needed. Drain turkey-onion mixture.

3. To the mixture, add tomatoes with their juice, tomato sauce, tomato paste, red wine, 2 tablespoons parsley, basil, oregano, black pepper, and bay leaf. Simmer, uncovered, until sauce begins to thicken, about 1 hour. Remove bay leaf.

4. Bring water to a rapid boil in a large, covered pot. Slowly stir in pasta. Return water to a boil. Stir pasta with a long-handled wooden fork to prevent it from sticking together. Follow cooking time recommendation on package. Pasta should be cooked through but still firm. Check for doneness by biting into a piece of pasta rinsed in cold water. Drain cooked pasta into a colander in the sink.

5. Serve pasta with sauce. Garnish with remaining ½ cup parsley.

Calories Per Serving: 399	Carbohydrates: 64 g
Fat: 2 g	Dietary Fiber: 4 g
Cholesterol: 38 mg	Sodium: 128 mg
Protein: 29 g	

Ziti Rigati with Mushroom–Ground Turkey Sauce

Ziti rigati is served with a sauce of turkey, tomatoes, and mushrooms, flavored with basil and oregano.

YIELD: *4 servings* • PREPARATION TIME: *15 minutes* •
COOKING TIME: *35 minutes plus pasta cooking time*

¼ cup nonfat chicken broth
½ pound ground turkey breast
1 cup sliced fresh white mushrooms
½ cup chopped onion
½ cup chopped carrot
½ cup chopped red bell pepper
½ cup chopped celery
1 clove garlic, minced
2 cups low-sodium canned tomatoes,
   chopped, juice reserved

⅓ cup low-sodium tomato paste
½ teaspoon dried basil
¼ teaspoon dried oregano
1 bay leaf
¼ teaspoon ground black pepper
¼ cup plus 4 quarts water
8 ounces ziti rigati
2 tablespoons grated nonfat Parmesan

1. Heat broth in a large skillet. Add turkey, mushrooms, onion, carrot, red bell pepper, celery, and garlic. Sauté until turkey is done through, about 5 minutes.

2. Stir in tomatoes with their juice, tomato paste, basil, oregano, bay leaf, ¼ cup water, and black pepper. Bring to a boil, reduce heat, cover, and simmer for 30 minutes.

3. Bring 4 quarts water to a rapid boil in a large, covered pot. Slowly stir in pasta. Return water to a boil. Stir pasta with a long-handled wooden fork to prevent it from sticking together. Follow cooking time recommendation on package. Pasta should be cooked through but still firm. Check for doneness by biting into a piece of pasta rinsed in cold water. Drain cooked pasta into a colander in the sink.

4. Top pasta with sauce. Sprinkle with Parmesan.

Calories Per Serving: 336
Fat: 2 g
Cholesterol: 31 mg
Protein: 24 g

Carbohydrates: 57 g
Dietary Fiber: 3 g
Sodium: 116 mg

Mezzani Rigati with Easy Turkey-Tomato Sauce

Ridged, tubular pasta is served with a sauce that includes ground turkey and cayenne pepper.

YIELD: 4 servings • *PREPARATION TIME: 5 minutes* •
COOKING TIME: 20 minutes plus pasta cooking time

¾ cup nonfat chicken broth
½ pound ground turkey breast
2 cloves garlic, minced
¼ teaspoon cayenne pepper

2 cups low-sodium tomato sauce
4 quarts water
8 ounces mezzani rigati
2 tablespoons grated nonfat Parmesan

1. Heat ¼ cup of broth in a large skillet. Add turkey, garlic, and cayenne pepper. Sauté until turkey is cooked through, about 5 minutes. Drain liquid.

2. Stir in tomato sauce and remaining broth. Bring to a boil, reduce heat, and simmer for 15 minutes.

3. Bring water to a rapid boil in a large, covered pot. Slowly stir in pasta. Return water to a boil. Stir pasta with a long-handled wooden fork to prevent it from sticking together. Follow cooking time recommendation on package. Pasta should be cooked through but still firm. Check for doneness by biting

into a piece of pasta rinsed in cold water. Drain cooked pasta into a colander in the sink.

4. Top pasta with sauce. Sprinkle with Parmesan.

Calories Per Serving: 325
Fat: 2 g
Cholesterol: 31 mg
Protein: 24 g

Carbohydrates: 53 g
Dietary Fiber: 2 g
Sodium: 148 mg

Penne Rigate with Quick and Spicy Turkey-Tomato Sauce

Ribbed penne are served with a zesty tomato sauce flavored with three kinds of peppers, plus paprika, oregano, and thyme.

YIELD: 4 servings ▪ *PREPARATION TIME: 15 minutes* ▪
COOKING TIME: 15 minutes plus pasta cooking time

¼ cup nonfat chicken broth
1 medium onion, minced
2 celery stalks, minced
1 green bell pepper, diced
¾ pound ground turkey breast
½ teaspoon paprika
½ teaspoon cayenne pepper
½ teaspoon ground black pepper

½ teaspoon ground white pepper
½ teaspoon dried oregano
½ teaspoon dried thyme
1 cup low-sodium canned tomatoes,
    drained and chopped
4 quarts water
8 ounces penne rigate

1. Heat broth in a skillet. Add onion, celery, and green bell pepper and sauté until onion is translucent, about 5 minutes.
2. Add turkey, paprika, cayenne pepper, black pepper, white pepper, oregano, and thyme. Sauté until the turkey is cooked through, about 5 minutes. Add tomatoes and simmer until tomatoes are heated through.
3. Bring water to a rapid boil in a large, covered pot. Slowly stir in pasta. Return water to a boil. Stir pasta with a long-handled wooden fork to prevent it from sticking together. Follow cooking time recommendation on package. Pasta should be cooked through but still firm. Check for doneness by biting into a piece of pasta rinsed in cold water. Drain cooked pasta into a colander in the sink.
4. Top pasta with sauce.

Calories Per Serving: 337
Fat: 2 g
Cholesterol: 43 mg
Protein: 29 g

Carbohydrates: 51 g
Dietary Fiber: 2 g
Sodium: 91 mg

Linguine with Turkey-Clam Sauce

Linguine is served with a tomato-mushroom sauce featuring both ground turkey and clams.

YIELD: 6 servings • PREPARATION TIME: 15 minutes •
COOKING TIME: 25 minutes plus pasta cooking time

¼ cup nonfat chicken broth
¾ pound ground turkey breast
1 medium onion, chopped
1 red bell pepper, chopped
1 stalk celery, finely chopped
1 clove garlic, minced
4 cups low-sodium tomato sauce
¾ cup low-sodium tomato paste
1 cup canned minced clams, with liquid

1 cup sliced fresh white mushrooms
½ teaspoon ground black pepper
½ teaspoon dried basil
½ teaspoon dried oregano
¼ teaspoon dried thyme
6 quarts water
12 ounces linguine
2 tablespoons grated nonfat Parmesan

1. Heat broth in a large skillet. Add turkey, onion, red bell pepper, celery, and garlic. Sauté until turkey is done, about 5 minutes. Drain.
2. Add tomato sauce, tomato paste, clams and their liquid, mushrooms, black pepper, basil, oregano, and thyme. Bring to a boil. Reduce heat and simmer for 20 minutes.
3. Bring water to a rapid boil in a large, covered pot. Slowly stir in pasta. Return water to boil. Stir pasta with a long-handled wooden fork to prevent it from sticking together. Follow cooking time recommendation on package. Pasta should be cooked through but still firm. Check for doneness by biting into a piece of pasta rinsed in cold water. Drain cooked pasta into a colander in the sink.
4. Divide pasta among individual plates, top with sauce, sprinkle with Parmesan, and serve immediately.

Calories Per Serving: 421
Fat: 2 g
Cholesterol: 48 mg
Protein: 33 g

Carbohydrates: 68 g
Dietary Fiber: 6 g
Sodium: 145 mg

Conchiglie and Vegetables in Wine Sauce

Little pasta shells and vegetables meet in this tasty treat.

YIELD: 6 servings   •   PREPARATION TIME: 15 minutes   •
COOKING TIME: 25 minutes plus pasta cooking time

6 quarts water
12 ounces conchiglie
¼ cup nonfat chicken broth
1 medium onion, chopped
1 carrot, shredded
½ teaspoon dried thyme

2 cloves garlic, minced
4 cups fresh or low-sodium canned
  tomatoes
½ cup dry white wine
2 cups chopped cauliflower
3 tablespoons grated nonfat Parmesan

1. Bring water to a rapid boil in a large, covered pot. Slowly stir in pasta. Return water to a boil. Stir pasta with a long-handled wooden fork to prevent it from sticking together. Follow cooking time recommendation on package. Pasta should be cooked through but still firm. Check for doneness by biting into a piece of pasta rinsed in cold water. Drain cooked pasta into a colander in the sink.
2. Heat broth in a large skillet. Add onion, carrot, and thyme and sauté for 5 minutes. Stir in garlic, tomatoes, and wine and simmer for 10 minutes.
3. Add cauliflower and continue to simmer for 10 more minutes.
4. Toss pasta with the vegetables and top with Parmesan.

Calories Per Serving: 293
Fat: 1 g
Cholesterol: 3 mg
Protein: 11 g

Carbohydrates: 57 g
Dietary Fiber: 2 g
Sodium: 106 mg

Rigatoni with Black Bean— Ground Turkey Sauce

Rigatoni is served with a cumin-chili–flavored tomato sauce, black beans, and ground turkey.

YIELD: 4 servings   •   PREPARATION TIME: 5 minutes   •
COOKING TIME: 13 minutes plus pasta cooking time

¼ cup nonfat chicken broth
1 medium onion, diced
1 clove garlic, minced
¾ pound ground turkey breast
1 cup low-sodium canned tomatoes,
    crushed, with their juice
¼ teaspoon dried oregano
¾ teaspoon ground cumin

¾ teaspoon chili powder
⅛ teaspoon cayenne pepper
2 cups low-sodium canned black beans,
    rinsed and drained
4 quarts water
8 ounces rigatoni
¼ cup chopped fresh parsley

1. Heat broth in a skillet. Add onion and garlic and sauté until onion is translucent, about 3 minutes. Stir in turkey and sauté until it is cooked through, about 6 minutes.
2. Add tomatoes, oregano, cumin, chili powder, cayenne, and black beans. Simmer for 5 minutes.
3. Bring water to a rapid boil in a large, covered pot. Slowly stir in pasta. Return water to a boil. Stir pasta with a long-handled wooden fork to prevent it from sticking together. Follow cooking time recommendation on package. Pasta should be cooked through but still firm. Check for doneness by biting into a piece of pasta rinsed in cold water. Drain cooked pasta into a colander in the sink.
4. Transfer pasta to individual plates, top with sauce, garnish with parsley, and serve immediately.

Calories Per Serving: 235
Fat: 2 g
Cholesterol: 43 mg
Protein: 29 g

Carbohydrates: 28 g
Dietary Fiber: 8 g
Sodium: 79 mg

Ziti with White Bean–Chili Sauce

Ziti is served with white beans and ground turkey in a tomato sauce enhanced with eight spices.

YIELD: 6 servings • PREPARATION TIME: 15 minutes •
COOKING TIME: 50 minutes plus pasta cooking time

¼ cup nonfat chicken broth
1 pound ground turkey breast
1½ cups finely chopped onion
2 cloves garlic, minced
3½ cups low-sodium canned tomatoes,
   with juice
1 cup water
2 tablespoons chili powder
1 teaspoon dry mustard
1 teaspoon ground cumin
1 teaspoon paprika

¼ teaspoon cayenne pepper
¼ teaspoon ground black pepper
⅛ teaspoon ground allspice
⅛ teaspoon ground cardamom
⅛ teaspoon ground cinnamon
⅛ teaspoon ground cloves
6 quarts water
12 ounces ziti
2 cups low-sodium canned Great
   Northern beans, rinsed and drained
¾ cup shredded nonfat cheddar

1. Heat broth in a large saucepan. Add turkey, onion, and garlic. Sauté until turkey is cooked through, about 5 minutes. Drain liquid.
2. Stir in tomatoes with their juice, 1 cup water, chili powder, dry mustard, cumin, paprika, cayenne pepper, black pepper, allspice, cardamom, cinnamon, and cloves. Bring to a boil. Reduce heat and simmer 45 minutes.
3. Bring water to a rapid boil in a large, covered pot. Slowly stir in pasta. Return water to a boil. Stir pasta with a long-handled wooden fork to prevent it from sticking together. Follow cooking time recommendation on package. Pasta should be cooked through but still firm. Check for doneness by biting into a piece of pasta rinsed in cold water. Drain cooked pasta into a colander in the sink.
4. Stir beans into tomato mixture and heat through.
5. Top pasta with white bean sauce and cheese.

Calories Per Serving: 420
Fat: 3 g
Cholesterol: 38 mg
Protein: 32 g

Carbohydrates: 68 g
Dietary Fiber: 7 g
Sodium: 104 mg

Penne with Kidney Bean–
Ground Turkey Sauce

Penne are simmered in a chili-like sauce of red kidney beans, ground turkey, onion, chili powder, and tomatoes.

YIELD: *4 servings* ▪ PREPARATION TIME: *5 minutes* ▪
COOKING TIME: *20 minutes plus pasta cooking time*

4 quarts water
8 ounces penne
2 tablespoons nonfat chicken broth
½ pound ground turkey breast
1 small onion, chopped

2 cups canned low-sodium tomatoes,
   chopped, with their juice
1¼ cups canned low-sodium kidney
   beans, with their liquid
2 teaspoons chili powder

1. Bring water to a rapid boil in a large, covered pot. Slowly stir in pasta. Return water to a boil. Stir pasta with a long-handled wooden fork to prevent it from sticking together. Follow cooking time recommendation on package. Pasta should be cooked through but still firm. Check for doneness by biting into a piece of pasta rinsed in cold water. Drain cooked pasta into a colander in the sink.
2. Heat broth in a large skillet. Add turkey and onion, and sauté until turkey is lightly browned, about 5 minutes. Drain liquid.
3. Stir in tomatoes with their juice, and beans with their liquid. Stir in chili powder. Cover; simmer until heated through, about 5 minutes. Transfer penne to individual bowls, top with sauce, and serve immediately.

Calories Per Serving: 281
Fat: 2 g
Cholesterol: 32 mg
Protein: 25 g

Carbohydrates: 42 g
Dietary Fiber: 7 g
Sodium: 75 mg

Mostaccioli with Ground Turkey and Snow Peas

"Little mustaches" are served with ground turkey, snow peas, mushrooms, and tomato sauce, and are flavored with soy sauce and ginger.

YIELD: 4 servings • PREPARATION TIME: 20 minutes •
COOKING TIME: 13 minutes plus pasta cooking time

4 quarts water
8 ounces mostaccioli
¼ cup nonfat chicken broth
½ pound ground turkey breast
6 scallions, chopped
3 tablespoons reduced-sodium soy sauce
¼ teaspoon ground ginger

2 stalks celery, chopped
1 cup sliced fresh mushrooms
1 cup snow peas
1 cup low-sodium tomato sauce
3 large ripe tomatoes, cut into wedges
1 yellow bell pepper, cut into thin strips

1. Bring water to a rapid boil in a large, covered pot. Slowly stir in pasta. Return water to a boil. Stir pasta with a long-handled wooden fork to prevent it from sticking together. Follow cooking time recommendation on package. Pasta should be cooked through but still firm. Check for doneness by biting into a piece of pasta rinsed in cold water. Drain cooked pasta into a colander in the sink.

2. Heat broth in a large skillet. Add turkey, scallions, soy sauce, and ginger. Sauté until turkey is almost cooked through, about 5 minutes. Add celery and mushrooms and sauté for 2 more minutes.

3. Add snow peas and tomato sauce. Simmer, stirring occasionally, for 4 minutes.

4. Stir in pasta, fresh tomatoes, and yellow bell pepper. Simmer for 3 minutes.

Calories Per Serving: 450
Fat: 2 g
Cholesterol: 31 mg
Protein: 33 g

Carbohydrates: 75 g
Dietary Fiber: 4 g
Sodium: 583 mg

Conchiglie Rigate with Curried Tomato Sauce and Ground Turkey

Ribbed shells are topped with ground turkey and an apple-tomato sauce flavored with curry powder, apple juice, cumin, and onion.

YIELD: 4 servings • *PREPARATION TIME: 15 minutes* •
COOKING TIME: 10 minutes plus pasta cooking time

¼ cup nonfat chicken broth
½ pound ground turkey breast
½ cup chopped onion
1 clove garlic, minced
1 tart apple, cored and chopped
¼ cup apple juice
¼ cup chopped fresh parsley
1½ teaspoons curry powder

½ teaspoon ground cumin
⅛ teaspoon cayenne pepper
2 cups low-sodium canned tomatoes, chopped, juice reserved
4 quarts water
8 ounces conchiglie rigate
1 tablespoon chopped dry-roasted peanuts

1. Heat broth in a large skillet. Add turkey, onion, and garlic, and sauté until turkey is cooked through, about 5 minutes.

2. Stir in apple, apple juice, parsley, curry powder, cumin, cayenne pepper, and tomatoes with their juice. Bring to a boil; reduce heat and simmer until apple is just tender, about 5 minutes.
3. Bring water to a rapid boil in a large, covered pot. Slowly stir in pasta. Return water to a boil. Stir pasta with a long-handled wooden fork to prevent it from sticking together. Follow cooking time recommendation on package. Pasta should be cooked through but still firm. Check for doneness by biting into a piece of pasta rinsed in cold water. Drain cooked pasta into a colander in the sink.
4. Toss pasta with sauce. Sprinkle with peanuts.

Calories Per Serving: 348
Fat: 3 g
Cholesterol: 29 mg
Protein: 23 g

Carbohydrates: 58 g
Dietary Fiber: 2 g
Sodium: 71 mg

Maruzze Stuffed with Eggplant-Tomato Sauce

Large pasta shells are stuffed with a mixture of eggplant, tomatoes, red wine, and onion.

YIELD: 8 servings ▪ *PREPARATION TIME: 20 minutes* ▪
COOKING TIME: 50 minutes plus pasta cooking time

¼ cup nonfat chicken broth
1 pound ground turkey breast
1 cup minced onion
1 cup peeled, grated eggplant
3 cloves garlic, minced
¼ teaspoon ground black pepper
3½ cups low-sodium canned tomatoes, chopped, with juice
1 cup low-sodium tomato sauce

1 cup red wine
1 teaspoon dried oregano
1 teaspoon dried basil
⅛ teaspoon red pepper flakes
6 quarts water
12 ounces maruzze
¾ cup shredded nonfat mozzarella
½ cup grated nonfat Parmesan

1. Heat broth in a large skillet. Add turkey, onion, eggplant, two thirds of the minced garlic, and black pepper. Sauté until turkey is no longer pink, about 5 minutes. Set aside.
2. In a separate pot, combine tomatoes (with their juice), remaining minced garlic, tomato sauce, wine, oregano, basil, and red pepper flakes. Simmer for 15 minutes.

3. Preheat oven to 350 degrees.
4. Bring water to a rapid boil in a large, covered pot. Slowly stir in pasta. Return water to a boil. Stir pasta with a long-handled wooden fork to prevent it from sticking together. Follow cooking time recommendation on package. Pasta should be cooked through but still firm. Check for doneness by biting into a piece of pasta rinsed in cold water. Drain cooked pasta into a colander in the sink.
5. Mix together turkey mixture and half of the tomato sauce. Stuff shells. Place finished shells in a nonstick baking pan, spoon remaining sauce over them, and bake for 20 minutes.
6. Sprinkle with mozzarella and bake for 10 more minutes.
7. Sprinkle with Parmesan and serve.

Calories Per Serving: 328
Fat: 2 g
Cholesterol: 36 mg
Protein: 27 g

Carbohydrates: 48 g
Dietary Fiber: 3 g
Sodium: 205 mg

Turkey Manicotti in Marinara Sauce

Manicotti are stuffed with a filling of red bell pepper and turkey breast in tomato marinara sauce.

YIELD: *6 servings* • PREPARATION TIME: *15 minutes* •
COOKING TIME: *30 minutes plus pasta cooking time*

6 quarts water
12 manicotti shells
cooking oil spray
¼ cup nonfat chicken broth
½ cup chopped onion
1½ pounds ground turkey breast

1 red bell pepper, chopped
½ teaspoon ground black pepper
2 cups low-sodium tomato sauce
½ cup shredded nonfat mozzarella
¼ cup chopped fresh parsley

1. Bring water to a rapid boil in a large, covered pot. Slowly stir in pasta. Return water to boil. Stir pasta with a long-handled wooden fork to prevent it from sticking together. Follow cooking time recommendation on package. Check for doneness by biting into a piece of pasta rinsed in cold water. Since pasta will cook further in the oven, it should be slightly underdone. Drain cooked pasta into a colander in the sink and rinse with cold water.

2. Preheat oven to 350 degrees. Lightly spray a 9-inch-by-13-inch baking dish with cooking oil spray.
3. Heat broth in a large skillet. Sauté onion 2 minutes. Add turkey and red bell pepper and cook until turkey is no longer pink, about 5 minutes. Drain liquid. Add black pepper and 1 cup of tomato sauce and simmer until mixture is heated through, about 3 minutes.
4. Fill the cooked manicotti shells with the turkey mixture. Arrange the stuffed shells in the baking dish, top with remaining cup of tomato sauce, cover with foil, and bake for 10 minutes.
5. Sprinkle with mozzarella and bake for 10 minutes more.
6. Serve garnished with parsley.

Calories Per Serving: 329
Fat: 2 g
Cholesterol: 61 mg
Protein: 40 g

Carbohydrates: 35 g
Dietary Fiber: 2 g
Sodium: 222 mg

Turkey-Jalapeño Lasagna

Ground turkey, jalapeño-tomato sauce, and nonfat cottage cheese are featured in this low-fat lasagna.

YIELD: 8 servings ▪ *PREPARATION TIME: 20 minutes* ▪
COOKING TIME: 55 minutes plus pasta cooking time and standing time

¼ cup nonfat chicken broth
1½ pounds ground turkey breast
1¼ cups chopped onion
1 cup chopped red bell pepper
2 cloves garlic, minced
½ teaspoon ground oregano
½ cup chopped fresh parsley
1½ cups low-sodium tomato paste
1¼ cups low-sodium canned tomatoes,
   with juice

1 jalapeño pepper, seeded and minced
1½ cups plus 6 quarts water
12 ounces lasagna noodles
2 egg whites, lightly beaten
2 cups nonfat cottage cheese
olive oil cooking spray
½ cup grated nonfat Parmesan
½ cup shredded nonfat mozzarella

1. Preheat oven to 350 degrees.
2. Heat broth in a large skillet over medium heat. Add turkey, onion, red bell pepper, and garlic. Sauté until turkey is no longer pink, about 5 minutes. Drain well.

3. Add oregano, ¼ cup parsley, tomato paste, tomatoes, jalapeño pepper, and 1½ cups water. Cover and simmer, stirring occasionally, for 30 minutes.

4. Bring 6 quarts water to a rapid boil in a large, covered pot. Add pasta by holding it in a bundle at one end and slowly bending it inside the pot as the pasta softens. Keep water boiling; stir pasta with a long-handled wooden fork to prevent it from sticking together. Follow cooking time recommendation on package. Check for doneness by biting into a piece of pasta rinsed in cold water. Since pasta will cook further in the oven, it should be slightly under-done. Drain cooked pasta into a colander in the sink and rinse with cold water.

5. Combine egg whites, cottage cheese, and remaining parsley, and set aside.

6. Lightly coat a 13-inch-by-9-inch baking dish with olive oil cooking spray. Cover the bottom of the dish with a layer of noodles; top with half the turkey mixture and then half the cottage cheese mixture. Repeat. Cover with foil and bake for 25 minutes.

7. Remove the foil, sprinkle the Parmesan and mozzarella cheeses over the top, and continue to bake until cheese melts, about 5 minutes. Allow to stand for 10 minutes before serving.

Calories Per Serving: 376
Fat: 2 g
Cholesterol: 69 mg
Protein: 39 g

Carbohydrates: 49 g
Dietary Fiber: 4 g
Sodium: 242 mg

Turkey-Vegetable Lasagna

Ground turkey, green bell pepper, and corn are layered with lasagna noodles and tomato sauce.

YIELD: *8 servings* • PREPARATION TIME: *15 minutes* •
COOKING TIME: *45 minutes plus pasta cooking time and 10 minutes standing time*

6 quarts water
9 lasagna noodles
¼ cup nonfat chicken broth
1½ pounds ground turkey breast
1 medium onion, chopped
¼ cup pitted chopped black olives
2 cups sliced fresh mushrooms

2 cups low-sodium canned tomato sauce
¼ teaspoon ground black pepper
¼ teaspoon dried oregano
1¼ cups frozen corn kernels, thawed
1¼ cups chopped green bell pepper
1 cup shredded nonfat mozzarella

1. Preheat oven to 350 degrees.
2. Bring water to a rapid boil in a large, covered pot. Add pasta by holding it in a bundle at one end and slowly bending it inside the pot as the pasta softens. Keep water boiling; stir pasta with a long-handled wooden fork to prevent it from sticking together. Follow cooking time recommendation on package. Check for doneness by biting into a piece of pasta rinsed in cold water. Since pasta will cook further in the oven, it should be slightly underdone. Drain cooked pasta into a colander in the sink and rinse with cold water.
3. Heat broth in a large skillet. Add turkey and sauté until no longer pink, about 5 minutes.
4. Add onion, olives, and mushrooms. Sauté for 3 minutes. Stir in tomato sauce, black pepper, and oregano. Simmer for 2 minutes. Remove from heat and set aside.
5. In separate dish, combine corn and green pepper.
6. Arrange 3 lasagna noodles in the bottom of a 9-inch-by-13-inch nonstick baking dish. Add half the turkey mixture; top with half the corn–green pepper mixture. Repeat the layers, top with the remaining 3 lasagna noodles, and bake for 25 minutes.
7. Sprinkle top with mozzarella and bake until the cheese begins to melt. Allow to stand for 10 minutes before cutting and serving.

Calories: 310	Carbohydrates: 41 g
Fat: 3 g	Dietary Fiber: 4 g
Cholesterol: 58 mg	Sodium: 326 mg
Protein: 30 g	

Turkey Lasagna with Yogurt Sauce

This dish, inspired by an eggplant dish called *aushak,* is made with ground turkey and tomato sauce, then topped with garlic-yogurt sauce.

YIELD: 4 servings • *PREPARATION TIME: 15 minutes* •
COOKING TIME: 25 minutes plus pasta cooking time

4 quarts water
8 ounces lasagna noodles
¼ cup nonfat chicken broth
12 scallions, chopped
1 small onion, minced
1 pound ground turkey breast

2 cups low-sodium tomato sauce
1½ tablespoons ground cinnamon
3 teaspoons dried mint
2 cups nonfat plain yogurt
2 cloves garlic, minced

1. Bring water to a rapid boil in a large, covered pot. Add pasta by holding it in a bundle at one end and slowly bending it inside the pot as the pasta softens. Keep water boiling; stir pasta with a long-handled wooden fork to prevent it from sticking together. Follow cooking time recommendation on package. Check for doneness by biting into a piece of pasta rinsed in cold water. Since pasta will cook further in the oven, it should be slightly underdone. Drain cooked pasta into a colander in the sink and rinse with cold water.
2. Preheat oven to 375 degrees.
3. Heat broth in a large skillet over medium heat. Add scallions and onion and sauté for 3 minutes. Remove scallions and onion from pan and set aside.
4. Add turkey and sauté until meat is no longer pink, about 5 minutes. Add tomato sauce, cinnamon, and 2 teaspoons mint. Mix thoroughly and heat through.
5. Place a layer of lasagna noodles in the bottom of a 9-inch-by-9-inch nonstick baking dish. Sprinkle the noodles with the scallion-onion mixture. Cover this with the remaining noodles, spoon the turkey mixture over the noodles, and bake for 15 minutes.
6. Combine the yogurt, garlic, and remaining mint in a mixing bowl. Stir well.
7. Cut lasagna into 8 portions and top with yogurt mixture.

Calories Per Serving: 450
Fat: 2 g
Cholesterol: 76 mg
Protein: 41 g

Carbohydrates: 66 g
Dietary Fiber: 3 g
Sodium: 192 mg

Cavatelli with Turkey and Artichokes

Short, curled noodles are served with turkey, artichoke hearts, red bell pepper, celery, and olives.

YIELD: *4 servings* • PREPARATION TIME: *15 minutes* •
COOKING TIME: *15 minutes plus pasta cooking time*

4 quarts water
8 ounces cavatelli
1¼ cups nonfat chicken broth
4 turkey breast cutlets, about 4 ounces each
2 stalks celery, sliced
1 cup chopped artichoke hearts

1 large red bell pepper, cut into thin strips
4 pitted black olives, sliced
1½ teaspoons dried thyme
¼ teaspoon ground black pepper
2 tablespoons chopped fresh parsley

1. Bring water to a rapid boil in a large, covered pot. Slowly stir in pasta. Return water to boil. Stir pasta with a long-handled wooden fork to prevent it from sticking together. Follow cooking time recommendation on package. Pasta should be cooked through but still firm. Check for doneness by biting into a piece of pasta rinsed in cold water. Drain cooked pasta into a colander in the sink.

2. Heat ¼ cup broth in a large skillet. Add turkey and sauté until turkey is cooked through, about 4 minutes on each side. Remove turkey and set aside.

3. Add celery to skillet and sauté until just tender-crisp, about 3 minutes. Stir in artichoke hearts, red bell pepper, olives, remaining chicken broth, thyme, and black pepper. Bring to a boil, reduce heat, and simmer until artichoke hearts are heated through, about 4 minutes.

4. Add turkey and pasta and simmer until turkey is heated through, about 1 minute. Sprinkle with parsley.

Calories Per Serving: 363
Fat: 3 g
Cholesterol: 50 mg
Protein: 35 g

Carbohydrates: 51 g
Dietary Fiber: 3 g
Sodium: 348 mg

Rotelle-Chicken Salad

A chicken-pasta salad with cherry tomatoes, scallions, and a mustard-yogurt dressing.

YIELD: 2 servings • PREPARATION TIME: 15 minutes plus chicken cooking time •
COOKING TIME: 12 minutes plus pasta cooking time

2 quarts water
4 ounces rotelle
3 tablespoons nonfat mayonnaise
3 tablespoons nonfat plain yogurt
1 tablespoon red wine vinegar
½ teaspoon Dijon mustard

¼ teaspoon dried basil
⅛ teaspoon ground black pepper
8 ounces skinless chicken breast cutlets,
   cooked and chopped
1 cup halved cherry tomatoes
2 scallions, thinly sliced

1. Bring water to a rapid boil in a large, covered pot. Slowly stir in pasta. Return water to a boil. Stir pasta with a long-handled wooden fork to prevent it from sticking together. Follow cooking time recommendation on package. Pasta should be cooked through but still firm. Check for doneness by biting into a piece of pasta rinsed in cold water. Drain cooked pasta into a colander in the sink. Allow to cool to room temperature.

2. Mix mayonnaise, yogurt, vinegar, mustard, basil, and black pepper in a large bowl.
3. Pour dressing over chicken, rotelle, tomatoes, and scallions. Serve.

Calories Per Serving: 240
Fat: 2 g
Cholesterol: 74 mg
Protein: 29 g

Carbohydrates: 26 g
Dietary Fiber: 2 g
Sodium: 289 mg

Rotini-Chicken Salad with Red Grapes and Sugar Snap Peas

Chicken and small pasta twists are partnered with artichoke hearts, red grapes, sugar snap peas, spinach, kiwi, and cucumber.

YIELD: 6 servings • *PREPARATION TIME: 15 minutes plus chicken cooking time* • *COOKING TIME: 10 minutes plus pasta cooking time*

4 quarts water
8 ounces rotini
1½ pounds skinless chicken breast cutlets, cooked and chopped
6 ounces marinated artichoke hearts, drained and ¼ cup liquid reserved
2 cups seedless red grapes

1 cup sugar snap peas
6 cups chopped fresh spinach
1 kiwi, peeled and sliced
½ cucumber, peeled and sliced
1 scallion, chopped
½ cup nonfat Italian dressing

1. Bring water to a rapid boil in a large, covered pot. Slowly stir in pasta. Return water to a boil. Stir pasta with a long-handled wooden fork to prevent it from sticking together. Follow cooking time recommendation on package. Pasta should be cooked through but still firm. Check for doneness by biting into a piece of pasta rinsed in cold water. Drain cooked pasta into a colander in the sink. Allow to cool to room temperature.
2. Combine chicken, pasta, artichoke hearts and their reserved liquid, grapes, sugar snap peas, spinach, kiwi, cucumber, and scallion in a large serving bowl.
3. Pour dressing over salad, toss to coat all ingredients, and serve immediately.

Calories Per Serving: 367
Fat: 3 g
Cholesterol: 73 mg
Protein: 34 g

Carbohydrates: 54 g
Dietary Fiber: 7 g
Sodium: 402 mg

Farfalle with Chicken and
Yellow Bell Pepper

Butterfly-shaped pasta is tossed with shredded chicken, yellow bell pepper, and water chestnuts, with a yogurt dressing.

YIELD: 4 servings • PREPARATION TIME: 15 minutes •
COOKING TIME: chicken cooking time and pasta cooking time

4 quarts water
4 ounces farfalle
2 cups shredded cooked skinless chicken
    breast cutlets
1½ cups snow peas sliced into ½-inch
    diagonal pieces
1 cup diced yellow bell pepper
½ small onion, sliced

1 8-ounce can sliced water chestnuts,
    drained
⅓ cup plain nonfat yogurt
1½ tablespoons low-sodium soy sauce
2 tablespoons nonfat mayonnaise
¼ teaspoon ground black pepper
⅛ teaspoon ground ginger
1 tablespoon slivered almonds

1. Bring water to a rapid boil in a large, covered pot. Slowly stir in pasta. Return water to a boil. Stir pasta with a long-handled wooden fork to prevent it from sticking together. Follow cooking time recommendation on package. Pasta should be cooked through but still firm. Check for doneness by biting into a piece of pasta rinsed in cold water. Drain cooked pasta into a colander in the sink. Allow to cool to room temperature.
2. Combine chicken, pasta, snow peas, yellow bell pepper, onion, and water chestnuts in a large bowl. Toss gently and set aside.
3. Mix yogurt, soy sauce, mayonnaise, black pepper, and ginger.
4. Add the dressing to the salad and toss to coat all ingredients. Garnish with almonds. Serve immediately at room temperature or chilled.

Calories Per Serving: 246
Fat: 3 g
Cholesterol: 55 mg
Protein: 25 g

Carbohydrates: 32 g
Dietary Fiber: 3 g
Sodium: 499 mg

Fusilli-Chicken Salad with Tropical Fruit Dressing

Pasta twists are tossed with chicken, mandarin oranges, pineapple chunks, and green bell pepper in a pineapple-curry dressing.

YIELD: 4 servings • PREPARATION TIME: 10 minutes plus chicken cooking time • COOKING TIME: pasta cooking time plus 1 hour chilling time

4 quarts water
8 ounces fusilli
1 cup juice-packed pineapple chunks, with ¼ cup juice reserved
½ cup nonfat mayonnaise
2 teaspoons brown sugar
1 teaspoon curry powder

1 cup drained, juice-packed mandarin orange sections
2 cooked skinless chicken breast cutlets, about 4 ounces each, cut into thin strips
½ cup chopped green bell pepper
2 scallions, chopped

1. Bring water to a rapid boil in a large, covered pot. Slowly stir in pasta. Return water to a boil. Stir pasta with a long-handled wooden fork to prevent it from sticking together. Follow cooking time recommendation on package. Pasta should be cooked through but still firm. Check for doneness by biting into a piece of pasta rinsed in cold water. Drain cooked pasta into a colander in the sink. Allow to cool to room temperature.
2. Combine reserved pineapple juice, mayonnaise, brown sugar, and curry powder in a large bowl.
3. Stir in fusilli, pineapple chunks, mandarin oranges, chicken, green bell pepper, and scallions and mix well. Chill for 1 hour before serving.

Calories Per Serving: 269
Fat: 2 g
Cholesterol: 41 mg
Protein: 18 g

Carbohydrates: 45 g
Dietary Fiber: 2 g
Sodium: 266 mg

Penne-Chicken Salad

Penne are tossed with cubes of chicken breast, carrots, and broccoli in a Parmesan-yogurt dressing.

YIELD: 4 servings • PREPARATION TIME: 15 minutes • COOKING TIME: 10 minutes plus pasta cooking time and 1 hour chilling time

2 quarts plus 2 cups water
4 ounces penne
1 cup diced carrots
1 cup broccoli florets
½ cup plain nonfat yogurt
3 scallions, minced

2 tablespoons nonfat mayonnaise
2 tablespoons grated nonfat Parmesan
½ teaspoon dried oregano
⅛ teaspoon ground black pepper
8 ounces skinless chicken breast cutlets,
   cooked and cut into ¾-inch cubes

1. Bring 2 quarts water to a rapid boil in a large, covered pot. Slowly stir in pasta. Return water to a boil. Stir pasta with a long-handled wooden fork to prevent it from sticking together. Follow cooking time recommendation on package. Pasta should be cooked through but still firm. Check for doneness by biting into a piece of pasta rinsed in cold water. Drain cooked pasta into a colander in the sink. Allow to cool to room temperature.
2. Bring 2 cups water to a boil in a saucepan. Add carrots and broccoli. Simmer, covered, until vegetables are just tender-crisp, about 10 minutes.
3. Mix yogurt, scallions, mayonnaise, Parmesan, oregano, and black pepper.
4. Combine dressing, chicken, pasta, and vegetables, and toss to coat all ingredients. Cover and chill for 1 hour before serving.

Calories Per Serving: 183
Fat: 1 g
Cholesterol: 28 mg
Protein: 15 g

Carbohydrates: 28 g
Dietary Fiber: 2 g
Sodium: 129 mg

Chicken, Fruit, and Fusilli Salad

Grapes, pineapple, and celery are features of this delightful dish.

YIELD: 4 servings • *PREPARATION TIME: 15 minutes* •
COOKING TIME: 7 minutes plus 1 hour chilling time

4 quarts water
8 ounces fusilli
¾ pound skinless chicken breast cutlets,
   cut into ¾-inch cubes
1 stalk celery, chopped
1 red bell pepper, chopped
4 scallions, sliced

1 cup juice-packed pineapple chunks,
   juice reserved
1 cup seedless grapes
1 cup nonfat plain yogurt
1 teaspoon lemon juice
¼ teaspoon ground black pepper

1. Bring water to a rapid boil in a large, covered pot. Slowly stir in pasta. Return water to a boil. Stir pasta with a long-handled wooden fork to prevent it from sticking together. Follow cooking time recommendation on package. Pasta should be cooked through but still firm. Check for doneness by biting into a piece of pasta rinsed in cold water. Drain cooked pasta into a colander in the sink. Allow to cool to room temperature.
2. Place chicken pieces on a broiler pan, 4 inches from heat. Broil for 4 minutes. Turn and broil for 3 additional minutes.
3. Combine pasta, chicken, celery, red bell pepper, scallions, pineapple, and grapes.
4. Mix yogurt, reserved pineapple juice, lemon juice, and black pepper.
5. Add dressing to the salad and toss to coat. Chill for 1 hour before serving.

Calories Per Serving: 286 Carbohydrates: 46 g
Fat: 2 g Dietary Fiber: 4 g
Cholesterol: 58 mg Sodium: 74 mg
Protein: 27 g

Conchiglie with Smoked Turkey— Asparagus Salad

Shell-shaped pasta is mixed with smoked turkey, tomatoes, and watercress, in a ricotta dressing.

YIELD: 6 servings • PREPARATION TIME: 15 minutes •
COOKING TIME: pasta cooking time plus 1 hour chilling time

6 quarts water
12 ounces conchiglie
3 cups chopped smoked turkey breast
4 large ripe tomatoes, chopped
1 pound asparagus, cut into 1-inch lengths
2 cups chopped watercress

1 cup plain nonfat yogurt
½ cup nonfat ricotta
2 tablespoons white wine vinegar
1 clove garlic, minced
½ teaspoon dried basil
¼ teaspoon ground black pepper

1. Bring water to a rapid boil in a large, covered pot. Slowly stir in pasta. Return water to a boil. Stir pasta with a long-handled wooden fork to prevent it from sticking together. Follow cooking time recommendation on package. Pasta should be cooked through but still firm. Check for doneness by biting

into a piece of pasta rinsed in cold water. Drain cooked pasta into a colander in the sink. Allow to cool to room temperature.

2. Combine turkey, tomatoes, asparagus, and watercress and set aside.
3. In small bowl, mix yogurt, ricotta, vinegar, garlic, basil, and black pepper.
4. Pour dressing over pasta and turkey mixture. Chill for 1 hour before serving.

Calories Per Serving: 330   Carbohydrates: 49 g
Fat: 2 g   Dietary Fiber: 2 g
Cholesterol: 35 mg   Sodium: 170 mg
Protein: 28 g

Mostaccioli with Apples and Turkey Salad

In this version of Waldorf salad, medium-size pasta tubes are combined with turkey breast, apple, celery, mayonnaise, and walnuts.

YIELD: 8 servings • PREPARATION TIME: 15 minutes •
COOKING TIME: pasta cooking and cooling time

6 quarts water   ¼ cup finely diced celery
1 pound mostaccioli   4 teaspoons cider vinegar
3 cups chopped cooked turkey breast   ½ cup nonfat mayonnaise
2 cups chopped fresh apple   ¼ cup chopped walnuts

1. Bring water to a rapid boil in a large, covered pot. Slowly stir in pasta. Return water to a boil. Stir pasta with a long-handled wooden fork to prevent it from sticking together. Follow cooking time recommendation on package. Pasta should be cooked through but still firm. Check for doneness by biting into a piece of pasta rinsed in cold water. Drain cooked pasta into a colander in the sink. Allow to cool to room temperature.
2. Thoroughly mix cooled pasta, turkey, apple, celery, vinegar, and mayonnaise. Top with walnuts.

Calories Per Serving: 303   Carbohydrates: 51 g
Fat: 3 g   Dietary Fiber: 1 g
Cholesterol: 25 mg   Sodium: 223 mg
Protein: 19 g

Radiatore-Turkey-Cantaloupe Salad

Radiatore are tossed with turkey, cantaloupe chunks, celery, scallion, and a lime-accented yogurt dressing.

YIELD: 4 servings ▪ *PREPARATION TIME: 10 minutes plus 1 hour chilling time* ▪
COOKING TIME: pasta cooking time

4 quarts water
8 ounces radiatore
¼ cup nonfat plain yogurt
2 tablespoons nonfat mayonnaise
1 teaspoon lime juice

1½ cups chopped cooked turkey breast
2 cups cubed cantaloupe
½ cup sliced celery
1 scallion, minced

1. Bring water to a rapid boil in a large, covered pot. Slowly stir in pasta. Return water to a boil. Stir pasta with a long-handled wooden fork to prevent it from sticking together. Follow cooking time recommendation on package. Pasta should be cooked through but still firm. Check for doneness by biting into a piece of pasta rinsed in cold water. Drain cooked pasta into a colander in the sink. Allow to cool to room temperature.
2. Whisk together yogurt, mayonnaise, and lime juice.
3. Combine pasta, turkey, cantaloupe, celery, and scallions in a large serving bowl.
4. Pour dressing over salad and mix well.
5. Chill for 1 hour.

Calories Per Serving: 314
Fat: 2 g
Cholesterol: 38 mg
Protein: 25 g

Carbohydrates: 49 g
Dietary Fiber: 1 g
Sodium: 168 mg

RICE

LOW-FAT RICE RECIPES

❖

Like pasta, rice is a nutritionally sound food that fits perfectly into the current recommended low-fat American diet. One pound of rice, which is a principal food crop for half the world's population, delivers four times the food energy of a similar amount of potatoes.

Rice is primarily carbohydrate, composed of 80 percent starch and 12 percent water. It provides protein, thiamine (B_1), phosphorus, and potassium. It is low in fat and calories and cholesterol-free.

The average American eats only 20 pounds of rice a year (in contrast to the Burmese, who consume an average of 1¼ pounds a day, or 500 pounds a year). American rice consumption has doubled in the past decade as interest has grown in high-carbohydrate foods and rice-based cuisines such as Thai, Vietnamese, Indonesian, and Japanese.

▪ ABOUT RICE ▪

Rice originated in India and Southeast Asia. It was brought to Europe by Alexander the Great in 300 B.C., but did not become a European crop until the Moors introduced it into Spain in the ninth century. It was grown early in the United States; records indicate its presence in South Carolina in 1685. Now it is grown commercially in California, Texas, Louisiana, Arkansas, Mississippi, Missouri, South Carolina, and Florida. It requires wet soil and a growing season four to six months long with an average temperature of 70 degrees.

More than 7,000 varieties of rice are grown around the world. Rice is available in various grain sizes. Long-grain rice is long and slender, with grains 4 or

5 times as long as they are wide. Cooked grains of this rice remain separate, light, and fluffy. Medium-grain rices are plump, but not round. When cooked, they are more moist and tender than long-grain. Short-grain rices are almost round, and the grains tend to cling together when cooked.

▪   TYPES OF RICE USED IN THE RECIPES   ▪

Brown rice is rice from which only the inedible outer hull has been removed, leaving the bran layer. It takes longer to cook than white rice, but contains more nutrients. When cooked it has a slightly chewy texture and nutlike flavor. It is a natural source of rice bran and adds fiber to the diet. All rice begins as brown rice.

Polished white rice is rice that has had its hulls, bran, germ, and endosperm removed in the polishing. Most regular milled white rice is "enriched," which means that is has added iron, calcium, and assorted B-complex vitamins to make up the deficiencies caused by the removal of the husk, bran, and germ. These lost nutrients are replaced in a special coating, so avoid washing polished white rice or they will be lost.

Converted or parboiled white or brown rice is rice that has been soaked and steamed before milling to retain more of its vitamins and nutrients. It should not be confused with instant rice, which has been partly or fully cooked before being dehydrated and packaged.

Basmati rice is a long-grain rice that is thin-grained and aromatic. It is grown mostly in India and Pakistan. Its long, slender shape elongates rather than widens when it cooks. (Texmati rice, a hybrid grown in the United States, is less flavorful than basmati.)

Wild rice is not a true rice. It is a self-propagating aquatic grass whose large, dark grains stand on long stalks in the lakes of Canada and the north-central United States, where it is harvested in the old-fashioned way by Native Americans who paddle along the water's edge, bending the grasses and beating the seeds into their boats. Much of the "wild" rice produced today is cultivated in manmade paddies in Minnesota and California. After harvest, wild rice is left to ferment in the hull, to intensify its flavor and help loosen the hull. It is then lightly toasted to stabilize the grain. Its distinctive taste blends well with strong-flavored dishes. Since wild rice is both assertive in flavor and expensive, it is often mixed with other rices. Shop for wild rice that has long, slender, uniformly shaped grains. The best wild rice, which has one-inch grains, is classified as "giant." "Fancy" wild rice is of medium-length grain, and "Select" is short-grain. A cup of wild rice contains 72 milligrams of carbohydrate, in addition to phosphorus, magnesium, potassium, and zinc, and only 130 calories.

Arborio rice is short-grain and cultivated in Italy's Po and Ticino valleys. It is the only rice used to make risotto, a stirred Italian rice dish. It has shorter and rounder kernels than other short-grain rices, and the exact amount of starch needed to provide the creamy texture of this dish.

Instant rice is not suggested for use in these recipes because it lacks texture, taste, and sufficient nutritional value.

Organically grown rices, raised without pesticides or chemical fertilizers, are available.

▪ RECIPE SUBSTITUTIONS ▪

You can substitute one type of rice for another in these recipes with appropriate adjustments in cooking time and method.

▪ COOKING WITH RICE ▪

- Check rice for the presence of foreign matter such as small stones or other particles. Pick over rice and wash it by placing it in a saucepan under a running tap and letting the water flow over the top. You can also shake the rice in water in an enclosed container and pour away the water through a strainer to get rid of dirt and dust that may adhere to rice.
- Overcooking or adding too much liquid results in mushy rice.
- If rice is cooked too long or not enough liquid is added during cooking, the rice may be too firm.
- Firm rice can also result if rice is cooked in too large a pan or if a loose lid caused evaporation.
- Serve rice soon after cooking or it can become sticky.
- Avoid stirring during cooking. During the cooking process, water is absorbed into the interior of the grain, softening and moistening the starch cells. Eventually there is no water left between the grains, and the rice is cooked. Stirring during cooking disturbs this process and breaks the skins of the grains, causing stickiness and starchiness.
- Salting the water when preparing rice is optional. You can substitute a tablespoon of dried herbs.
- Rinse wild rice in a sieve before cooking to remove tiny pieces of hull. In cooking wild rice, use three cups of liquid to one cup of wild rice.
- Wild rice is cooked when most of the grains are cracked or open, revealing the fluffy white interior, and the texture is just slightly chewy, like al dente

pasta. Wild rice can take from 25 to 60 minutes to cook depending on grain length. If there is a small amount of water in the pan at the end of the cooking period, let the rice stand for 10 minutes to absorb it.

▪ S T O R I N G R I C E ▪

- White rice will keep indefinitely as long as the package remains sealed. However, brown rice has a more abbreviated shelf life because the oil in the bran oxidizes. Refrigerate or freeze brown rice in airtight sealed plastic bags to keep it fresh. Defrost before using.
- Once the package is opened, brown and white rice should be transferred to airtight jars. Glass or ceramic containers with screw-top or vacuum-sealed lids are excellent containers for rice. Store rice in a cool, dry, semidark place.
- Wild rice should keep indefinitely if stored in a tightly covered container in a cool, dry place. It should be kept refrigerated in warm weather. Cooked wild rice can be refrigerated for a week in an airtight sealed plastic bag or a glass jar or Tupperware container.

BASIC RICE

Boiled White Rice ▪ Cantonese Rice ▪ Stovetop-Reheated White Rice ▪ Microwave-Reheated White Rice ▪ Boiled Brown Rice ▪ Basic Baked Brown Rice ▪ Toasty Baked Brown Rice ▪ Spicy Baked White Rice ▪ Microwave Wild Rice ▪ Baked Wild Rice ▪ Sushi Rice ▪ Microwave Basmati Rice

Boiled White Rice

This method of cooking rice resembles the usual way of cooking pasta. It produces fluffy rice, with each grain remaining intact.

YIELD: 2 servings, 1 cup each • COOKING TIME: 12 minutes

1 cup white rice   *3 quarts boiling water*

1. Add rice to boiling water. Stir once, return water to a boil, and reduce heat.
2. Simmer uncovered for 12 minutes, or until tender. Drain.

Calories Per Serving: 351   Carbohydrates: 78 g
Fat: 1 g   Dietary Fiber: 0 g
Cholesterol: 0 mg   Sodium: 1 mg
Protein: 6 g

Cantonese Rice

This method of cooking white rice is based on a ratio of 1 cup of rice to 1 cup less 1 tablespoon of water.

YIELD: 4 servings • COOKING TIME: 17 minutes

2 cups white rice   *1¾ cups plus two tablespoons water*

1. Place rice and water in pot. Begin cooking, uncovered over high heat, and bring the water to a boil. Stir with a wooden spoon and cook for 4 minutes or until the water evaporates.
2. Cover the pot and cook over low heat for 8 minutes more.
3. Turn off heat and loosen rice with wooden spoon to retain fluffiness. Cover until ready to serve. Stir just before serving.

Calories Per Serving: 351   Carbohydrates: 78 g
Fat: 1 g   Dietary Fiber: 0 g
Cholesterol: 0 mg   Sodium: 1 mg
Protein: 6 g

Stovetop-Reheated White Rice

If you have leftover rice, it can easily be reheated.

YIELD: 2 servings • *COOKING TIME: 5 minutes*

2 cups leftover rice *¼ cup water*

1. Place rice and water in heavy saucepan.
2. Cover and cook over low heat about 5 minutes or until hot.

Calories Per Serving: 242 Carbohydrates: 53 g
Fat: 0 g Dietary Fiber: 0 g
Cholesterol: 0 mg Sodium: 1 mg
Protein: 4 g

Microwave-Reheated White Rice

Leftover rice can also be reheated in your microwave.

YIELD: 2 servings • *COOKING TIME: 2 to 3 minutes*

2 cups leftover rice *¼ cup water*

1. Place rice and water in a microwave-safe bowl and cover with vented microwave-safe plastic wrap.
2. Heat on HIGH for 2 to 3 minutes.

Calories Per Serving: 242 Carbohydrates: 53 g
Fat: 0 g Dietary Fiber: 0 g
Cholesterol: 0 mg Sodium: 1 mg
Protein: 4 g

Boiled Brown Rice

This method of cooking rice resembles the usual way of cooking pasta. It produces fluffy rice, with each grain remaining intact.

YIELD: 2 servings • COOKING TIME: 35 minutes

1 cup brown rice   *3 quarts boiling water*

1. Add rice to boiling water. Stir once, return water to a boil, and reduce heat.
2. Simmer uncovered for 35 minutes, or until tender. Drain.

Calories Per Serving: 344   Carbohydrates: 73 g
Fat: 3 g   Dietary Fiber: 2 g
Cholesterol: 0 mg   Sodium: 4 mg
Protein: 7 g

Basic Baked Brown Rice

Baked brown rice has a nuttier flavor and is lighter and fluffier than boiled brown rice.

YIELD: 4 servings • PREPARATION TIME: 5 minutes • COOKING TIME: 50 minutes

¼ cup nonfat chicken broth   *3½ cups water*
1½ cups brown rice

1. Preheat oven to 350 degrees. Heat chicken broth in a skillet over medium heat. Cook and stir the rice for 5 minutes.
2. Combine the rice and water in an oven-safe casserole. Cover and bake for 45 minutes, or until the water is absorbed.
3. Uncover rice and allow it to cool 10 minutes before serving.

Calories Per Serving: 258   Carbohydrates: 54 g
Fat: 2 g   Dietary Fiber: 4 g
Cholesterol: 0 mg   Sodium: 26 mg
Protein: 6 g

Toasty Baked Brown Rice

Brown rice is toasted in a nonstick skillet before baking, producing a nutty flavor.

YIELD: 4 servings • *PREPARATION TIME: 5 minutes* • *COOKING TIME: 45 minutes*

2 cups uncooked brown rice   *3 cups boiling water*

1. Preheat oven to 350 degrees.
2. Heat a nonstick skillet. Add rice and stir constantly until toasted, about 5 minutes.
3. Transfer rice to an oven-safe baking dish and pour boiling water over it.
4. Bake until rice is tender, about 40 minutes.

Calories Per Serving: 344   Carbohydrates: 73 g
Fat: 3 g   Dietary Fiber: 2 g
Cholesterol: 0 mg   Sodium: 9 mg
Protein: 7 g

Spicy Baked White Rice

This version is spiced with cayenne.

YIELD: 4 servings • *PREPARATION TIME: 5 minutes* • *COOKING TIME: 29 minutes*

3¼ cups nonfat chicken broth   *⅛ teaspoon cayenne pepper*
1½ cups uncooked white rice   *2 tablespoons chopped fresh parsley*

1. Preheat oven to 400 degrees.
2. Heat ¼ cup broth in an oven-safe saucepan. Add rice and sauté until lightly browned, about 4 minutes.
3. Add remaining broth, pepper, and parsley; bring to a boil. Stir well; cover the pan, set it in the oven, and bake until rice is tender, about 25 minutes.

Calories Per Serving: 283   Carbohydrates: 59 g
Fat: 1 g   Dietary Fiber: 0 g
Cholesterol: 0 mg   Sodium: 274 mg
Protein: 9 g

Microwave Wild Rice

Wild rice is steamed in the microwave.

YIELD: 3 servings ▪ *PREPARATION TIME: 3 minutes* ▪
COOKING TIME: 32 minutes plus 5 minutes standing time

¾ cup uncooked wild rice   *1½ cups water*

1. Place rice and water in a 3-quart microwave-safe casserole. Cover tightly and microwave on HIGH for 7 minutes, or until the water begins to boil.
2. Microwave on MEDIUM for 20 to 25 minutes.
3. Let stand for 5 minutes. Drain.

Calories Per Serving: 142   Carbohydrates: 30 g
Fat: 0 g   Dietary Fiber: 0 g
Cholesterol: 0 mg   Sodium: 3 mg
Protein: 6 g

Baked Wild Rice

Wild rice is baked with carrots, onions, and bay leaves.

YIELD: 6 servings ▪ *PREPARATION TIME: 15 minutes* ▪
COOKING TIME: 1 hour and 40 minutes

4 cups nonfat chicken broth   *¼ cup grated carrot*
1 cup uncooked wild rice, rinsed *3 bay leaves*
¼ cup chopped onion   *¼ teaspoon ground black pepper*

1. Preheat oven to 325 degrees.
2. Heat ½ cup chicken broth in an ovenproof casserole over medium heat. Add the rice, onion, and carrot and sauté for 5 minutes, stirring constantly.
3. Add the remaining chicken stock, bay leaves, and black pepper. Bring to a boil.
4. Cover the casserole and bake for 1½ hours, or until rice is tender and has absorbed the liquid. Add water if needed while rice is cooking.
5. Remove bay leaves.

Calories Per Serving: 174   Carbohydrates: 33 g
Fat: 2 g   Dietary Fiber: 1 g
Cholesterol: 0 mg   Sodium: 341 mg
Protein: 11 g

Sushi Rice

This vinegar-flavored rice is used in making sushi and can also be served as a side dish with seafood.

YIELD: 2 servings • *PREPARATION TIME: 5 minutes* • *COOKING TIME: 17 minutes*

¾ cup white rice   3 tablespoons distilled white vinegar
1 cup water   2 tablespoons sugar

1. Combine rice and water. Bring to a boil. Reduce heat and simmer rice for 20 minutes, or until the water has been absorbed.
2. Combine vinegar and sugar in a saucepan over low heat. Bring to a boil, stirring constantly. When sugar is dissolved, remove from heat.
3. Stir vinegar into hot rice and let sit until liquid is absorbed.

Calories Per Serving: 312   Carbohydrates: 72 g
Fat: 2 g   Dietary Fiber: 1 g
Cholesterol: 0 mg   Sodium: 1 mg
Protein: 5 g

Microwave Basmati Rice

Fragrant basmati rice is quickly prepared in the microwave.

YIELD: 2 servings • *PREPARATION TIME: 3 minutes* •
COOKING TIME: 20 minutes plus 5 minutes standing time

1 cup basmati rice, rinsed   1 tablespoon chopped fresh parsley
2 cups nonfat chicken broth   ¼ teaspoon ground black pepper

1. Place rice and broth in a large microwave-safe casserole. Cover tightly. Cook on HIGH for 20 minutes.

2. Let stand, covered, for 5 minutes.
3. Stir in parsley and black pepper.

Calories Per Serving: 376
Fat: 2 g
Cholesterol: 0 mg
Protein: 11 g

Carbohydrates: 79 g
Dietary Fiber: 1 g
Sodium: 338 mg

RICE SOUPS

❖

Garlic Peasant Soup ▪ Corn-and-Rice Soup ▪ Black-Eyed Pea Soup ▪ Curried Plum Tomato–Spinach Soup ▪ Mushroom-Kale Soup with Rice ▪ Broccoli–Yellow Pepper Soup ▪ Saffron Vegetable Bowl ▪ Many-Vegetable Minestrone ▪ Zucchini–Red Bell Pepper–Tomato Soup ▪ Carrot Soup with Parsnips and Wild Rice ▪ Butternut-Pear Soup ▪ Shrimp-Rice Soup ▪ Very Quick Turkey Soup ▪ Chicken and Brown Rice Soup with Escarole ▪ Potato-Turkey Soup ▪ Mulligatawny Soup ▪ Curried Chicken-Apple Soup ▪ Jalapeño-Tomato Chicken Stew ▪ Jalapeño-Chicken Chili with Great Northern Beans

Garlic Peasant Soup

This simple soup, a garlic lover's delight, features minced garlic, onions, brown rice, and fresh parsley in chicken broth. It's a great choice for a chilly winter night.

YIELD: 4 servings • PREPARATION TIME: 20 minutes plus rice cooking time • COOKING TIME: 15 minutes

¼ cup nonfat chicken broth	1 tablespoon reduced-sodium soy sauce
2 medium onions, finely chopped	2 cups cooked brown rice (see p. 192)
12 cloves garlic, minced	1 cup chopped fresh parsley
6 cups vegetable broth	

1. Heat chicken broth in a skillet over medium heat. Add onions and garlic and sauté until onion is lightly browned, about 4 minutes.
2. Bring vegetable broth and soy sauce to a boil in a large saucepan. Stir in rice.
3. Add onions and garlic and simmer for 10 minutes.
4. Stir in parsley and serve.

Calories Per Serving: 193	Carbohydrates: 35 g
Fat: 3 g	Dietary Fiber: 3 g
Cholesterol: 0 mg	Sodium: 673 mg
Protein: 12 g	

Corn-and-Rice Soup

This chicken-rice soup is enhanced with corn, celery, onion, and leek and seasoned with soy sauce. Serve as a first course with your favorite Chinese entrées.

YIELD: 4 servings • PREPARATION TIME: 15 minutes plus rice cooking time • COOKING TIME: 40 minutes

4¼ cups nonfat chicken broth	1 stalk celery, thinly sliced
1 medium onion, diced	3 cups cooked white rice (see p. 190)
1 leek, rinsed and chopped	1 tablespoon reduced-sodium soy sauce
2 cups fresh, frozen, thawed, or canned corn kernels	

1. Heat ¼ cup chicken broth in a large saucepan over medium heat. Add onion and leek. Sauté until onion is lightly browned, about 4 minutes.
2. Add corn and celery and sauté for 2 additional minutes.
3. Add the rice, remaining 4 cups chicken broth, and soy sauce and bring to a boil.
4. Reduce heat and simmer for 30 minutes.

Calories Per Serving: 291
Fat: 3 g
Cholesterol: 0 mg
Protein: 13 g

Carbohydrates: 60 g
Dietary Fiber: 6 g
Sodium: 515 mg

Black-Eyed Pea Soup

Black-eyed peas are small beige beans with black circular "eyes" in their inner curves. They can be purchased dried or canned. Here they are combined with herbs, onion, and brown rice in a quick, hearty soup.

YIELD: 6 servings • *PREPARATION TIME: 10 minutes plus rice cooking time and bean cooking time* • *COOKING TIME: 15 minutes*

¼ cup nonfat chicken broth
1 cup chopped onion
8 cups vegetable broth
1 cup cooked brown rice (see p. 192)
⅛ teaspoon dried thyme

⅛ teaspoon dried marjoram
1 tablespoon reduced-sodium soy sauce
1 cup cooked or low-sodium canned black-eyed peas, drained

1. Heat chicken broth in a skillet over medium heat. Add onion and sauté until lightly browned, about 4 minutes.
2. Bring vegetable broth to a boil in a large saucepan. Add sautéed onions, rice, thyme, marjoram, soy sauce, and black-eyed peas.
3. Reduce heat and simmer for 5 minutes.
4. Serve immediately.

Calories Per Serving: 139
Fat: 2 g
Cholesterol: 0 mg
Protein: 12 g

Carbohydrates: 22 g
Dietary Fiber: 6 g
Sodium: 559 mg

Curried Plum Tomato–Spinach Soup

Flavorful egg-shaped plum tomatoes are combined with fresh spinach, onion, and brown rice in this curried soup.

YIELD: 6 servings • *PREPARATION TIME: 15 minutes plus rice cooking time* • *COOKING TIME: 40 minutes*

1¼ cups nonfat chicken broth
1 cup chopped onion
2 teaspoons curry powder
1 teaspoon ground cumin

8 cups canned low-sodium plum tomatoes, with their juice
2 cups chopped fresh spinach
1 cup cooked brown rice (see p. 192)
¼ teaspoon ground black pepper

1. Heat ¼ cup chicken broth in a large saucepan over medium heat. Add onion and sauté until the onion is lightly browned, about 4 minutes.
2. Stir in the curry powder and cumin and sauté 1 more minute.
3. Add tomatoes and bring to a boil.
4. Reduce heat and simmer, covered, for 20 minutes.
5. Stir in the spinach and rice. Simmer for 10 minutes.
6. Add remaining chicken broth and black pepper. Continue cooking until broth is hot.

Calories Per Serving: 133
Fat: 2 g
Cholesterol: 0 mg
Protein: 7 g

Carbohydrates: 26 g
Dietary Fiber: 4 g
Sodium: 144 mg

Mushroom-Kale Soup with Rice

Kale, which has been cultivated for over 2,000 years, is rich in vitamins A and C, folic acid, calcium, and iron. Here it is added to a mushroom-rice soup with Asian accents.

YIELD: 4 servings • *PREPARATION TIME: 25 minutes plus rice cooking time* • *COOKING TIME: 25 minutes*

4½ cups nonfat chicken broth
2 cups chopped onion
10 ounces chopped fresh mushrooms

1 clove garlic, minced
¼ teaspoon ground black pepper
1 cup cooked white rice (see p. 190)

1 cup chopped kale leaves
1 tablespoon reduced-sodium soy sauce

1 teaspoon sesame oil
2 tablespoons chopped fresh parsley

1. Heat ¼ cup chicken broth in a large saucepan over medium heat. Add onion and sauté until it softens thoroughly, about 5 minutes.
2. Add the mushrooms and garlic and sauté until mushrooms are lightly browned, about 5 minutes.
3. Add the black pepper, the remaining broth, the rice, and kale. Bring to a boil; reduce heat, cover, and simmer for 15 minutes.
4. Stir in soy sauce and sesame oil. Sprinkle with parsley.

Calories Per Serving: 143
Fat: 3 g
Cholesterol: 0 mg
Protein: 10 g

Carbohydrates: 24 g
Dietary Fiber: 4 g
Sodium: 553 mg

Broccoli–Yellow Pepper Soup

This zesty soup is not only delicious, but rich in vitamins A and C as well as calcium and iron.

YIELD: 8 servings • *PREPARATION TIME: 20 minutes* • *COOKING TIME: 25 minutes*

8 cups nonfat chicken broth
1 carrot, thinly sliced
¾ cup uncooked white rice
4 cups chopped broccoli stems and florets
1 tablespoon olive oil

½ cup very thinly sliced yellow bell pepper
1 teaspoon crushed hot pepper flakes
5 cloves garlic, minced
½ teaspoon ground black pepper

1. Heat chicken broth in a large saucepan over medium heat. Add carrot and rice. Bring to a boil. Reduce heat; cover and simmer for 10 minutes.
2. Add broccoli and simmer until it is just tender, about 10 minutes.
3. While soup is cooking, heat olive oil in a small skillet. Add the yellow bell pepper and the hot pepper flakes. Sauté for 2 minutes.
4. Using a slotted spoon, transfer the bell pepper mixture to the soup mixture.
5. Add garlic to the oil and sauté for 1 minute.
6. Stir the garlic mixture and the black pepper into the soup.

Calories Per Serving: 74
Fat: 3 g
Cholesterol: 0 mg
Protein: 7 g

Carbohydrates: 9 g
Dietary Fiber: 2 g
Sodium: 354 mg

Saffron Vegetable Bowl

This tempting soup is made with spinach, green beans, carrot, peas, and tomatoes that are added to a saffron-flavored chicken broth.

YIELD: *6 servings* • PREPARATION TIME: *20 minutes plus 15 minutes standing time* • COOKING TIME: *35 minutes*

8 cups nonfat chicken broth
pinch of saffron threads (crushed)
2 cups green beans cut into ½-inch
　lengths
1 cup diced carrot
⅓ cup uncooked white rice
2 cups chopped fresh spinach

1 cup diced yellow summer squash
½ cup frozen peas, thawed
½ cup fresh or canned low-sodium
　tomatoes, chopped
½ teaspoon ground black pepper
2 tablespoons grated nonfat Parmesan

1. Heat ¼ cup chicken broth in a small saucepan over medium heat. Add saffron and bring to a boil; cover, remove from heat, and allow to stand for 15 minutes.
2. Heat the remaining broth in a large saucepan. Stir in the saffron-broth mixture, green beans, carrot, and rice. Bring to a boil.
3. Reduce heat, cover, and cook, stirring frequently, until rice and vegetables are just tender, about 15 minutes.
4. Add the spinach, squash, peas, tomatoes, and black pepper. Simmer until peas are tender, about 10 minutes.
5. Transfer to serving bowls, sprinkle with Parmesan, and serve.

Calories Per Serving: 100
Fat: 2 g
Cholesterol: 2 mg
Protein: 10 g

Carbohydrates: 16 g
Dietary Fiber: 3 g
Sodium: 486 mg

Many-Vegetable Minestrone

Served with a loaf of warm Italian bread, this hearty soup is a meal in a bowl.

YIELD: 10 servings ▪ *PREPARATION TIME: 35 minutes* ▪
COOKING TIME: 40 minutes

½ cup nonfat chicken broth
1 clove garlic, minced
1 medium onion, chopped
3 stalks celery, chopped
2 cups fresh or low-sodium canned
    tomatoes, chopped, with juice
2 medium red potatoes, cubed
2 carrots, diced
3 cups yellow summer squash, chopped

2 cups string beans cut into 1-inch
    lengths
1 cup fresh or frozen, thawed green peas
1 cup chopped fresh parsley
2 cups cooked or canned low-sodium red
    kidney beans, rinsed and drained
2 quarts water
1 cup chopped cabbage
1½ cups uncooked white rice
¼ cup grated nonfat Parmesan

1. Heat broth in a large stockpot over medium heat. Add garlic, onion, celery, tomatoes, potatoes, carrots, squash, string beans, peas, parsley, and kidney beans. Sauté for 5 minutes.
2. Add water; bring to a boil.
3. Reduce heat and simmer until potatoes are just tender, about 20 minutes. Add cabbage; return to a boil and stir in rice.
4. Reduce heat, cover, and simmer until rice is tender, about 15 minutes.
5. Serve immediately, topped with Parmesan.

Calories Per Serving: 164
Fat: 1 g
Cholesterol: 0 mg
Protein: 6 g

Carbohydrates: 36 g
Dietary Fiber: 6 g
Sodium: 37 mg

Zucchini–Red Bell Pepper–Tomato Soup

This attractive red and green soup is made aromatic with basil and oregano and topped with nonfat Parmesan.

YIELD: 8 servings ▪ *PREPARATION TIME: 20 minutes plus rice cooking time* ▪
COOKING TIME: 35 minutes

5 cups nonfat chicken broth
½ cup chopped onion
1 clove garlic, minced
3½ cups chopped zucchini
2 red bell peppers, seeded and chopped
2 tablespoons dried basil

1 teaspoon dried oregano
¼ teaspoon ground black pepper
1 cup cooked brown rice (see p. 192)
4 cups fresh or canned low-sodium plum
    tomatoes, chopped, with juice
3 tablespoons grated nonfat Parmesan

1. Heat ½ cup chicken broth in a large saucepan over medium heat. Add onion and garlic and sauté until onion is just tender, about 3 minutes. Stir in zucchini, red bell pepper, basil, oregano, and black pepper. Sauté until vegetables are just tender, about 6 to 8 minutes.
2. Add remaining chicken broth, brown rice, and tomatoes. Bring to a boil, reduce heat, cover, and simmer for 15 minutes.
3. Sprinkle cheese over individual bowls of soup, and serve immediately.

Calories Per Serving: 196
Fat: 2 g
Cholesterol: 2 mg
Protein: 9 g

Carbohydrates: 39 g
Dietary Fiber: 2 g
Sodium: 291 mg

Carrot Soup with Parsnips and Wild Rice

This soup blends the nutty flavor and chewy texture of wild rice with sweet parsnips and carrots, zesty gingerroot, and nutmeg.

YIELD: 10 servings • PREPARATION TIME: 20 minutes •
COOKING TIME: 1 hour, 25 minutes plus 10 minutes cooling time

10 cups nonfat chicken broth
½ cup uncooked wild rice
½ teaspoon dried thyme
1 medium onion, chopped
2 pounds carrots, diced

2 parsnips, peeled and diced
1 tablespoon minced fresh gingerroot
2 cups skim milk
¼ teaspoon ground nutmeg
¼ teaspoon ground black pepper

1. Bring 2 cups chicken broth to a boil in a large saucepan. Stir in wild rice and thyme.
2. Return to a boil; reduce heat, cover, and simmer until rice is just tender, about 50 minutes.
3. While the rice is cooking, heat ½ cup chicken broth in another saucepan. Add onion and sauté until lightly browned, about 4 minutes.

4. Add carrots, parsnips, gingerroot, and remaining broth. Bring to a boil; reduce heat and simmer until vegetables are just tender, about 20 minutes.
5. Allow to cool for 10 minutes.
6. Puree the vegetables in a food processor or blender.
7. Combine the pureed vegetables, milk, cooked rice, nutmeg, and black pepper in the large saucepan. Mix thoroughly, heat through, and serve.

Calories Per Serving: 124   Carbohydrates: 23 g
Fat: 2 g   Dietary Fiber: 4 g
Cholesterol: 1 mg   Sodium: 425 mg
Protein: 9 g

Butternut-Pear Soup

Sweet orange butternut squash chunks are combined with pear, gingerroot, apple juice, and wild rice in this pureed soup.

YIELD: 6 servings • *PREPARATION TIME: 20 minutes plus rice cooking time* •
COOKING TIME: 40 minutes plus 10 minutes cooling time

4 cups butternut squash, peeled, seeded,   2 cups apple juice
   and cut into 1-inch cubes   1½ cups cooked wild rice (see p. 194)
¾ cup nonfat chicken broth   1½ cups skim milk
⅓ cup chopped onion   ¼ teaspoon ground black pepper
1 pear, peeled, cored, and diced   ¼ teaspoon ground cinnamon
1 tablespoon minced fresh gingerroot   1 tablespoon chopped fresh parsley

1. Steam the squash for 15 minutes.
2. Heat ¼ cup chicken broth in a large saucepan over medium heat. Add the onion and pear; sauté for 5 minutes or until tender.
3. Stir in the gingerroot and sauté for 1 additional minute.
4. Add apple juice and steamed squash and bring to a boil. Reduce heat, cover, and simmer for 10 minutes.
5. Remove lid and allow to cool for 10 minutes. Puree in a food processor or blender until smooth. Return puree to saucepan.
6. Add cooked rice, milk, black pepper, cinnamon, parsley, and remaining chicken broth.
7. Gently reheat before serving.

Calories Per Serving: 166
Fat: 1 g
Cholesterol: 1 mg
Protein: 6 g

Carbohydrates: 37 g
Dietary Fiber: 3 g
Sodium: 84 mg

Shrimp-Rice Soup

Shrimp, scallions, corn, and rice are seasoned with thyme, bay leaf, and hot pepper sauce to create this chowder.

YIELD: 4 servings ▪ *PREPARATION TIME: 15 minutes* ▪ *COOKING TIME: 55 minutes*

2¼ cups nonfat chicken broth
2 scallions, chopped
½ bay leaf
¾ teaspoon dried thyme
⅓ cup uncooked white rice
2 cups skim milk

1 cup fresh, canned, or thawed frozen
    corn kernels
¼ pound small shrimp, peeled
⅛ teaspoon hot pepper sauce
¼ cup minced green bell pepper

1. Heat ¼ cup broth in a large saucepan over medium heat. Add the scallions and sauté until just tender, about 3 minutes.
2. Add remaining broth, bay leaf, and thyme. Bring to a boil; reduce heat, cover, and simmer for 20 minutes.
3. Stir in the rice. Return to a boil; reduce heat, cover, and simmer until rice is soft, about 20 minutes.
4. Stir in 1 cup of the milk and the corn kernels and simmer for 10 minutes.
5. Add the shrimp; cover and cook for 5 minutes or until shrimp are done.
6. Discard bay leaf. Add hot pepper sauce and mix well. Transfer to serving bowls, sprinkle with minced green pepper, and serve.

Calories Per Serving: 277
Fat: 3 g
Cholesterol: 23 mg
Protein: 15 g

Carbohydrates: 50 g
Dietary Fiber: 5 g
Sodium: 356 mg

Very Quick Turkey Soup

If you get a hankering for turkey soup any season of the year, this recipe provides a delicious shortcut. Onion, carrots, tomatoes, and brown rice are simmered with pieces of turkey cutlet.

YIELD: *6 servings* • PREPARATION TIME: *20 minutes plus rice cooking time* • COOKING TIME: *25 minutes*

6¼ cups nonfat chicken broth
1 cup diced onion
1 cup diced carrots
1 clove garlic, minced

2 cups chopped fresh or canned low-sodium tomatoes
2 turkey cutlets, cubed
1 cup cooked brown rice (see p. 192)
3 tablespoons chopped fresh parsley

1. Heat ¼ cup broth in a large saucepan over medium heat. Add onion and carrots. Sauté until carrots begin to soften, about 5 minutes.
2. Add garlic and sauté for an additional minute.
3. Add remaining broth, tomatoes, turkey, and rice. Simmer for 20 minutes. Sprinkle with parsley before serving.

Calories Per Serving: 132
Fat: 2 g
Cholesterol: 17 mg
Protein: 14 g

Carbohydrates: 18 g
Dietary Fiber: 2 g
Sodium: 369 mg

Chicken and Brown Rice Soup with Escarole

Escarole, which has broad, slightly curved, rich green leaves, is combined with chicken, brown rice, and tomatoes in this classic soup. Escarole has a milder flavor than either Belgian or curly endive.

YIELD: *6 servings* • PREPARATION TIME: *20 minutes* • COOKING TIME: *25 minutes*

7¼ cups nonfat chicken broth
1 medium onion
4 cups escarole cut into thin strips
1 cup uncooked brown rice
¾ pound skinless chicken breast cutlets,
  cut into ½-inch cubes

2 cups fresh or low-sodium canned tomatoes, chopped
¼ teaspoon ground black pepper
2 tablespoons grated nonfat Parmesan

1. Heat ¼ cup chicken broth in a large soup pot over medium heat. Add onions and sauté until golden, about 3 minutes.
2. Add escarole and 1 cup of broth. Bring to a boil; reduce heat, cover, and simmer for 15 minutes.
3. Stir in remaining broth and return to a simmer. Add rice, chicken, and tomatoes and continue to simmer until chicken is cooked through, about 8 to 10 minutes.
4. Stir in black pepper. Sprinkle with Parmesan before serving.

Calories Per Serving: 181

Fat: 2 g

Cholesterol: 39 mg

Protein: 22 g

Carbohydrates: 22 g

Dietary Fiber: 2 g

Sodium: 453 mg

Potato-Turkey Soup

This sherry-laced turkey soup is accented with scallions, onion, and garlic.

YIELD: 8 servings • PREPARATION TIME: 30 minutes • COOKING TIME: 35 minutes

4¼ cups nonfat chicken broth

1 pound skinless turkey breast cutlets, cubed

1 cup chopped scallions

1 cup diced onion

1 clove garlic, minced

1 cup peeled, cubed turnip

2 cups cubed potato

½ cup uncooked white rice

2 cups skim milk

¼ teaspoon ground black pepper

2 teaspoons dry sherry

1. Heat ¼ cup broth in a large stockpot over medium heat. Add turkey, scallions, onion, and garlic. Sauté for 8 minutes, or until turkey is no longer pink. Remove turkey from pot and set aside.
2. Add turnip, potato, rice, and remaining broth. Bring to a boil; reduce heat, cover, and simmer until turnips and potato are just tender and rice is cooked, about 20 minutes.
3. Puree potato-turnip mixture in a food processor or blender until smooth.
4. In the stockpot, combine turnip puree, milk, and black pepper with the turkey mixture. Stir well. Simmer 5 minutes.
5. Stir in sherry and serve.

Calories Per Serving: 181
Fat: 1 g
Cholesterol: 41 mg
Protein: 22 g

Carbohydrates: 23 g
Dietary Fiber: 2 g
Sodium: 386 mg

Mulligatawny Soup

Mulligatawny soup—the name means "pepper water"—originated in southern India. The seasonings in this soup include coriander, ginger, turmeric, and cayenne.

YIELD: 4 servings • *PREPARATION TIME: 15 minutes* • *COOKING TIME: 25 minutes*

4¼ cups water
4 skinless chicken breast cutlets, about 4
   ounces each
1 teaspoon ground black pepper
1 tablespoon ground coriander
½ teaspoon ground ginger

2 teaspoons ground turmeric
½ teaspoon cayenne pepper
¼ cup nonfat chicken broth
2 medium onions, sliced
2 cups cooked white rice (see p. 190)
1 tablespoon lemon juice

1. Bring 4 cups water to a boil in a saucepan. Add chicken, reduce heat, and stir in black pepper, coriander, ginger, turmeric, and cayenne pepper. Simmer until meat is tender, about 15 minutes.
2. Heat chicken broth in a skillet. Add onions and sauté until they are lightly browned.
3. Add onions, rice, and lemon juice to saucepan. Reduce heat and simmer until rice is heated through.

Calories Per Serving: 258
Fat: 2 g
Cholesterol: 75 mg
Protein: 31 g

Carbohydrates: 34 g
Dietary Fiber: 2 g
Sodium: 51 mg

Curried Chicken-Apple Soup

Apples and curry powder are prominent ingredients in this tangy soup. Garnish with raisins and serve with white wine.

*YIELD: 4 servings ▪ PREPARATION TIME: 30 minutes plus chicken cooking time ▪
COOKING TIME: 45 minutes*

2 cups low-sodium tomato juice
2 cups nonfat chicken broth
2 cups water
2 carrots, sliced
2 medium onions, chopped
2 stalks celery, chopped
4 tablespoons chopped fresh parsley

¼ cup uncooked brown rice
2 teaspoons curry powder
¾ pound skinless chicken breast cutlets,
   cooked and cubed
2 apples, cored and diced
¼ cup raisins

1. Combine tomato juice, chicken broth, water, carrots, onions, celery, parsley, rice, and curry powder in a large stockpot. Bring to a boil; reduce heat, cover, and simmer until rice is tender, about 45 minutes.
2. Add chicken, apples, and raisins; heat all ingredients through and serve.

Calories Per Serving: 244
Fat: 2 g
Cholesterol: 56 mg
Protein: 26 g

Carbohydrates: 35 g
Dietary Fiber: 6 g
Sodium: 238 mg

Jalapeño-Tomato Chicken Stew

Jalapeño peppers, cumin, chili powder, and lime juice give this soup a special zing.

*YIELD: 4 servings ▪ PREPARATION TIME: 20 minutes plus rice and chicken
cooking time ▪ COOKING TIME: 25 minutes*

2 cups nonfat chicken broth
2 cups fresh or low-sodium canned
   tomatoes, chopped, with juice
½ cup minced onion
3 jalapeño peppers, seeded and minced
¼ teaspoon cumin
¼ teaspoon chili powder

1 cup cooked white rice (see p. 190)
½ pound skinless chicken breast cutlets,
   cooked and diced
1 cup fresh or thawed frozen corn
   kernels
2 tablespoons lime juice

1. In a large saucepan combine the broth, tomatoes, onion, jalapeños, cumin, and chili powder. Bring to a boil, reduce heat, and simmer for 10 minutes.
2. Stir in the rice, chicken, corn, and lime juice. Simmer until all ingredients are heated through.

Calories Per Serving: 33
Fat: 3 g
Cholesterol: 38 mg
Protein: 22 g

Carbohydrates: 56 g
Dietary Fiber: 6 g
Sodium: 519 mg

Jalapeño-Chicken Chili with Great Northern Beans

Great Northern beans, chicken, jalapeño peppers, rice, and oregano are simmered with chicken broth to create this soup, which has been popular since pioneer days.

YIELD: 8 servings • *PREPARATION TIME: 20 minutes plus rice and chicken cooking time* • *COOKING TIME: 15 minutes*

8 cups nonfat chicken broth
½ pound skinless chicken breast cutlets, cooked and cubed
2 cups canned Great Northern beans, drained and rinsed

2 jalapeño peppers, seeded and minced
2 cups cooked white rice (see p. 190)
2 teaspoons dried oregano
6 ounces grated nonfat cheddar

1. Bring chicken broth to a boil in a large saucepan. Add chicken, beans, jalapeño peppers, rice, and oregano. Simmer for 10 minutes.
2. Transfer soup into serving bowls, sprinkle with cheese, and serve.

Calories Per Serving: 212
Fat: 2 g
Cholesterol: 18 mg
Protein: 22 g

Carbohydrates: 30 g
Dietary Fiber: 0 g
Sodium: 603 mg

RICE WITH VEGETABLES

❖

Cumin Rice ▪ Curried Rice ▪ Turmeric Rice ▪ Pineapple–Almond Rice ▪ Almond-Raisin Rice ▪ Sunflower-Leek Rice ▪ Leek-Thyme Rice ▪ Orange-Honey Rice ▪ Rice with Pumpkin Seeds ▪ Almond-Thyme Wild Rice ▪ Almond-Garlic Rice ▪ Jalapeño Rice ▪ Lemon Rice ▪ Microwave Mandarin-Ginger Rice ▪ Orange-Ginger Rice ▪ Brown Rice with Mushrooms ▪ Arborio Rice Salad ▪ Brown Rice Salad ▪ Basic Rice Pilaf ▪ Mediterranean Pilaf ▪ Layered Mushroom Pilaf ▪ Spicy Carrot-Basmati Pilaf ▪ Basmati–Red Bell Pepper Pilaf ▪ Nectarine-Strawberry Rice ▪ Grape Pilaf ▪ Fruited Rice ▪ Baked Pear-Raisin Rice Pilaf ▪ Rice Pilaf with Corn and Saffron ▪ Asparagus Rice ▪ Eggplant-Rice Casserole ▪ Gingered Broccoli Rice ▪ Carrot–Plum Tomato Rice ▪ Garlic-Cauliflower Rice ▪ Tomato-Garlic Rice with Corn and Scallion ▪ Rice with Green Beans, Zucchini, Carrot, and Peas ▪ Rice and Kale ▪ Rice and Spinach ▪ Tomato-Chile Rice ▪ Honey-Lemon Brown Rice and Spinach ▪ Ginger-Scallion Rice with Spinach ▪ Tomato-Okra Rice ▪ Zucchini Rice ▪ Green and Yellow Rice ▪ Vegetable-Rice Scramble ▪ Summer Vegetables and Rice ▪ Chickpea-Vegetable Paella ▪ Shiitake Mushrooms and Rice ▪ Brown Rice–Spinach Casserole ▪ Red Bell Peppers, Lima Beans, and Rice ▪ Tomato-Vegetable Rice ▪ Zucchini and Rice ▪ Basic Risotto ▪

Mixed-Vegetable Risotto · Spinach Risotto · Brazilian Rice · Vegetable-Rice Bake · Rice-Stuffed Peppers · Peppers Stuffed with Chicken, Corn, and Cannellini Beans · Acorn Squash with Rice Stuffing · Rice-Stuffed Tomatoes · Wild and White Rices with Asparagus · Grape Leaves Stuffed with Rice · Dilled Artichoke Salad · Rice Salad with Carrots and Leeks · Carrot-Mushroom Rice · Rice Salad with Tomato and Corn · Corn–Wild Rice Salad · Middle Eastern Rice Salad · Mini Molded Rice and Vegetable Salad · Rice Salad with Pineapple and Vegetables · Rice Salad with Pineapple and Cucumber · Rice Salad with Mandarin Oranges and Cucumber · Rice Salad with Mango and Jalapeños · Apricot Rice Salad · Apple–Wild Rice Salad with Citrus Dressing · Rice Salad with Peaches and Raspberries · Microwave Pear-Date Pilaf

Cumin Rice

This flavorful dish features white rice, cumin, and parsley.

YIELD: 3 servings • PREPARATION TIME: 5 minutes • COOKING TIME: 20 minutes

3 cups water
1½ cups uncooked white rice

¾ teaspoon ground cumin
2 tablespoons chopped fresh parsley

1. Bring water to boil in a saucepan. Stir in rice and cumin. Return to a boil; reduce heat, cover, and simmer until rice is tender. Drain any excess liquid, sprinkle parsley over the top of the rice, and serve.

Calories Per Serving: 354
Fat: 1 g
Cholesterol: 0 mg
Protein: 7 g

Carbohydrates: 78 g
Dietary Fiber: 0 g
Sodium: 10 mg

Curried Rice

This simple curried rice is made with sautéed onion and garlic, raisins, curry powder, bay leaf, and thyme.

YIELD: 2 servings • PREPARATION TIME: 15 minutes •
COOKING TIME: 22 minutes

¼ cup nonfat chicken broth
½ cup chopped onion
½ teaspoon finely chopped garlic
1 cup uncooked white rice
2 tablespoons raisins

1 tablespoon curry powder
1½ cups water
1 bay leaf
½ teaspoon dried thyme
¼ teaspoon ground black pepper

1. Heat the chicken broth in a skillet over medium heat. Sauté onion and garlic until onion is slightly golden, about 3 minutes.
2. Add rice, raisins, curry powder, water, bay leaf, thyme, and black pepper and bring to a boil.
3. Cover and simmer for 20 minutes.
4. Remove bay leaf.

Calories Per Serving: 411
Fat: 1 g
Cholesterol: 0 mg
Protein: 8 g

Carbohydrates: 91 g
Dietary Fiber: 3 g
Sodium: 47 mg

Turmeric Rice

Pungent turmeric, lemon juice, scallions, parsley, and raisins flavor simmered rice. Serve with curried entrées.

YIELD: 4 servings • *PREPARATION TIME: 10 minutes plus 10 minutes standing time* • *COOKING TIME: 24 minutes*

3¼ cups nonfat chicken broth
4 scallions, finely chopped
1½ cups uncooked white rice
1 tablespoon lemon juice

¼ teaspoon ground turmeric
½ cup golden raisins
¼ cup chopped fresh parsley

1. Heat ¼ cup broth in a large saucepan. Add the scallions and sauté until just tender, about 3 minutes.
2. Stir in rice; sauté for an additional 3 minutes.
3. Add remaining broth, lemon juice, and turmeric. Bring to a boil; reduce heat, cover, and simmer until rice is tender, about 20 minutes.
4. Remove from heat and stir in raisins. Let stand, covered, for 10 minutes. Garnish with parsley and serve.

Calories Per Serving: 346
Fat: 1 g
Cholesterol: 0 mg
Protein: 11 g

Carbohydrates: 73 g
Dietary Fiber: 1 g
Sodium: 144 mg

Pineapple-Almond Rice

White rice is simmered in pineapple juice and gingerroot, then mixed with almonds and scallions.

YIELD: 4 servings • *PREPARATION TIME: 5 minutes* • *COOKING TIME: 25 minutes*

1 cup pineapple juice
1 cup water
1 teaspoon minced fresh gingerroot

1 cup uncooked white rice
2 tablespoons slivered toasted almonds
2 scallions, finely chopped

1. Combine pineapple juice, water, and gingerroot in a saucepan. Bring to boil. Stir in rice; return to boil, reduce heat, cover, and simmer until rice is just tender and liquid is absorbed, about 20 minutes.
2. Remove from heat. Stir in almonds and scallions and mix well. Serve immediately.

Calories Per Serving: 24
Fat: 3 g
Cholesterol: 0 mg
Protein: 4 g

Carbohydrates: 50 g
Dietary Fiber: 1 g
Sodium: 9 mg

Almond-Raisin Rice

White rice is simmered with saffron and cardamom and accented with almonds, currants, and citrus.

YIELD: 4 servings • PREPARATION TIME: 20 minutes plus 30 minutes currant soaking time • COOKING TIME: 35 minutes

¼ cup dried currants
enough hot water to cover currants
3¼ cups nonfat chicken broth
1 medium onion, finely chopped
1½ cups uncooked white rice
2 egg whites, beaten
¼ teaspoon ground white pepper

1 tablespoon saffron, mixed with 2 tablespoons hot water
2 tablespoons reduced-sodium soy sauce
½ teaspoon ground cardamom
2 tablespoons slivered blanched almonds
1 tablespoon minced orange peel
1 tablespoon minced lemon peel

1. Cover currants with hot water and allow to soak for 30 minutes.
2. Meanwhile, heat ¼ cup broth in a small saucepan. Add onion and sauté until translucent, about 3 minutes. Remove from heat and set aside.
3. Preheat oven to 350 degrees.
4. In a large saucepan, stir the rice into the beaten egg whites, mixing until rice is well coated. Stir over moderate heat until rice is dry and kernels separate. Add onion, white pepper, saffron, remaining broth, and soy sauce. Stir gently as you bring the mixture to a boil.

5. Add cardamom, almonds, currants, orange peel, and lemon peel. Mix thoroughly. Cover with a tight-fitting lid and bake until rice is tender, about 30 minutes. Turn into a large bowl and serve immediately.

Calories Per Serving: 355
Fat: 3 g
Cholesterol: 0 mg
Protein: 12 g

Carbohydrates: 72 g
Dietary Fiber: 2 g
Sodium: 585 mg

Sunflower-Leek Rice

Garlic, leek, sunflower seeds, mushrooms, parsley, and soy sauce are combined with brown rice.

YIELD: 4 servings • *PREPARATION TIME: 15 minutes, plus rice cooking time* • *COOKING TIME: 11 minutes*

¼ cup nonfat chicken broth
1 clove garlic, minced
½ cup minced leek
1 tablespoon sunflower seeds

2 cups sliced fresh mushrooms
2 cups cooked brown rice (see p. 192)
1 tablespoon chopped fresh parsley
1 teaspoon reduced-sodium soy sauce

1. Heat 2 tablespoons broth in a saucepan. Add garlic, leek, and sunflower seeds. Sauté for 2 minutes.
2. Add mushrooms and remaining broth. Bring to a boil; reduce heat, cover, and simmer until leek is translucent, about 4 minutes.
3. Stir in rice, parsley, and soy sauce. Heat gently until rice is warmed through, about 5 minutes, and serve.

Calories Per Serving: 148
Fat: 3 g
Cholesterol: 0 mg
Protein: 4 g

Carbohydrates: 27 g
Dietary Fiber: 3 g
Sodium: 98 mg

Leek-Thyme Rice

White rice is prepared with leek, red onion, and red bell pepper.

YIELD: 4 servings ▪ *PREPARATION TIME: 15 minutes* ▪ *COOKING TIME: 22 minutes*

2¼ cups nonfat chicken broth
1 cup finely chopped leek
1½ cups uncooked white rice
1 cup water

½ teaspoon dried thyme
⅛ teaspoon ground black pepper
¼ cup chopped red onion
¼ cup chopped red bell pepper

1. Heat ¼ cup broth in a large saucepan. Stir in leek and sauté for 2 minutes.
2. Add rice, remaining broth, water, thyme, and black pepper. Bring to a boil. Reduce heat, cover, and simmer until liquid is absorbed, about 20 minutes.
3. Toss with onion and red bell pepper and serve.

Calories Per Serving: 408
Fat: 1 g
Cholesterol: 0 mg
Protein: 10 g

Carbohydrates: 88 g
Dietary Fiber: 2 g
Sodium: 204 mg

Orange-Honey Rice

White rice is mixed with raisins, nutmeg, honey, almonds, and mandarin oranges.

YIELD: 6 servings ▪ *PREPARATION TIME: 25 minutes* ▪ *COOKING TIME: 5 minutes*

1½ cups water
¾ cup uncooked white rice
⅓ cup raisins
½ teaspoon ground nutmeg

2 tablespoons honey
2 tablespoons slivered toasted almonds
1 11-ounce can mandarin orange sections, drained and chopped

1. Bring water to a boil in a saucepan. Stir in rice. Return to a boil, reduce heat, cover, and simmer until rice is tender, about 20 minutes.
2. Stir in raisins, nutmeg, and honey. Continue simmering until raisins are heated through, about 3 minutes.
3. Remove from heat; fold in almonds and chopped orange sections. Allow to stand for 1 minute before serving.

Calories Per Serving: 172
Fat: 2 g
Cholesterol: 0 mg
Protein: 3 g

Carbohydrates: 36 g
Dietary Fiber: 1 g
Sodium: 8 mg

Rice with Pumpkin Seeds

Rice is prepared with garlic, cilantro, red pepper flakes, and pumpkin seeds.

*YIELD: 4 servings • PREPARATION TIME: 10 minutes plus 5 minutes standing time •
COOKING TIME: 21 minutes*

2¼ cups nonfat chicken broth
2 cloves garlic, minced
1 cup uncooked white rice
¼ cup roasted pumpkin seeds

2 tablespoons minced fresh cilantro
    leaves
¼ teaspoon dried red pepper flakes

1. Heat ¼ cup chicken broth in a large saucepan. Add garlic and sauté for 1 minute.
2. Add remaining chicken broth and bring to a boil. Stir in rice and return to a boil; reduce heat, cover, and simmer until rice is just tender and liquid is absorbed, about 20 minutes.
3. Remove from heat. Stir in pumpkin seeds, cilantro, and red pepper flakes. Cover and allow to stand for 5 minutes before serving.

Calories Per Serving: 229
Fat: 3 g
Cholesterol: 0 mg
Protein: 7 g

Carbohydrates: 46 g
Dietary Fiber: 2 g
Sodium: 192 mg

Almond-Thyme Wild Rice

Wild rice is seasoned with thyme, lemon peel, almonds, and raisins.

*YIELD: 4 servings • PREPARATION TIME: 10 minutes •
COOKING TIME: 30 minutes*

3½ cups water
1 cup uncooked wild rice
1 teaspoon olive oil
2 shallots, peeled and chopped
½ teaspoon dried thyme

1 teaspoon minced lemon peel
1 tablespoon slivered almonds
¼ cup raisins
¼ teaspoon ground black pepper

1. Bring water to a boil in a saucepan. Stir in wild rice. Return to a boil; reduce heat, cover, and simmer until rice is tender, about 30 minutes.
2. Remove from heat. Stir in olive oil, shallots, thyme, lemon peel, almonds, raisins, and pepper. Serve immediately.

Calories Per Serving: 200
Fat: 3 g
Cholesterol: 0 mg
Protein: 7 g

Carbohydrates: 49 g
Dietary Fiber: 1 g
Sodium: 29 mg

Almond-Garlic Rice

Rice is mixed with red and green bell pepper strips, garlic, and almonds.

YIELD: 4 servings • PREPARATION TIME: 10 minutes •
COOKING TIME: 25 minutes

3¼ cups nonfat chicken broth
1½ cups uncooked white rice
1 green bell pepper, cut into thin strips
1 red bell pepper, cut into thin strips

2 tablespoons slivered almonds
4 cloves garlic, minced
2 tablespoons chopped fresh parsley

1. Bring 3 cups broth to a boil in a large saucepan. Stir in rice; return to a boil, reduce heat, cover, and simmer until rice is just tender, about 20 minutes.
2. Heat remaining ¼ cup of broth in a large skillet. Add green and red peppers, almonds, and garlic. Sauté until peppers begin to soften, about 5 minutes.
3. Combine rice and vegetables in a serving bowl. Top with the parsley and serve immediately.

Calories Per Serving: 133
Fat: 3 g
Cholesterol: 0 mg
Protein: 7 g

Carbohydrates: 22 g
Dietary Fiber: 2 g
Sodium: 272 mg

Jalapeño Rice

Rice is prepared with a Mexican-influenced combination of jalapeño, onion, garlic, coriander, cumin, and turmeric.

YIELD: *4 servings* • PREPARATION TIME: *10 minutes* •
COOKING TIME: *25 minutes*

¼ cup nonfat chicken broth
1 medium onion, coarsely chopped
1 jalapeño pepper, seeded and minced
3 cloves garlic, minced
1 teaspoon ground coriander

1 teaspoon ground cumin
½ teaspoon ground turmeric
3 cups water
1½ cups uncooked white rice

1. Heat broth in a large, heavy saucepan. Add onion, jalapeño, garlic, coriander, cumin, and turmeric. Sauté until the onion is translucent, about 3 minutes.
2. Add water and bring to a boil. Stir in the rice; return to a boil, reduce heat, cover, and simmer until rice is just tender, about 20 minutes. Drain any excess liquid and serve immediately.

Calories Per Serving: 296
Fat: 1 g
Cholesterol: 0 mg
Protein: 6 g

Carbohydrates: 65 g
Dietary Fiber: 2 g
Sodium: 129 mg

Lemon Rice

Rice prepared with garlic, lemon peel, and parsley can be served with Middle Eastern dishes.

YIELD: *4 servings* • PREPARATION TIME: *10 minutes* •
COOKING TIME: *25 minutes*

2 cloves garlic, minced
1 tablespoon minced lemon peel
¼ teaspoon ground black pepper

3 cups nonfat chicken broth
2 cups uncooked white rice
¼ cup chopped fresh parsley

1. Combine garlic, lemon peel, pepper, and chicken broth in a saucepan. Bring to a boil. Stir in rice; return to a boil, reduce heat, cover, and simmer until rice is just tender, about 20 minutes.
2. Stir in parsley and serve immediately.

Calories Per Serving: 373 Carbohydrates: 79 g
Fat: 1 g Dietary Fiber: 1 g
Cholesterol: 0 mg Sodium: 255 mg
Protein: 10 g

Microwave Mandarin-Ginger Rice

Rice with ground ginger, pineapple juice, chopped mandarin oranges, green bell pepper, and water chestnuts is prepared in the microwave.

YIELD: 4 servings • PREPARATION TIME: 15 minutes •
COOKING TIME: 18 to 21 minutes plus 7 minutes standing time

1 cup white rice *1 cup drained juice-packed mandarin*
1½ cups pineapple juice *oranges, chopped*
¼ teaspoon ground ginger *½ cup minced green bell pepper*
  ½ cup minced water chestnuts

1. Place rice, pineapple juice, and ginger in a 3-quart microwave-safe casserole. Cover tightly. Cook on HIGH for 4 to 7 minutes, until the liquid boils.
2. Cook on MEDIUM for 10 minutes, or until all the liquid is absorbed. Let stand, covered, for 5 minutes.
3. Place mandarin oranges, green bell pepper, and water chestnuts in another microwave-safe bowl and microwave on HIGH for 2 minutes.
4. Stir pineapple mixture into rice. Microwave on HIGH for 2 minutes.

Calories Per Serving: 260 Carbohydrates: 60 g
Fat: 0 g Dietary Fiber: 4 g
Cholesterol: 0 mg Sodium: 3 mg
Protein: 4 g

Orange-Ginger Rice

A dish of white rice with orange peel, onion, currants, and gingerroot.

YIELD: 2 servings • PREPARATION TIME: 10 minutes •
COOKING TIME: 21 minutes

¼ cup nonfat chicken broth
¼ cup finely chopped onion
1 cup uncooked white rice
1 tablespoon dried currants

1 teaspoon minced orange peel
1 teaspoon minced fresh gingerroot
1¾ cups water

1. Heat broth in a large saucepan. Add onion and sauté for 3 minutes.
2. Add rice, currants, orange peel, and gingerroot. Sauté for 3 additional minutes.
3. Stir in water and bring to a boil. Reduce heat, cover, and simmer until water is absorbed and rice is just tender, about 18 minutes.
4. Allow to stand, uncovered, for 5 minutes before serving.

Calories Per Serving: 376
Fat: 1 g
Cholesterol: 0 mg
Protein: 7 g

Carbohydrates: 83 g
Dietary Fiber: 1 g
Sodium: 50 mg

Brown Rice with Mushrooms

Cooked brown rice in a richly flavored dish with soy sauce, chicken broth, mushrooms, and parsley.

YIELD: 4 servings • *PREPARATION TIME: 10 minutes plus rice cooking time* • *COOKING TIME: 12 minutes*

¼ cup nonfat chicken broth
1 medium onion, chopped
1½ cups sliced fresh mushrooms
4 cups cooked brown rice (see p. 192)

2 tablespoons low-sodium soy sauce
3 tablespoons water
¼ cup chopped fresh parsley

1. Heat broth in a large skillet. Add onion and sauté until translucent, about 3 minutes.
2. Add mushrooms and sauté until mushrooms are cooked through, about 6 minutes.
3. Stir in rice, soy sauce, and water. Cover and simmer until liquid is absorbed, about 3 minutes.
4. Sprinkle parsley over rice and serve immediately.

Calories Per Serving: 245

Carbohydrates: 50 g

Fat: 2 g

Dietary Fiber: 4 g

Cholesterol: 0 mg

Sodium: 298 mg

Protein: 7 g

Arborio Rice Salad

In this simple salad, arborio rice is dressed with olive oil, lemon juice, and parsley.

YIELD: 6 servings • PREPARATION TIME: 10 minutes •
COOKING TIME: 20 minutes

2 quarts water
2 cups uncooked arborio rice
1 tablespoon olive oil

⅓ cup lemon juice
½ cup chopped fresh parsley

1. Bring water to a boil in a large saucepan. Stir in rice; return to a boil, reduce heat, and simmer about 17 minutes, until rice is al dente, done but still firm to the bite. Drain to remove any excess liquid.
2. Transfer to a large serving dish. Whisk the oil and lemon juice together and drizzle over the rice. Sprinkle with the parsley and serve immediately.

Calories Per Serving: 266

Carbohydrates: 55 g

Fat: 3 g

Dietary Fiber: 0 g

Cholesterol: 0 mg

Sodium: 13 mg

Protein: 5 g

Brown Rice Salad

Brown rice is chilled in a mayonnaise-mustard dressing and enhanced with sweet pickles and celery. Green olives and hard-cooked egg whites are added as a finishing touch.

YIELD: 4 servings • PREPARATION TIME: 15 minutes plus rice cooking time
and 2 hours chilling time

2 cups cooked brown rice, cooled to room
   temperature
¼ cup diced onion
2 tablespoons pickle relish
¼ cup chopped celery
¼ teaspoon ground black pepper

½ cup nonfat mayonnaise
½ teaspoon prepared mustard
¼ teaspoon celery seeds
lettuce leaves
2 tablespoons sliced green olives
2 hard-boiled egg whites, sliced

1. Combine the rice, onion, pickle relish, celery, pepper, mayonnaise, mustard, and celery seed. Chill for 2 hours.
2. Surround with lettuce leaves on a serving platter. Serve topped with the olive slices and sliced egg whites.

Calories Per Serving: 163
Fat: 1 g
Cholesterol: 0 mg
Protein: 5 g

Carbohydrates: 33 g
Dietary Fiber: 3 g
Sodium: 558 mg

Basic Rice Pilaf

Rice and onion are sautéed in chicken broth, then simmered with bay leaf.

YIELD: *6 servings* · PREPARATION TIME: *15 minutes* ·
COOKING TIME: *32 minutes*

3¼ cups nonfat chicken broth
1 medium onion, finely chopped
1½ cups uncooked white rice

¼ teaspoon ground black pepper
1 bay leaf
1 tablespoon chopped fresh parsley

1. Heat ¼ cup of broth in a skillet over medium heat. Add onion and sauté over low heat, stirring, about 3 minutes or until soft but not brown.
2. Add rice and sauté, stirring, for 2 minutes.
3. Bring 3 cups of chicken broth to a boil. Add broth, pepper, and bay leaf to rice. Stir once with a fork and cover.
4. Simmer over low heat, without stirring, for 20 minutes. Remove bay leaf. Stir in parsley and serve.

Calories Per Serving: 306
Fat: 2 g
Cholesterol: 0 mg
Protein: 11 g

Carbohydrates: 63 g
Dietary Fiber: 1 g
Sodium: 380 mg

Mediterranean Pilaf

Rice richly seasoned with onion, garlic, and orange peel is combined with tomatoes and then garnished with olives.

YIELD: 4 servings • PREPARATION TIME: 20 minutes •
COOKING TIME: 11 minutes

¾ cup nonfat chicken broth
½ cup chopped onion
1 clove garlic, minced
1 teaspoon grated orange peel

2 cups low-sodium canned tomato puree
4 cups cooked white rice (see p. 190)
1 teaspoon dried basil
4 pitted black olives, sliced

1. Heat ¼ cup chicken broth in a skillet over medium heat. Add onion and garlic and sauté until onion is lightly golden, about 4 minutes.
2. Stir in orange peel, tomato puree, and remaining broth, and bring to a boil. Boil for 5 minutes.
3. Stir in rice and basil. Cover and cook over low heat for 5 minutes. Garnish with olives before serving.

Calories Per Serving: 286
Fat: 1 g
Cholesterol: 0 mg
Protein: 7 g

Carbohydrates: 61 g
Dietary Fiber: 1 g
Sodium: 118 mg

Layered Mushroom Pilaf

Sautéed onions and mushrooms are layered with steamed rice.

YIELD: 6 servings • PREPARATION TIME: 5 minutes plus 10 minutes standing time •
COOKING TIME: 32 minutes

1 cup uncooked white rice
2 cups water
¼ cup nonfat chicken broth
3 medium onions, coarsely chopped

1 pound fresh white button mushrooms,
    coarsely chopped
¼ teaspoon ground black pepper

1. In a saucepan, bring rice and water to a boil. Reduce heat, cover, and simmer for 20 minutes, or until the liquid is absorbed.

2. Heat chicken broth in a skillet over medium heat. Sauté onions in a small skillet until just tender, about 3 minutes.
3. Add mushrooms and cook for 5 minutes.
4. Season rice with pepper. In a serving bowl, layer rice with onion-mushroom mixture. Let stand for 10 minutes before serving.

Calories Per Serving: 168
Fat: 1 g
Cholesterol: 0 mg
Protein: 5 g

Carbohydrates: 36 g
Dietary Fiber: 3 g
Sodium: 20 mg

Spicy Carrot-Basmati Pilaf

Basmati rice is prepared with a fragrant array of 5 exotic spices.

Yield: 4 servings • *Preparation Time: 15 minutes* • *Cooking Time: 27 minutes*

¼ cup nonfat chicken broth
1 medium onion, finely chopped
3 cloves garlic, minced
1 tablespoon curry powder
2 teaspoons chili powder
½ teaspoon ground ginger

1 cup uncooked basmati rice
2½ cups water
½ cup grated carrot
1 cinnamon stick
¼ teaspoon ground cardamom

1. Heat chicken broth in a skillet over medium heat. Sauté onion and garlic until onion is lightly golden, about 5 minutes.
2. Stir in the curry powder, chili powder, and ginger. Sauté for 30 seconds. Add rice and stir for 2 minutes, to coat.
3. Add water and bring to a boil. Reduce heat to low.
4. Stir in carrots, cinnamon stick, and cardamom. Cook, covered, for 20 minutes, or until rice is tender. Discard cinnamon stick before serving.

Calories Per Serving: 212
Fat: 1 g
Cholesterol: 0 mg
Protein: 5 g

Carbohydrates: 47 g
Dietary Fiber: 2 g
Sodium: 42 mg

Basmati–Red Bell Pepper Pilaf

Basmati rice is prepared with onion, garlic, red bell pepper, and currants.

YIELD: *4 servings*   ▪   PREPARATION TIME: *15 minutes*   ▪
COOKING TIME: *28 minutes*

1¾ cups nonfat chicken broth
½ cup chopped onion
1 clove garlic, minced
1 red bell pepper, finely chopped

1 cup uncooked basmati rice
¼ cup dried currants
¼ teaspoon ground black pepper

1. Heat ¼ cup chicken broth in a saucepan over medium heat.
2. Add onion, garlic, and red bell pepper, sautéing for 3 minutes.
3. Add rice and cook over low heat until the rice is opaque.
4. Add remaining 1½ cups chicken broth, currants, and black pepper. Cover pan and simmer for 20 minutes, or until all the liquid is absorbed and the rice is tender.

Calories Per Serving: 239
Fat: 1 g
Cholesterol: 0 mg
Protein: 7 g

Carbohydrates: 52 g
Dietary Fiber: 1 g
Sodium: 192 mg

Nectarine-Strawberry Rice

Rice is tossed with fresh fruit, gingerroot, mint, and lemon peel. Serve with grilled chicken and roasted peppers.

YIELD: *4 servings*   ▪   PREPARATION TIME: *20 minutes*   ▪
COOKING TIME: *25 minutes plus rice cooling time*

1 cup uncooked white rice
1½ cups water
2 scallions, minced
2 tablespoons chopped fresh parsley
1 teaspoon dried mint leaves
1 teaspoon minced fresh gingerroot

½ teaspoon grated lemon peel
⅛ teaspoon ground cloves
3 tablespoons plain nonfat yogurt
1 teaspoon brown sugar, firmly packed
1 large nectarine or peach, chopped
¾ cup sliced fresh strawberries

1. Place rice and water in a medium saucepan. Bring water to a boil. Reduce heat, cover, and simmer for 20 minutes, or until rice is tender. Drain rice. Let cool to room temperature.
2. Mix scallions, parsley, mint, gingerroot, lemon peel, cloves, yogurt, brown sugar, nectarine (or peach), and strawberries. Toss with rice.

Calories Per Serving: 196
Fat: 0 g
Cholesterol: 0 mg
Protein: 4 g

Carbohydrates: 43 g
Dietary Fiber: 1 g
Sodium: 11 mg

Grape Pilaf

White rice combined with red seedless grapes, onion, and mushrooms.

YIELD: *3 servings* • PREPARATION TIME: *15 minutes* •
COOKING TIME: *25 minutes*

1¼ cups nonfat chicken broth
2 tablespoons minced onion
1 cup uncooked white rice
½ cup sliced fresh mushrooms

⅛ teaspoon dried thyme
⅛ teaspoon dried marjoram
1 cup whole seedless red grapes

1. Heat ¼ cup chicken broth in saucepan and sauté onion for 3 minutes until tender. Add rice and sauté until lightly browned, about 3 minutes.
2. In a second saucepan, heat remaining chicken broth to a boil. Stir broth, mushrooms, thyme, and marjoram into rice. Simmer for 20 minutes.
3. Stir in grapes and cook for 5 minutes longer.

Calories Per Serving: 273
Fat: 1 g
Cholesterol: 0 mg
Protein: 8 g

Carbohydrates: 59 g
Dietary Fiber: 1 g
Sodium: 198 mg

Fruited Rice

Brown rice is cooked with dried apricots, dates, and pears. Serve with baked fish and steamed broccoli.

YIELD: 4 servings • *PREPARATION TIME: 15 minutes* •
COOKING TIME: 35 minutes

¼ cup nonfat chicken broth
1 cup uncooked brown rice
1 medium onion, chopped
2 teaspoons curry powder

3 cups water
¼ cup chopped dried apricots
¼ cup chopped dates
¼ cup chopped dried pears

1. Heat chicken broth in a skillet over medium heat. Add rice, onion, and curry powder. Sauté, stirring, for 2 minutes.
2. Add water; cover and simmer for 25 minutes.
3. Add apricots, dates, and pears. Simmer for 10 minutes.
4. Remove from heat and let stand for 5 minutes before serving.

Calories Per Serving: 265
Fat: 2 g
Cholesterol: 0 mg
Protein: 5 g

Carbohydrates: 60 g
Dietary Fiber: 5 g
Sodium: 26 mg

Baked Pear-Raisin Rice Pilaf

Rice is combined with pear, onion, raisins, thyme, sage, and apple juice and then baked.

YIELD: 5 servings • *PREPARATION TIME: 15 minutes* •
COOKING TIME: 32 minutes

4¼ cups nonfat chicken broth
1 small onion, chopped
1 pear, peeled, cored, and diced
¼ cup raisins
1 tablespoon chopped fresh parsley

¼ teaspoon ground sage
¼ teaspoon dried thyme
¼ teaspoon ground black pepper
1½ cups uncooked rice
½ cup apple juice

1. Preheat oven to 350 degrees. Heat ¼ cup chicken broth in an oven-safe pot over medium heat. Sauté onion for 5 minutes.
2. Stir in pear, raisins, parsley, sage, and thyme. Season with pepper. Stir in rice and cook over low heat for 2 minutes.
3. Pour remaining chicken broth and apple juice into pot. Bring to a boil and stir.
4. Transfer pot to oven and bake for 25 minutes, or until the broth and apple juice are absorbed and the rice is tender.

Calories Per Serving: 293
Fat: 2 g
Cholesterol: 0 mg
Protein: 9 g

Carbohydrates: 63 g
Dietary Fiber: 2 g
Sodium: 289 mg

Rice Pilaf with Corn and Saffron

Rice pilaf is accented with saffron, corn, and parsley.

YIELD: 4 servings • PREPARATION TIME: 20 minutes •
COOKING TIME: 25 minutes

2¾ cups nonfat chicken broth
1 small onion, chopped
1 cup uncooked white rice
⅛ teaspoon ground saffron

¾ cup fresh, canned, or thawed frozen
 corn kernels
¼ teaspoon ground black pepper
1 tablespoon chopped fresh parsley

1. Heat ¼ cup chicken broth in a skillet over medium heat. Sauté the onion for 5 minutes.
2. Add the rice and cook over moderate heat for 2 minutes.
3. Add saffron and corn and cook for 1 minute.
4. Stir in pepper and parsley and remaining chicken broth. Bring to a boil.
5. Lower heat, cover, and simmer for 20 minutes, or until the liquid is absorbed and the rice is tender.

Calories Per Serving: 232
Fat: 1 g
Cholesterol: 0 mg
Protein: 8 g

Carbohydrates: 49 g
Dietary Fiber: 2 g
Sodium: 234 mg

Asparagus Rice

Fresh asparagus and rice are flavored with thyme and lemon peel.

YIELD: 4 servings   •   PREPARATION TIME: 10 minutes   •
COOKING TIME: 25 minutes

2½ cups nonfat chicken broth
½ cup chopped scallions
1½ cups uncooked white rice
½ cup water
¼ teaspoon dried thyme

⅛ teaspoon ground black pepper
½ pound fresh asparagus, cut into ¾-
   inch pieces
½ tablespoon minced lemon peel

1. Heat ¼ cup broth in a large saucepan. Add scallions and sauté for 2 minutes. Stir in rice and sauté for an additional 3 minutes.
2. Add remaining broth, water, thyme, and pepper. Stir well. Bring to a boil; reduce heat, cover, and simmer for 18 minutes.
3. Blend asparagus pieces and lemon peel into the rice mixture. Cover and cook over low heat for 5 minutes.

Calories Per Serving: 297
Fat: 2 g
Cholesterol: 0 mg
Protein: 10 g

Carbohydrates: 61 g
Dietary Fiber: 2 g
Sodium: 222 mg

Eggplant-Rice Casserole

Tomatoes complement eggplant and brown rice in this casserole.

YIELD: 6 servings   •   PREPARATION TIME: 15 minutes   •
COOKING TIME: 45 minutes

4½ cups nonfat chicken broth
3 large ripe tomatoes, sliced
2 cups uncooked brown rice

2 medium eggplants, cut into ½-inch
   slices
3 tablespoons grated nonfat Parmesan
¼ cup chopped fresh parsley

1. Heat ¼ cup broth in a large saucepan. Add tomato slices and sauté for 2 minutes. Stir in rice and 4 cups broth, cover, and simmer for 15 minutes.
2. Preheat oven to 350 degrees.

3. Heat remaining ¼ cup broth in another skillet. Add eggplant and sauté for 3 minutes.
4. Arrange the eggplant slices in a nine-by-thirteen-inch nonstick baking dish, top with the tomato-rice mixture, and bake for 25 minutes.
5. Remove from oven; sprinkle with Parmesan and garnish with parsley before serving.

Calories Per Serving: 288
Fat: 3 g
Cholesterol: 3 mg
Protein: 11 g

Carbohydrates: 57 g
Dietary Fiber: 4 g
Sodium: 273 mg

Gingered Broccoli Rice

Crisp broccoli and brown rice are prepared with a sherry, ginger, garlic, and soy sauce.

YIELD: 4 servings • *PREPARATION TIME: 15 minutes plus rice cooking time* •
COOKING TIME: 6 minutes

6 cups water
3 cups broccoli florets cut into 2-inch-
    long pieces
½ cup nonfat chicken broth
1 tablespoon dry sherry

2 teaspoons reduced-sodium soy sauce
4 cloves garlic, minced
2 teaspoons minced fresh gingerroot
3 cups cooked brown rice (see p. 192)

1. Bring water to a boil in a large saucepan. Add broccoli and cook for 2 minutes. Drain well and set aside.
2. Combine ¼ cup chicken broth, sherry, and soy sauce. Set aside.
3. Heat remaining ¼ cup broth in a skillet. Add garlic and gingerroot and sauté for 1 minute.
4. Add the blanched broccoli and sauté for an additional minute. Add the broth–soy sauce mixture.
5. Stir, cover, and cook for 2 minutes.
6. Stir in rice and heat through.

Calories Per Serving: 199
Fat: 2 g
Cholesterol: 0 mg
Protein: 6 g

Carbohydrates: 40 g
Dietary Fiber: 5 g
Sodium: 150 mg

Carrot–Plum Tomato Rice

White rice is topped with a mixture of carrot, plum tomatoes, and onion.

YIELD: 4 servings   ▪   PREPARATION TIME: 15 minutes   ▪
COOKING TIME: 42 minutes

¼ cup nonfat chicken broth
1 medium onion, minced
1 carrot, finely chopped
3½ cups canned low-sodium plum
    tomatoes, drained and coarsely
    chopped

¼ teaspoon ground black pepper
4 cups water
2 cups uncooked white rice

1. Heat broth in a large skillet. Add onion and carrot and sauté for 2 minutes. Add tomatoes and black pepper and simmer for 20 minutes. Remove from heat and let stand, covered.
2. Bring water to a boil in a large saucepan. Stir in the rice; return to a boil, cover, and simmer until rice is just tender, about 20 minutes. Drain thoroughly.
3. Arrange rice on individual serving plates and top with the hot sauce. Serve immediately.

Calories Per Serving: 418
Fat: 1 g
Cholesterol: 0 mg
Protein: 9 g

Carbohydrates: 92 g
Dietary Fiber: 3 g
Sodium: 379 mg

Garlic-Cauliflower Rice

Cauliflower and rice are flavored with onion, gingerroot, and soy sauce.

YIELD: 4 servings   ▪   PREPARATION TIME: 15 minutes   ▪
COOKING TIME: 26 minutes

3 cups water
1½ cups uncooked white rice
¼ cup nonfat chicken broth
2 cups cauliflower florets
¼ teaspoon ground black pepper

1 medium onion, chopped
6 cloves garlic, minced
1 teaspoon minced fresh gingerroot
1 tablespoon reduced-sodium soy sauce

1. Bring water to a boil in a large saucepan. Stir in rice; return to a boil, reduce heat, cover, and simmer until rice is just tender, about 20 minutes.
2. Heat broth in a large skillet. Add cauliflower and pepper and sauté for 4 minutes. Remove cauliflower from the skillet and set aside.
3. Add onion and garlic to the skillet. Stir in gingerroot. Sauté until onion is translucent, about 3 minutes.
4. Return the cauliflower to the skillet. Stir in the soy sauce, add rice, mix well, and serve immediately.

Calories Per Serving: 300
Fat: 2 g
Cholesterol: 0 mg
Protein: 8 g

Carbohydrates: 63 g
Dietary Fiber: 2 g
Sodium: 179 mg

Tomato-Garlic Rice with Corn and Scallion

White rice is prepared with corn kernels, tomato, scallion, and garlic.

YIELD: 5 servings • PREPARATION TIME: 10 minutes • COOKING TIME: 24 minutes

2 cups nonfat chicken broth
1 cup uncooked white rice
1 clove garlic, minced
⅛ teaspoon ground black pepper

1½ cups fresh, canned, or frozen, thawed corn kernels
1 tablespoon minced scallion
1 large ripe tomato, finely chopped

1. Heat ¼ cup broth in a saucepan. Add rice and garlic and sauté for 4 minutes. Stir in remaining broth and black pepper and bring to a boil. Reduce heat, cover, and simmer for 15 minutes.
2. Stir in the corn and scallion and simmer for an additional 5 minutes, or until rice is cooked.
3. Add the tomato and heat through. Serve hot.

Calories Per Serving: 191
Fat: 1 g
Cholesterol: 0 mg
Protein: 5 g

Carbohydrates: 43 g
Dietary Fiber: 2 g
Sodium: 55 mg

Rice with Green Beans,
Zucchini, Carrot, and Peas

Rice is tossed with sautéed scallions, green beans, zucchini, carrot, and peas.

YIELD: 4 servings • *PREPARATION TIME: 25 minutes* • *COOKING TIME: 24 minutes*

2¼ cups nonfat chicken broth
1 cup uncooked white rice
1 cup sliced carrot
2 tablespoons minced scallions
1 cup fresh green beans, cut diagonally
    into ½-inch lengths

1 cup frozen, thawed green peas
1 cup sliced zucchini
2 tablespoons grated nonfat Parmesan
¼ teaspoon ground black pepper
1 scallion, chopped
¼ cup chopped fresh parsley

1. Bring 2 cups broth to a boil in a large saucepan. Stir in rice and return to a boil; reduce heat, cover, and simmer until rice is just tender, about 20 minutes.
2. Heat remaining broth in a large skillet. Stir in carrot and sauté for 2 minutes. Add the minced scallions and green beans. Sauté for 2 minutes. Stir in the peas; cover and simmer for 2 additional minutes.
3. Remove from heat and stir in zucchini.
4. Mix the rice with the vegetables. Transfer to a serving dish; sprinkle with Parmesan, black pepper, chopped scallion, and parsley.

Calories Per Serving: 286
Fat: 3 g
Cholesterol: 3 mg
Protein: 11 g

Carbohydrates: 55 g
Dietary Fiber: 5 g
Sodium: 258 mg

Rice and Kale

Rice and kale are cooked with garlic, scallions, and tomatoes.

YIELD: 4 servings • *PREPARATION TIME: 15 minutes* • *COOKING TIME: 29 minutes*

2 cups water
1 cup uncooked white rice
¾ cup nonfat chicken broth
4 cloves garlic, minced

4 scallions, thinly sliced
2 cups finely chopped fresh kale
2 large ripe tomatoes, cut into small
    wedges

1. Bring water to a boil in a large saucepan. Stir in rice; return to a boil, reduce heat, cover, and simmer until rice is just tender, about 20 minutes. Drain and set aside.
2. Heat ¼ cup broth in a large skillet. Add garlic and scallions. Sauté for 2 minutes.
3. Stir in the remaining broth and the kale and simmer for 2 minutes. Add rice and tomatoes, cover, and simmer for 5 minutes. Drain any excess liquid and serve immediately.

Calories Per Serving: 232   Carbohydrates: 46 g
Fat: 3 g   Dietary Fiber: 3 g
Cholesterol: 0 mg   Sodium: 88 mg
Protein: 6 g

Rice and Spinach

An easy pairing of spinach and rice, prepared with chicken broth and onion.

YIELD: 4 servings • PREPARATION TIME: 10 minutes •
COOKING TIME: 24 minutes plus 5 minutes standing time

2 cups nonfat chicken broth   *1 cup uncooked white rice*
1 medium onion, chopped   *1 10-ounce package frozen chopped*
                                        spinach

1. Heat ¼ cup broth in a large saucepan. Add onion and sauté until just tender, about 3 minutes.
2. Add remaining broth and rice. Bring to a boil. Reduce heat, cover, and simmer for 10 minutes. Add spinach; return to a boil, reduce heat, cover, and simmer until rice is just tender, about 15 minutes.
3. Remove from heat and allow to stand for 5 minutes. Drain unabsorbed liquid and serve.

Calories Per Serving: 217   Carbohydrates: 45 g
Fat: 1 g   Dietary Fiber: 3 g
Cholesterol: 0 mg   Sodium: 182 mg
Protein: 8 g

Tomato-Chile Rice

Scallions, green chiles, and fresh tomato help define this fresh adaptation of an old favorite.

YIELD: 4 servings • PREPARATION TIME: 10 minutes • COOKING TIME: 28 minutes

3¼ cups nonfat chicken broth
1 cup uncooked white rice
2 cloves garlic, minced

4 scallions, chopped
½ cup canned mild green chiles, chopped
1 cup fresh diced tomato

1. Heat ¼ cup broth in a large skillet. Add rice and sauté for 3 minutes.
2. Stir in garlic, scallions, chiles, and tomato.
3. Add remaining chicken broth. Bring to a boil; reduce heat, cover, and simmer for 20 minutes.

Calories Per Serving: 214
Fat: 2 g
Cholesterol: 0 mg
Protein: 8 g

Carbohydrates: 44 g
Dietary Fiber: 1 g
Sodium: 389 mg

Honey-Lemon Brown Rice and Spinach

Brown rice and spinach are combined with scallions, garlic, parsley, lemon juice, and honey.

YIELD: 6 servings • PREPARATION TIME: 10 minutes • COOKING TIME: 30 minutes

2 cups nonfat chicken broth
¾ cup uncooked brown rice
3 scallions, chopped
2 cloves garlic, minced
2 tablespoons chopped fresh parsley
1 teaspoon dried dill

1 10-ounce package frozen chopped
  spinach, thawed and drained
1½ tablespoons lemon juice
1 tablespoon honey
1 lemon, cut into wedges

1. Heat 1 tablespoon broth in a saucepan. Add rice, scallions, and garlic. Sauté until liquid has been absorbed, about 2 minutes.
2. Add remaining broth and bring to a boil. Stir in parsley and dill. Reduce heat, cover, and simmer until rice is tender, about 25 minutes.

3. Stir spinach into rice and simmer for 5 minutes.
4. Mix together the lemon juice and honey until well blended. Stir into the rice mixture. Serve with a lemon wedge.

Calories Per Serving: 125
Fat: 1 g
Cholesterol: 0 mg
Protein: 5 g

Carbohydrates: 26 g
Dietary Fiber: 3 g
Sodium: 156 mg

Ginger-Scallion Rice with Spinach

Fresh spinach and rice are given an Asian seasoning of ginger, scallions, lemon peel, sesame oil, soy sauce, and onion.

YIELD: 3 servings • PREPARATION TIME: 15 minutes • COOKING TIME: 27 minutes

3 cups water
1½ cups uncooked white rice
¼ cup nonfat chicken broth
1 medium onion, sliced
2 cloves garlic, minced
6 scallions, thinly sliced

3 cups fresh spinach, cut into thin strips
1 teaspoon minced fresh gingerroot
1 teaspoon minced lemon peel
1 tablespoon lemon juice
1 teaspoon sesame oil
2 teaspoons reduced-sodium soy sauce

1. Bring water to a boil in a large saucepan. Stir in rice; return to a boil, reduce heat, cover, and simmer until rice is just tender, about 20 minutes. Drain well and set aside.
2. Heat broth in a large saucepan. Add onion, garlic, and scallions and sauté for 4 minutes. Add spinach and gingerroot and sauté until spinach just begins to wilt, about 3 minutes.
3. Fold in the cooked rice, lemon peel, lemon juice, sesame oil, and soy sauce and combine all ingredients well.

Calories Per Serving: 436
Fat: 3 g
Cholesterol: 0 mg
Protein: 10 g

Carbohydrates: 92 g
Dietary Fiber: 6 g
Sodium: 158 mg

Tomato-Okra Rice

Fresh okra and tomatoes are prepared with rice and hot pepper sauce.

YIELD: 4 servings • *PREPARATION TIME: 15 minutes* • *COOKING TIME: 28 minutes*

¼ cup nonfat chicken broth
1 medium onion, finely chopped
1 cup uncooked white rice
2 cups fresh okra, trimmed and cut into
   ½-inch pieces

2 cups fresh or low-sodium canned
   tomatoes, chopped, with juice
1¼ cups water
⅛ teaspoon ground black pepper
⅛ teaspoon hot pepper sauce

1. Heat broth in a large saucepan. Add onion and sauté until it is just tender, about 3 minutes.
2. Add rice, okra, tomatoes and juice, water, black pepper, and hot pepper sauce.
3. Bring to a boil. Reduce heat, cover, and simmer until rice is just tender, about 20 minutes. Serve immediately.

Calories Per Serving: 242
Fat: 1 g
Cholesterol: 0 mg
Protein: 7 g

Carbohydrates: 53 g
Dietary Fiber: 3 g
Sodium: 45 mg

Zucchini Rice

Rice cooked with zucchini is seasoned with onion, garlic, bay leaf, basil, and cayenne pepper.

YIELD: 4 servings • *PREPARATION TIME: 10 minutes* • *COOKING TIME: 23 minutes*

¼ cup nonfat chicken broth
½ cup chopped onion
3 cloves garlic, minced
2 small zucchini, thinly sliced
⅛ teaspoon ground black pepper

1 cup uncooked white rice
1 bay leaf
½ teaspoon dried basil
¼ teaspoon cayenne pepper
1½ cups water

1. Heat broth in a saucepan. Add onion and garlic and sauté until onion is translucent, about 3 minutes.

2. Add zucchini, black pepper, rice, bay leaf, basil, cayenne pepper, and water. Bring to a boil. Reduce heat, cover, and simmer until rice is just tender, about 20 minutes. Remove the bay leaf and serve immediately.

Calories Per Serving: 197
Fat: 0 g
Cholesterol: 0 mg
Protein: 5 g

Carbohydrates: 43 g
Dietary Fiber: 1 g
Sodium: 27 mg

Green and Yellow Rice

Rice is partnered with green peas and yellow bell pepper.

YIELD: 4 servings • *PREPARATION TIME: 15 minutes* • *COOKING TIME: 28 minutes*

4 cups water
2 cups uncooked white rice
¼ cup nonfat chicken broth
1 small onion, minced

1 yellow bell pepper, cored and cut into
    ¼-inch strips
1 10-ounce package frozen green peas,
    thawed
⅛ teaspoon ground black pepper

1. Bring water to a boil in a large saucepan. Add rice; return to a boil, reduce heat, cover, and simmer until rice is just tender, about 20 minutes. Remove from heat and drain well.
2. Heat broth in a large skillet. Add onion and sauté until translucent, about 2 minutes. Add bell pepper strips and peas and sauté 1 additional minute.
3. Transfer the hot rice to a serving bowl, stir in the vegetables, season with black pepper, and serve immediately.

Calories Per Serving: 436
Fat: 1 g
Cholesterol: 0 mg
Protein: 11 g

Carbohydrates: 94 g
Dietary Fiber: 4 g
Sodium: 85 mg

Vegetable-Rice Scramble

Try this combination of rice, vegetables, and egg substitute for a late weekend breakfast.

*YIELD: 4 servings   •   PREPARATION TIME: 15 minutes   •
COOKING TIME: 6 minutes plus rice cooking time*

¼ cup nonfat chicken broth
½ stalk celery, sliced thinly crosswise
½ cup diced red bell pepper
½ cup sliced fresh mushrooms

1 cup liquid egg substitute
¼ cup skim milk
¼ teaspoon ground black pepper
2 cups cooked white rice (see p. 190)

1. Heat broth in a large skillet over medium heat. Add celery, red bell pepper, and mushrooms and sauté for 3 minutes.
2. Combine egg substitute, skim milk, and black pepper and pour over the vegetables. Continue to cook, stirring, until "eggs" are almost cooked, about 1 minute. Add rice; stir to mix all ingredients and cook until heated through. Serve immediately.

Calories Per Serving: 188
Fat: 2 g
Cholesterol: 1 mg
Protein: 11 g

Carbohydrates: 29 g
Dietary Fiber: 1 g
Sodium: 154 mg

Summer Vegetables and Rice

Rice is prepared with green bell pepper, tomatoes, and yellow summer squash and seasoned with jalapeño.

YIELD: 6 servings   •   PREPARATION TIME: 20 minutes   •   COOKING TIME: 50 minutes

2½ cups nonfat chicken broth
1 jalapeño pepper, seeded and minced
1 medium onion, chopped
*2 green bell peppers, cored and cut into
    thin strips*
2 cloves garlic, minced
1½ teaspoons paprika

1 teaspoon dried thyme
*2 cups yellow summer squash cut into
    ½-inch cubes*
4 large ripe tomatoes, chopped
¼ teaspoon ground black pepper
1¼ cups uncooked white rice
2 tablespoons lemon juice

1. Heat ¼ cup broth in a large skillet. Add jalapeño pepper, onion, and green bell peppers. Cover and cook until vegetables are just tender, about 15 minutes. Add a little water if needed.
2. Stir in the garlic, paprika, thyme, summer squash, tomatoes, and pepper. Cover and cook for additional 10 minutes.
3. Add remaining broth and bring to a boil. Stir in rice; return to a boil, reduce heat, cover, and simmer until rice is just tender, about 20 minutes.
4. Sprinkle with the lemon juice.

Calories Per Serving: 194
Fat: 1 g
Cholesterol: 0 mg
Protein: 6 g

Carbohydrates: 41 g
Dietary Fiber: 3 g
Sodium: 207 mg

Chickpea-Vegetable Paella

Protein-rich chickpeas highlight this delicious vegetable medley.

YIELD: 8 servings • PREPARATION TIME: 20 minutes • COOKING TIME: 32 minutes

4 cups water
2 cups uncooked white rice
¼ cup nonfat chicken broth
2 cups asparagus cut into 2-inch pieces
3 cups broccoli florets
1 red bell pepper, cored and chopped
2 cups chopped zucchini

½ cup chopped onion
½ teaspoon saffron threads
2 large ripe tomatoes, chopped
2 cups canned chickpeas, rinsed and
    drained
2 cups fresh green peas

1. Bring water to a boil in a large saucepan. Stir in rice; return to a boil, reduce heat, cover, and simmer until rice is just tender, about 20 minutes.
2. Heat broth in a large skillet. Add asparagus, broccoli, bell pepper, zucchini, and onion. Sauté until just tender-crisp, about 5 minutes.
3. Stir in rice, saffron, tomatoes, chickpeas, and peas. Cook, stirring frequently, until all ingredients are heated through, about 5 minutes. Serve immediately.

Calories Per Serving: 307
Fat: 2 g
Cholesterol: 0 mg
Protein: 11 g

Carbohydrates: 61 g
Dietary Fiber: 8 g
Sodium: 296 mg

Shiitake Mushrooms and Rice

A Chinese-influenced dish of rice topped with bean sprouts, bamboo shoots, carrot, and snow peas, and flavored with soy sauce.

YIELD: 4 servings   •   PREPARATION TIME: 20 minutes   •   COOKING TIME: 30 minutes

2 cups water
1 cup uncooked white rice
¾ cup nonfat chicken broth
1 small onion, chopped
2 cloves garlic, minced
½ cup bean sprouts

½ cup sliced fresh shiitake mushrooms
1 carrot, sliced into thin rounds
½ cup sliced bamboo shoots
1 cup snow peas
2 tablespoons reduced-sodium soy sauce

1. Bring water to a boil in a large saucepan. Stir in rice; return to a boil, reduce heat, cover, and simmer until rice is just tender, about 20 minutes.
2. Heat ¼ cup broth in a large skillet. Add onion and garlic and sauté for 3 minutes.
3. Add remaining broth, bean sprouts, mushrooms, carrot, bamboo shoots, snow peas, and soy sauce. Simmer for 2 minutes.
4. Spoon the rice onto individual serving plates, top with the vegetables and broth, and serve immediately.

Calories Per Serving: 252
Fat: 3 g
Cholesterol: 0 mg
Protein: 8 g

Carbohydrates: 50 g
Dietary Fiber: 4 g
Sodium: 404 mg

Brown Rice–Spinach Casserole

Brown rice, spinach, onion, mushrooms, and cottage cheese are baked to create this hearty casserole.

YIELD: 8 servings   •   PREPARATION TIME: 20 minutes   •   COOKING TIME: 1 hour

3 cups water
1½ cups uncooked brown rice
¼ cup nonfat chicken broth
1 medium onion, chopped
2 cups sliced fresh mushrooms
1 clove garlic, minced

2 egg whites
2 cups nonfat cottage cheese
2 cups frozen chopped spinach, thawed
¼ teaspoon ground black pepper
½ teaspoon dried thyme
2 tablespoons grated nonfat Parmesan

1. Bring water to a boil in a large saucepan. Stir in rice; return to a boil, reduce heat, cover, and simmer until rice is just tender, about 25 minutes.
2. Preheat oven to 375 degrees.
3. Heat broth in a large saucepan. Add onion, mushrooms, and garlic and sauté until onions are lightly golden, about 4 minutes.
4. Whisk together the egg whites and cottage cheese in a small bowl.
5. Thoroughly mix egg white–cheese mixture, onion-mushroom mixture, spinach, cooked rice, black pepper, and thyme.
6. Transfer to a nonstick baking dish and bake for 30 minutes.
7. Sprinkle with Parmesan immediately after removing from oven.

Calories Per Serving: 221   Carbohydrates: 38 g
Fat: 2 g   Dietary Fiber: 2 g
Cholesterol: 1 mg   Sodium: 290 mg
Protein: 13 g

Red Bell Peppers, Lima Beans, and Rice

Lima beans and red bell peppers are simmered with onion, celery, tomato, and spices.

YIELD: 4 servings • *PREPARATION TIME: 24 minutes* • *COOKING TIME: 16 minutes*

¼ cup nonfat chicken broth   1 large ripe tomato, chopped
¾ cup diced red bell pepper   1 teaspoon paprika
½ cup chopped onion   1 teaspoon dried basil
1 stalk celery, chopped   ½ teaspoon dried thyme
3 cloves garlic, minced   1½ cups thawed frozen lima beans
¾ cup water   ¼ teaspoon hot pepper sauce
1 cup uncooked white rice

1. Heat broth in a large skillet. Add red bell pepper, onion, celery, and garlic. Sauté until onion is tender, about 3 minutes.
2. Stir in water, rice, tomato, paprika, basil, and thyme. Bring to a boil. Reduce heat, cover, and simmer for 15 minutes. Add lima beans and continue to simmer until lima beans are just tender, about 7 minutes.
3. Remove from heat. Stir in hot pepper sauce. Allow to stand, covered, until liquid is absorbed and rice is tender, about 5 minutes. Serve immediately.

Calories Per Serving: 260
Fat: 1 g
Cholesterol: 0 mg
Protein: 8 g

Carbohydrates: 55 g
Dietary Fiber: 5 g
Sodium: 71 mg

Tomato-Vegetable Rice

White rice, onion, celery, red bell pepper, and zucchini are simmered in tomato juice.

YIELD: 6 servings • PREPARATION TIME: 10 minutes • COOKING TIME: 25 minutes

1½ cups water
1 cup low-sodium tomato juice
½ cup sliced onion
½ stalk celery, sliced crosswise
½ cup chopped red bell pepper

½ teaspoon dried basil
1 cup uncooked white rice
½ cup chopped zucchini
½ cup chopped yellow summer squash

1. Combine water and tomato juice in a large saucepan. Add onion, celery, red bell pepper, and basil. Bring to a boil. Simmer for 15 minutes. Stir in rice. Return to a boil; add zucchini and yellow squash, reduce heat, cover, and simmer until rice is tender, about 20 minutes.
2. Remove from heat. Stir to distribute ingredients evenly through the dish, and serve at once.

Calories Per Serving: 165
Fat: 1 g
Cholesterol: 0 mg
Protein: 4 g

Carbohydrates: 35 g
Dietary Fiber: 2 g
Sodium: 57 mg

Zucchini and Rice

Zucchini and rice are cooked with red bell pepper, onion, herbs, and hot pepper sauce.

YIELD: 4 servings • PREPARATION TIME: 15 minutes • COOKING TIME: 24 minutes

1½ cups nonfat chicken broth
½ cup finely chopped onion
1 red bell pepper, cut into 1½-inch-long
  strips
2 cups yellow squash, cut into ½-inch
  cubes

1 cup uncooked white rice
1 bay leaf
½ teaspoon dried thyme
⅛ teaspoon hot pepper sauce
¼ teaspoon ground black pepper

1. Heat ¼ cup broth in a saucepan. Add onion and sauté for 2 minutes. Add bell pepper and sauté 2 additional minutes.
2. Stir in squash, rice, bay leaf, thyme, hot pepper sauce, remaining broth, and black pepper. Cover and simmer until rice is just tender, about 20 minutes.
3. Discard bay leaf and serve immediately.

Calories Per Serving: 209
Fat: 1 g
Cholesterol: 0 mg
Protein: 6 g

Carbohydrates: 44 g
Dietary Fiber: 2 g
Sodium: 217 mg

Basic Risotto

Risotto is a northern Italian dish that is traditionally made with arborio rice. Constant stirring and medium heat are the two most important elements in cooking successful risotto.

YIELD: 3 servings • *PREPARATION TIME: 15 minutes* • *COOKING TIME: 20 minutes*

2 cups water
1¼ cups nonfat chicken broth
olive oil cooking spray

½ cup chopped onion
1 cup uncooked arborio rice

1. Combine water and broth in a saucepan. Bring to a simmer over low heat.
2. Spray a second saucepan with olive oil spray. Set over medium heat. Sauté onion until tender, about 4 minutes.
3. Add rice to onion and cook for 3 minutes, stirring.
4. Gradually add ½ cup warm broth. Cook for 3 minutes, or until liquid is nearly absorbed, stirring constantly.
5. Gradually add another ½ cup of warm broth, stirring constantly until it is absorbed.
6. Continue adding broth in ½-cup increments, stirring constantly until each portion is absorbed before adding the next. Serve at once.

Calories Per Serving: 254
Fat: 1 g
Cholesterol: 0 mg
Protein: 7 g

Carbohydrates: 54 g
Dietary Fiber: 1 g
Sodium: 146 mg

Mixed-Vegetable Risotto

This risotto is made with white wine, Parmesan, onion, yellow squash, and red bell peppers.

YIELD: 6 servings • *PREPARATION TIME: 20 minutes* • *COOKING TIME: 30 minutes*

3⅔ cups nonfat chicken broth
1 medium onion, chopped
2 medium yellow squash, cut into julienne strips
2 red bell peppers, cut into julienne strips

⅓ cup dry white wine
2 cups uncooked arborio or other short-grain rice
1 cup skim milk
½ teaspoon ground black pepper
2 tablespoons grated nonfat Parmesan

1. Heat ⅓ cup chicken broth in a skillet over medium heat. Sauté onion until tender.
2. Add yellow squash and red bell peppers. Sauté for 5 minutes, or until tender.
3. Stir in white wine. Cook until wine has evaporated.
4. Stir in rice. Stir until rice begins to brown.
5. Combine remaining chicken broth, milk, and pepper.
6. Gradually pour ½ cup of the broth-milk mixture over rice.
7. Cook, stirring, until liquid is absorbed.
8. Repeat with remaining broth-milk mixture, ½ cup at a time.
9. Sprinkle with cheese and serve.

Calories Per Serving: 307
Fat: 1 g
Cholesterol: 2 mg
Protein: 11 g

Carbohydrates: 62 g
Dietary Fiber: 2 g
Sodium: 251 mg

Spinach Risotto

Arborio rice is simmered with garlic and onion, then combined with cannellini beans, spinach, and nonfat Parmesan.

YIELD: *4 servings*   •   PREPARATION TIME: *15 minutes*   •
COOKING TIME: *23 minutes plus 5 minutes standing time*

3¼ cups nonfat chicken or vegetable
   broth
1 medium onion, chopped
1 clove garlic, minced
1 cup arborio rice
¼ teaspoon ground turmeric

1 16-ounce can cannellini beans, rinsed
   and drained
1 10-ounce package frozen spinach,
   thawed and drained
½ cup grated nonfat Parmesan

1. Heat ¼ cup of broth in a skillet over medium heat. Sauté onion and garlic in broth until onion is slightly tender, about 3 minutes.
2. Stir in rice.
3. Gradually stir in half the remaining broth. Add turmeric. Bring to a boil, stirring constantly. Reduce heat. Gradually stir in remaining broth and simmer, stirring, until liquid is absorbed, about 20 minutes.
4. Stir in beans, spinach, and cheese. Let stand for 5 minutes before serving.

Calories Per Serving: 287
Fat: 3 g
Cholesterol: 3 mg
Protein: 16 g

Carbohydrates: 66 g
Dietary Fiber: 7 g
Sodium: 628 mg

Brazilian Rice

Brown rice is mixed with onion, garlic, and tomatoes and topped with a lemon-chile sauce.

YIELD: *4 servings*   •   PREPARATION TIME: *25 minutes*   •
COOKING TIME: *10 minutes plus rice cooking time*

½ cup nonfat chicken broth or vegetable
   broth
2 small onions, chopped
4 cloves garlic, minced

2 cups cooked brown rice (see p. 192)
¼ cup lemon juice
2 large ripe tomatoes, diced
¼ cup diced canned green chiles

1. Heat broth in a skillet over medium heat. Sauté half the onions and half the garlic until onion is lightly browned, about 4 minutes.
2. Stir rice into skillet; reduce heat to low.
3. Place remaining onions and garlic, lemon juice, diced tomato, and green chiles in a blender or food processor and process until smooth.
4. Serve sauce over warm rice.

Calories Per Serving: 176
Fat: 1 g
Cholesterol: 0 mg
Protein: 5 g

Carbohydrates: 38 g
Dietary Fiber: 5 g
Sodium: 36 mg

Vegetable-Rice Bake

Onion, carrot, zucchini, and cabbage are sautéed and baked with brown rice.

YIELD: 6 servings   •   PREPARATION TIME: 20 minutes   •
COOKING TIME: 38 minutes plus 10 minutes standing time

4½ cups nonfat chicken broth
1 medium onion, chopped
2 carrots, diced
2 cups zucchini cut into matchstick-size
   pieces

1 cup shredded cabbage
1½ cups uncooked brown rice
3 cloves garlic, minced
¼ teaspoon ground black pepper
3 tablespoons chopped fresh parsley

1. Preheat oven to 350 degrees.
2. Heat ¼ cup broth in a heavy oven-safe casserole. Add onion, carrots, zucchini, and cabbage. Sauté until vegetables are just tender.
3. Add rice and sauté for 3 minutes. Stir in remaining 4¼ cups broth, garlic, pepper, and parsley. Bring to a boil.
4. Place casserole in oven and bake, uncovered, for 35 minutes.
5. Remove from the oven; allow to stand for 10 minutes before serving.

Calories Per Serving: 227
Fat: 1 g
Cholesterol: 0 mg
Protein: 9 g

Carbohydrates: 45 g
Dietary Fiber: 3 g
Sodium: 113 mg

Rice-Stuffed Peppers

Green peppers are baked with a stuffing of rice, olives, anchovies, capers, oregano, and parsley.

YIELD: 4 servings ▪ *PREPARATION TIME: 20 minutes* ▪
COOKING TIME: 50 minutes

4 cups water
2 cups uncooked white rice
8 green bell peppers, cut in half horizontally and cored
1 teaspoon olive oil
6 pitted green olives, minced

4 anchovy fillets, minced
1 tablespoon capers, rinsed and minced
¼ teaspoon ground black pepper
½ teaspoon dried oregano
1 cup chopped fresh parsley

1. Bring water to a boil in a large saucepan. Stir in rice; return to a boil, reduce heat, cover, and simmer until rice is just tender, about 20 minutes. Drain rice thoroughly when cooked.
2. Preheat oven to 350 degrees.
3. Arrange pepper halves in a shallow, nonstick baking dish.
4. Combine the olive oil, olives, anchovies, capers, black pepper, oregano, and parsley. Add to the rice and stir gently to blend.
5. Fill the pepper halves with the rice mixture and bake for 30 minutes.

Calories Per Serving: 422
Fat: 3 g
Cholesterol: 3 mg
Protein: 10 g

Carbohydrates: 88 g
Dietary Fiber: 3 g
Sodium: 301 mg

Peppers Stuffed with Chicken, Corn, and Cannellini Beans

Minced broiled chicken, corn, and cannellini beans are mixed with ricotta cheese and egg whites, then stuffed into green pepper halves and baked.

YIELD: 4 servings ▪ *PREPARATION TIME: 20 minutes plus chicken cooking time* ▪
COOKING TIME: 1 hour 8 minutes

1 cup water
½ cup uncooked brown rice
2 egg whites
8 ounces skinless chicken breast, broiled and minced
1 cup frozen, thawed corn kernels
1 cup low-sodium canned cannellini beans, rinsed and drained

½ cup nonfat ricotta
1 clove garlic, minced
¼ teaspoon ground black pepper
4 green bell peppers, cut in half horizontally and cored
½ cup nonfat chicken broth
¼ cup chopped fresh parsley

1. Bring water to a boil in a large saucepan. Stir in rice; return to a boil, reduce heat, cover, and simmer until rice is just tender, about 20 minutes.
2. Preheat oven to 450 degrees.
3. Beat egg whites. In large bowl, combine egg whites, rice, chicken, corn, beans, ricotta cheese, garlic, and black pepper. Stuff green pepper halves with this mixture.
4. Arrange in a nonstick baking dish and bake until peppers are tender, basting with chicken broth, about 40 minutes. Sprinkle with parsley and serve immediately.

Calories Per Serving: 305
Fat: 2 g
Cholesterol: 42 mg
Protein: 31 g

Carbohydrates: 45 g
Dietary Fiber: 6 g
Sodium: 193 mg

Acorn Squash with Rice Stuffing

Acorn squash is stuffed with rice, walnuts, raisins, and nutmeg.

YIELD: 4 servings ▪ PREPARATION TIME: 15 minutes ▪ COOKING TIME: 72 minutes

2 acorn squash, cut in half lengthwise, seeds removed
1½ cups water
½ cup uncooked white rice

2 tablespoons chopped walnuts
¼ cup raisins
¼ teaspoon ground nutmeg

1. Wrap squash in microwave-safe plastic wrap. Microwave for 15 minutes on HIGH.
2. Bring water to a boil in a large saucepan. Stir in rice; return to a boil, reduce heat, cover, and simmer until rice is just tender and liquid is absorbed, about 20 minutes.

3. Preheat oven to 400 degrees. Mix walnuts, raisins, and nutmeg into rice.
4. Stuff squash halves with the rice mixture and bake in a nonstick baking pan until squash is tender, about 12 minutes.

Calories Per Serving: 254	Carbohydrates: 57 g
Fat: 3 g	Dietary Fiber: 5 g
Cholesterol: 0 mg	Sodium: 53 mg
Protein: 5 g	

Rice-Stuffed Tomatoes

Large, ripe tomatoes are stuffed with rice seasoned with olives, green bell peppers, celery, parsley, and lemon juice.

YIELD: 4 servings　•　PREPARATION TIME: 20 minutes　•
COOKING TIME: 20 minutes

3 cups water	3 tablespoons chopped fresh parsley
1½ cups uncooked white rice	1 teaspoon dried basil
4 large, firm, ripe tomatoes	½ cup lemon juice
4 black olives, pitted and minced	1 teaspoon olive oil
3 green bell peppers, cored and minced	¼ teaspoon ground black pepper
1 stalk celery, minced	

1. Bring water to a boil in a large saucepan. Stir in rice; return to a boil, reduce heat, cover, and simmer until rice is just tender, about 20 minutes. Allow rice to cool to room temperature.
2. Slice off the stem end of the tomatoes and remove most of the pulp from inside, leaving a ¼-inch shell.
3. In a large mixing bowl, combine the tomato pulp with the rice, olives, green bell peppers, celery, parsley, basil, lemon juice, olive oil, and black pepper.
4. Stuff the tomato shells with the rice mixture.

Calories Per Serving: 330	Carbohydrates: 72 g
Fat: 3 g	Dietary Fiber: 4 g
Cholesterol: 0 mg	Sodium: 62 mg
Protein: 7 g	

Wild and White Rices with Asparagus

Wild rice and white rice are prepared with mushrooms, tomatoes, and asparagus.

YIELD: 4 servings · PREPARATION TIME: 25 minutes · COOKING TIME: 42 minutes

2¾ cups nonfat chicken broth
⅔ cup uncooked wild rice
½ cup uncooked white rice
1 tablespoon chopped fresh parsley
1 small onion, chopped

1 pound fresh white mushrooms, sliced
1 pound asparagus, cut into 2-inch
  pieces
2 cups canned stewed tomatoes

1. Bring 2½ cups broth to a boil in a large saucepan. Stir in wild rice. Return to a boil; reduce heat, cover, and simmer 10 minutes. Stir in white rice. Return to a boil; reduce heat, cover, and simmer until rices are tender, about 20 additional minutes. Remove from heat, stir in parsley, and set aside.
2. Heat remaining ¼ cup broth in a large skillet. Add onion and sauté for 2 minutes. Stir in mushrooms and asparagus and sauté for an additional 6 minutes. Stir in tomatoes, cover, and simmer until asparagus is just tender, about 4 minutes.
3. Serve asparagus-tomato mixture over rice.

Calories Per Serving: 354
Fat: 2 g
Cholesterol: 0 mg
Protein: 14 g

Carbohydrates: 68 g
Dietary Fiber: 7 g
Sodium: 374 mg

Grape Leaves Stuffed with Rice

This classic Greek dish features a rice stuffing seasoned with garlic, onion, allspice, pine nuts, lemon juice, and parsley.

YIELD: 6 servings · PREPARATION TIME: 30 minutes · COOKING TIME: 45 minutes

1 8-ounce jar grape leaves
2 tablespoons nonfat chicken broth
1 medium onion, finely chopped
2 cloves garlic, minced
1⅔ cups uncooked white rice
½ teaspoon ground allspice
1 cinnamon stick
1⅔ cups water

¼ teaspoon ground black pepper
2 tablespoons chopped toasted pine nuts
2 tablespoons chopped raisins
1 teaspoon dried mint
1 tablespoon fresh parsley, minced
2 teaspoons olive oil
¼ cup lemon juice
6 lemon wedges

1. Rinse and thoroughly dry the grape leaves. Cut off the stems.
2. Heat broth in a saucepan. Add onion and garlic. Sauté until just tender, about 3 minutes. Add rice, allspice, and cinnamon and sauté for 1 additional minute.
3. Add ⅔ cup water and black pepper. Bring to a boil. Reduce heat, cover, and simmer until the liquid is absorbed, about 15 minutes. Remove from heat, discard cinnamon stick, and stir in pine nuts, raisins, mint, and parsley.
4. Place grape leaves on a smooth surface, shiny side down. Place a tablespoon of rice mixture on each leaf and roll up, tucking in the ends. Make 24 rolls.
5. Line a large skillet with the remaining grape leaves. Arrange the rolled leaves in a single layer on the lining.
6. Whisk together the olive oil and lemon juice and drizzle over the grape leaves. Return skillet to the stove, add remaining water, and bring to a boil. Cover with a tight-fitting lid and simmer for 25 minutes, or until liquid is absorbed. Remove from heat and allow to cool to room temperature before serving. Serve with lemon wedges.

Calories Per Serving: 102
Fat: 3 g
Cholesterol: 0 mg
Protein: 3 g

Carbohydrates: 17 g
Dietary Fiber: 1 g
Sodium: 391 mg

Dilled Artichoke Salad

Artichokes and dill in a delightful merger of mild flavors.

YIELD: 6 servings ⋅ PREPARATION TIME: 25 minutes ⋅ COOKING TIME: 25 minutes

2 cups nonfat chicken broth
1 cup uncooked white rice
3 scallions, chopped
1 green bell pepper, chopped
1 7-ounce jar marinated artichokes

hearts, drained and chopped
¼ cup chopped celery
⅓ cup nonfat mayonnaise
¾ teaspoon dried dill
¼ teaspoon ground black pepper

1. Bring broth to a boil. Stir in rice; return to a boil, reduce heat, cover, and simmer until rice is just tender, about 20 minutes. Remove from heat and allow to cool, uncovered, to room temperature.
2. Combine scallions, green bell pepper, artichoke hearts, celery, mayonnaise, dill, and black pepper.
3. Add dressing to rice, toss to coat thoroughly, and chill before serving.

Calories Per Serving: 155
Fat: 1 g
Cholesterol: 0 mg
Protein: 5 g

Carbohydrates: 33 g
Dietary Fiber: 2 g
Sodium: 404 mg

Rice Salad with Carrots and Leeks

Brown rice is blended with celery, leeks, and carrots in this refreshing salad.

YIELD: *4 servings* • PREPARATION TIME: *15 minutes plus rice cooking time*

2 leeks, minced
3 stalks celery, chopped
2 carrots, grated
1 cup cooked brown rice (see p. 458)
4 tablespoons nonfat Italian dressing

1 teaspoon lemon juice
½ teaspoon Dijon mustard
¼ teaspoon ground black pepper
¼ cup chopped fresh parsley

1. Combine the leeks, celery, carrots, and rice in a serving bowl.
2. Whisk together the Italian dressing, lemon juice, mustard, and black pepper.
3. Toss dressing with salad, top with the parsley, and serve.

Calories Per Serving: 121
Fat: 1 g
Cholesterol: 0 mg
Protein: 3 g

Carbohydrates: 26 g
Dietary Fiber: 3 g
Sodium: 274 mg

Carrot-Mushroom Rice

White rice is cooked with sliced carrots and mushrooms and then seasoned with balsamic vinegar and parsley.

YIELD: 3 servings ▪ *PREPARATION TIME: 15 minutes* ▪ *COOKING TIME: 20 minutes*

2 cups water
1 cup uncooked white rice
2 carrots, thinly sliced
1½ cups sliced fresh mushrooms

1 tablespoon balsamic vinegar
1 teaspoon olive oil
2 tablespoons chopped fresh parsley

1. Bring water to a boil in a heavy saucepan. Stir in rice; return to a boil, reduce heat, cover, and simmer until rice is tender, about 20 minutes.
2. Ten minutes before rice is done, stir in carrots; 5 minutes later, stir in mushrooms.
3. Whisk together vinegar and olive oil.
4. When rice is done, remove from heat; stir in vinegar and olive oil. Mix well, garnish with parsley, and serve immediately.

Calories Per Serving: 287
Fat: 2 g
Cholesterol: 0 mg
Protein: 6 g

Carbohydrates: 61 g
Dietary Fiber: 2 g
Sodium: 28 mg

Rice Salad with Tomato and Corn

Corn, tomato, and red onion are mixed into brown rice with a garlic-accented dressing.

YIELD: 6 servings ▪ *PREPARATION TIME: 20 minutes* ▪ *COOKING TIME: 20 minutes*

2 cups water
1 cup uncooked brown rice
3 tablespoons nonfat Italian dressing
1 clove garlic, minced
¼ teaspoon ground black pepper

1¼ cups fresh or thawed frozen corn
  kernels, drained
1 large ripe tomato, diced
¼ cup diced red onion
½ teaspoon dried basil

1. Bring water to a boil in a large saucepan. Stir in rice; return to a boil, reduce heat, cover, and simmer until rice is just tender, about 25 minutes. Remove lid and allow rice to cool.
2. Whisk together Italian dressing, garlic, and black pepper.
3. Combine rice, corn, tomato, onion, and basil. Add dressing and toss to coat all ingredients.

Calories Per Serving: 112
Fat: 1 g
Cholesterol: 0 mg
Protein: 3 g

Carbohydrates: 24 g
Dietary Fiber: 2 g
Sodium: 175 mg

Corn–Wild Rice Salad

Corn and wild rice are flavored with tomato, red onion, and scallions and tossed with a dressing of honey and mustard.

YIELD: 6 servings • PREPARATION TIME: 20 minutes •
COOKING TIME: 25 minutes plus 60 minutes standing time

2 cups water
1 cup uncooked wild rice
1½ cups cooked fresh, canned, or
*   thawed frozen corn kernels*
¾ cup chopped fresh tomato

⅓ cup chopped red onion
2 tablespoons minced scallions
1 tablespoon Dijon mustard
1 tablespoon honey

1. Bring water to a boil in a large saucepan. Stir in rice; return to a boil, reduce heat, cover, and simmer until rice is tender, about 25 minutes. Remove from heat. Allow to stand, covered, for 10 minutes.
2. Combine the rice, corn, tomato, onion, and scallions and mix well.
3. Whisk the mustard and honey together briskly. Stir into the rice mixture and toss to distribute the dressing. Allow to stand at room temperature for at least 1 hour before serving.

Calories Per Serving: 148
Fat: 1 g
Cholesterol: 0 mg
Protein: 6 g

Carbohydrates: 33 g
Dietary Fiber: 2 g
Sodium: 72 mg

Middle Eastern Rice Salad

Chopped tomatoes, cucumber, scallions, parsley, mint, and a lemon-garlic dressing are classic accents for white rice.

YIELD: 6 servings   ·   *PREPARATION TIME: 20 minutes*   ·   *COOKING TIME: 20 minutes*

2 cups water
1 cup uncooked white rice
¼ cup nonfat Italian dressing
1 tablespoon lemon juice
1 clove garlic, minced
¼ teaspoon ground black pepper

2 cups chopped fresh tomatoes
1 cup diced cucumber
½ cup chopped scallions
1 cup chopped fresh parsley
1 teaspoon dried mint

1. Bring water to a boil in a large saucepan. Stir in rice; return to a boil, reduce heat, cover, and simmer until rice is just tender, about 20 minutes. Remove lid and allow rice to stand.
2. Whisk together the Italian dressing, lemon juice, garlic, and black pepper.
3. Combine the rice, tomatoes, cucumber, scallions, parsley, and mint. Add the dressing, toss to coat all ingredients, and serve.

Calories Per Serving: 133
Fat: 0 g
Cholesterol: 0 mg
Protein: 3 g

Carbohydrates: 28 g
Dietary Fiber: 1 g
Sodium: 238 mg

Mini Molded Rice and Vegetable Salad

Chilled rice is mixed with a medley of vegetables, packed into custard cups, and chilled for 2 hours.

YIELD: 6 servings   ·   *PREPARATION TIME: 20 minutes plus 2 hours chilling time*

2 cups cooked, cooled white rice
1 large ripe tomato, finely chopped
1½ cups finely diced cucumber
3 scallions, finely chopped
½ cup finely diced celery

10 pitted green olives, chopped
2 tablespoons red wine vinegar
1 tablespoon olive oil
⅛ teaspoon cayenne pepper
olive oil cooking spray

1. Combine rice, tomato, cucumber, scallions, celery, olives, vinegar, olive oil, and cayenne pepper in a large bowl.
2. Spray 6 custard cups with olive oil cooking spray. Pack rice mixture into cups, cover with plastic wrap, and refrigerate for 2 hours.
3. Invert molded rice onto small plates.

Calories Per Serving: 121
Fat: 3 g
Cholesterol: 0 mg
Protein: 2 g

Carbohydrates: 21 g
Dietary Fiber: 1 g
Sodium: 154 mg

Rice Salad with Pineapple and Vegetables

Bean sprouts, green bell pepper, celery, scallions, and pineapple chunks are mixed with brown rice and a soy dressing.

YIELD: 6 servings ▪ PREPARATION TIME: 20 minutes, plus rice cooking time and 30 minutes chilling time

2 cups cooked brown rice, at room temperature (see p. 192)
½ cup bean sprouts, rinsed and drained
1 green bell pepper, chopped
1 stalk celery, chopped
2 scallions, chopped

½ cup seedless raisins
½ cup juice-packed pineapple chunks, drained, ¼ cup juice reserved
1 tablespoon olive oil
2 tablespoons reduced-sodium soy sauce
¼ teaspoon ground black pepper

1. Combine rice, bean sprouts, green bell pepper, celery, scallions, raisins, and pineapple.
2. Whisk together reserved pineapple juice, olive oil, soy sauce, and black pepper. Toss the rice mixture with the dressing. Chill 30 minutes and serve.

Calories Per Serving: 152
Fat: 3 g
Cholesterol: 0 mg
Protein: 3 g

Carbohydrates: 30 g
Dietary Fiber: 2 g
Sodium: 188 mg

Rice Salad with Pineapple and Cucumber

Rice and a medley of pineapple chunks, cucumber, red bell pepper, carrot, scallions, and peanuts are bonded with a sherry–ginger dressing.

YIELD: *6 servings* • PREPARATION TIME: *20 minutes plus rice cooking time and 2 hours chilling time*

1 cup juice-packed pineapple chunks, drained, 3 tablespoons juice reserved	*3 scallions, chopped*
	1 tablespoon chopped peanuts
3 cups cooked white rice (see p. 190)	*2 tablespoons lime juice*
1 cup diced cucumber	*2 tablespoons dry sherry*
1 red bell pepper, diced	*1 tablespoon rice wine vinegar*
1 cup grated carrot	*1 teaspoon minced fresh gingerroot*

1. Combine pineapple, rice, cucumber, red bell pepper, carrot, scallions, and peanuts in a large serving bowl.
2. Whisk together lime juice, sherry, vinegar, gingerroot, and pineapple juice.
3. Add dressing to rice mixture. Toss to coat all ingredients.
4. Cover salad and chill for 2 hours.

Calories Per Serving: 159
Fat: 2 g
Cholesterol: 0 mg
Protein: 4 g

Carbohydrates: 33 g
Dietary Fiber: 2 g
Sodium: 28 mg

Rice Salad with Mandarin Oranges and Cucumber

Rice is simmered in pineapple juice and mixed with mandarin oranges, crushed pineapple, cucumber, and red onion.

YIELD: *4 servings* • PREPARATION TIME: *5 minutes* • COOKING TIME: *15 minutes plus 10 minutes standing time*

⅔ cup pineapple juice	*1 cup drained juice-packed crushed pineapple*
⅓ cup water	
1 cup uncooked white rice	*½ cup chopped cucumber*
1 cup drained juice-packed mandarin oranges	*⅓ cup chopped red onion*
	1 teaspoon dried mint

1. Bring pineapple juice and water to a boil in a large saucepan. Stir in rice; return to a boil, reduce heat, cover, and simmer until rice is just tender, about 20 minutes. Remove from heat and allow to stand for 10 minutes.
2. Combine rice, mandarin oranges, crushed pineapple, cucumber, onion, and mint in a serving bowl.
3. Refrigerate for 1 hour.

Calories Per Serving: 245
Fat: 1 g
Cholesterol: 0 mg
Protein: 5 g

Carbohydrates: 55 g
Dietary Fiber: 2 g
Sodium: 6 mg

Rice Salad with Mango and Jalapeños

White rice is combined with the exotic tastes of mango, cilantro, jalapeño, and a lime-flavored dressing.

YIELD: 6 servings • PREPARATION TIME: 20 minutes •
COOKING TIME: 20 minutes plus cooling time

2 cups water
1 cup uncooked white rice
1½ tablespoons olive oil
2 tablespoons lime juice
1 cup peeled, diced ripe mango

¼ cup diced red onion
2 tablespoons chopped fresh parsley
½ teaspoon dried cilantro
2 teaspoons seeded, minced fresh
   jalapeño pepper

1. Bring water to a boil in a saucepan. Stir in rice; return to a boil, reduce heat, cover, and simmer until just tender, about 20 minutes. Remove from heat, uncover, and allow rice to cool to room temperature.
2. Whisk together olive oil and lime juice.
3. Combine rice, mango, onion, parsley, olive oil, lime juice, cilantro, and jalapeño pepper.
4. Refrigerate for 1 hour.

Calories Per Serving: 182
Fat: 3 g
Cholesterol: 1 mg
Protein: 4 g

Carbohydrates: 36 g
Dietary Fiber: 1 g
Sodium: 26 mg

Apricot Rice Salad

Dried plus fresh or canned apricots are the main feature of this sweet rice salad.

YIELD: 6 servings • PREPARATION TIME: 25 minutes •
COOKING TIME: 15 minutes plus cooling time

2 cups water
1 cup uncooked white rice
1 tablespoon olive oil
2 tablespoons lemon juice
1 tablespoon honey
¼ teaspoon ground black pepper

½ cup diced dried apricots
2 cups diced fresh apricots, or canned
  apricots, drained and diced
3 scallions, sliced
½ cup chopped celery

1. Bring water to a boil in a saucepan. Stir in rice; return to a boil, reduce heat, cover, and simmer until rice is just tender, about 20 minutes. Allow to cool, uncovered, to room temperature.
2. Whisk together the olive oil, lemon juice, honey, and black pepper.
3. Combine the cooled rice, dried and fresh apricots, scallions, and celery. Add honey-lemon dressing, toss to coat all ingredients, and serve.

Calories Per Serving: 314
Fat: 3 g
Cholesterol: 0 mg
Protein: 5 g

Carbohydrates: 71 g
Dietary Fiber: 1 g
Sodium: 31 mg

Apple–Wild Rice Salad with Citrus Dressing

Orange and lime juices are combined with olive oil, orange peel, and black pepper as a dressing for a salad of wild rice, white rice, apple, and celery.

YIELD: 6 servings • PREPARATION TIME: 15 minutes plus rice cooking time

2 cups cooked wild rice, cooled (see p. 194)
2 cups cooked white rice, cooled (see p. 190)
1 cup chopped apple
1 cup chopped celery

½ cup orange juice
3 tablespoons lime juice
1 teaspoon dried mint
1 tablespoon olive oil
1½ teaspoons grated orange peel
¼ teaspoon ground black pepper

1. In a large serving bowl, toss wild rice, white rice, apple, and celery.
2. Combine orange juice, lime juice, mint, olive oil, orange peel, and black pepper. Whisk briskly and pour over the rice mixture.

Calories Per Serving: 195   Carbohydrates: 38 g
Fat: 3 g   Dietary Fiber: 3 g
Cholesterol: 0 mg   Sodium: 26 mg
Protein: 5 g

Rice Salad with Peaches and Raspberries

Peaches and raspberries are combined with chilled microwaved rice, yogurt, brown sugar, and lime juice.

YIELD: 4 servings ▪ PREPARATION TIME: 15 minutes ▪
COOKING TIME: 17 minutes plus 5 minutes standing time and 1 hour chilling time

1 cup uncooked white rice   *¾ cup nonfat plain yogurt*
1¼ cups water   *¼ cup brown sugar, firmly packed*
1 cup fresh or frozen, thawed raspberries   *1 tablespoon lime juice*
1 cup sliced fresh or frozen, thawed
    peaches

1. Place rice and water in a 3-quart microwave-safe casserole. Cover tightly. Microwave on HIGH for 4 to 7 minutes, or until the water boils. Microwave on MEDIUM for 10 minutes, or until the liquid is absorbed. Let stand, covered, for 5 minutes.
2. Chill rice for 1 hour.
3. Combine rice with raspberries and peaches.
4. Combine yogurt, sugar, and lime juice, pour over rice-fruit mixture, and toss.

Calories Per Serving: 90   Carbohydrates: 20 g
Fat: 0 g   Dietary Fiber: 1 g
Cholesterol: 1 mg   Sodium: 39 mg
Protein: 3 g

Microwave Pear-Date Pilaf

Rice is cooked with dried pears, dates, and onion.

YIELD: 4 servings   ▪   *PREPARATION TIME: 15 minutes*   ▪   *COOKING TIME: 21 minutes*

¼ cup finely chopped onion	*¼ teaspoon ground black pepper*
¼ cup skim milk	*2 teaspoons curry powder*
1 cup uncooked white rice	*¼ cup chopped dried pears*
2 cups nonfat chicken broth	*¼ cup chopped dried dates*

1. Place onion and milk in a large, microwave-safe bowl. Cover and microwave on HIGH for 3 minutes.
2. Add the rice, broth, pepper, curry powder, pears, and dates. Cover and microwave on HIGH for 18 minutes, or until all the liquid is absorbed.

Calories Per Serving: 239	Carbohydrates: 52 g
Fat: 1 g	Dietary Fiber: 2 g
Cholesterol: 0 mg	Sodium: 177 mg
Protein: 7 g	

RICE WITH BEANS

Bombay Vegetables and Rice ▪ Jalapeño and Kidney Beans with Rice ▪ Rice and Pinto Bean Toss ▪ Navy Beans and Rice ▪ Great Northern Beans, Vegetables, and Rice ▪ Saffron Spinach, Rice, and Beans ▪ Rice with Black Beans and Bell Peppers ▪ Microwave Rice and Black Beans ▪ Papaya and Black Beans with Orange Rice ▪ Hopping John ▪ Rice and Chickpeas ▪ Spicy Chickpea Stew with Rice ▪ Jalapeño Rice with Winter Squash and Chickpeas ▪ Curried Tomato Rice with Lentils and Peas ▪ Spiced Lentils with Rice ▪ Dilled Lentils with Rice ▪ Baked Bean–and–Rice Salad ▪ Red Bean–and–Rice Salad ▪ Golden Rice Salad with Black Beans ▪ Cannellini Bean–and–Rice Salad ▪ Tomato-Scallion Rice Salad with Lentils ▪ Rice Salad with Lentils and Vegetables ▪ Squash-Rice Salad

Bombay Vegetables and Rice

Rice, cauliflower, sweet potato, green beans, and carrot are flavored with eight herbs and spices.

YIELD: 6 servings • *PREPARATION TIME: 25 minutes* • *COOKING TIME: 23 minutes plus 15 minutes standing time*

2¼ cups nonfat chicken broth
1 medium onion, coarsely chopped
1 tablespoon minced fresh gingerroot
2 cloves garlic, minced
1 tablespoon curry powder
1 teaspoon ground cumin
1 cinnamon stick, about 2 inches long
½ teaspoon ground coriander
½ teaspoon ground cardamom
¼ teaspoon red pepper flakes

1 cup uncooked white rice
2 cups chopped cauliflower
2 cups sweet potato, peeled and cut into ½-inch cubes
1 cup fresh green beans, cut into 1-inch lengths
1 cup frozen, thawed lima beans
1 cup chopped carrot
¼ teaspoon ground black pepper

1. Heat ¼ cup broth in a large saucepan. Add the onion, gingerroot, and garlic. Sauté for 4 minutes.
2. Stir in the curry powder, cumin, cinnamon stick, coriander, cardamom, and red pepper flakes. Sauté for 2 minutes. Add the rice; stir well and cook for 1 additional minute.
3. Add the cauliflower, sweet potato, green beans, lima beans, and carrot. Stir well. Add the remaining 2 cups chicken broth and black pepper. Bring to a boil; reduce heat, cover, and simmer until the liquid is absorbed and the rice and vegetables are just tender, about 15 minutes.
4. Remove from heat and let stand, covered, for 15 minutes before serving.

Calories Per Serving: 311
Fat: 2 g
Cholesterol: 0 mg
Protein: 9 g

Carbohydrates: 67 g
Dietary Fiber: 7 g
Sodium: 175 mg

Jalapeño and Kidney Beans with Rice

Jalapeño pepper, onion, green chiles, and chili powder flavor white rice and kidney beans.

YIELD: 6 servings ▪ *PREPARATION TIME: 15 minutes* ▪
COOKING TIME: 23 minutes, plus 2 minutes standing time

¼ cup nonfat chicken broth
1 jalapeño pepper, seeds removed, half
  minced, half sliced crosswise into
  ⅛-inch pieces
1 medium onion, chopped
2 cups water
1 cup uncooked white rice

4 cups drained low-sodium canned kidney beans
½ teaspoon chili powder
1 4-ounce can green chiles, diced
½ cup shredded nonfat cheddar
1 large ripe tomato, chopped
2 scallions, thinly sliced

1. Heat broth in a large skillet. Add minced jalapeño and onion. Sauté until onion is just tender, about 3 minutes.
2. Add water, rice, beans, chili powder, and chiles. Slowly bring mixture to a boil. Reduce heat, cover, and simmer until rice is tender, about 20 minutes.
3. Remove from heat, sprinkle the cheese over the top, and allow to stand until cheese is melted, about 2 minutes. Garnish with the sliced jalapeño pieces, tomato, and scallions. Serve immediately.

Calories Per Serving: 306
Fat: 1 g
Cholesterol: 0 mg
Protein: 15 g

Carbohydrates: 59 g
Dietary Fiber: 10 g
Sodium: 227 mg

Rice and Pinto Bean Toss

Cinnamon-accented pinto beans, zucchini, carrot, onion, and green bell pepper are served with garlic and onion-flavored white rice.

YIELD: 8 servings ▪ *PREPARATION TIME: 20 minutes* ▪ *COOKING TIME: 25 minutes*

2½ cups nonfat chicken broth
2½ cups chopped onion
3 cloves garlic, minced
2 cups uncooked white rice
½ cup finely chopped carrot
½ cup finely chopped celery

½ cup finely chopped red onion
½ cup finely chopped green bell pepper
½ teaspoon ground cinnamon
4 cups low-sodium canned red pinto
    beans, rinsed and drained

1. Heat ¼ cup chicken broth in a large saucepan. Add 2 cups onion and the garlic and sauté until onion is just tender, about 3 minutes. Add the rice and stir
   until it is coated with liquid. Add 2 cups broth and bring to a boil. Reduce
   heat, cover, and simmer until rice is just tender, about 15 minutes.
2. Heat remaining ¼ cup broth in a large skillet. Add the carrot, celery, and red
   onion. Sauté until vegetables are tender-crisp, about 5 minutes. Stir in the
   green bell pepper and cinnamon and sauté an additional 2 minutes. Remove
   from heat and set aside.
3. Heat beans. Toss half the sautéed vegetables with the cooked rice. Place a
   mound of the rice mixture in individual serving bowls, top each with beans
   and the remaining sautéed vegetables, and serve.

Calories Per Serving: 326
Fat: 2 g
Cholesterol: 0 mg
Protein: 14 g

Carbohydrates: 66 g
Dietary Fiber: 8 g
Sodium: 197 mg

Navy Beans and Rice

Navy beans and cooked brown rice are prepared with a spicy mixture of onion,
garlic, black pepper, coriander, cumin, and lemon juice.

Yield: 4 servings ▪ *Preparation Time: 10 minutes* ▪
Cooking Time: 8 minutes plus rice cooking time

¼ cup nonfat chicken broth
1 small onion, chopped
4 cloves garlic, minced
2 cups canned navy beans, rinsed and
    drained
½ teaspoon ground black pepper

1 teaspoon ground coriander
½ teaspoon ground cumin
¼ cup lemon juice
1 cup water
3 cups cooked brown rice (see p. 192)
2 tablespoons chopped fresh parsley

1. Heat broth in a large skillet. Add onion and garlic and sauté for 3 minutes.
2. Add beans and sauté for another 3 minutes.
3. Add pepper, coriander, cumin, lemon juice, and water. Bring to a boil. Reduce heat and simmer for 5 minutes.
4. Stir in rice, cover, and simmer until the liquid is absorbed, about 15 to 18 minutes.
5. Sprinkle with parsley before serving.

Calories Per Serving: 342   Carbohydrates: 68 g
Fat: 2 g   Dietary Fiber: 3 g
Cholesterol: 0 mg   Sodium: 35 mg
Protein: 14 g

Great Northern Beans, Vegetables, and Rice

Beans, rice, corn, peas, and tomatoes are flavored with turmeric, cumin, and cinnamon.

YIELD: 6 servings • PREPARATION TIME: 15 minutes • COOKING TIME: 24 minutes

¼ cup nonfat chicken broth   about 1 cup water
1 medium onion, finely chopped   1 bay leaf
2 cloves garlic, minced   1 cup frozen, thawed corn kernels
1 cup uncooked white rice   1 cup frozen, thawed green peas
½ teaspoon ground turmeric   1 cup low-sodium canned Great North-
½ teaspoon ground cumin   ern beans, drained
¼ teaspoon ground cinnamon   ½ cup seedless raisins
2 cups fresh or low-sodium canned   1 tablespoon sliced toasted almonds
   tomatoes, chopped, juice reserved   ¼ cup chopped fresh parsley

1. Heat broth in a large skillet. Add onion and sauté for 3 minutes. Add garlic and sauté for 1 additional minute. Stir in rice, turmeric, cumin, and cinnamon.
2. Combine reserved tomato juice with enough water to total 1¾ cups liquid. Add liquid to skillet. Add bay leaf. Bring to a boil. Reduce heat, cover, and simmer for 10 minutes.
3. Stir in tomatoes, corn, peas, beans, and raisins. Cover and simmer until rice is done, about 10 minutes. Drain any excess liquid. Remove bay leaf.
4. Transfer to a serving bowl. Sprinkle with almonds and parsley and serve immediately.

Calorics Per Serving: 348
Fat: 3 g
Cholesterol: 0 mg
Protein: 11 g

Carbohydrates: 72 g
Dietary Fiber: 8 g
Sodium: 65 mg

Saffron Spinach, Rice, and Beans

Spinach, white rice, Great Northern beans, artichokes, red bell pepper, and onion are simmered with saffron and paprika.

YIELD: 6 servings • *PREPARATION TIME: 25 minutes* • *COOKING TIME: 33 minutes plus 15 minutes standing time*

½ cup water
¼ teaspoon saffron threads
3¼ cups nonfat chicken broth
1 red bell pepper, diced
1 medium onion, diced
1 9-ounce package frozen artichokes, thawed and coarsely chopped
2 cloves garlic, minced
1½ cups uncooked white rice

2 cups chopped chard or endive
1 cup drained low-sodium canned tomatoes
¼ teaspoon paprika
2 cups canned Great Northern beans, rinsed and drained
½ cup fresh or frozen, thawed green peas

1. Bring water to a boil in a small saucepan. Stir in saffron; remove from heat, cover, and let stand for 10 minutes.
2. Heat ¼ cup broth in a large saucepan. Add red bell pepper and onion and sauté until onion is translucent, about 5 minutes.
3. Add artichokes and garlic and sauté for 5 more minutes. Add rice, remaining chicken broth, chard, and tomatoes. Bring to a boil, stirring often. Add saffron water and paprika. Reduce heat, cover, and simmer for 15 minutes.
4. Stir in beans and peas and allow to simmer until liquid is absorbed and rice is tender, about 5 minutes.
5. Remove from heat and allow to stand for 5 minutes before serving.

Calories Per Serving: 344
Fat: 2 g
Cholesterol: 0 mg
Protein: 15 g

Carbohydrates: 70 g
Dietary Fiber: 4 g
Sodium: 262 mg

Rice with Black Beans and Bell Peppers

The perennial combination of black beans, rice, and green and red bell peppers, flavored with onion, garlic, and cider vinegar. Serve topped with yogurt.

YIELD: 4 servings ▪ PREPARATION TIME: 15 minutes ▪ COOKING TIME: 35 minutes

2 cups water
1 cup uncooked white rice
¼ cup nonfat chicken broth
1 small onion, chopped
1 green bell pepper, finely chopped
1 red bell pepper, finely chopped
1 stalk celery, finely chopped

2 cloves garlic, minced
¼ teaspoon dried thyme
2 cups canned low-sodium black beans, rinsed and drained
2 tablespoons cider vinegar
½ cup nonfat plain yogurt
1 scallion, minced

1. Bring water to a boil in a large saucepan. Stir in rice; return to a boil, reduce heat, cover, and simmer until rice is just tender, about 20 minutes.
2. Heat broth in a large skillet. Add the onion, green and red bell peppers, celery, garlic, and thyme. Sauté until vegetables are just tender, about 7 minutes.
3. Stir in the beans and vinegar. Sauté until the beans are heated through, about 3 minutes.
4. Transfer bean mixture to individual bowls, top each with yogurt and minced scallion, and serve.

Calories Per Serving: 330
Fat: 1 g
Cholesterol: 1 mg
Protein: 13 g

Carbohydrates: 68 g
Dietary Fiber: 8 g
Sodium: 498 mg

Microwave Rice and Black Beans

This combination of baked brown rice, fresh tomatoes, beans, onion, celery, carrots, and herbs is ready for dinner in about 30 minutes.

*YIELD: 6 servings ▪ PREPARATION TIME: 15 minutes ▪
COOKING TIME: 11 minutes plus rice cooking time*

¼ cup water
2 cloves garlic, minced
1 large onion, chopped
2 carrots, chopped
½ cup chopped fresh parsley
1 stalk celery, chopped
½ teaspoon dried oregano

½ teaspoon dried basil
2 cups low-sodium canned black beans,
    rinsed and drained
2⅔ cups cooked brown rice (see p. 192)
3 large ripe tomatoes, coarsely chopped
¼ teaspoon ground black pepper

1. Combine water, garlic, onion, carrots, parsley, celery, oregano, and basil in a microwave-safe casserole. Microwave on HIGH, stirring once, for 4 minutes.
2. Add beans, rice, tomatoes, and black pepper. Stir and microwave on MEDIUM until heated through, about 7 minutes.

Calories Per Serving: 205
Fat: 1 g
Cholesterol: 0 mg
Protein: 8 g

Carbohydrates: 41 g
Dietary Fiber: 8 g
Sodium: 31 mg

Papaya and Black Beans with Orange Rice

Black beans, green bell pepper, and papaya are served with orange-flavored rice.

YIELD: 8 servings ▪ *PREPARATION TIME: 20 minutes* ▪ *COOKING TIME: 40 minutes*

4 cups water
2 cups uncooked white rice
¼ cup nonfat chicken broth
½ cup finely chopped red onion
2 cloves garlic, minced
1 green bell pepper, finely chopped

1 papaya, peeled, seeded, and diced
½ teaspoon cayenne pepper
½ cup orange juice
¼ cup lime juice
4 cups canned black beans, rinsed and
    drained

1. Bring water to a boil in a large saucepan. Stir in rice; return to a boil, reduce heat, cover, and simmer until rice is just tender, about 20 minutes.
2. Heat broth in a large skillet. Add onion and garlic and sauté until onion is just tender, about 3 minutes.
3. Stir in green bell pepper, papaya, and cayenne pepper. Sauté for 3 minutes. Add orange juice and lime juice. Simmer until bell pepper is just tender, about 5 minutes.
4. Stir in beans. Cook until they are heated through.
5. Place a mound of rice in individual bowls, top with the beans, and serve hot.

Calories Per Serving: 135
Fat: 1 g
Cholesterol: 0 mg
Protein: 7 g

Carbohydrates: 27 g
Dietary Fiber: 7 g
Sodium: 456 mg

Hopping John

A low-fat variation of the Deep South's traditional New Year's Day good-luck dish.

YIELD: 6 servings • PREPARATION TIME: 20 minutes • COOKING TIME: 25 minutes

3 cups water
1½ cups uncooked brown rice
¼ cup nonfat chicken broth
1 cup chopped onion
1 clove garlic, minced
2 cups chopped canned tomatoes, juice
    reserved

½ teaspoon dried basil
¼ teaspoon dried thyme
2 cups canned low-sodium black-eyed
    peas, rinsed and drained
¼ teaspoon ground black pepper

1. Bring water to a boil in a large saucepan. Stir in rice; return to a boil, reduce heat, cover, and simmer until rice is just tender, about 25 minutes.
2. Heat broth in a large skillet. Add onion and sauté for 3 minutes. Add garlic and sauté 2 additional minutes. Add tomatoes and their juice, basil, and thyme and cook for 5 minutes.
3. Add the cooked rice, black-eyed peas, and pepper. Simmer for 15 minutes. (Add water or chicken broth if needed.) Serve immediately.

Calories Per Serving: 262
Fat: 2 g
Cholesterol: 0 mg
Protein: 9 g

Carbohydrates: 54 g
Dietary Fiber: 6 g
Sodium: 317 mg

Rice and Chickpeas

Rice and chickpeas are flavored with onion and black pepper.

YIELD: 4 servings • PREPARATION TIME: 10 minutes • COOKING TIME: 40 minutes

1½ cups water
⅔ cup uncooked white rice
¼ cup nonfat chicken broth

1 small onion, finely chopped
1½ cups canned chickpeas, drained
⅛ teaspoon ground black pepper

1. Bring water to a boil in a large saucepan. Stir in rice; return to a boil, reduce heat, cover, and simmer until rice is just tender, about 20 minutes.
2. Heat broth in a large skillet. Add onion and sauté until translucent, about 3 minutes.
3. Add rice, chickpeas, and black pepper. Cover and cook over low heat until liquid is absorbed, about 15 minutes.

Calories Per Serving: 304
Fat: 3 g
Cholesterol: 0 mg
Protein: 10 g

Carbohydrates: 60 g
Dietary Fiber: 9 g
Sodium: 589 mg

Spicy Chickpea Stew with Rice

A savory mixture of chickpeas, onions, garlic, tomatoes, and tomato paste is spiced with turmeric, cayenne, coriander, and cumin, then served with white rice.

YIELD: 8 servings ▪ *PREPARATION TIME: 20 minutes* ▪ *COOKING TIME: 45 minutes*

7 cups water
3 cups uncooked white rice
¼ cup nonfat chicken broth
2 medium onions, sliced
1 clove garlic, minced
3 large ripe tomatoes, chopped
¾ cup low-sodium tomato paste

1 teaspoon ground turmeric
1 teaspoon cayenne pepper
1 teaspoon ground coriander
½ teaspoon ground cumin
4 cups canned chickpeas, rinsed and drained

1. Bring 6 cups water to a boil in a large saucepan. Stir in rice; return to a boil, reduce heat, cover, and simmer until rice is just tender, about 20 minutes.
2. Heat chicken broth in a large skillet. Add onions and garlic and sauté until onions are translucent.
3. Stir in the tomatoes, tomato paste, remaining cup of water, turmeric, cayenne pepper, coriander, and cumin. Bring to a boil; stir in chickpeas, reduce heat, and simmer for 20 minutes.
4. Place a mound of rice on each plate, top with chickpea stew, and serve immediately.

Calories Per Serving: 498
Fat: 3 g
Cholesterol: 0 mg
Protein: 17 g

Carbohydrates: 100 g
Dietary Fiber: 3 g
Sodium: 109 mg

Jalapeño Rice with Winter Squash and Chickpeas

A delight for a cold winter evening.

YIELD: 5 servings • PREPARATION TIME: 25 minutes •
COOKING TIME: 35 minutes plus 5 minutes standing time

2½ cups nonfat chicken broth
½ cup chopped onion
1 fresh jalapeño pepper, seeded and
   minced
1 clove garlic, minced
2 teaspoons ground coriander

1 teaspoon ground cumin
1 cup uncooked brown rice
2 cups butternut squash, peeled and cut
   into ½-inch cubes
2 cups canned chickpeas, rinsed and
   drained

1. Heat ¼ cup of the chicken broth in a large skillet. Add the onion and sauté 3
   minutes. Stir in the jalapeño and garlic and sauté for 1 minute. Stir in the coriander and cumin and sauté another minute.
2. Add the rice, squash, and chickpeas. Stir well. Add the remaining broth and
   bring to a boil. Reduce heat, cover, and simmer until the broth is absorbed
   and the rice is tender, about 25 minutes.
3. Remove from heat and allow to stand, uncovered, for 5 minutes before serving.

Calories Per Serving: 241
Fat: 3 g
Cholesterol: 0 mg
Protein: 10 g

Carbohydrates: 46 g
Dietary Fiber: 6 g
Sodium: 519 mg

Curried Tomato Rice with Lentils and Peas

Lentils and rice are simmered in tomato juice and seasoned with curry powder.

YIELD: 4 servings • PREPARATION TIME: 15 minutes • COOKING TIME: 37 minutes

¼ cup nonfat chicken broth
½ cup chopped green bell pepper
½ cup chopped onion
2 cloves garlic, minced
1 cup dry lentils

1 cup uncooked brown rice
1 teaspoon curry powder
5 cups low-sodium tomato juice
1½ cups frozen peas, thawed

1. Heat chicken broth in a large skillet. Add green bell pepper, onion, and garlic. Sauté for 2 minutes.
2. Stir in lentils, rice, and curry powder. Add tomato juice and bring to a boil. Reduce heat and simmer for 25 minutes. Stir in peas and continue to simmer until rice is tender, about 10 minutes. Serve hot.

Calories Per Serving: 401
Fat: 2 g
Cholesterol: 0 mg
Protein: 19 g

Carbohydrates: 81 g
Dietary Fiber: 13 g
Sodium: 109 mg

Spiced Lentils with Rice

Rice and lentils are seasoned with turmeric, garlic, and cumin.

YIELD: 4 servings ▪ *PREPARATION TIME: 10 minutes* ▪ *COOKING TIME: 43 minutes*

7 cups water
1 cup dry lentils
1 teaspoon ground turmeric
2 cups uncooked white rice
¼ cup or more nonfat chicken broth

1 small onion, chopped
2 cloves garlic, minced
1 teaspoon ground cumin
¼ teaspoon ground cardamom

1. Bring 3 cups water to a boil in a saucepan. Stir in lentils and turmeric. Return to a boil; reduce heat, cover, and simmer until lentils are tender, about 20 minutes.
2. Bring remaining 4 cups water to a boil in a large saucepan. Stir in rice; return to a boil, reduce heat, cover, and simmer until rice is just tender, about 20 minutes.
3. Heat ¼ cup broth in a large skillet. Add onion, garlic, cumin, and cardamom. Sauté until onion is just tender, about 3 minutes.
4. Add lentils to onion mixture. Cook, stirring several times, over low heat for 20 minutes. Add more broth if necessary.
5. Arrange the rice on individual serving plates, top with the lentils, and serve.

Calories Per Serving: 482
Fat: 1 g
Cholesterol: 0 mg
Protein: 16 g

Carbohydrates: 100 g
Dietary Fiber: 6 g
Sodium: 31 mg

Dilled Lentils with Rice

Lentils and rice are seasoned with dill, mint, onion, garlic, and fresh lemon juice.

YIELD: 4 servings • PREPARATION TIME: 15 minutes •
COOKING TIME: 32 minutes plus 5 minutes standing time

3 cups water
½ cup dry lentils
2¾ cups nonfat chicken broth
½ cup chopped onion
1 clove garlic, minced

1½ cups uncooked white rice
2 tablespoons fresh lemon juice
1 teaspoon dried dill
1 teaspoon dried mint

1. Bring water to a boil in a saucepan. Stir in lentils. Boil until they are just turning tender, about 10 minutes. Drain and set aside.
2. Heat ¼ cup chicken broth in a large skillet. Add onion and garlic and sauté until onion becomes translucent, about 4 minutes. Add rice and cooked lentils. Sauté for 2 minutes. Add remaining 2½ cups broth and bring to a boil; reduce heat, cover, and simmer until rice is just tender and liquid is absorbed, about 20 minutes. Remove from heat and let stand for 5 minutes.
3. Transfer to a serving bowl. Stir in the lemon juice, sprinkle with dill and mint, and serve.

Calories Per Serving: 345
Fat: 1 g
Cholesterol: 0 mg
Protein: 13 g

Carbohydrates: 71 g
Dietary Fiber: 3 g
Sodium: 218 mg

Baked Bean–and–Rice Salad

Cold baked beans and rice are tossed with mustard-garlic dressing.

YIELD: 6 servings • PREPARATION TIME: 15 minutes, plus rice cooking and cooling time

5 cups cooked brown rice, cooled to room
   temperature (see p. 192)
2 cups low-sodium baked beans
3 scallions, sliced thin
2 stalks celery, finely chopped
1 red bell pepper, finely chopped
½ cup nonfat Italian dressing
2 cloves garlic, minced
1 teaspoon prepared mustard
¼ teaspoon ground black pepper

1. Combine the rice, beans, scallions, celery, and red bell pepper in a large serving bowl.
2. Combine the Italian dressing with the garlic, mustard, and black pepper, pour over the rice, toss to coat all ingredients, and serve.

Calories Per Serving: 262
Fat: 2 g
Cholesterol: 0 mg
Protein: 7 g

Carbohydrates: 55 g
Dietary Fiber: 5 g
Sodium: 318 mg

Red Bean–and–Rice Salad

Red kidney beans and brown rice are mixed with a lemon-parsley dressing and chilled. Raw vegetables are added just before serving.

Yield: 6 servings • *Preparation Time: 20 minutes plus rice cooking and cooling time*

1 cup low-sodium canned red kidney
   beans, rinsed and drained
2 cups cooked brown rice, cooled to room
   temperature (see p. 192)
3 tablespoons nonfat mayonnaise
3 tablespoons cider vinegar
2 cloves garlic, minced
1 tablespoon lemon juice
2 tablespoons minced fresh parsley
¼ teaspoon ground black pepper
1 carrot, cut into matchstick-size pieces
1 green bell pepper, diced
1 stalk celery, finely chopped

1. Combine the beans and rice.
2. Whisk together the mayonnaise, vinegar, garlic, lemon juice, parsley, and black pepper. Stir into the rice-bean mixture and toss to coat all ingredients. Refrigerate for 30 minutes.
3. Stir in the carrot, green bell pepper, and celery, and serve.

Calories Per Serving: 129
Fat: 1 g
Cholesterol: 0 mg
Protein: 5 g

Carbohydrates: 27 g
Dietary Fiber: 4 g
Sodium: 111 mg

Golden Rice Salad with Black Beans

Rice is simmered until golden in turmeric and cumin, then mixed with black beans and a tomato-cilantro dressing.

YIELD: 6 servings • PREPARATION TIME: 20 minutes • COOKING TIME: 20 minutes

1½ cups water
1 teaspoon ground turmeric
½ teaspoon ground cumin
1 cup uncooked white rice
⅓ cup nonfat Italian dressing
2 teaspoons seeded, minced jalapeño
   pepper

½ cup chopped red onion
½ cup seeded, chopped fresh tomato
½ cup chopped green bell pepper
1 tablespoon dried cilantro
¼ teaspoon cayenne pepper
2 cups cooked or canned low-sodium
   black beans, rinsed and drained

1. Combine the water, turmeric, and cumin in a large saucepan. Bring to a boil. Stir in rice; return to a boil, reduce heat, cover, and simmer until rice is just tender, about 20 minutes. Drain away excess liquid and cool, uncovered, to room temperature.
2. Whisk together the Italian dressing and jalapeño pepper.
3. Mix the cooled rice, onion, tomato, green bell pepper, cilantro, cayenne, and black beans. Add the dressing and toss to coat all ingredients.

Calories Per Serving: 95
Fat: 0 g
Cholesterol: 0 mg
Protein: 6 g

Carbohydrates: 17 g
Dietary Fiber: 3 g
Sodium: 205 mg

Cannellini Bean–and–Rice Salad

White Italian kidney beans are combined with white rice, green bell pepper, onion, garlic, and parsley in a dressing of oil and cider vinegar.

YIELD: 10 servings • PREPARATION TIME: 25 minutes •
COOKING TIME: 25 minutes plus 30 minutes cooling time

4¼ cups nonfat chicken broth
½ yellow bell pepper, finely chopped
½ red bell pepper, finely chopped
½ green bell pepper, finely chopped
½ onion, finely chopped
2 cloves garlic, minced
2 cups uncooked white or basmati rice

1 cup minced fresh parsley
2 scallions, minced
1½ tablespoons olive oil
2 tablespoons cider vinegar
¼ teaspoon ground black pepper
2 cups cooked or canned, rinsed, and
 drained cannellini beans

1. Heat ¼ cup chicken broth in a large skillet. Add the yellow, red, and green bell peppers, onion, and garlic and sauté until onion is just tender, about 3 minutes. Drain and allow to cool to room temperature, about 30 minutes.
2. Bring 4 cups broth to a boil in a saucepan. Stir in rice; return to a boil, reduce heat, cover, and simmer until rice is just tender, about 20 minutes. Remove from heat, drain any excess liquid, and allow to cool to room temperature.
3. In a large serving bowl, combine the cooked peppers and onion, rice, parsley, scallions, oil, vinegar, and black pepper. Stir in the beans. Toss gently to coat ingredients.
4. Serve immediately at room temperature, or refrigerate and serve chilled.

Calories Per Serving: 244
Fat: 3 g
Cholesterol: 0 mg
Protein: 9 g

Carbohydrates: 46 g
Dietary Fiber: 1 g
Sodium: 141 mg

Tomato-Scallion Rice Salad with Lentils

Tomato, scallions, and parsley flavor lentils and white rice.

YIELD: 4 servings ・ *PREPARATION TIME: 15 minutes* ・ *COOKING TIME: 40 minutes*

1½ cups nonfat chicken broth
¾ cup uncooked white rice
1 cup water
½ cup lentils
1 large ripe tomato, chopped
3 scallions, sliced

1 tablespoon chopped fresh parsley
1 clove garlic, minced
¼ teaspoon or more ground black pepper
¼ cup nonfat Italian salad dressing
enough lettuce leaves to make beds on 4
 plates

1. Bring broth to a boil in a saucepan. Stir in rice; return to a boil, reduce heat, cover, and simmer until rice is just tender, about 20 minutes. Uncover and allow to cool to room temperature, about 30 minutes.

2. Bring water to a boil in a saucepan. Stir in lentils; return to a boil, reduce heat, cover, and simmer until lentils are tender, about 20 minutes. Drain any excess liquid. Allow to cool to room temperature.
3. Combine rice, lentils, tomato, scallions, parsley, garlic, and black pepper. Add dressing; add more black pepper if desired. Serve on beds of lettuce on individual serving plates.

Calories Per Serving: 248
Fat: 1 g
Cholesterol: 0 mg
Protein: 10 g

Carbohydrates: 49 g
Dietary Fiber: 2 g
Sodium: 481 mg

Rice Salad with Lentils and Vegetables

Lentils are a good source of iron, calcium, and vitamins A and B. In this robust salad they are added to brown rice and an array of vegetables and finished with a lemon-mustard dressing.

YIELD: 8 servings • PREPARATION TIME: 25 minutes plus rice cooking and cooling time
• COOKING TIME: 20 minutes plus 30 minutes cooling time

1½ cups water
½ cup lentils
1½ cups cooked, cooled brown rice
1 large ripe tomato, chopped
3 scallions, sliced
½ cup diced celery
½ cup diced carrots

½ cup diced green bell pepper
1½ cups broccoli florets
1 tablespoon chopped fresh parsley
¼ cup rice vinegar
1 tablespoon lemon juice
1½ teaspoons Dijon mustard
1 tablespoon olive oil

1. Bring water to a boil in a saucepan. Stir in the lentils; return to a boil, reduce heat, cover, and simmer until they are tender, about 20 minutes. Remove from heat, drain, and allow to cool to room temperature, about 30 minutes.
2. Combine lentils, rice, tomato, scallions, celery, carrots, green bell pepper, broccoli, and parsley.
3. Whisk together the rice vinegar, lemon juice, mustard, and oil. Add the dressing to the lentil mixture, toss gently to coat all ingredients, and serve.

Calories Per Serving: 126
Fat: 2 g
Cholesterol: 0 mg
Protein: 5 g

Carbohydrates: 23 g
Dietary Fiber: 2 g
Sodium: 60 mg

Squash-Rice Salad

A delightful combination of vegetables and rice for a hot summer afternoon or evening.

YIELD: 6 servings ▪ *PREPARATION TIME: 15 minutes* ▪ *COOKING TIME: 17 minutes*

¼ cup sunflower seeds
2 medium yellow summer squash, sliced
    into ¼-inch rounds
1 zucchini, sliced into ¼-inch rounds
3 cups cooked white rice (see p. 190)

3 scallions, minced
1 teaspoon dried dill
¼ teaspoon ground black pepper
¼ cup nonfat Italian dressing

1. Preheat oven to 250 degrees.
2. Spread sunflower seeds on a nonstick baking sheet and bake until lightly browned, about 15 minutes.
3. Place 1 inch of water in the bottom of a steamer pot and bring to a boil. Place yellow squash and zucchini in a colander or steamer basket over the boiling water and steam, covered, until tender-crisp, about 2 minutes. Run cold water over the vegetables and drain well.
4. Combine the vegetables, rice, scallions, dill, black pepper, and sunflower seeds.
5. Pour dressing over salad and toss gently.

Calories Per Serving: 178
Fat: 3 g
Cholesterol: 0 mg
Protein: 5 g

Carbohydrates: 32 g
Dietary Fiber: 2 g
Sodium: 145 mg

SWEET RICE DISHES

❖

Microwave Rice Pudding ▪ Dried-Fruit Rice Pudding ▪ Apple-Cabbage Rice ▪ Maple-Raisin Rice Pudding ▪ Blueberry Rice Pudding ▪ Orange-Prune Rice Pudding ▪ Cranberry Rice Pudding ▪ Apricot Rice with Blueberries and Honey ▪ Molded Fresh Berry Delight ▪ Mango Rice Pudding ▪ Royal Melon Rice Salad ▪ Sweet Citrus Rice Pudding

Microwave Rice Pudding

Rice pudding is quick and easy in your microwave. This version is prepared with sugar and cinnamon.

YIELD: 2 servings • PREPARATION TIME: 5 minutes • COOKING TIME: 2 minutes

1 cup cooked white rice (see p. 190)	*1 tablespoon sugar*
⅔ cup skim milk	*¼ teaspoon ground cinnamon*

1. Combine, rice, milk, sugar, and cinnamon in a microwave-safe container.
2. Microwave on 100% HIGH until rice begins to thicken, about 2 minutes.

Calories Per Serving: 156	Carbohydrates: 33 g
Fat: 0 g	Dietary Fiber: 0 g
Cholesterol: 1 mg	Sodium: 43 mg
Protein: 5 g	

Dried-Fruit Rice Pudding

Dried peaches, apricots, and pineapple are layered with brown rice and baked.

YIELD: 8 servings • PREPARATION TIME: 15 minutes plus fruit soaking time and rice cooking time • COOKING TIME: 30 minutes

1 cup dried apricots	*1 teaspoon apple juice*
1 cup dried peaches	*1⅓ cups skim milk*
½ cup dried pineapple	*1 teaspoon ground cinnamon*
boiling water to soak fruit	*½ cup roasted slivered almonds*
5 cups cooked brown rice (see p. 192)	*(optional)*

1. Cover apricots, peaches, and pineapple with boiling water and soak until they are plump and soft, about 3 hours. Drain and chop.
2. Preheat oven to 350 degrees.
3. Place half the fruit in a single layer in an ovenproof dish.
4. Top the fruit layer with half the rice. Place the remaining fruit on the rice layer and cover with a last layer of rice.
5. Mix the apple juice, milk, and cinnamon, and pour over the rice.
6. Bake for 30 minutes, sprinkle the almonds over the rice, and serve hot.

Calories Per Serving: 270 Carbohydrates: 61 g
Fat: 1 g   Dietary Fiber: 3 g
Cholesterol: 1 mg   Sodium: 31 mg
Protein: 6 g

Apple-Cabbage Rice

Apples and cabbage are mixed with brown rice in a dish that combines fruits, vegetables, and grain.

YIELD: 4 servings ▪ PREPARATION TIME: 20 minutes ▪ COOKING TIME: 50 minutes

2¼ cups water   *2 apples, cored and diced*
1 cup uncooked brown rice   *2 cups shredded green cabbage*
1 teaspoon ground cumin   *1 tablespoon minced fresh gingerroot*
2 tablespoons nonfat chicken broth *½ cup chopped pitted prunes*
1 small onion, chopped   *2 cups apple juice*

1. Place water, rice, and cumin in a medium saucepan. Bring water to a boil. Reduce heat, cover, and simmer for 25 minutes.
2. Heat broth in a large skillet. Sauté onion for 5 minutes. Add apples and continue to sauté until they start to brown.
3. Add cabbage, gingerroot, prunes, and apple juice. Bring to a boil. Reduce heat, cover, and simmer for 5 minutes. Uncover and continue to cook until liquid is absorbed.
4. Combine rice with apple-cabbage mixture and serve.

Calories Per Serving: 308 Carbohydrates: 69 g
Fat: 2 g   Dietary Fiber: 4 g
Cholesterol: 0 mg   Sodium: 38 mg
Protein: 5 g

Maple-Raisin Rice Pudding

This sweet pudding is flavored with vanilla, cinnamon, and maple syrup.

*YIELD: 6 servings ▪ PREPARATION TIME: 10 minutes plus rice cooking time ▪
COOKING TIME: 15 minutes plus 10 minutes standing time*

1 quart skim milk
1½ cups cooked white rice (see p. 190)
½ cup maple syrup
½ cup raisins
½ teaspoon vanilla extract
½ teaspoon ground cinnamon

1. Combine the milk and rice in a large saucepan. Bring to a gentle simmer and cook for 10 minutes, stirring often. Stir in the syrup and simmer an additional 5 minutes.
2. Remove from heat, mix in the raisins, and allow to stand for 10 minutes. Stir in the vanilla extract and mix well. Transfer to individual bowls, sprinkle with cinnamon, and serve warm.

Calories Per Serving: 193
Fat: 0 g
Cholesterol: 3 mg
Protein: 7 g

Carbohydrates: 41 g
Dietary Fiber: 0 g
Sodium: 88 mg

Blueberry Rice Pudding

Dried blueberries add a flavor burst to rice pudding.

YIELD: 6 servings • PREPARATION TIME: 10 minutes •
COOKING TIME: 20 minutes plus 30 minutes cooling time

5½ cups skim milk
½ cup sugar
2 teaspoons vanilla extract
¾ cup uncooked white rice
¾ cup dried blueberries
½ cup nonfat plain yogurt

1. Combine the milk, sugar, and vanilla extract in a large saucepan. Bring to a boil. Stir in rice; return to a boil, reduce heat, and simmer until the rice is tender, about 20 minutes. Remove from heat.
2. Stir in blueberries and cool to room temperature, about 30 minutes.
3. Transfer to individual serving bowls and top with yogurt.

Calories Per Serving: 272
Fat: 1 g
Cholesterol: 5 mg
Protein: 12 g

Carbohydrates: 54 g
Dietary Fiber: 1 g
Sodium: 147 mg

Orange-Prune Rice Pudding

The lovely pairing of orange juice and prunes combines with white rice, cinnamon, and brown sugar.

YIELD: 5 servings • *PREPARATION TIME: 10 minutes plus rice cooking time* •
COOKING TIME: 8 minutes plus 2 hours chilling time

2 cups orange juice
¼ teaspoon ground cinnamon
2 tablespoons cornstarch
2 tablespoons brown sugar

1 teaspoon vanilla extract
2 cups cooked brown rice (see p. 192)
¼ cup chopped pitted prunes

1. Combine orange juice and cinnamon in a large saucepan. Slowly add cornstarch, stirring to ensure that it dissolves thoroughly.
2. Stirring constantly, bring to a boil. Keep at a boil, continuing to stir, for 2 minutes. Remove from heat.
3. Stir in brown sugar, and allow to dissolve. Add vanilla extract, rice, and prunes. Mix well. Transfer to a shallow bowl, cover, and chill for 2 hours.

Calories Per Serving: 192
Fat: 1 g
Cholesterol: 0 mg
Protein: 3 g

Carbohydrates: 43 g
Dietary Fiber: 3 g
Sodium: 8 mg

Cranberry Rice Pudding

A warm, wintry pudding of white rice and skim milk flavored with dried cranberries, cinnamon, nutmeg, and vanilla.

YIELD: 4 servings • *PREPARATION TIME: 15 minutes* •
COOKING TIME: 30 minutes plus 30 minutes cooling time

3 cups skim milk
½ cup uncooked white rice
½ cup maple syrup
½ teaspoon ground cinnamon

¼ teaspoon ground nutmeg
½ cup dried cranberries
½ teaspoon vanilla extract

1. Bring milk to a boil in a large saucepan. Stir in rice. Return to a boil, reduce heat, and simmer until rice is tender, about 20 minutes.
2. Stir in maple syrup, cinnamon, and nutmeg. Simmer for 10 additional minutes.
3. Stir the cranberries into the hot rice. Allow the pudding to cool for 30 minutes; stir in vanilla extract and serve.

Calories Per Serving: 261
Fat: 1 g
Cholesterol: 3 mg
Protein: 8 g

Carbohydrates: 57 g
Dietary Fiber: 0 g
Sodium: 105 mg

Apricot Rice with Blueberries and Honey

Rice pudding with dried apricots is topped with fresh fruit, honey, and cinnamon.

YIELD: *4 servings* • PREPARATION TIME: *15 minutes* • COOKING TIME: *25 minutes*

2¼ cups water
¼ cup diced dried apricots
1 cup uncooked white rice
1½ cups skim milk
2 tablespoons honey

1 cup sliced fresh or canned apricots,
  drained
1 cup fresh or frozen, thawed, drained
  blueberries
½ teaspoon ground cinnamon

1. Place the water and dried apricots in a large saucepan. Bring to a boil and stir in the rice. Return to a boil; reduce heat, cover, and simmer, stirring often, until the rice is tender, about 20 minutes.
2. Add milk and continue simmering until the mixture thickens, about 5 minutes.
3. Transfer to individual bowls, top with honey, apricots, and blueberries, sprinkle with cinnamon, and serve.

Calories Per Serving: 292
Fat: 1 g
Cholesterol: 2 mg
Protein: 7 g

Carbohydrates: 65 g
Dietary Fiber: 3 g
Sodium: 57 mg

Molded Fresh Berry Delight

Simply irresistible.

YIELD: 6 servings   ▪   PREPARATION TIME: 20 minutes   ▪
COOKING TIME: 35 minutes plus 40 minutes standing time and 1 hour chilling time

2 cups water
2 cups skim milk
2 cups uncooked white rice
3½ tablespoons sugar

3 tablespoons water plus boiling water
  as needed
4 cups strawberries, hulled and cut into
  ¾-inch pieces
¼ cup lemon juice

1. Bring the water and milk to a boil in a large saucepan. Stir in the rice. Return to a boil, reduce heat, cover, and simmer until rice is just tender, but still firm to the bite, about 20 minutes.
2. Preheat oven to 350 degrees.
3. Combine ½ tablespoon sugar and 3 tablespoons water in a small saucepan. Bring the mixture to a boil and cook until the liquid begins to turn caramel-colored. Pour the syrup into a 2-quart ring mold. Swirl the syrup around to coat the mold.
4. When the rice is cooked, stir in the remaining 3 tablespoons sugar and transfer the rice to the mold. Place the mold in a baking pan at least 4 inches deep. Pour 3 inches of boiling water into the baking dish; place the dish in the oven and bake until pudding has a golden-brown crust, about 20 minutes.
5. Remove from oven and allow to stand for 10 minutes. Place the pudding in the refrigerator and chill for at least 30 minutes.
6. Combine strawberries and lemon juice. Chill for 1 hour.
7. When pudding is chilled, loosen the edges of the mold with a sharp knife and turn the pudding onto a serving platter. Place the fruit mixture in the center of the mold and serve.

Calories Per Serving: 323
Fat: 1 g
Cholesterol: 1 mg
Protein: 8 g

Carbohydrates: 71 g
Dietary Fiber: 2 g
Sodium: 44 mg

Mango Rice Pudding

Rice pudding is brightened with vanilla yogurt, almonds, and mango.

YIELD: 6 servings · PREPARATION TIME: 15 minutes ·
COOKING TIME: 25 minutes plus 5 minutes standing time

2½ cups water
1 cup uncooked white rice
½ cup nonfat plain yogurt
¼ cup sugar

1 teaspoon vanilla extract
¾ cup peeled, diced ripe mango
2 tablespoons chopped almonds

1. Bring the water to a boil in a large saucepan. Stir in rice. Return to a boil; reduce heat, cover, and simmer until rice is tender, about 20 minutes. Remove from heat and allow to stand, covered, for 5 minutes.
2. Combine the hot rice, yogurt, sugar, vanilla extract, and mango.
3. Sprinkle with almonds and serve.

Calories Per Serving: 201
Fat: 2 g
Cholesterol: 0 mg
Protein: 5 g

Carbohydrates: 41 g
Dietary Fiber: 1 g
Sodium: 39 mg

Royal Melon Rice Salad

A delightful refresher for a sultry day.

YIELD: 6 servings · PREPARATION TIME: 10 minutes ·
COOKING TIME: 18 minutes plus 30 minutes chilling time

4 cups water
2 cups uncooked white rice
2 cups skim milk

1 ripe cantaloupe
5 tablespoons sugar
1 tablespoon ground cinnamon

1. Bring water to a boil in a large pot. Stir in the rice. Return to a boil; reduce heat, cover, and simmer for 10 minutes. Remove from heat; drain rice, rinse it with cold water, and drain again.
2. Bring the milk to a boil in a saucepan. Stir in the partly cooked rice; reduce heat, cover, and simmer until rice is just tender, but still firm to the bite, about 10 minutes. Remove from heat and allow to cool.

3. Cut the cantaloupe in half lengthwise. Scoop out the flesh with a melon baller. Do not discard the rinds.
4. When the rice is cooled, stir in the sugar and cinnamon. Add the melon balls and mix thoroughly.
5. Transfer the rice mixture to the hollowed-out melon rinds and chill in the refrigerator for 30 minutes before serving.

Calories Per Serving: 362
Fat: 1 g
Cholesterol: 1 mg
Protein: 9 g

Carbohydrates: 81 g
Dietary Fiber: 3 g
Sodium: 87 mg

Sweet Citrus Rice Pudding

Lemon and raisins are shown off here.

YIELD: 4 servings ▪ PREPARATION TIME: 5 minutes ▪
COOKING TIME: 20 minutes plus 30 minutes cooling time

2 cups water
1 cup uncooked white rice
¼ cup raisins
⅛ teaspoon ground nutmeg
1 cup skim milk

¼ cup sugar
½ teaspoon vanilla extract
1 teaspoon grated lemon peel
1 teaspoon lemon juice

1. Combine water, rice, raisins, and nutmeg in the upper portion of a double boiler. Cover; cook over boiling water for 20 minutes.
2. Stir in milk and continue to cook, uncovered, until milk is absorbed, about 10 more minutes. Remove from heat, stir in sugar and vanilla, and allow to cool about 30 minutes.
3. Mix in the lemon peel and juice and chill until ready to serve.

Calories Per Serving: 276
Fat: 0 g
Cholesterol: 1 mg
Protein: 6 g

Carbohydrates: 62 g
Dietary Fiber: 1 g
Sodium: 37 mg

RICE WITH SEAFOOD

❖

Kidney Bean and Shrimp Jumble ▪ Mushroom-Shrimp Brown Rice Toss ▪ Saffron, Shrimp, and Rice Pilaf ▪ Shrimp in Vegetable-Wine Sauce ▪ Green Bean–Tuna–Tomato Rice Bowl ▪ Orange Roughy in Chile-Wine Sauce ▪ Salsa Shrimp Salad with Black Beans ▪ Snow Pea–Plum Tomato–Scallop Salad ▪ Red Bell Pepper–Scallop Salad ▪ Molded Parsleyed Rice Salad with Shrimp ▪ Jalapeño-Crab Salad ▪ Watercress-Tuna Salad with Beans and Rice ▪ Tomatoes Stuffed with Curried Rice and Tuna ▪ Great Northern Bean and Tuna Salad ▪ Salmon-Honeydew Salad ▪ Tuna–Vegetable–Wild Rice Salad ▪ Molded Rice Salad with Tuna and Peas ▪ Dilled Brown Rice and Salmon Salad

Kidney Bean and Shrimp Jumble

Fresh shrimp are simmered in a spicy tomato broth with rice and kidney beans.

YIELD: *8 servings* • PREPARATION TIME: *30 minutes* • COOKING TIME: *30 minutes*

1 cup water
1¼ cups nonfat chicken broth
2 teaspoons chili powder
1 teaspoon ground cumin
½ teaspoon paprika
½ teaspoon ground black pepper
3 cloves garlic, minced
1 cup uncooked white rice

1½ cups coarsely chopped fresh or low-sodium canned tomatoes, drained
1 yellow bell pepper, chopped
1 red bell pepper, chopped
¾ pound medium shrimp, shelled and deveined
3 scallions, cut into ½-inch pieces
¼ cup chopped fresh parsley
2½ cups cooked or canned low-sodium kidney beans, rinsed and drained

1. Combine water, chicken broth, chili powder, cumin, paprika, black pepper, and garlic. Bring to a boil.
2. Stir in rice; return to a boil, reduce heat, cover, and simmer for 10 minutes.
3. Stir in tomatoes, yellow bell pepper, and red bell pepper. Simmer for 10 minutes.
4. Add shrimp, scallions, parsley, and beans. Simmer for 10 minutes.

Calories Per Serving: 229
Fat: 2 g
Cholesterol: 65 mg
Protein: 17 g

Carbohydrates: 37 g
Dietary Fiber: 5 g
Sodium: 157 mg

Mushroom-Shrimp Brown Rice Toss

This Louisiana-style dish features fresh mushrooms, shrimp, red bell pepper, and celery in a pungent Creole sauce.

YIELD: *8 servings* • PREPARATION TIME: *30 minutes plus rice and shrimp cooking time* • COOKING TIME: *22 minutes*

¼ cup nonfat chicken broth
1 cup chopped celery
6 scallions, chopped

2½ cups sliced fresh mushrooms
2 cloves garlic, minced
3½ cups pureed tomatoes

1 red bell pepper, seeded, cored, and cut
   into ¼-inch-wide strips
1 bay leaf
⅛ teaspoon hot pepper sauce

1½ pounds cooked medium shrimp,
   peeled and deveined
½ cup chopped fresh parsley
5 cups cooked brown rice (see p. 192)

1. Heat chicken broth in a large skillet over medium heat. Sauté celery, scallions, mushrooms, and garlic for 5 minutes, or until vegetables are just tender.
2. Add tomatoes, red bell pepper, bay leaf, and hot pepper sauce. Bring to a boil, reduce heat, and simmer, stirring occasionally, for 15 minutes.
3. Discard bay leaf. Stir in shrimp and parsley; simmer until all ingredients are warmed through.
4. Toss with warm brown rice.

Calories Per Serving: 258
Fat: 2 g
Cholesterol: 129 mg
Protein: 22 g

Carbohydrates: 37 g
Dietary Fiber: 3 g
Sodium: 484 mg

Saffron, Shrimp, and Rice Pilaf

Aromatic saffron, cayenne pepper, onion, and garlic accent this combination of shrimp and peas.

YIELD: 4 servings • *PREPARATION TIME: 15 minutes* • *COOKING TIME: 27 minutes*

1½ cups nonfat chicken broth
½ cup chopped onion
1 clove garlic, minced
1 cup uncooked white rice
⅛ teaspoon saffron threads

⅛ teaspoon cayenne pepper
½ pound medium shrimp, peeled and
   deveined
1 cup frozen, thawed green peas
1 yellow bell pepper, diced

1. Heat 2 tablespoons chicken broth in a large skillet over medium heat. Add onion and garlic and sauté until lightly browned.
2. Stir in rice and sauté for 2 additional minutes.
3. Combine remaining broth and saffron. Add to the rice and bring to a boil. Reduce heat, cover, and simmer for 10 minutes.
4. Stir in cayenne pepper, shrimp, peas, and yellow bell pepper. Simmer, covered, for 10 minutes, or until shrimp are cooked and peas are tender.

Calories Per Serving: 300
Fat: 3 g
Cholesterol: 87 mg
Protein: 19 g

Carbohydrates: 48 g
Dietary Fiber: 2 g
Sodium: 230 mg

Shrimp in Vegetable-Wine Sauce

Fresh shrimp and corn are served with rice that has been simmered in a wine sauce.

YIELD: 4 servings   •   PREPARATION TIME: 20 minutes   •   COOKING TIME: 20 minutes

1 cup dry white wine
3 scallions, chopped
1½ cups uncooked white rice
1¼ cups water
1 cup fresh, canned, or thawed frozen
   corn kernels

½ pound medium shrimp, peeled and
   deveined
1 teaspoon dried basil
½ teaspoon dried thyme

1. Heat 1 tablespoon wine in a large saucepan over medium heat. Add scallions and sauté for 2 minutes.
2. Stir in the rice and sauté 2 more minutes. Add water and remaining wine. Bring to a boil, stirring. Reduce heat, cover, and simmer for 15 minutes.
3. Stir in the corn, shrimp, basil, and thyme. Cover and simmer until shrimp are cooked through, about 4 minutes.

Calories Per Serving: 415
Fat: 2 g
Cholesterol: 86 mg
Protein: 18 g

Carbohydrates: 70 g
Dietary Fiber: 2 g
Sodium: 99 mg

Green Bean—Tuna—Tomato Rice Bowl

This easy tuna dish is a great dinner-in-a-hurry when you've got green beans in the freezer, tuna in the pantry, and leftover rice.

*YIELD: 4 servings   •   PREPARATION TIME: 15 minutes plus rice cooking time   •
COOKING TIME: 8 minutes*

1½ cups nonfat chicken broth
1 cup chopped onion
⅓ cup water
1½ cups cooked fresh or thawed frozen
   green beans
1½ cups cooked brown rice (see p. 192)

1 teaspoon dried basil
¼ teaspoon ground black pepper
1 13-ounce can solid white water-
   packed tuna, broken into small
   chunks
1 cup chopped fresh plum tomatoes

1. Heat ¼ cup chicken broth in a large skillet over medium heat. Add onion and sauté until it is lightly browned.
2. Stir in remaining chicken broth, water, green beans, rice, basil, and pepper. Return to a boil, reduce heat, cover, and simmer for 3 minutes, or until liquid is mostly absorbed.
3. Stir in tuna and tomatoes. Cover and simmer until all ingredients are heated through, about 1 minute.

Calories Per Serving: 150
Fat: 2 g
Cholesterol: 11 mg
Protein: 18 g

Carbohydrates: 18 g
Dietary Fiber: 1 g
Sodium: 127 mg

Orange Roughy in Chile-Wine Sauce

Serve this delicious fish dish with steamed broccoli and a bowl of mandarin orange slices and pineapple chunks.

YIELD: 4 servings • PREPARATION TIME: 20 minutes plus rice cooking time • COOKING TIME: 30 minutes

¼ cup nonfat chicken broth
1 cup chopped onion
2 cloves garlic, minced
1¾ cups fresh or canned low-sodium
   tomatoes, chopped and drained
½ cup white wine
½ teaspoon dried oregano
½ teaspoon dried basil

¼ teaspoon ground black pepper
¼ teaspoon hot pepper sauce
1 4-ounce can green chiles, drained and
   chopped
1 pound filleted orange roughy, cut into
   4 pieces
2 cups warm cooked brown rice (see p. 192)

1. Heat chicken broth in a large skillet over medium heat. Add onion and garlic and sauté for 4 minutes, or until onion is slightly browned.

2. Stir in tomatoes, wine, oregano, basil, black pepper, hot pepper sauce, and chiles. Reduce heat and simmer for 10 minutes.
3. Add fish to skillet and spoon sauce over fish. Cover skillet and simmer for 10 minutes.
4. Turn fillets and simmer until fish flakes when tested with fork, about 5 additional minutes.
5. Place warm brown rice on a platter. Top with fish and sauce.

Calories Per Serving: 307 | Carbohydrates: 33 g
Fat: 3 g | Dietary Fiber: 2 g
Cholesterol: 77 mg | Sodium: 158 mg
Protein: 32 g

Salsa Shrimp Salad with Black Beans

This simple-to-prepare salad of shrimp, black beans, and rice is accented with salsa and sour cream.

*YIELD: 4 servings ▪ PREPARATION TIME: 10 minutes plus rice cooking time ▪
COOKING TIME: 25 minutes plus cooling time and 30 minutes chilling time*

*4 cups water
½ pound medium shrimp, peeled and deveined
2 cups cooked white rice (see p. 190)*

*2 cups cooked or canned low-sodium black beans, rinsed and drained
¼ cup prepared salsa
2 tablespoons nonfat sour cream*

1. Bring water to a boil in a large saucepan. Add shrimp. Return to a boil, reduce heat, and simmer until shrimp are cooked through, about 3 minutes.
2. Combine shrimp, rice, and beans in a serving bowl. Allow to cool to room temperature.
3. Combine salsa and sour cream and stir into shrimp mixture. Toss gently to combine ingredients.
4. Cover and refrigerate at least 30 minutes before serving.

Calories Per Serving: 304 | Carbohydrates: 50 g
Fat: 1 g | Dietary Fiber: 6 g
Cholesterol: 114 mg | Sodium: 250 mg
Protein: 22 g

Snow Pea–Plum Tomato–Scallop Salad

Petite bay scallops join crisp snow peas, garlic, scallion, dill, rice vinegar, olive oil, and Dijon mustard in this splendid seafood salad. Serve with chilled gazpacho for a great summer lunch.

YIELD: 5 servings • *PREPARATION TIME: 20 minutes plus rice cooking time* • *COOKING TIME: 5 minutes*

1 cup water
1 tablespoon lemon juice
½ pound bay scallops
20 snow peas, ends trimmed
2 cloves garlic, minced
¼ cup chopped scallion
1 teaspoon dried dill

3 tablespoons rice vinegar
2 teaspoons olive oil
1½ teaspoons Dijon mustard
¼ teaspoon ground white pepper
2 cups shredded romaine lettuce
2 cups cooked brown rice (see p. 192)
3 fresh plum tomatoes, sliced

1. Bring ½ cup water and the lemon juice to a boil in a large sauce pan. Add scallops. Return to a boil, reduce heat, and cook until the scallops just turn opaque, about 1 minute. Drain scallops, transfer to a bowl, and set aside.
2. Bring remaining ½ cup of water to a boil in a skillet. Add snow peas; cover and blanch peas for 30 seconds. Drain, rinse, and set aside.
3. Combine the garlic, scallion, dill, rice vinegar, oil, mustard, and white pepper in a food processor or blender and process until smooth.
4. Arrange the lettuce on a serving platter. Mix the rice, snow peas, tomato slices, and scallops and spoon into center of platter. Drizzle with the dressing.

Calories Per Serving: 191
Fat: 3 g
Cholesterol: 15 mg
Protein: 12 g

Carbohydrates: 30 g
Dietary Fiber: 3 g
Sodium: 158 mg

Red Bell Pepper–Scallop Salad

Bay scallops are simmered in white wine and thyme, then tossed with red bell pepper, brown rice, and a lemon-accented dressing.

YIELD: 6 servings • *PREPARATION TIME: 20 minutes plus rice cooking time* • *COOKING TIME: 3 minutes*

1 pound bay scallops
1 cup white wine
1 medium onion, sliced
½ teaspoon ground thyme leaves
about 1 cup water
4 cups cooked brown rice (see p. 192)
1 cup minced fresh parsley or watercress

1 red bell pepper, cored and minced
¼ cup nonfat mayonnaise
¼ cup nonfat sour cream
2 tablespoons lemon juice
¼ teaspoon ground black pepper
6 lemon wedges

1. Combine scallops, wine, onion, thyme, and enough water to cover the scallops in a saucepan. Bring to a boil, reduce heat, and simmer until scallops are just cooked through.
2. Drain liquid.
3. Add scallop-onion mixture to rice. Stir in ¾ cup parsley and red bell pepper.
4. Combine mayonnaise, sour cream, lemon juice, and black pepper in a blender or food processor. Blend until mixture is smooth. Pour the dressing over the scallop-rice mixture.
5. Arrange the lettuce leaves on individual plates and top with the salad. Divide the remaining parsley and the lemon wedges among the plates and serve.

Calories Per Serving: 304
Fat: 1 g
Cholesterol: 30 mg
Protein: 12 g

Carbohydrates: 50 g
Dietary Fiber: 1 g
Sodium: 253 mg

Molded Parsleyed Rice Salad with Shrimp

Shrimp, red bell pepper, parsley, and green peas are combined with rice in this cooling molded salad.

YIELD: 8 servings • PREPARATION TIME: 20 minutes •
COOKING TIME: 35 minutes plus 2 hours chilling time

3½ quarts water
2 cups uncooked arborio or other short-
    grain white rice
1 pound fresh medium shrimp, peeled
    and deveined

1 10-ounce package frozen green peas
1 small red bell pepper, minced
6 tablespoons nonfat Italian dressing
½ cup minced fresh parsley
¼ teaspoon ground black pepper

1. Bring 1 quart of water to a boil in a large saucepan. Stir in rice; return to a boil, reduce heat, and simmer until rice is just tender, about 20 minutes.

Remove from heat, drain excess liquid, and allow rice to cool to room temperature, about 30 minutes.

2. Bring 2 quarts of water to a boil in another large saucepan. Add the shrimp and simmer until shrimp are pink throughout, about 5 minutes. Remove from heat; drain shrimp and allow them to cool.

3. Bring remaining ½ quart water to a boil. Add the peas and simmer until the peas just become tender, about 15 minutes.

4. Combine the cooled rice, shrimp, peas, and red pepper in a large bowl. Add the dressing, ¼ cup of parsley, and black pepper and toss to coat all ingredients.

5. Transfer to a 2-quart mold and refrigerate for 2 hours.

6. Invert the mold onto a serving plate, garnish with remaining parsley, and serve.

Calories Per Serving: 272
Fat: 1 g
Cholesterol: 86 mg
Protein: 17 g

Carbohydrates: 45 g
Dietary Fiber: 1 g
Sodium: 372 mg

Jalapeño-Crab Salad

An array of crabmeat, rice, peppers, corn kernels, scallions, and parsley is tossed with nonfat Italian dressing in this refreshing salad.

YIELD: 6 servings • *PREPARATION TIME: 25 minutes plus rice and corn cooking time and 20 minutes standing time*

2 cups fresh, frozen, or canned corn kernels, cooked
½ green bell pepper, chopped
½ red bell pepper, chopped
1 jalapeño pepper, seeded and minced
2 large ripe tomatoes, chopped

6 scallions, chopped
½ pound fresh crabmeat
1 cup nonfat Italian dressing
¼ cup chopped fresh parsley
2 cups cooked white rice (see p. 190)

1. In a large salad bowl, combine the corn, green bell pepper, red bell pepper, jalapeño, tomatoes, and scallions. Stir in the crabmeat and mix thoroughly.

2. Add the dressing to the salad, stir in the parsley and rice, and allow the salad to stand for 20 minutes before serving.

Calories Per Serving: 172
Fat: 1 g
Cholesterol: 38 mg
Protein: 12 g

Carbohydrates: 30 g
Dietary Fiber: 3 g
Sodium: 186 mg

Watercress-Tuna Salad with Beans and Rice

Black beans, kidney beans, and rice are tossed with tuna, watercress leaves, bell pepper, and scallions. Serve with sliced tomatoes and multigrain baguettes.

YIELD: 6 servings • PREPARATION TIME: 20 minutes plus rice cooking time

2 cups cooked or canned low-sodium
    black beans, rinsed and drained
2 cups cooked or low-sodium kidney
    beans, rinsed and drained
2½ cups chopped green bell pepper
½ cup chopped scallions

1 6½-ounce can water-packed tuna
2 cups cooked white rice (see p. 190)
¼ cup nonfat Italian dressing
4 cups chopped watercress
6 romaine lettuce leaves

1. Combine black beans, kidney beans, green bell pepper, scallions, and tuna in a large bowl.
2. Add rice and dressing and mix thoroughly.
3. Arrange chopped watercress and romaine leaves on individual serving plates. Serve the salad on the greens.

Calories Per Serving: 294
Fat: 2 g
Cholesterol: 6 mg
Protein: 21 g

Carbohydrates: 50 g
Dietary Fiber: 11 g
Sodium: 478 mg

Tomatoes Stuffed with Curried Rice and Tuna

This tuna-rice combination, flavored with lemon juice, curry powder, and parsley, makes a great filling for plump, vine-ripened tomatoes.

YIELD: 5 servings • PREPARATION TIME: 15 minutes plus rice cooking time

4 large ripe tomatoes, cut in half horizontally, pulp removed and reserved
1 6½-ounce can water-packed tuna,
  flaked
1 cup cooked brown rice (see p. 192)

¼ cup nonfat mayonnaise
2 tablespoons chopped fresh parsley
1 teaspoon curry powder
1 teaspoon lemon juice
⅛ teaspoon ground black pepper

1. Chop the tomato pulp. Combine pulp, tuna, rice, mayonnaise, parsley, curry powder, lemon juice, and black pepper.
2. Stuff the tomato shells with the tuna mixture.

Calories Per Serving: 127
Fat: 1 g
Cholesterol: 13 mg
Protein: 12 g

Carbohydrates: 18 g
Dietary Fiber: 1 g
Sodium: 177 mg

Great Northern Bean and Tuna Salad

Albacore tuna and white rice are combined with scallions, beans, celery, and Italian dressing.

YIELD: 6 servings • *PREPARATION TIME: 15 minutes* • *COOKING TIME: 20 minutes*

1 quart water
2 cups uncooked white rice
½ cup chopped scallions
1 6½-ounce can water-packed solid
  white albacore tuna

1 stalk celery, minced
1½ cups canned Great Northern beans,
  rinsed and drained
¼ cup nonfat Italian dressing

1. Bring water to a boil in a large saucepan. Stir in rice. Return to a boil, reduce heat, and simmer until rice is just tender, about 20 minutes. Drain excess liquid and allow rice to cool to room temperature.
2. Combine the rice, scallions, tuna, celery, and beans and toss with the dressing.

Calories Per Serving: 364
Fat: 1 g
Cholesterol: 6 mg
Protein: 17 g

Carbohydrates: 70 g
Dietary Fiber: 1 g
Sodium: 256 mg

Salmon-Honeydew Salad

Fresh salmon and honeydew provide a delicious surprise.

YIELD: 4 servings • PREPARATION TIME: 30 minutes plus rice cooking time •
COOKING TIME: 10 minutes plus 45 minutes cooling time

3 cups water
½ pound fresh salmon fillet
3 scallions, thinly sliced
½ teaspoon dried mint
1 tablespoon honey
4 drops hot pepper sauce

1 small honeydew melon, cubed
3 cups cooked white rice (see p. 190)
2 stalks celery, sliced
½ cup nonfat plain yogurt
2 tablespoons nonfat mayonnaise
3 tablespoons lime juice

1. Bring water to a boil in a large skillet. Add salmon; reduce heat, cover, and cook until salmon flakes with a fork, about 8 minutes. Remove salmon from skillet and allow to cool for 15 minutes. Break into small pieces.
2. Combine 1 scallion, mint, honey, and hot pepper sauce in a large bowl. Stir in the cubed honeydew; cover and refrigerate for 1 hour.
3. Combine the salmon, rice, and celery in a large bowl.
4. In another bowl combine the yogurt, mayonnaise, and lime juice.
5. Combine the yogurt mixture with the salmon and toss gently to coat all ingredients. Stir in the honeydew mixture. Cover and refrigerate for 45 minutes.

Calories Per Serving: 389
Fat: 3 g
Cholesterol: 39 mg
Protein: 22 g

Carbohydrates: 70 g
Dietary Fiber: 4 g
Sodium: 251 mg

Tuna–Vegetable–Wild Rice Salad

Tuna, broccoli, cauliflower, yellow bell pepper, and red bell pepper are combined with wild rice and nonfat Italian dressing.

YIELD: 8 servings • PREPARATION TIME: 25 minutes •
COOKING TIME: 20 minutes plus 30 minutes cooling time

4 cups water
2 cups uncooked wild rice
13 ounces water-packed albacore tuna,
    flaked
½ cup chopped broccoli, steamed until
    just tender

½ cup chopped cauliflower, steamed
    until just tender
¼ cup diced red bell pepper
¼ cup diced yellow bell pepper
¼ cup nonfat Italian dressing

1. Bring water to a boil in a large saucepan. Stir in wild rice; return to a boil, reduce heat, cover, and simmer until rice is just tender, about 25 minutes. Remove from heat, remove cover, and allow rice to cool to room temperature, about 30 minutes.
2. Combine wild rice, tuna, broccoli, cauliflower, and red and yellow bell peppers. Toss gently with Italian dressing.

Calories Per Serving: 220
Fat: 1 g
Cholesterol: 17 mg
Protein: 21 g

Carbohydrates: 32 g
Dietary Fiber: 1 g
Sodium: 372 mg

Molded Rice Salad with Tuna and Peas

Albacore tuna and peas are combined with rice, olives, and nonfat Italian dressing in this molded salad.

YIELD: 6 servings • PREPARATION TIME: 10 minutes plus rice cooking time and 2 hours molding time

2 cups cooked white rice (see p. 190)
1 10-ounce package frozen peas, cooked
    according to package directions
1 6½-ounce can water-packed solid
    white albacore tuna, drained and
    flaked

3 green olives, pitted and minced
½ cup nonfat Italian dressing
¼ teaspoon ground black pepper
olive oil cooking spray
2 hardboiled egg whites, sliced

1. Combine rice and peas in a large bowl. Stir in tuna and olives. Pour dressing over the mixture, add pepper, and toss to coat all ingredients.
2. Spray a 2-quart mold with olive oil cooking spray. Transfer the salad to the mold and refrigerate for 2 hours.
3. Invert mold on serving plate, garnish with the sliced egg whites, and serve.

Calories Per Serving: 326
Fat: 1 g
Cholesterol: 6 mg
Protein: 16 g

Carbohydrates: 60 g
Dietary Fiber: 2 g
Sodium: 573 mg

Dilled Brown Rice and Salmon Salad

Brown rice and flaked broiled salmon are tossed with a lemon-honey-yogurt dressing and served over spinach leaves.

YIELD: 5 servings ▪ *PREPARATION TIME: 15 minutes plus rice and salmon cooking time*

2½ cups cooked brown rice (see p. 192)
1 cup frozen, thawed green peas
1 red bell pepper, chopped
1 green bell pepper, chopped
¼ cup nonfat plain yogurt
¼ cup nonfat mayonnaise
1 scallion, chopped
2 teaspoons dried dill

2 teaspoons Dijon mustard
1 teaspoon honey
1 teaspoon lemon juice
¼ teaspoon ground black pepper
½ pound salmon fillet, broiled
enough spinach leaves to make beds on
   5 serving plates

1. Stir rice into peas and bell peppers.
2. Combine yogurt, mayonnaise, scallion, dill, mustard, honey, lemon juice, and black pepper. Stir into rice and peas.
3. Remove skin from salmon. Flake fish coarsely and fold into the rice-pea mixture. Toss gently to combine all ingredients. Arrange spinach leaves on individual serving plates, top with the salmon salad, and serve.

Calories Per Serving: 232
Fat: 3 g
Cholesterol: 28 mg
Protein: 15 g

Carbohydrates: 34 g
Dietary Fiber: 2 g
Sodium: 244 mg

RICE WITH POULTRY

❖

Paprika-Garlic Chicken over Cilantro Rice ▪ Brown Rice with
Chicken and Capers ▪ Chicken with Zucchini, Salsa, and Brown Rice
▪ Chicken and Rice in Tomato-Vegetable Sauce ▪ Curried Summer
Squash, Chicken, and Rice ▪ Paella ▪ Sherried Saffron Chicken
Cutlets and Bell Peppers ▪ Lima Beans, Chicken, and Rice ▪ Curried
Chicken and Red Bell Pepper with Rice ▪ Chicken–Black Bean Chili
▪ Chili Rice ▪ Chicken, Spinach, and Tomatoes with Rice ▪
Curried Apples and Chicken with Lemon Rice ▪ Pineapple Chicken
and Rice ▪ Brown Rice with Chicken, Cranberries, and Pears ▪
Spiced Wild Rice and Chicken Salad ▪ Pineapple-Chicken Salad ▪
Chicken-Spinach Salad with Wild Rice ▪ Rice Salad with Chicken
and Shrimp ▪ Wild Rice–White Rice–Smoked Turkey Salad ▪
Chicken and Broccoli Salad with Yogurt Dressing ▪ Broiled Lime
Chicken–Rice Salad ▪ Tomatoes Stuffed with Chicken-Rice Salad ▪
Molded Chicken-Rice Salad ▪ Spicy Chicken and Brown Rice

Paprika-Garlic Chicken over Cilantro Rice

Chicken cutlets are spiced with paprika, baked with olives, and served over rice flavored with cilantro.

YIELD: 6 servings • PREPARATION TIME: 15 minutes, plus rice cooking time • COOKING TIME: 50 minutes

1 tablespoon paprika	¼ cup lemon juice
2 cloves garlic, minced	8 pitted black olives, quartered
6 skinless chicken breast cutlets, about 4 ounces each	6 cups water
⅓ cup all-purpose flour	3 cups uncooked white rice
½ cup nonfat chicken broth	1 teaspoon dried cilantro
	1 tablespoon minced lemon peel

1. Preheat oven to 350 degrees.
2. Combine paprika and garlic and rub over all surfaces of chicken. Dredge chicken in flour.
3. Arrange chicken in nonstick 9-inch-by-13-inch baking dish. Mix broth and lemon juice and pour over chicken. Sprinkle olives over chicken.
4. Bake, basting chicken with the broth several times, until chicken is done through, about 50 minutes.
5. Bring water to a boil in a large saucepan. Stir in rice; bring to a boil, reduce heat, cover, and simmer until rice is tender, about 20 minutes.
6. Combine cilantro, lemon peel, and hot rice.
7. Divide the rice mixture among individual serving plates, top each with a chicken cutlet, and serve.

Calories Per Serving: 370	Carbohydrates: 62 g
Fat: 3 g	Dietary Fiber: 0 g
Cholesterol: 55 mg	Sodium: 104 mg
Protein: 24 g	

Brown Rice with Chicken and Capers

Chicken breast strips are prepared with scallions, garlic, brown rice, lemon peel, lemon juice, and capers.

YIELD: 6 servings • PREPARATION TIME: 20 minutes plus rice cooking time • COOKING TIME: 10 minutes

1 cup nonfat chicken broth
6 scallions, chopped
2 cloves garlic, minced
1½ pounds skinless chicken breast cutlets, cut into ¼-inch-wide strips 3 inches long

3 cups cooked brown rice (see p. 192)
2 teaspoons minced lemon peel
⅓ cup lemon juice
1 tablespoon capers, rinsed and drained
¼ teaspoon ground black pepper
3 tablespoons chopped fresh parsley

1. Heat broth in a large skillet; add scallions and garlic. Cook until scallions are just tender, about 3 minutes.
2. Stir in chicken and cook 3 additional minutes.
3. Add rice, lemon peel, lemon juice, capers, and black pepper. Continue cooking until chicken is done through, about 4 minutes. Stir in parsley and serve.

Calories Per Serving: 201
Fat: 2 g
Cholesterol: 55 mg
Protein: 21 g

Carbohydrates: 25 g
Dietary Fiber: 2 g
Sodium: 94 mg

Chicken with Zucchini, Salsa, and Brown Rice

Brown rice is combined with chicken strips, zucchini, corn, chili powder, olives, salsa, and cheddar cheese.

YIELD: 6 servings · PREPARATION TIME: 20 minutes plus rice cooking time ·
COOKING TIME: 15 minutes

1½ pounds skinless chicken breast cutlets, cut into ½-inch strips
2 cloves garlic
1 teaspoon chili powder
¼ cup nonfat chicken broth
2 cups chopped zucchini

2 cups cooked brown rice (see p. 192)
1 cup fresh, canned, or thawed frozen corn kernels
1 cup shredded nonfat cheddar
1 cup commercially prepared salsa
8 pitted black olives, quartered

1. Rub the chicken cutlets with the garlic cloves. Sprinkle the chili powder on the chicken.
2. Heat 2 tablespoons of the chicken broth in a large skillet. Sauté garlic for 1 minute. Add the chicken cutlets and sauté until cooked through and lightly brown. Remove from skillet.

3. Heat the remaining 2 tablespoons broth in the skillet. Add zucchini and sauté until just tender, about 2 minutes. Add rice and corn and continue to cook, stirring several times, until all ingredients are heated through.
4. Place salsa in small saucepan and warm through.
5. Transfer rice mixture to a large serving platter. Cover rice with chicken strips, cheddar cheese, salsa, and olives.

Calories Per Serving: 232
Fat: 2 g
Cholesterol: 59 mg
Protein: 27 g

Carbohydrates: 27 g
Dietary Fiber: 2 g
Sodium: 506 mg

Chicken and Rice in Tomato-Vegetable Sauce

Rice and chicken in a variation of the traditional favorite.

YIELD: *4 servings* • PREPARATION TIME: *20 minutes* • COOKING TIME: *45 minutes*

2¼ cups nonfat chicken broth
4 4-ounce skinless chicken breast cutlets
1 cup uncooked white rice
1 small onion, chopped

1 yellow bell pepper, chopped
1 cup low-sodium tomato juice
1¼ cups fresh or frozen, thawed green peas

1. Heat ¼ cup broth in a large skillet. Add chicken and sauté until it begins to brown. Remove chicken and add rice, onion, and yellow bell pepper. Sauté for 5 minutes.
2. Stir in remaining broth and tomato juice. Bring to a boil; reduce heat, add chicken, cover, and simmer until rice is almost tender and chicken almost cooked through.
3. Add peas. Return to a boil; reduce heat, cover, and simmer until chicken is done and peas are hot, about 10 minutes.

Calories Per Serving: 419
Fat: 2 g
Cholesterol: 75 mg
Protein: 41 g

Carbohydrates: 62 g
Dietary Fiber: 8 g
Sodium: 367 mg

Curried Summer Squash, Chicken, and Rice

Chicken breast cutlets, yellow summer squash, and zucchini are prepared with curry powder, ginger, and scallions, then served over rice.

YIELD: 4 servings   •   PREPARATION TIME: 20 minutes   •
COOKING TIME: 30 minutes plus 5 minutes standing time

2¼ cups nonfat chicken broth
1¼ cups uncooked white rice
2 teaspoons curry powder
1 teaspoon ground ginger
4 skinless chicken breast cutlets, about 4
   ounces each

½ teaspoon ground black pepper
2 scallions, chopped
2 cups chopped yellow summer squash
2 cups chopped zucchini

1. Bring 1½ cups broth to a boil in a large saucepan. Stir in rice; return to a boil, reduce heat, cover, and simmer until rice is just tender, about 20 minutes. Remove from heat and allow to stand.
2. Combine 1 teaspoon curry powder and ½ teaspoon ginger. Rub into chicken.
3. Heat ½ cup broth in a large skillet. Add chicken and sauté until brown on all sides, about 6 minutes. Stir in remaining 1 teaspoon curry powder and ½ teaspoon ginger, black pepper, and scallions, and sauté for 1 minute.
4. Add squash, zucchini, and remaining ¼ cup broth. Bring to a boil; remove from heat, cover, and allow to stand for 5 minutes.
5. Serve over rice.

Calories Per Serving: 419
Fat: 2 g
Cholesterol: 75 mg
Protein: 36 g

Carbohydrates: 68 g
Dietary Fiber: 3 g
Sodium: 200 mg

Paella

This classic dish is made with onion, garlic, thyme, turmeric, tomatoes, green peas, rice, and shrimp.

YIELD: 6 servings   •   PREPARATION TIME: 30 minutes   •   COOKING TIME: 30 minutes

5 cups nonfat chicken broth
1½ cups chopped onion
3 cloves garlic, minced
½ teaspoon dried thyme
¼ teaspoon ground turmeric
2 cups water
3 cups uncooked white rice

2 cups canned low-sodium tomatoes, chopped
2 cups frozen, thawed green peas
1 pound skinless chicken breast cutlets, cut into 1-inch cubes
½ pound medium shrimp, peeled and deveined

1. Heat ¼ cup chicken broth in a large pot. Add onion, garlic, thyme, and turmeric. Sauté until onion is lightly golden, about 4 minutes.
2. Add remaining broth and water and bring to a boil. Stir in rice; return to a boil, reduce heat, cover, and simmer for 15 minutes, or until rice is almost tender.
3. Stir in tomatoes, green peas, chicken, and shrimp. Cover and cook, stirring occasionally, until chicken and shrimp are done through, about 10 minutes.

Calories Per Serving: 517
Fat: 3 g
Cholesterol: 93 mg
Protein: 34 g

Carbohydrates: 90 g
Dietary Fiber: 5 g
Sodium: 630 mg

Sherried Saffron Chicken Cutlets and Bell Peppers

Marinated chicken breast chunks are baked with onion, rice, bay leaf, saffron, and tomatoes.

YIELD: 6 servings　•　PREPARATION TIME: 20 minutes　•
COOKING TIME: 35 minutes plus 30 minutes marinating time

1½ pounds skinless chicken breast cut-lets, cut into 1-inch cubes
¾ cup orange juice
3 cloves garlic, minced
4½ cups nonfat chicken broth
1 medium onion, chopped
1 yellow bell pepper, chopped
2 green bell peppers, chopped

1 red bell pepper, chopped
1½ cups uncooked white rice
1 bay leaf
⅛ teaspoon saffron threads
2 cups low-sodium canned tomatoes, chopped
3 tablespoons sherry

1. Arrange the chicken cutlets in a glass baking dish. (Do not use metal, or the orange juice and chicken will pick up a metallic taste.) Combine ½ cup orange juice with the garlic and pour over the chicken. Allow to marinate for 30 minutes. Drain chicken and discard the orange juice.
2. Preheat oven to 350 degrees.
3. Heat ½ cup broth in a large, ovenproof casserole. Add onion and yellow, green, and red bell peppers and sauté until onion is lightly golden, about 4 minutes. Add chicken and brown on all sides, about 4 minutes. Add more broth as necessary.
4. Add remaining chicken broth. Stir in the rice, bay leaf, saffron, tomatoes, and remaining ¼ cup orange juice. Bring to a boil, reduce heat, and simmer for 5 minutes.
5. Transfer casserole to oven and bake, covered, for 30 minutes.
6. Sprinkle with sherry and serve.

Calories Per Serving: 366   Carbohydrates: 55 g
Fat: 3 g   Dietary Fiber: 4 g
Cholesterol: 55 mg   Sodium: 544 mg
Protein: 31 g

Lima Beans, Chicken, and Rice

Lima beans are simmered with chicken breast cutlets, tomatoes, white rice, and thyme.

YIELD: 6 servings • *PREPARATION TIME: 15 minutes* • *COOKING TIME: 50 minutes*

4¼ cups chicken broth
6 skinless chicken breast cutlets, about 4
    ounces each
1 teaspoon dried thyme
1½ cups uncooked white rice

1 cup canned low-sodium tomatoes,
    chopped and drained
1 10-ounce package frozen lima beans,
    thawed
12 pitted green olives

1. Heat ¼ cup chicken broth in a large skillet. Add chicken cutlets and brown on all sides, about 10 minutes.
2. Add remaining broth and bring to a boil. Stir in thyme, rice, tomatoes, and lima beans. Return to a boil; reduce heat, cover, and simmer for 25 minutes.
3. Transfer to a serving bowl, top with the olives, and serve.

Calories Per Serving: 343
Fat: 3 g
Cholesterol: 55 mg
Protein: 28 g

Carbohydrates: 52 g
Dietary Fiber: 4 g
Sodium: 354 mg

Curried Chicken and Red Bell Pepper
with Rice

Chicken cutlets are baked with wild rice, curry powder, paprika, mushrooms, onions, and red bell pepper.

YIELD: 6 servings ▪ *PREPARATION TIME: 20 minutes* ▪ *COOKING TIME: 55 minutes*

2 cups nonfat chicken broth
1 teaspoon curry powder
½ teaspoon paprika
1 cup uncooked wild rice
½ pound fresh white mushrooms, sliced

1 red bell pepper, chopped
2 cups chopped onions
6 skinless chicken breast cutlets, about 4
    ounces each

1. Preheat oven to 350 degrees.
2. Combine broth, curry powder, and paprika in a shallow baking pan.
3. Stir in wild rice, mushrooms, red bell pepper, and onions. Arrange chicken cutlets in the pan. Cover with foil and bake until chicken is cooked through, about 50 minutes.

Calories Per Serving: 303
Fat: 3 g
Cholesterol: 57 mg
Protein: 31 g

Carbohydrates: 42 g
Dietary Fiber: 3 g
Sodium: 229 mg

Chicken—Black Bean Chili

A chili variation with chicken, black beans, red bell pepper, onion, and carrots.

YIELD: 4 servings ▪ *PREPARATION TIME: 15 minutes plus rice cooking time* ▪
COOKING TIME: 24 minutes

¼ cup nonfat chicken broth

2 skinless chicken breast cutlets, about 4 ounces each, minced or ground

1⅓ cups canned black beans, rinsed and drained

½ cup diced red bell pepper

½ cup diced onion

½ cup diced carrots

2 teaspoons chili powder

1 clove garlic, minced

1 bay leaf

¼ teaspoon cayenne pepper

1½ cups low-sodium tomato juice

1⅓ cups hot cooked white rice (see p. 190)

1. Heat broth in a large saucepan. Add chicken and sauté until it is no longer pink, about 3 minutes. Stir in beans, red bell pepper, onion, carrots, chili powder, garlic, bay leaf, cayenne pepper, and tomato juice. Bring to a boil, reduce heat, and simmer for 20 minutes.
2. Remove from heat and discard bay leaf. Serve chili over rice.

Calories Per Serving: 212
Fat: 1 g
Cholesterol: 28 mg
Protein: 17 g

Carbohydrates: 34 g
Dietary Fiber: 7 g
Sodium: 268 mg

Chili Rice

This simple dish includes ground turkey, rice, onion, and red bell pepper in a chili-tomato sauce.

YIELD: *6 servings* • PREPARATION TIME: *10 minutes* • COOKING TIME: *24 minutes*

¼ cup nonfat chicken broth

¾ pound ground turkey breast

1 cup chopped onion

½ cup diced red bell pepper

2 cups uncooked white rice

1 teaspoon chili powder

½ teaspoon ground cumin

½ teaspoon ground black pepper

1 cup low-sodium tomato sauce

1½ cups water

1. Heat broth in a large skillet. Add turkey, onion, and red bell pepper. Sauté until turkey is browned, about 4 minutes.
2. Stir in rice, chili powder, cumin, black pepper, tomato sauce, and water. Bring to a boil. Reduce heat, cover, and simmer until rice is tender, about 20 minutes. Serve immediately.

Calories Per Serving: 318
Fat: 1 g
Cholesterol: 37 mg
Protein: 18 g

Carbohydrates: 58 g
Dietary Fiber: 2 g
Sodium: 54 mg

Chicken, Spinach, and Tomatoes with Rice

Chicken cutlets are sautéed with onion and garlic and simmered with spinach and tomato.

YIELD: 4 servings • *PREPARATION TIME: 20 minutes* • *COOKING TIME: 30 minutes*

2¼ cups nonfat chicken broth
1 small onion, cut into thin slices
2 cloves garlic, minced
4 skinless chicken breast cutlets, about 4
*   ounces each*

1 10-ounce package frozen chopped
*   spinach, thawed*
1 cup uncooked white rice
½ teaspoon ground black pepper
1 cup fresh or low-sodium canned toma-
*   toes, chopped and drained*

1. Heat 2 tablespoons broth in a large saucepan. Add onion and garlic and sauté until onion is translucent, about 3 minutes.
2. Move onion to one side of pan. Add 2 tablespoons broth and chicken cutlets and sauté until chicken is no longer pink, about 3 minutes.
3. Add spinach, rice, remaining 2 cups broth, and black pepper. Bring to a boil, reduce heat, cover, and simmer for 10 minutes.
4. Stir in tomatoes, cover, and simmer until rice is tender and chicken is cooked through, about 12 minutes.

Calories Per Serving: 315
Fat: 3 g
Cholesterol: 55 mg
Protein: 26 g

Carbohydrates: 48 g
Dietary Fiber: 3 g
Sodium: 403 mg

Curried Apples and Chicken with Lemon Rice

Chicken chunks, apple, and onion are simmered with garlic and curry powder and served over rice flavored with lemon peel, currants, and parsley.

YIELD: 4 servings ▪ *PREPARATION TIME: 25 minutes plus rice cooking time* ▪
COOKING TIME: 15 minutes

1½ cups nonfat chicken broth
1 pound skinless chicken breast cutlets,
   cut into 1-inch cubes
⅛ teaspoon cayenne pepper
1 apple, cored and chopped
1 small onion, chopped
1 clove garlic, minced

2 teaspoons curry powder
2 tablespoons minced lemon peel
¼ cup currants
3 tablespoons chopped fresh parsley
4 cups hot cooked white rice (see p.
   190)

1. Heat 2 tablespoons broth in a large skillet. Stir in chicken, add cayenne pepper, and sauté until chicken is no longer pink, about 7 minutes. Remove chicken from skillet and set aside.
2. Heat another 2 tablespoons broth in skillet. Add apple, onion, garlic, curry powder, and 2 teaspoons lemon peel. Sauté for 6 minutes.
3. Stir in remaining broth and add chicken. Bring to a boil, stirring constantly.
4. Toss parsley, currants, and remaining lemon peel with the hot rice. Divide rice among 4 serving plates, top each with chicken-apple mixture, and serve.

Calories Per Serving: 408
Fat: 2 g
Cholesterol: 55 mg
Protein: 25 g

Carbohydrates: 74 g
Dietary Fiber: 2 g
Sodium: 135 mg

Pineapple Chicken and Rice

Rice is simmered in pineapple juice and served with sautéed chicken, pineapple chunks, scallions, garlic, and ginger.

YIELD: 6 servings ▪ *PREPARATION TIME: 20 minutes plus rice cooking time* ▪
COOKING TIME: 10 minutes

1 cup water
2 cups pineapple juice
1½ cups uncooked white rice
1 cup nonfat chicken broth
3 skinless chicken breast cutlets, about 4
  ounces each, cut into ½-inch cubes
2½ cups water-packed or juice-packed
  pineapple chunks, drained, with 4
  tablespoons liquid reserved

¼ cup raisins
3 scallions, chopped
½ teaspoon ground ginger
1 clove garlic, minced
2 tablespoons low-sodium soy sauce

1. Bring water and pineapple juice to a boil in a saucepan. Stir in rice; bring to a boil, reduce heat, cover, and simmer until rice is tender, about 20 minutes.
2. Heat broth in a skillet over medium heat. Add chicken and simmer until it is cooked through, about 12 minutes. Remove chicken from skillet. Discard broth.
3. Heat 2 tablespoons pineapple liquid in the skillet. Stir in raisins, scallions, ginger, and garlic. Sauté for 3 minutes.
4. Add pineapple, chicken, soy sauce, and remaining pineapple liquid. Continue to cook until all ingredients are heated through.
5. Serve over pineapple rice.

Calories Per Serving: 235
Fat: 1 g
Cholesterol: 28 mg
Protein: 13 g

Carbohydrates: 46 g
Dietary Fiber: 1 g
Sodium: 197 mg

Brown Rice with Chicken, Cranberries, and Pears

Brown rice and chicken cutlets are baked with dried cranberries and pears.

YIELD: 4 servings • PREPARATION TIME: 25 minutes • COOKING TIME: 70 minutes

2 cups unsweetened apple juice
1 cup water
1 cup uncooked brown rice
2 pears, cored and cut into chunks

1 pound skinless chicken breast cutlets,
  cut into 1-inch cubes
½ cup dried cranberries
2 teaspoons sugar
½ teaspoon ground cinnamon

1. Bring apple juice and water to a boil in a saucepan. Stir in rice; return to a boil, reduce heat, cover, and simmer until rice is tender, about 25 minutes. Remove from heat and drain.
2. Preheat oven to 450 degrees.
3. Arrange pear chunks in a single layer on a nonstick baking sheet and bake until tender, about 10 minutes.
4. Mix together rice, chicken, cranberries, sugar, cinnamon, and baked pear chunks. Transfer to an 11-by-7-by-2-inch nonstick baking dish.
5. Reduce oven temperature to 350 degrees. Cover chicken–rice mixture with foil and bake for 30 minutes, or until chicken is done.

Calories Per Serving: 350
Fat: 2 g
Cholesterol: 55 mg
Protein: 25 g

Carbohydrates: 62 g
Dietary Fiber: 3 g
Sodium: 45 mg

Spiced Wild Rice and Chicken Salad

Wild rice is seasoned with onion, green bell pepper, garlic, curry powder, cayenne, and cilantro, and served with chicken and a lemon-yogurt dressing.

YIELD: 4 servings • *PREPARATION TIME: 20 minutes plus chicken cooking time* • *COOKING TIME: 55 minutes plus 2 hours chilling time*

3 cups water
½ cup uncooked wild rice
½ cup uncooked brown rice
¼ cup nonfat chicken broth
1 small onion, chopped
1 green bell pepper, chopped
1 clove garlic, minced
1½ teaspoons curry powder

1 teaspoon cayenne pepper
¾ pound skinless chicken breast cutlets, cooked and cubed
1 teaspoon dried cilantro
½ cup nonfat plain yogurt
2 tablespoons lemon juice
3 tablespoons minced lemon peel

1. Bring water to a boil in a large saucepan. Stir in wild rice and brown rice. Return to a boil; reduce heat, cover, and simmer until rice is tender, about 25 minutes.
2. Remove from heat, drain excess liquid, and allow to stand for 10 minutes.
3. Heat chicken broth in a large, heavy pot over medium heat. Add onion, green bell pepper, garlic, curry powder, and cayenne pepper. Sauté for 2 minutes.

4. Remove pot from heat and stir in chicken and cilantro.
5. Combine chicken mixture and rice.
6. Whisk together yogurt, lemon juice, and lemon peel. Stir into the chicken-rice mixture.
7. Chill for at least 2 hours before serving.

Calories Per Serving: 294   Carbohydrates: 43 g
Fat: 3 g   Dietary Fiber: 4 g
Cholesterol: 57 mg   Sodium: 68 mg
Protein: 27 g

Pineapple-Chicken Salad

Pineapple and tomato chunks, green bell pepper, and celery are tossed with diced chicken breast, brown rice, and a curried mayonnaise dressing.

YIELD: 6 servings ▪ PREPARATION TIME: 20 minutes plus rice cooking time and 1½ hours chilling time

3 cups cooked brown rice (see p. 192)   2 cups water-packed pineapple chunks
3 skinless chicken breast cutlets, cooked   2 large ripe tomatoes, cut into chunks
   and diced   1 cup nonfat mayonnaise
1 cup celery, sliced   ¾ teaspoon curry powder
1 green bell pepper, seeded and chopped   ¼ teaspoon ground ginger

1. Combine rice, chicken, celery, green bell pepper, pineapple, and tomatoes.
2. Whisk together mayonnaise, curry powder, and ginger.
3. Pour dressing over rice mixture and stir to coat all ingredients. Chill for 1½ hours or until ready to serve.

Calories Per Serving: 235   Carbohydrates: 45 g
Fat: 1 g   Dietary Fiber: 2 g
Cholesterol: 28 mg   Sodium: 547 mg
Protein: 12 g

Chicken-Spinach Salad with Wild Rice

Chicken, fresh spinach, and wild rice are a stellar trio when combined in this simple salad.

YIELD: 4 servings • *PREPARATION TIME: 15 minutes plus rice cooking time*

2 cups water
4 skinless chicken breast cutlets, about 4
   ounces each
2 cups cooked wild rice (see p. 192)

2 cups fresh spinach torn into small
   pieces
3 scallions, thinly sliced
½ cup nonfat Italian dressing

1. Bring water to a boil in a large skillet. Add chicken cutlets; reduce heat, cover, and simmer until they are cooked through, about 12 minutes. Remove from heat; drain chicken and chop it into bite-size pieces.
2. Combine rice, spinach, and scallions.
3. Combine chicken and rice-spinach mixture; add dressing and toss to coat all ingredients.

Calories Per Serving: 187
Fat: 1 g
Cholesterol: 55 mg
Protein: 22 g

Carbohydrates: 21 g
Dietary Fiber: 2 g
Sodium: 612 mg

Rice Salad with Chicken and Shrimp

Chicken chunks, saffron-flavored white rice, shrimp, scallion, peas, artichoke hearts, and green bell pepper are tossed with Italian dressing.

YIELD: 6 servings • *PREPARATION TIME: 25 minutes plus green pea cooking time* •
COOKING TIME: 25 minutes plus rice, chicken, and shrimp cooling time

7 cups water
1 cup uncooked white rice
¼ teaspoon powdered saffron
1 pound skinless chicken breast cutlets
1 cup raw, unpeeled medium shrimp
1 cup canned artichoke hearts, drained
   and diced

½ cup frozen green peas, cooked according to package directions
1 scallion, thinly sliced
2 tablespoons chopped green bell pepper
1 tablespoon minced fresh parsley
½ cup nonfat Italian dressing
1 clove garlic, minced
¼ cup lemon juice

1. Bring 2 cups water to a boil in a large saucepan. Stir in rice and saffron. Return to a boil; reduce heat, cover, and simmer until rice is just tender, about 20 minutes. Remove from heat, drain, and cool.
2. Bring another 2 cups water to a boil in a large skillet. Add chicken; reduce heat, cover, and simmer until it is cooked through, about 15 minutes. Allow to cool; cut into ½-inch cubes.
3. Bring remaining 3 cups water to a boil in a saucepan. Add shrimp and cook until they are pink throughout, about three minutes. Allow shrimp to cool; then peel and devein them.
4. Combine cooled rice, chicken, shrimp, artichoke hearts, peas, scallion, green bell pepper, and parsley in a large bowl.
5. Whisk together the Italian dressing, the minced garlic, and the lemon juice. Drizzle over the rice-chicken mixture and toss to combine.

Calories Per Serving: 241
Fat: 1 g
Cholesterol: 80 mg
Protein: 22 g

Carbohydrates: 34 g
Dietary Fiber: 3 g
Sodium: 596 mg

Wild Rice–White Rice–Smoked Turkey Salad

Two kinds of rice, smoked turkey, celery, apples, and scallions are combined in this tasty salad.

YIELD: 4 servings • *PREPARATION TIME: 25 minutes* • *COOKING TIME: 50 minutes*

3 cups water
¾ cup uncooked wild rice
½ cup uncooked white rice
½ pound smoked turkey breast, diced

2 apples, cored and diced
5 scallions, thinly sliced
1 stalk celery, diced
¾ cup nonfat Italian dressing

1. Bring 2 cups of water to a boil in a large saucepan. Stir in wild rice; return to a boil, reduce heat, cover, and simmer until rice is just tender, about 25 minutes.
2. Meanwhile, bring remaining water to a boil in another saucepan. Stir in white rice; return to a boil, reduce heat, cover, and simmer until rice is just tender, about 20 minutes.
3. Rinse both rices with cold water and drain.
4. Combine rices, turkey, apples, scallions, and celery.
5. Toss dressing with rice mixture.

Calories Per Serving: 378
Fat: 1 g
Cholesterol: 23 mg
Protein: 19 g

Carbohydrates: 75 g
Dietary Fiber: 3 g
Sodium: 601 mg

Chicken and Broccoli Salad with Yogurt Dressing

Chicken slices, steamed broccoli, carrots, and rice are tossed with a cucumber-yogurt dressing.

YIELD: *4 servings* • PREPARATION TIME: *25 minutes* • COOKING TIME: *45 minutes plus chicken cooling time*

4 cups nonfat chicken broth
1 cup uncooked brown rice
4 cups water
3 skinless chicken breast cutlets, about 4 ounces each
2 cups broccoli florets

2 carrots, cut diagonally into ¼-inch slices
2 scallions, cut diagonally into ½-inch pieces
1 cucumber, finely chopped
¾ cup nonfat plain yogurt
2 tablespoons chopped fresh parsley

1. Bring 2 cups chicken broth to a boil in a saucepan. Add rice. Return to a boil; reduce heat, cover, and simmer until rice is just tender, about 25 minutes.
2. Bring water to a boil in a large skillet. Add chicken; cover, reduce heat, and simmer until it is cooked through, about 12 minutes. Remove from heat and allow to cool to room temperature, about 30 minutes.
3. Bring remaining 2 cups chicken broth to a boil in a saucepan. Add broccoli and carrots; reduce heat, cover, and simmer for 5 minutes. Transfer vegetables to a bowl.
4. Cut cooled chicken into diagonal slices about ¼ inch thick. Mix with rice, broccoli, carrots, and scallions.
5. Combine cucumber, yogurt, and parsley and add to the chicken mixture. Toss gently to coat all ingredients and serve.

Calories Per Serving: 253
Fat: 3 g
Cholesterol: 34 mg
Protein: 21 g

Carbohydrates: 39 g
Dietary Fiber: 3 g
Sodium: 344 mg

Broiled Lime Chicken—Rice Salad

Chicken is marinated in jalapeño pepper and lime juice, then tossed with rice, cilantro, and mint.

YIELD: 4 servings • PREPARATION TIME: 20 minutes plus rice cooking time and 1 hour marinating time • COOKING TIME: 8 minutes

2 jalapeño peppers, seeded and minced
2 cloves garlic, minced
½ teaspoon minced lime peel
5 tablespoons lime juice
2 skinless chicken breast cutlets, about 4 ounces each
2 cups cooked white rice (see p. 190)

1 tablespoon chopped fresh parsley
1 teaspoon dried cilantro
1 teaspoon dried mint
2 teaspoons olive oil
¼ teaspoon ground black pepper
2 tablespoons minced fresh parsley

1. Combine one jalapeño pepper, garlic, lime peel, and 4 tablespoons lime juice in a bowl. Add the chicken cutlets and marinate in the refrigerator for 1 hour, turning several times.
2. Preheat broiler.
3. Broil marinated chicken, 5 minutes on each side. Cool sufficiently to handle; then cut into half-inch pieces.
4. Combine the rice, parsley, cilantro, mint, and remaining jalapeño pepper in a large bowl and add the chicken.
5. Toss the remaining tablespoon of lime juice, the olive oil, and the black pepper with the chicken-rice mixture. Sprinkle with minced parsley.

Calories Per Serving: 194
Fat: 3 g
Cholesterol: 28 mg
Protein: 11 g

Carbohydrates: 30 g
Dietary Fiber: 0 g
Sodium: 227 mg

Tomatoes Stuffed with Chicken-Rice Salad

Chicken, rice, celery, olives, cilantro, parsley, and capers are used as a stuffing for large, fresh tomatoes.

YIELD: 6 servings • PREPARATION TIME: 40 minutes •
COOKING TIME: 35 minutes plus rice and chicken cooling time and 1 hour chilling time

6 cups water
1¼ cups uncooked white rice
½ pound skinless chicken breast cutlets
2 celery stalks, diced
¾ cup pitted green olives, sliced
1 teaspoon dried basil

1 teaspoon dried cilantro
1 tablespoon chopped fresh parsley
2 teaspoons capers
½ cup nonfat Italian dressing
¼ teaspoon ground black pepper
6 large ripe tomatoes

1. Bring 3 cups of water to a boil in a saucepan. Stir in rice; return to boil, reduce heat, cover, and simmer until rice is just tender, about 20 minutes. Drain excess liquid, rinse with cold water, and drain well. Allow rice to cool to room temperature.
2. Bring remaining 3 cups water to a boil in a large skillet. Add chicken cutlets and simmer until they are cooked through, about 15 minutes. Remove from heat and cool to room temperature. Cut chicken into half-inch cubes.
3. Combine rice, chicken, celery, olives, basil, cilantro, parsley, and capers in a large bowl.
4. Toss the dressing with the salad; add black pepper. Refrigerate for 1 hour.
5. Halve tomatoes. Scoop out seeds; place the halves cut side down and allow them to drain.
6. Turn the tomatoes onto a large serving platter, fill each with the salad mixture, and serve.

Calories Per Serving: 221
Fat: 3 g
Cholesterol: 18 mg
Protein: 10 g

Carbohydrates: 38 g
Dietary Fiber: 3 g
Sodium: 710 mg

Molded Chicken-Rice Salad

Chicken cubes, rice, peas, olives, and basil are the ingredients in this easy-to-assemble molded salad.

YIELD: *4 servings* ▪ PREPARATION TIME: *15 minutes* ▪
COOKING TIME: *45 minutes plus cooling time and 1 hour molding time*

9 cups water
2 cups uncooked white rice
1 10-ounce package frozen peas
¾ pound skinless chicken breast cutlets
4 black olives, pitted

1 teaspoon dried basil
7 tablespoons nonfat Italian dressing
4 hardboiled egg whites, sliced, for garnish

1. Bring 4 cups water to a boil in a large saucepan. Stir in rice; return to a boil, reduce heat, cover, and simmer until rice is just tender, about 20 minutes. Remove from heat, rinse rice in cold water, and drain.
2. Bring 2 cups water to a boil. Stir in peas and simmer until just tender, about 10 minutes. Drain.
3. Bring remaining 3 cups water to a boil in a large skillet. Add chicken cutlets, reduce heat, cover, and cook until they are cooked through, about 15 minutes. Remove from heat, allow to cool, and cut into 1-inch cubes.
4. Combine the cooled rice and peas. Add the chicken, olives, and basil.
5. Toss the chicken-rice mixture with Italian dressing, then transfer the salad to a 2-quart mold and refrigerate for at least 1 hour.
6. Turn the mold onto a serving plate and garnish with egg slices.

Calories Per Serving: 509
Fat: 2 g
Cholesterol: 41 mg
Protein: 28 g

Carbohydrates: 90 g
Dietary Fiber: 3 g
Sodium: 700 mg

Spicy Chicken and Brown Rice

Chicken breasts are coated with spices, seasoned with lemon juice, baked, and served over brown rice. Serve with steamed broccoli and orange slices.

YIELD: 6 servings • *PREPARATION TIME: 20 minutes plus rice cooking time* • *COOKING TIME: 45 minutes*

1 tablespoon paprika
2 teaspoons ground cumin
½ teaspoon ground turmeric
½ teaspoon ground ginger
1 large clove garlic, minced
6 skinless chicken breast cutlets, about 4 ounces each

⅓ cup unbleached all-purpose flour
½ cup nonfat chicken broth
¼ cup lemon juice
¼ cup chopped fresh parsley
1 tablespoon grated lemon peel
6 cups hot, cooked brown rice (see p. 192)

1. Preheat oven to 350 degrees. Combine paprika, cumin, turmeric, ginger, and garlic in a shallow bowl. Rub chicken pieces in spices.
2. Spread flour in another shallow bowl. Rub spice-coated chicken pieces in flour.
3. Place chicken in a baking dish.
4. Combine chicken broth and lemon juice. Pour over chicken.

5. Bake for 45 minutes, or until chicken is done.
6. Mix parsley and lemon peel into rice.
7. Spoon rice onto a large serving platter and serve with chicken on top.

Calories Per Serving: 336
Fat: 3 g
Cholesterol: 55 mg
Protein: 24 g

Carbohydrates: 54 g
Dietary Fiber: 4 g
Sodium: 68 mg

GRAINS

LOW-FAT GRAIN RECIPES

✦

▪ ABOUT GRAINS ▪

Grains have been vitally important to the human diet for thousands of years. One of our earliest-known foods was a paste made from either cooked or raw grain mixed with water. The history of civilization became connected to the search for grain-bearing lands. The need for grain was a primary reason nomadic tribes settled into permanent locations. As people became more settled, they started to cook these pastes, possibly as early as 5000 B.C. in China.

Grains are the dried seeds of grass plants; those used for food are called cereals. All cereals contain a high percentage of carbohydrate, with varying amounts of protein, minerals, and vitamins. While they don't provide complete protein on their own, their complement of protein is completed when they are combined with milk products, eggs, beans, or animal proteins. Grains are low in fat and calories and high in fiber; they are one of the best sources of complex carbohydrates. One cup of grain provides less than 2 grams of fat and no cholesterol, and has from 120 to 280 calories. Grain provides both soluble and insoluble fiber. In many areas of the world where meat is in short supply, the population lives largely on grain.

▪ THE GRAINS USED IN THE RECIPES ▪

Barley   Barley is thought to be the first cereal cultivated by humans. Native to Ethiopia, it was the most significant European grain until the sixteenth century.

"Pearled" barley has been processed to remove both the hull and the germ, leaving small cream-colored balls that look like pearls. Recipes in this book have been tested with pearl barley unless they specify instant barley. Cooked barley has a mild flavor, a nutlike taste, and a chewy texture.

Buckwheat or Kasha   Buckwheat is a low, shrublike plant whose seeds are often ground into flour. Kasha is buckwheat groats that have been roasted to produce a more intense, nutlike flavor.

Bulgur Wheat   Bulgur is made by boiling, drying, and cooking whole wheat grains. It resembles brown rice in its chewy texture, hearty flavor, and nutritional composition. Because bulgur is dehydrated, it must be reconstituted by soaking in liquid for an hour if you are using it raw, as in a salad. In cooking bulgur, use a ratio of one part bulgur to two parts water, broth, tomato juice, or other liquid.

Cornmeal   The only native American grain, corn was used by the Indians before Columbus arrived, and was introduced to Europe by the early explorers of this continent. Cornmeal is made of ground corn kernels. Water-ground meal retains the vitamin-rich germ, while commercially ground cornmeal is made from only the starchy part of the kernel. The texture of the meal can range from coarse to fine; which to use depends on the dish being prepared. Coarse cornmeal is suggested in the polenta recipes that follow. Both yellow and white cornmeal are available, and differ only in color.

Couscous   Couscous is the bulgur of North Africa. It is made by steaming finely cracked millet or wheat. Packaged couscous is precooked and dried granular semolina. It resembles grits.

Hominy   Hominy is a staple in the American South. It is dried corn that has had its hull and germ removed with lye or soda. Hominy grits are toasted hominy grains. They are white and about the size of toast crumbs. When cooked, they have a thick, chewy texture and a mild flavor.

Millet   Millet, a grain that has been found in Asia since prehistoric times, is a protein-rich cereal grass. It has a bland flavor that takes seasoning well. Millet is cooked like rice.

Wheat Berries   This chewy grain is made from whole wheat kernels with only the outer layer removed. Without the strawlike chaff or husk, wheat berries have a nutlike taste and are packed with nutrients.

Many of these grains can be found in supermarkets. If they are not available from your supermarket, look for them in health-food stores and Asian markets.

▪   L E F T O V E R   G R A I N S   ▪

- Store leftover grains in the refrigerator for 1 to 2 days or in the freezer (in 1- or 2-cup portions) for up to 6 months. Freezing hominy is not recommended.
- To reheat frozen grain, place it in the microwave on HIGH for 2 minutes or cook it on top of the stove in a saucepan with 3 tablespoons of water until heated through.

▪   S T O R I N G   G R A I N S   ▪

- Store grain in tightly sealed containers in a cool, dry location.
- Unprocessed grains can be stored in the refrigerator for a month or in the freezer for up to 6 months.

COUSCOUS

✦

Morning Couscous ▪ Breakfast Couscous with Yogurt ▪ Prune-Apricot Couscous ▪ Raisin Couscous ▪ Currant-Almond-Date Couscous ▪ Scallion Couscous ▪ Roasted Red Bell Pepper Couscous ▪ Saffron-Tomato Couscous ▪ Minted Couscous with Green Peas ▪ Green Bell Peppers with Black Bean–Couscous Stuffing ▪ Couscous and Chili-Cumin Vegetables ▪ Microwave Couscous-Stuffed Eggplant ▪ Garlic-Tomato Couscous ▪ Microwave Paella with Couscous ▪ Couscous with Chicken and Vegetables ▪ Red Pepper Salsa Couscous with Chicken ▪ Chicken and Green Beans with Couscous ▪ Couscous-Chicken Salad with Lemon-Garlic Dressing ▪ Curried Zucchini-Tuna Couscous ▪ Garlicky Tuna-Couscous Salad

Morning Couscous

A hot cereal of couscous and raisins.

YIELD: 2 servings • *PREPARATION TIME: 2 minutes* •
COOKING TIME: 5 minutes plus 5 minutes standing time

1 cup skim milk   *1 tablespoon raisins*
½ cup uncooked couscous

1. Bring milk to a slow boil in a small saucepan. Stir in couscous and raisins. Remove from heat, cover, and allow to stand for 5 minutes.

Calories Per Serving: 230   Carbohydrates: 45 g
Fat: 1 g   Dietary Fiber: 7 g
Cholesterol: 2 mg   Sodium: 68 mg
Protein: 10 g

Breakfast Couscous with Yogurt

Couscous flavored with brown sugar and cinnamon is served with yogurt.

YIELD: 4 servings • *PREPARATION TIME: 5 minutes* •
COOKING TIME: 5 minutes plus 5 minutes standing time

¾ cup water   *¼ teaspoon ground cinnamon*
¾ cup uncooked couscous   *3 tablespoons plain nonfat yogurt*
1 tablespoon firmly packed brown sugar

1. Bring water to a boil in a small saucepan. Stir in couscous, brown sugar, and cinnamon. Remove from heat.
2. Stir in yogurt. Cover and let stand for 5 minutes before serving.

Calories Per Serving: 152   Carbohydrates: 31 g
Fat: 1 g   Dietary Fiber: 6 g
Cholesterol: 0 mg   Sodium: 11 mg
Protein: 5 g

Prune-Apricot Couscous

Prunes, apricots, and couscous simmered in orange juice are combined in this breakfast treat.

YIELD: 4 servings ▪ PREPARATION TIME: 5 minutes ▪
COOKING TIME: 7 minutes plus 5 minutes standing time

1 cup orange juice
1¼ cups water
1 cup uncooked couscous
¼ cup chopped pitted prunes

¼ cup chopped dried apricots
2 tablespoons slivered almonds
1 teaspoon ground cinnamon

1. Bring juice and 1 cup of water to a boil in a small saucepan. Stir in couscous. Remove from heat and allow to stand for 5 minutes.
2. Meanwhile, heat remaining ¼ cup water in a skillet. Add prunes, apricots, almonds, and cinnamon. Sauté for 2 minutes. Stir in cooked couscous, mix well, and serve.

Calories Per Serving: 265
Fat: 3 g
Cholesterol: 0 mg
Protein: 8 g

Carbohydrates: 53 g
Dietary Fiber: 9 g
Sodium: 42 mg

Raisin Couscous

Couscous is cooked in chicken broth and served with raisins.

YIELD: 2 servings ▪ PREPARATION TIME: 5 minutes ▪
COOKING TIME: 5 minutes plus 5 minutes standing time

1½ cups nonfat chicken broth
1 cup uncooked couscous

¼ cup chopped raisins

1. Bring broth to a boil in a saucepan. Stir in couscous. Return to a boil; remove from heat, cover, and allow to stand for 5 minutes.
2. Stir in raisins. Transfer to individual bowls and serve.

Calories Per Serving: 423
Fat: 1 g
Cholesterol: 0 mg
Protein: 18 g

Carbohydrates: 85 g
Dietary Fiber: 15 g
Sodium: 139 mg

Currant-Almond-Date Couscous

Couscous is mixed with dates, scallions, currants, and almonds.

YIELD: 6 servings • *PREPARATION TIME: 5 minutes* •
COOKING TIME: 5 minutes plus 5 minutes standing time

1 cup nonfat chicken broth
½ teaspoon ground cinnamon
⅛ teaspoon ground nutmeg
⅔ cup uncooked couscous

⅔ cup chopped pitted dates
3 scallions, chopped
⅓ cup currants
3 tablespoons slivered almonds

1. Bring broth, cinnamon, and nutmeg to a boil in a saucepan.
2. Stir in couscous, dates, scallions, and currants. Remove from heat; cover and allow to stand for 5 minutes.
3. Transfer to serving bowl, sprinkle with almonds, and serve.

Calories Per Serving: 159
Fat: 3 g
Cholesterol: 0 mg
Protein: 5 g

Carbohydrates: 31 g
Dietary Fiber: 4 g
Sodium: 65 mg

Scallion Couscous

Couscous and scallions are tossed with lemon peel.

YIELD: 4 servings • *PREPARATION TIME: 5 minutes* •
COOKING TIME: 5 minutes plus 5 minutes standing time

1½ cups water
2 scallions, chopped

1 cup uncooked couscous
1½ teaspoons minced lemon peel

1. Bring water to a boil in a saucepan. Stir in scallions and couscous. Remove from heat; stir in lemon peel, cover, and allow to stand for 5 minutes before serving.

Calories Per Serving: 174
Fat: 0 g
Cholesterol: 0 mg
Protein: 6 g

Carbohydrates: 36 g
Dietary Fiber: 7 g
Sodium: 7 mg

Roasted Red Bell Pepper Couscous

The smoky flavor of roasted red bell pepper mingles with garlic and couscous in this classic dish.

YIELD: 4 servings • PREPARATION TIME: 20 minutes • COOKING TIME: 5 minutes plus 15 minutes pepper cooling time and 5 minutes couscous standing time

1 red bell pepper
1¼ cups water
1 teaspoon olive oil

2 cloves garlic, minced
1 cup uncooked couscous
¼ teaspoon ground black pepper

1. Broil the red pepper, turning several times, until skin is blackened and blistered, about 10 minutes. Allow the pepper to cool in a closed paper bag for approximately 15 minutes. (This will make the skin easier to remove.) Peel off the skin, discard the core and seeds, and dice the flesh.
2. Bring water to a boil in a saucepan. Add the oil and garlic. Stir in the couscous. Cover, remove from heat, and allow to stand for 5 minutes.
3. Drain any excess liquid, combine the couscous and the red pepper, sprinkle the black pepper over the dish, and serve immediately.

Calories Per Serving: 191
Fat: 1 g
Cholesterol: 0 mg
Protein: 6 g

Carbohydrates: 37 g
Dietary Fiber: 7 g
Sodium: 7 mg

Saffron-Tomato Couscous

Saffron, tomatoes, onion, and coriander are partnered with couscous.

YIELD: 4 servings • *PREPARATION TIME: 15 minutes* •
COOKING TIME: 6 minutes plus 5 minutes standing time

2 tablespoons nonfat chicken broth
½ cup minced onion
¼ teaspoon ground saffron
3 plum tomatoes, seeded and cut into
  ½-inch cubes

1⅓ cups water
1 cup uncooked couscous
3 teaspoons ground coriander

1. Heat chicken broth in a saucepan. Add onion and sauté until lightly golden, about 4 minutes.
2. Add saffron and tomatoes, stir well, and simmer for 2 minutes. Add water and bring to a boil.
3. Stir in couscous and cover tightly. Remove from heat and allow to stand for 5 minutes. Drain any excess liquid; stir in coriander and serve immediately.

Calories Per Serving: 220
Fat: 0 g
Cholesterol: 0 mg
Protein: 1 g

Carbohydrates: 5 g
Dietary Fiber: 1 g
Sodium: 19 mg

Minted Couscous with Green Peas

Couscous is paired with green peas and seasoned with mint.

YIELD: 2 servings • *PREPARATION TIME: 2 minutes* •
COOKING TIME: 5 minutes plus 5 minutes standing time

1½ cups nonfat chicken broth
1 10-ounce package frozen green peas
1 cup uncooked couscous

1 teaspoon dried mint
¼ teaspoon ground black pepper

1. Bring broth to a boil in a saucepan. Stir in peas and couscous. Return to a boil; remove from heat, cover, and allow to stand for 5 minutes.
2. Drain any excess liquid, stir in mint, sprinkle with black pepper, and serve.

Calories Per Serving: 475
Fat: 2 g
Cholesterol: 0 mg
Protein: 23 g

Carbohydrates: 92 g
Dietary Fiber: 20 g
Sodium: 384 mg

Green Bell Peppers with Black Bean—Couscous Stuffing

Green pepper halves are broiled, stuffed with a mixture of couscous and black beans, and topped with cheese.

YIELD: 4 servings • PREPARATION TIME: 20 minutes •
COOKING TIME: 18 minutes plus 5 minutes standing time

8 green bell peppers, halved lengthwise and seeded
1 teaspoon olive oil
2 tablespoons nonfat chicken broth
1 small onion, minced
1 teaspoon dried cilantro
½ teaspoon cayenne pepper
1 cup water

3 cups low-sodium black beans, rinsed and drained
1 cup uncooked couscous
½ cup chopped fresh parsley
¼ cup low-sodium tomato sauce
2 slices nonfat cheddar, cut into 4 strips each

1. Preheat broiler.
2. Arrange green bell peppers, cut side down, on a nonstick baking sheet. Brush the peppers with the oil. Broil 4 to 6 inches from heat until skins are slightly charred, about 6 minutes.
3. Heat broth in a large Dutch oven. Add onion, cilantro, and cayenne pepper. Sauté until onion is just tender-crisp, about 3 minutes.
4. Bring water to a boil in a saucepan. Stir in beans, couscous, parsley, and tomato sauce.
5. Reduce heat and simmer for 5 minutes. Remove from heat, cover, and allow to stand for 5 minutes.
6. Combine onion mixture with bean mixture.
7. Fill bell pepper halves with the onion-bean mixture. Top each with strips of cheese and broil just until cheese melts.

Calories Per Serving: 444
Fat: 3 g
Cholesterol: 0 mg
Protein: 25 g

Carbohydrates: 81 g
Dietary Fiber: 18 g
Sodium: 535 mg

Couscous and Chili-Cumin Vegetables

Couscous is served with a mixture of corn, red bell pepper, and mushrooms seasoned with onion, garlic, and chili powder.

YIELD: 6 servings • *PREPARATION TIME: 25 minutes* •
COOKING TIME: 25 minutes plus 5 minutes standing time

1¼ cups nonfat chicken broth
½ cup chopped onion
1 clove garlic, minced
¾ cup fresh, canned, or frozen, thawed
    corn kernels
½ cup chopped red bell pepper

½ cup chopped fresh mushrooms
3 cups chopped plum tomatoes
1 teaspoon chili powder
1 teaspoon ground cumin
1 cup uncooked couscous

1. Heat ¼ cup of broth in a skillet over medium heat. Add onion and garlic. Sauté for 5 minutes.
2. Add corn, red bell pepper, and mushrooms. Cook, stirring, for 5 minutes.
3. Add tomatoes, chili powder, and cumin. Simmer for 15 minutes.
4. Bring the remaining 1½ cups broth to a boil in a saucepan; add couscous. Cover pan and remove from heat. Let stand for 5 minutes.
5. Spoon vegetables over couscous.

Calories Per Serving: 158
Fat: 1 g
Cholesterol: 0 mg
Protein: 7 g

Carbohydrates: 36 g
Dietary Fiber: 6 g
Sodium: 81 mg

Microwave Couscous-Stuffed Eggplant

Small eggplants are stuffed with couscous, tomatoes, garlic, and jalapeño.

YIELD: 8 servings • *PREPARATION TIME: 25 minutes* •
COOKING TIME: 20 minutes plus 10 minutes standing time

4 small eggplants
2 cups water
2 cups uncooked couscous
4 large ripe tomatoes, diced
6 cloves garlic, minced

1 teaspoon dried cilantro
1 jalapeño pepper, seeded and minced
1 tablespoon lemon juice
2 teaspoons ground cumin
¼ teaspoon ground black pepper

1. Place a sheet of paper towel on a microwave-safe glass pie plate. Cut eggplant in half lengthwise. Arrange eggplant on plate, cut side down, with narrower ends toward center of dish. Cover with microwave-safe vented plastic wrap. Microwave on 100% HIGH for 3 minutes.

2. Allow eggplant to cool and carefully scoop out the flesh, leaving a shell about ⅛ inch thick. Reserve the flesh and set the eggplant shells aside.

3. Bring water to a boil in a saucepan. Stir in couscous; remove from heat, cover, and allow to stand for 5 minutes.

4. Combine the eggplant flesh, couscous, tomatoes, garlic, cilantro, jalapeño pepper, lemon juice, cumin, and black pepper. Mix well and spoon the mixture into the eggplant shells.

5. On a microwave-safe plate, arrange stuffed eggplant halves with narrow ends pointing to outside of plate. Cover with a paper towel and then vented plastic wrap. Microwave on 100% HIGH for 4 minutes. Remove from microwave. Loosen plastic and allow to stand for 5 minutes before serving.

Calories Per Serving: 242
Fat: 3 g
Cholesterol: 0 mg
Protein: 9 g

Carbohydrates: 47 g
Dietary Fiber: 9 g
Sodium: 97 mg

Garlic-Tomato Couscous

Couscous is combined with garlic, basil, balsamic vinegar, olive oil, and tomato.

YIELD: 4 servings • PREPARATION TIME: 6 minutes •
COOKING TIME: 9 minutes plus 5 minutes standing time

1 cup nonfat chicken broth
1 teaspoon dried basil
1 clove garlic, minced
¾ cup uncooked couscous

1½ tablespoons balsamic vinegar
1 teaspoon olive oil
¼ teaspoon ground black pepper
1 medium ripe tomato, chopped

1. Bring broth to a boil in a saucepan over medium heat. Add basil and garlic. Stir in couscous. Remove from heat, cover, and allow to stand for 5 minutes.
2. Whisk together the vinegar, oil, and pepper. Add the tomato.
3. Pour tomato dressing over couscous and toss gently.

Calories Per Serving: 160
Fat: 2 g
Cholesterol: 0 mg
Protein: 6 g

Carbohydrates: 30 g
Dietary Fiber: 6 g
Sodium: 92 mg

Microwave Paella with Couscous

A fast version of the classic—chicken breast, shrimp, peas, green bell pepper, and scallions are microwaved with garlic, saffron, and couscous.

YIELD: 5 servings • *PREPARATION TIME: 15 minutes* •
COOKING TIME: 8 minutes plus 5 minutes standing time

8 ounces skinless chicken breast cutlets,
    cubed
¼ cup water
1¼ cups nonfat chicken broth
¾ pound medium shrimp, peeled and
    deveined
½ cup fresh or thawed frozen green peas

½ cup chopped green bell pepper
2 scallions, chopped
2 cloves garlic, minced
¼ teaspoon ground black pepper
⅛ teaspoon ground saffron
1 cup uncooked couscous

1. Combine chicken, water, and chicken broth in a large microwave-safe covered casserole. Microwave on HIGH for 4 minutes.
2. Stir in shrimp, peas, green bell pepper, scallions, garlic, black pepper, and saffron. Microwave on HIGH until shrimp turn pink, about 4 minutes.
3. Stir in couscous; cover and allow to stand for 5 minutes before serving.

Calories Per Serving: 273
Fat: 2 g
Cholesterol: 163 mg
Protein: 32 g

Carbohydrates: 32 g
Dietary Fiber: 7 g
Sodium: 265 mg

Couscous with Chicken and Vegetables

Chicken is simmered with onion, carrot, celery, tomatoes, orange peel, rosemary, and garlic and served over couscous.

YIELD: 2 servings • PREPARATION TIME: 25 minutes • COOKING TIME: 30 minutes

1 cup water
1 cup uncooked couscous
½ cup nonfat chicken broth
½ pound skinless chicken breast cutlets
½ cup chopped onion
½ cup chopped carrot
½ cup diced celery

1 cup fresh or low-sodium canned tomatoes, chopped and drained
½ teaspoon minced orange peel
¼ teaspoon dried rosemary
⅛ teaspoon ground black pepper
1 clove garlic, minced

1. Bring water to a boil. Stir in couscous and remove from heat. Let stand, covered, for 5 minutes.
2. Meanwhile, heat ¼ cup chicken broth in skillet. Add chicken cutlets and sauté until they brown, about 4 minutes on each side. Set aside.
3. Heat remaining ¼ cup broth in the skillet. Add onion, carrot, and celery. Cook over medium heat for 5 minutes. Add tomatoes, orange peel, rosemary, black pepper, garlic, and chicken pieces.
4. Reduce heat, cover, and simmer until chicken is cooked through, about 20 minutes.
5. Serve chicken and tomato mixture over couscous.

Calories Per Serving: 516
Fat: 2 g
Cholesterol: 75 mg
Protein: 41 g

Carbohydrates: 84 g
Dietary Fiber: 17 mg
Sodium: 104 mg

Red Pepper Salsa Couscous with Chicken

Couscous is made with prepared salsa and served with broiled chicken.

YIELD: 4 servings • PREPARATION TIME: 20 minutes • COOKING TIME: 25 minutes

1⅓ cups commercially prepared red pepper salsa
½ cup water
1 cup uncooked couscous

4 skinless chicken breast cutlets, about 4
   ounces each
¼ cup chopped fresh parsley

1. Preheat broiler.
2. Combine salsa and water in a saucepan. Bring to a boil and stir in couscous.
   Remove from heat, cover, and allow to stand for 5 minutes.
3. Meanwhile, broil chicken 4 to 5 inches from heat for 5 minutes. Turn and
   continue to broil until meat is done, about 5 minutes.
4. Sprinkle couscous with parsley and serve chicken with couscous.

Calories Per Serving: 125
Fat: 1 g
Cholesterol: 75 mg
Protein: 28 g

Carbohydrates: 3 g
Dietary Fiber: 1 g
Sodium: 718 mg

Chicken and Green Beans with Couscous

Chicken cutlets, green beans, red bell peppers, tomato, and celery are combined
with couscous.

YIELD: *6 servings* ▪ PREPARATION TIME: *25 minutes plus chicken cooking time and
green bean steaming time* ▪ COOKING TIME: *10 minutes plus 5 minutes standing time*

1½ cups nonfat chicken broth
1 cup uncooked couscous
12 ounces skinless chicken breast cutlets,
   cooked and cut into ½-inch cubes
½ pound fresh green beans, steamed tender-crisp and cut into 2-inch pieces

2 red bell peppers, chopped
1 large ripe tomato, chopped
1 stalk celery, chopped
½ cup nonfat Italian dressing
2 tablespoons sliced toasted almonds

1. Bring broth to a boil in a saucepan over medium heat. Stir in couscous. Remove from heat, cover, and allow to stand for 5 minutes. Drain any excess
   liquid.
2. Combine couscous, chicken, green beans, red bell peppers, tomato, and celery in a serving bowl.
3. Stir in dressing and toss gently to coat all ingredients. Sprinkle with almonds
   and serve.

Calories Per Serving: 205
Fat: 3 g
Cholesterol: 28 mg
Protein: 16 g

Carbohydrates: 29 g
Dietary Fiber: 6 g
Sodium: 401 mg

Couscous-Chicken Salad
with Lemon-Garlic Dressing

Cooked, chopped chicken, spinach, and tomato are mixed with couscous and tossed with a lemon vinaigrette.

YIELD: 6 servings • PREPARATION TIME: 20 minutes •
COOKING TIME: 5 minutes plus 5 minutes standing time

1½ cups water
1½ cups uncooked couscous
3 skinless chicken breast cutlets, cooked
    and finely chopped
2 cups shredded spinach leaves
1 cup diced tomato
⅔ cup chopped fresh parsley

2 scallions, chopped
1 teaspoon dried mint
6 tablespoons lemon juice
3 tablespoons water
1 tablespoon olive oil
¼ teaspoon ground black pepper
1 clove garlic, minced

1. Bring water to a boil in a saucepan over medium heat. Stir in couscous. Remove from heat and allow to stand for 5 minutes. Fluff with a fork.
2. Combine couscous, chicken, spinach, tomato, parsley, scallions, and mint.
3. Whisk together lemon juice, water, olive oil, black pepper, and garlic.
4. Pour dressing over couscous mixture.

Calories Per Serving: 241
Fat: 3 g
Cholesterol: 28 mg
Protein: 15 g

Carbohydrates: 37 g
Dietary Fiber: 8 g
Sodium: 30 mg

Curried Zucchini-Tuna Couscous

Chopped zucchini, tomatoes, and canned albacore tuna are combined with couscous, onion, garlic, and curry powder.

YIELD: 6 servings • *PREPARATION TIME: 20 minutes*

2 tablespoons nonfat chicken broth
1 medium onion, chopped
3 cloves garlic, minced
1½ teaspoons curry powder
3 cups coarsely chopped zucchini
3 cups low-sodium canned tomatoes,
  chopped coarsely, juice reserved

¼ cup currants or raisins
⅓ cup uncooked couscous
1 13-ounce can water-packed solid albacore tuna, drained and flaked
¼ cup chopped fresh parsley

1. Heat chicken broth in a large skillet. Add onion, garlic, and curry powder and sauté until onion is lightly golden, about 4 minutes.
2. Add zucchini, tomatoes and their juice, currants, and couscous. Cover and simmer, stirring occasionally, until zucchini is just tender, about 5 minutes. Stir in tuna. Cover and allow to stand for 5 minutes.
3. Sprinkle with parsley before serving.

Calories Per Serving: 177
Fat: 2 g
Cholesterol: 10 mg
Protein: 18 g

Carbohydrates: 26 g
Dietary Fiber: 4 g
Sodium: 65 mg

Garlicky Tuna-Couscous Salad

Couscous cooked with 6 cloves of minced garlic is mixed with broiled tuna, celery, and tomatoes.

YIELD: 4 servings • *PREPARATION TIME: 30 minutes*

1½ teaspoons olive oil
¾ pound tuna steak
2 tablespoons nonfat chicken broth
¼ cup minced scallions
6 cloves garlic, minced
1 teaspoon ground cumin
1 cup water
¼ teaspoon ground black pepper

1 cup uncooked couscous
1 cup chopped celery
2 large ripe tomatoes, chopped
1 tablespoon dried basil
6 tablespoons red wine vinegar
1 tablespoon minced jalapeño pepper
¼ cup lemon juice

1. Preheat broiler and brush olive oil over the tuna steak.
2. Heat chicken broth in a saucepan. Add scallions, garlic, and cumin and sauté until onion is lightly golden, about 4 minutes. Add water and black pepper. Bring to a boil and stir in couscous. Remove from heat, cover, and allow to stand 5 minutes. Drain.
3. Meanwhile, broil tuna until done through, about 4 minutes on each side. Cut into bite-size pieces.
4. Combine celery, tomatoes, basil, vinegar, jalapeño pepper, lemon juice, tuna, and couscous.

Calories Per Serving: 321
Fat: 3 g
Cholesterol: 38 mg
Protein: 28 g

Carbohydrates: 47 g
Dietary Fiber: 9 g
Sodium: 260 mg

POLENTA

Basic Stovetop Polenta ▪ Microwave Polenta ▪ Microwave Parmesan Polenta ▪ Autumn Polenta ▪ Chili Polenta ▪ Scallion Polenta with Tomato Topping ▪ Polenta with Green Pepper–Wine Sauce ▪ Polenta with Tomato–Shiitake Mushroom Topping ▪ Polenta with Porcini Topping ▪ Corn–Lima Bean Polenta ▪ Polenta Topped with Great Northern Beans ▪ Polenta with Chicken and Mushrooms ▪ Polenta and Cinnamon Apples

Basic Stovetop Polenta

Simple polenta can be used as a base for a variety of vegetables.

YIELD: 6 servings • PREPARATION TIME: 5 minutes •
COOKING TIME: 15 to 20 minutes plus 5 to 10 minutes standing time

1 cup cornmeal

3½ cups nonfat chicken broth, skim milk, water, or a combination of these liquids

1. Stir cornmeal into 1 cup of liquid. Bring remaining 2½ cups of liquid to a boil in a large, heavy saucepan. Stir cornmeal mixture into boiling liquid. Return to boil, stirring constantly. Reduce heat and simmer, stirring constantly, until mixture thickens, about 15 minutes.
2. Form into a mound on a large platter or in a pie plate. Let cool for 5 to 10 minutes, until the polenta becomes slightly firm. Slice with a knife blade dipped in water.

Calories Per Serving: 87
Fat: 1 g
Cholesterol: 0 mg
Protein: 4 g

Carbohydrates: 16 g
Dietary Fiber: 3 g
Sodium: 203 mg

Microwave Polenta

Making polenta in your microwave is quick and easy. Microwave polenta can be used with any of the toppings in the following polenta recipes.

YIELD: 4 servings • PREPARATION TIME: 8 minutes •
COOKING TIME: 9 minutes plus 30 minutes cooling time

⅔ cup cornmeal
2 cups water
½ cup shredded nonfat cheddar

¼ cup minced fresh parsley
1 teaspoon ground cumin
¼ teaspoon hot pepper sauce

1. Mix the cornmeal and the water in a microwave-safe 3-quart casserole. Cover and microwave on HIGH for 6 minutes, stirring several times.
2. Remove from the microwave and stir in the cheese, parsley, cumin, and hot pepper sauce.

3. Spread cornmeal mixture in a nonstick 8-inch-by-8-inch baking pan and let stand for 30 minutes, or until firm.
4. Cut polenta into four squares. Arrange squares on a microwave-safe platter and heat in microwave for 3 minutes.

Calories Per Serving: 108

Fat: 1 g

Cholesterol: 2 mg

Protein: 7 g

Carbohydrates: 18 g

Dietary Fiber: 1 g

Sodium: 109 mg

Microwave Parmesan Polenta

Polenta, which is easily prepared in the microwave, can be served with tomato sauce.

YIELD: 4 servings ▪ *PREPARATION TIME: 10 minutes* ▪
COOKING TIME: 10 minutes plus 5 minutes standing time

1 cup skim milk

2½ cups water

1 cup cornmeal

¼ teaspoon dried basil

¼ cup grated nonfat Parmesan

1. Place milk, water, cornmeal, and basil in a microwave-safe 3-quart casserole. Cover with microwave-safe vented plastic wrap.
2. Microwave on HIGH for 5 minutes. Stir.
3. Microwave on HIGH for 5 more minutes. Polenta should be thickened, and almost all of the water should be absorbed.
4. Stir in the Parmesan.
5. Cover and let stand for 5 minutes, or until polenta is firm.

Calories Per Serving: 108

Fat: 0 g

Cholesterol: 1 mg

Protein: 4 g

Carbohydrates: 21 g

Dietary Fiber: 4 g

Sodium: 58 mg

Autumn Polenta

Sweet potatoes, cornmeal, and sage make a superb side dish with roast poultry.

YIELD: 6 servings • *PREPARATION TIME: 15 minutes* • *COOKING TIME: 20 minutes*

2 medium sweet potatoes, peeled and
    diced
⅓ cup water
3 cups skim milk

¾ cup cornmeal
¼ teaspoon dried sage
½ teaspoon ground black pepper

1. Place the sweet potatoes and water in a covered saucepan with an inch of water. Simmer for 10 minutes, or until potatoes are soft.
2. Drain the sweet potatoes and puree them in a blender or food processor until smooth.
3. Combine the milk, cornmeal, and sage in a microwave-safe 3-quart casserole. Cover and microwave for 8 minutes on HIGH, or until the liquid is absorbed. Stir vigorously several times while polenta is cooking.
4. Whisk together sweet potatoes, polenta, and black pepper, and serve.

Calories Per Serving: 138
Fat: 1 g
Cholesterol: 2 mg
Protein: 6 g

Carbohydrates: 27 g
Dietary Fiber: 4 g
Sodium: 73 mg

Chili Polenta

Polenta is accented with green chiles and served with a jalapeño-tomato topping.

YIELD: 6 servings • *PREPARATION TIME: 20 minutes* •
COOKING TIME: 35 minutes plus 1 hour cooling time

3½ cups skim milk
1 cup cornmeal
1 4-ounce can green chiles, chopped
1½ cups fresh or low-sodium canned
    tomatoes, chopped
¼ cup chopped scallions

¼ cup chopped fresh parsley
1 tablespoon lime juice
1 teaspoon minced jalapeño pepper
4 ounces nonfat cheddar
2 tablespoons grated nonfat Parmesan

1. Mix 1 cup skim milk with the cornmeal. Bring remaining skim milk to a boil in a large saucepan. Slowly add the cornmeal mixture to the boiling milk. Return to a boil, stirring constantly. Reduce heat and simmer, stirring often, until mixture is thickened.
2. Remove from heat and stir in chiles.
3. Pour the cornmeal mixture into a shallow, nonstick baking pan. Chill for 1 hour or until firm.
4. Preheat oven to 350 degrees.
5. Combine tomatoes, scallions, parsley, lime juice, and jalapeño pepper and mix well.
6. Cut chilled polenta into 2-inch squares. Arrange pieces on a shallow baking pan. Cover with foil and bake for 15 minutes. Remove foil; sprinkle with the cheeses and bake for 10 more minutes.
7. Serve with tomato topping.

Calories Per Serving: 176
Fat: 1 g
Cholesterol: 4 mg
Protein: 13 g

Carbohydrates: 29 g
Dietary Fiber: 4 g
Sodium: 388 mg

Scallion Polenta with Tomato Topping

Polenta is flavored with Parmesan and topped with a tomato-mushroom sauce.

Yield: 4 servings • Preparation Time: 25 minutes •
Cooking Time: 20 minutes plus 30 minutes cooling time

1 cup cornmeal
2¼ cups nonfat chicken broth
⅛ teaspoon ground red pepper
½ cup chopped scallions
½ cup skim milk
5 egg whites
⅓ cup grated nonfat Parmesan
½ cup sliced fresh mushrooms

¼ cup minced onion
2 cloves garlic, minced
2 tablespoons chopped fresh parsley
¾ teaspoon dried basil
½ teaspoon sugar
½ teaspoon dried oregano
3½ cups fresh or low-sodium canned
tomatoes, chopped

1. Combine cornmeal and 1 cup chicken broth with red pepper. Place another cup of broth in a saucepan and bring to a boil. Add cornmeal mixture. Reduce heat and simmer, stirring constantly, until mixture thickens.

2. Remove from heat and stir in scallions, milk, egg whites, and Parmesan. Return to heat and cook, stirring constantly, for 2 additional minutes.
3. Spread the polenta mixture in a nonstick 9-inch-by-13-inch baking pan. Set aside on a wire rack and allow to cool for 30 minutes.
4. Preheat oven to 350 degrees.
5. Heat remaining ¼ cup chicken broth in a saucepan over medium heat. Add mushrooms, onion, and garlic. Sauté for 3 minutes.
6. Add parsley, basil, sugar, oregano, and tomatoes and bring to a boil. Reduce heat and simmer, stirring often, for 15 minutes.
7. Cut polenta into 12 pieces. Place on a nonstick baking sheet and bake for 15 minutes.
8. Serve warm with the sauce.

Calories Per Serving: 231
Fat: 3 g
Cholesterol: 7 mg
Protein: 14 g

Carbohydrates: 40 g
Dietary Fiber: 7 g
Sodium: 224 mg

Polenta with Green Pepper–Wine Sauce

Polenta is topped with onion, garlic, mushrooms, thyme, white wine, and green bell peppers.

YIELD: 6 servings • *PREPARATION TIME: 20 minutes* •
COOKING TIME: 20 minutes plus 20 minutes standing time

2 cups cornmeal
7 cups water
3 tablespoons nonfat chicken broth
1 medium onion, sliced
2 cloves garlic, minced
1 pound fresh mushrooms, sliced

1 teaspoon dried thyme
½ cup white wine
5 green bell peppers, cut into ¼-inch strips
¼ teaspoon ground black pepper
¼ cup skim milk

1. Mix cornmeal with 4 cups of water. Bring remaining water to a boil in a large, heavy saucepan. Stir the cornmeal mixture into the boiling water. Return to boil and cook, stirring frequently, until mixture thickens.
2. Remove from heat, cover, and allow to stand for 20 minutes.
3. Heat the chicken broth in a large skillet over medium heat and sauté the onion and garlic for 5 minutes. Add mushrooms and sauté for an additional 5 minutes.

4. Add the thyme and wine and simmer until most of the wine has evaporated. Add the green bell pepper strips and cook until they are just tender. Season with black pepper. Stir in skim milk and cook until warmed through.
5. Turn the polenta onto a serving dish, slice, and serve with mushroom-pepper topping.

Calories Per Serving: 197
Fat: 2 g
Cholesterol: 0 mg
Protein: 6 g

Carbohydrates: 38 g
Dietary Fiber: 8 g
Sodium: 44 mg

Polenta with Tomato–Shiitake Mushroom Topping

Shiitake mushrooms and herbs are mixed with tomatoes and served over polenta.

YIELD: 6 servings • PREPARATION TIME: 20 minutes plus 10 minutes cooling time •
COOKING TIME: 20 minutes

4 cups low-sodium canned tomatoes, crushed and drained
½ teaspoon dried thyme
½ teaspoon dried oregano
¼ teaspoon ground black pepper

2½ tablespoons dried shiitake mushrooms, soaked in hot water, drained, and chopped
1 cup cornmeal
3½ cups nonfat chicken broth
2 tablespoons grated nonfat Parmesan

1. Mix tomatoes, thyme, oregano, and pepper in a large saucepan. Cook over medium heat for 10 minutes.
2. Add chopped mushrooms to tomatoes. Continue cooking for 5 minutes.
3. Stir cornmeal into 1 cup of the chicken broth. Bring remaining broth to a boil in a large saucepan and stir in the cornmeal mixture. Return to a boil; reduce heat and simmer, stirring often, until mixture thickens. Allow to stand for 10 minutes.
4. Serve polenta topped with the tomato-mushroom sauce and Parmesan.

Calories Per Serving: 122
Fat: 2 g
Cholesterol: 2 mg
Protein: 6 g

Carbohydrates: 23 g
Dietary Fiber: 4 g
Sodium: 269 mg

Polenta with Porcini Topping

Polenta is served with a topping of fragrant porcini mushrooms, green bell peppers, and fresh tomatoes.

YIELD: 6 servings ▪ *PREPARATION TIME: 35 minutes* ▪ *COOKING TIME: 35 minutes*

4 cups nonfat chicken broth
1 small onion, chopped
2 cloves garlic, minced
3 large ripe tomatoes, chopped
3 green bell peppers, finely chopped
¼ teaspoon dried thyme
½ teaspoon dried basil

1 teaspoon honey
½ teaspoon ground black pepper
10 porcini or other wild mushroom caps, finely chopped
1 cup cornmeal
2 tablespoons grated nonfat Parmesan
3 tablespoons chopped fresh parsley

1. Heat ¼ cup broth in a large nonstick skillet over medium heat. Sauté the onion for 2 minutes. Add garlic, tomatoes, green bell peppers, thyme, basil, honey, and ¼ teaspoon black pepper. Simmer until sauce thickens, about 15 minutes. Place in a blender or food processor and puree until smooth.
2. Heat ¼ cup chicken broth in a skillet and sauté mushrooms until tender, about 3 minutes.
3. Bring remaining chicken broth to a boil in a large saucepan. Stir in cornmeal and cook, stirring constantly, until mixture thickens, about 15 minutes. Stir in cheese and ¼ teaspoon black pepper.
4. Spoon polenta into shallow bowls and top with pepper sauce and mushrooms. Garnish with parsley and serve.

Calories Per Serving: 160
Fat: 2 g
Cholesterol: 4 mg
Protein: 8 g

Carbohydrates: 32 g
Dietary Fiber: 6 g
Sodium: 278 mg

Corn–Lima Bean Polenta

Polenta, flavored with garlic and sun-dried tomatoes, is topped with a sauce of tomatoes, corn, and lima beans.

YIELD: 8 servings • *PREPARATION TIME: 25 minutes* •
COOKING TIME: 25 minutes plus 25 minutes cooling time

1 cup cornmeal	*½ small onion, sliced*
2½ cups nonfat chicken broth	*3 cups fresh, canned, or thawed frozen*
1½ cups skim milk	*corn kernels*
1 teaspoon olive oil	*3 cups lima beans*
½ cup sun-dried tomatoes, finely	*1 cup low-sodium canned tomato puree*
chopped	*1 tablespoon grated nonfat Parmesan*
2 cloves garlic, minced	

1. Stir cornmeal into 1 cup of chicken broth. Bring another cup of broth, skim milk, and olive oil to a boil in a heavy saucepan. Stir cornmeal into boiling liquid. Return to a boil, stirring constantly.
2. Add the tomatoes and garlic. Reduce heat, cover, and simmer, stirring often, for 10 minutes, or until mixture thickens.
3. Pour the polenta into a nonstick 9-inch-by-9-inch pan and cool for 25 minutes. Meanwhile, preheat oven to 350 degrees.
4. Bake the polenta for 15 minutes.
5. While the polenta is baking, heat the remaining ½ cup broth in a saucepan over medium heat. Sauté onion in broth for 5 minutes. Add the corn and lima beans. Cover and cook, stirring frequently, for 10 minutes. Add the tomato puree and heat thoroughly.
6. Remove the baked polenta from the pan, cut into 8 pieces, sprinkle with Parmesan, and serve topped with the tomato-bean sauce.

Calories Per Serving: 208　　　Carbohydrates: 41 g
Fat: 2 g　　　　　　　　　　　Dietary Fiber: 8 g
Cholesterol: 2 mg　　　　　　　Sodium: 151 mg
Protein: 11 g

Polenta Topped with Great Northern Beans

Baked polenta is served with a topping of Great Northern beans, tomato, and parsley.

YIELD: 8 servings • PREPARATION TIME: 30 minutes •
COOKING TIME: 25 minutes plus 1 hour chilling time

3½ cups nonfat chicken broth
1 cup cornmeal
½ cup chopped red bell pepper
2 cups cooked or low-sodium canned
   Great Northern beans, rinsed and
   drained
¾ cup chopped scallions

1 large ripe tomato, chopped
¼ teaspoon ground black pepper
2 tablespoons chopped fresh parsley
3 cloves garlic, minced
1 tablespoon olive oil
1 tablespoon white wine vinegar
2 tablespoons grated nonfat Parmesan

1. Mix 1 cup broth with the cornmeal.
2. Bring remaining broth to a boil in a large saucepan. Slowly stir in cornmeal mixture and reduce heat to medium. Cook, stirring constantly, until mixture just returns to a boil and begins to thicken, about 15 minutes. Reduce heat to low and cook another 10 minutes.
3. Pour polenta into a 9-inch pie plate. Cover and chill for 1 hour, or until firm.
4. In a large bowl combine the red pepper, beans, scallions, tomato, black pepper, parsley, garlic, olive oil, and wine vinegar. Mix thoroughly, cover, and chill until ready to serve.
5. Preheat oven to 350 degrees.
6. Turn firm polenta onto a nonstick baking sheet. Bake for 15 minutes.
7. Sprinkle polenta with Parmesan. Serve slices topped with bean mixture.

Calories Per Serving: 174
Fat: 3 g
Cholesterol: 1 mg
Protein: 9 g

Carbohydrates: 30 g
Dietary Fiber: 1 g
Sodium: 164 mg

Polenta with Chicken and Mushrooms

Mushrooms and chicken cutlets are sautéed in wine and served with polenta.

YIELD: 6 servings • PREPARATION TIME: 25 minutes • COOKING TIME: 1 hour

1 cup cornmeal
2 cups nonfat chicken broth
1½ cups skim milk
5 tablespoons grated nonfat Parmesan

4 cups sliced fresh white mushrooms
3 tablespoons white wine
6 skinned chicken breast cutlets, about 4
   ounces each

1. Stir cornmeal into 1½ cups chicken broth. Bring milk to a boil. Stir in cornmeal mixture and return to a boil. Cook, stirring frequently, until mixture thickens.
2. Remove from heat and stir in 3 tablespoons of Parmesan.
3. Spread cornmeal mixture in a nonstick 6-inch-by-9-inch baking pan and set aside.
4. In a large skillet, heat ¼ cup broth over medium heat. Sauté mushrooms for 10 minutes. Remove mushrooms and set aside. Add wine and remaining chicken broth and sauté chicken until browned on all sides, about 15 minutes.
5. Preheat oven to 350 degrees.
6. Cut polenta into 12 pieces. Place on a nonstick baking sheet and bake for 15 minutes. Sprinkle remaining Parmesan over the hot polenta.
7. Return mushrooms to skillet with the chicken and warm through.
8. Spoon onto serving platter and arrange polenta pieces around chicken.

Calories Per Serving: 242
Fat: 3 g
Cholesterol: 79 mg
Protein: 32 g

Carbohydrates: 24 g
Dietary Fiber: 4 g
Sodium: 253 mg

Polenta and Cinnamon Apples

For dessert, slices of baked polenta are served with raisin-stuffed baked apples sprinkled with brown sugar and wine.

YIELD: *8 servings* • PREPARATION TIME: *35 minutes* •
COOKING TIME: *75 minutes plus 30 minutes cooling time and 4 hours chilling time*

1 cup cornmeal
3½ cups water
⅔ cup raisins
2 teaspoons ground cinnamon

1½ cups white wine
8 fresh apples, cored, peeled ⅓ of the way
   down, sides rubbed with lemon juice
⅓ cup brown sugar

1. Stir cornmeal into 1 cup of water. Bring remaining 2½ cups to a boil in a heavy saucepan. Stir cornmeal mixture into boiling liquid. Reduce heat and simmer, stirring constantly, until mixture thickens.
2. Place polenta in a nonstick 8-inch-by-4-inch loaf pan. Let mixture cool slightly and cover it with plastic food wrap, pressing it down on the surface of the polenta. Refrigerate for 4 hours.
3. Preheat oven to 350 degrees.
4. Combine raisins and cinnamon. Stuff into the apples.
5. Place apples on a nonstick baking dish. Pour the wine over the apples and sprinkle with brown sugar.
6. Bake for 50 minutes.
7. While apples are baking, cut polenta into 16 slices and arrange the slices on a baking sheet. Bake for 15 minutes.
8. Serve apples with slices of polenta drizzled with syrup from the baked apples.

Calories Per Serving: 251   Carbohydrates: 51 g
Fat: 3 g   Dietary Fiber: 5 g
Cholesterol: 0 mg   Sodium: 13 mg
Protein: 2 g

BARLEY

✦

Basic Barley ▪ White Bean–Barley Soup ▪ Three-Bean Barley Soup
▪ Vegetable-Barley Soup ▪ Lentil-Barley Soup ▪ Sherried
Mushroom-Barley Soup ▪ Shiitake-Barley Soup ▪ Tomato–Barley
Soup ▪ Turkey-Barley Soup ▪ Kale-Barley Soup ▪ Lemon-
Chicken-Barley Soup with Lentils ▪ Jalapeño-Barley Salad ▪ Sun-
Dried Tomato–Barley Salad ▪ Red Pepper–Broccoli–Barley Salad ▪
Artichoke-Barley Salad ▪ Black Bean–Barley Salad ▪ Barley–Kidney
Bean Salad ▪ Barley Pilaf ▪ Curried Vegetable-Barley Pilaf ▪
Barley–Green Pepper Salad ▪ Cranberry Barley ▪ Toasted Barley
Pilaf ▪ Barley with Capers ▪ Honey-Lemon Barley ▪ Barley-
Mushroom Trio ▪ Butternut-Barley Bake ▪ Red Pepper–Baked
Barley ▪ Chili with Barley ▪ Chili Loaf ▪ Microwave Barley with
Green Peas and Yellow Peppers ▪ Barley, Wild Rice, and Shiitake
Mushrooms ▪ Barley with Chicken and Vegetables ▪ Curried Barley
with Chicken, Lentils, and Spinach ▪ Barley Stuffing ▪ Chicken-
Apple Chowder with Barley

Basic Barley

YIELD: 2 servings · *COOKING TIME: 35 minutes*

3 cups water or nonfat chicken broth   *1 cup uncooked pearl barley*

1. Bring water to a boil over high heat in a saucepan.
2. Add barley; cover, reduce heat to low, and cook until the liquid is absorbed and the grain is tender, approximately 35 minutes.
3. Fluff with a fork and serve.

Calories Per Serving: 387   Carbohydrates: 79 g
Fat: 3 g   Dietary Fiber: 16 g
Cholesterol: 0 mg   Sodium: 512 mg
Protein: 17 g

White Bean—Barley Soup

Navy beans, corn, and barley are simmered with diced potato and onion in this robust soup.

YIELD: 6 servings · *PREPARATION TIME: 20 minutes* · *COOKING TIME: 70 minutes*

3 quarts nonfat chicken broth   *1 cup fresh, canned, or thawed frozen*
1 medium onion, chopped   *corn kernels*
2 cloves garlic, minced   *1 cup cooked or canned low-sodium*
1 cup uncooked pearl barley   *navy beans, rinsed and drained*
1 large boiling potato, diced   *¼ teaspoon ground black pepper*

1. Heat ¼ cup chicken broth in a large pot over medium heat, and sauté onion and garlic until tender, about 3 minutes.
2. Add remaining chicken broth, barley, and potato; reduce heat and simmer, stirring occasionally, until potato is tender, about 35 minutes.
3. Stir in corn and beans. Simmer for 10 minutes, or until barley is tender. Season with black pepper before serving.

Calories Per Serving: 153
Fat: 2 g
Cholesterol: 0 mg
Protein: 11 g

Carbohydrates: 28 g
Dietary Fiber: 4 g
Sodium: 511 mg

Three-Bean Barley Soup

This red wine–accented barley soup is a meal in itself, featuring green beans, lima beans, kidney beans, carrots, onion, and celery.

YIELD: 8 servings • *PREPARATION TIME: 25 minutes* • *COOKING TIME: 65 minutes*

2 quarts nonfat chicken broth
1 large onion, coarsely chopped
2 cloves garlic, minced
½ cup uncooked pearl barley
2 carrots, diced
2 stalks celery, diced
2 cups green beans, ends trimmed, cut
    into 2-inch lengths
2 cups low-sodium tomato puree
1½ cups red wine
2 tablespoons honey

1 tablespoon reduced-sodium Worcester-
    shire sauce
1 cup frozen lima beans
1 cup canned low-sodium red kidney
    beans, rinsed and drained
¼ cup low-sodium tomato paste
¼ teaspoon ground black pepper
1 teaspoon dried basil
1 teaspoon dried sage
1 teaspoon dried oregano
2 tablespoons red wine vinegar

1. Heat ¼ cup chicken broth in a large pot. Sauté onion and garlic until onion becomes transparent, about 3 minutes.
2. Add remaining broth and barley and simmer for 30 minutes.
3. Add carrots, celery, and green beans. Simmer for 15 minutes.
4. Process tomato puree, wine, honey, and Worcestershire sauce in a blender or food processor until well blended. Add to soup.
5. Add lima beans, kidney beans, black pepper, tomato paste, basil, sage, and oregano to soup. Simmer for 15 minutes.
6. Stir in vinegar.

Calories Per Serving: 198
Fat: 1 g
Cholesterol: 0 mg
Protein: 9 g

Carbohydrates: 35 g
Dietary Fiber: 7 g
Sodium: 258 mg

Vegetable-Barley Soup

This soup is quick and easy to prepare on a cold night when you want something warm, nutritious, and delicious in a rush.

YIELD: 6 servings • PREPARATION TIME: 25 minutes plus vegetable steaming time • COOKING TIME: 20 minutes

6 cups nonfat chicken broth
1 cup chopped zucchini, steamed tender-crisp
1 cup diced carrots, steamed tender-crisp
½ cup green beans cut into 1-inch lengths, steamed tender-crisp
2 cups sliced fresh white mushrooms
2 stalks celery, chopped
½ cup quick-cooking barley
⅓ cup chopped scallions
½ teaspoon dried thyme
½ teaspoon dried basil
1 clove garlic, minced

1. Combine broth, steamed zucchini, carrots, green beans, mushrooms, celery, barley, scallions, thyme, basil, and garlic in a large saucepan.
2. Bring to a boil, reduce heat, and simmer, covered, until barley is tender, about 15 minutes.

Calories Per Serving: 115
Fat: 2 g
Cholesterol: 0 mg
Protein: 8 g

Carbohydrates: 21 g
Dietary Fiber: 5 g
Sodium: 407 mg

Lentil-Barley Soup

This traditional barley soup, made with leek, carrots, and celery, freezes well. Make a big batch and freeze half for a busy day.

YIELD: 16 servings • PREPARATION TIME: 20 minutes • COOKING TIME: 1 hour

¼ cup nonfat chicken broth
1 large onion, chopped
2 cloves garlic, minced
1 leek, chopped
4 carrots, sliced
2 stalks celery, with leaves, sliced
½ teaspoon dried basil
1 teaspoon dried oregano, crushed
2 bay leaves
⅛ teaspoon cayenne pepper
¼ teaspoon ground black pepper
2 cups dried lentils
½ cup uncooked pearl barley
3 quarts water

1. Heat ¼ cup chicken broth in a large soup pot over medium heat. Sauté onion and garlic in broth until onions are tender, about 3 minutes. Add leek, carrots, celery, basil, oregano, bay leaves, cayenne pepper, black pepper, lentils, and barley. Stir well.
2. Add 3 quarts water and bring to a boil. Reduce heat, cover, and simmer until barley and lentils are tender, about 45 minutes. Add more water if needed.
3. Remove bay leaves before serving.

Calories Per Serving: 99
Fat: 0 g
Cholesterol: 0 mg
Protein: 6 g

Carbohydrates: 19 g
Dietary Fiber: 4 g
Sodium: 25 mg

Sherried Mushroom-Barley Soup

Mushrooms, scallions, garlic, parsley, and barley are the ingredients in this sherry-accented soup.

YIELD: 6 servings • *PREPARATION TIME: 20 minutes* • *COOKING TIME: 45 minutes*

6¼ cups nonfat chicken broth
1 pound fresh white mushrooms, sliced
2 scallions, chopped
2 cloves garlic, minced
¼ cup chopped fresh parsley

1 tablespoon dried thyme
¼ teaspoon ground black pepper
½ cup uncooked pearl barley
2 tablespoons dry sherry

1. Heat ¼ cup of chicken broth in a large Dutch oven or stockpot over medium heat. Add mushrooms and sauté for 4 minutes. Add the scallions, garlic, parsley, thyme, and black pepper. Stir well.
2. Add the remaining broth; bring to a boil. Stir in the barley and return to a boil. Reduce heat, cover, and simmer until barley is just tender, about 35 minutes.
3. Add sherry and serve.

Calories Per Serving: 339
Fat: 2 g
Cholesterol: 0 mg
Protein: 14 g

Carbohydrates: 73 g
Dietary Fiber: 11 g
Sodium: 353 mg

Shiitake-Barley Soup

Shiitake mushrooms are simmered with celery, carrot, onion, and barley in an herb-flavored chicken broth.

YIELD: 8 servings • *PREPARATION TIME: 30 minutes* •
COOKING TIME: 1 hour plus 15 minutes soaking time

1 ounce dried shiitake mushrooms
water for soaking mushrooms
8 cups nonfat chicken broth
1 medium onion, chopped
1 stalk celery, diced

1 carrot, diced
1 bay leaf
1 teaspoon dried thyme
¾ cup uncooked pearl barley

1. Rinse the mushrooms and cover with very hot water. Let stand for 15 minutes.
2. Remove the mushrooms from the water, slice, and reserve the liquid.
3. Heat ¼ cup of the broth in a large, heavy saucepan. Stir in the onion and sauté for 1 minute. Stir in the celery and carrot and sauté for another minute.
4. Add the mushrooms, the water in which they soaked, bay leaf, thyme, and remaining chicken broth and bring the mixture to a boil. Stir in the barley. Reduce heat, cover the pot, and simmer for 1 hour.
5. Discard the bay leaf and serve.

Calories Per Serving: 157
Fat: 2 g
Cholesterol: 0 mg
Protein: 9 g

Carbohydrates: 30 g
Dietary Fiber: 36 g
Sodium: 347 mg

Tomato-Barley Soup

This tomato-barley soup is thick, delicious, and easy. You can assemble the ingredients, put it in a pot, turn on the heat, and forget it.

YIELD: 8 servings • *PREPARATION TIME: 20 minutes* • *COOKING TIME: 70 minutes*

¼ cup nonfat chicken broth
2 medium onions, sliced

5 cups water
¾ cup uncooked pearl barley

2 carrots, sliced
1 turnip, diced
1 potato, peeled and diced
½ cup sliced celery

4 cups chopped low-sodium canned
   plum tomatoes, with liquid
2 bay leaves
¼ teaspoon ground black pepper

1. Heat broth in a large pot or Dutch oven over medium heat. Add the onions and sauté until lightly browned.
2. Add the water, barley, carrots, turnip, potato, celery, tomatoes, and bay leaves.
3. Bring to a boil; lower heat, cover, and simmer for 1 hour.
4. Add the black pepper.

Calories Per Serving: 145
Fat: 1 g
Cholesterol: 0 mg
Protein: 5 g

Carbohydrates: 32 g
Dietary Fiber: 6 g
Sodium: 240 mg

Turkey-Barley Soup

This simple turkey soup is a medley of onions, celery, turnip, parsley, carrots, pearl barley, and herbs.

YIELD: 12 servings • *PREPARATION TIME: 45 minutes* • *COOKING TIME: 1 hour*

3 pounds lowfat turkey cutlets, cut into
   1-inch pieces
10 cups nonfat chicken broth
4½ cups chopped onions
2 cups chopped celery
½ cup diced turnip
½ cup chopped fresh parsley
3 cups sliced carrots
⅔ cup uncooked pearl barley
½ teaspoon dried marjoram

¼ teaspoon dried thyme
¼ teaspoon ground black pepper
2 cups cooked or low-sodium canned
   Great Northern beans, rinsed and
   drained
1½ cups fresh, canned, or thawed frozen
   corn kernels
1 28-ounce can plum tomatoes, with
   liquid, crushed

1. Mix turkey, broth, onions, 1 cup celery, turnip, and parsley in a 6-quart pot and bring to a boil. Reduce heat and simmer, covered, for 30 minutes.
2. Add carrots, barley, remaining celery, marjoram, thyme, and black pepper. Simmer, covered, for additional 20 minutes.

3. Stir in beans, corn, and tomatoes and simmer, uncovered, for another 10 minutes.

Calories Per Serving: 271
Fat: 3 g
Cholesterol: 57 mg
Protein: 36 g

Carbohydrates: 31 g
Dietary Fiber: 5 g
Sodium: 490 mg

Kale-Barley Soup

Kale, cultivated for at least 2,000 years, is rich in vitamins A and C, folic acid, calcium, and iron. It is the star of this soup, which also features chicken and corn.

YIELD: 6 servings • *PREPARATION TIME: 20 minutes* • *COOKING TIME: 45 minutes*

3¼ cups nonfat chicken broth
1 medium onion, chopped
2 cups water
1 cup uncooked pearl barley
½ teaspoon ground black pepper

½ teaspoon ground nutmeg
4 cups kale, trimmed and cut into short strips
2 cups fresh, frozen, or canned corn kernels, cooked

1. Heat ¼ cup chicken broth in a large pot over medium heat. Sauté onion until tender.
2. Add rest of broth, 2 cups water, barley, pepper, nutmeg, and kale. Bring to a boil. Reduce heat and simmer, covered, for 20 minutes.
3. Add the corn to the soup, return to a boil, and simmer, covered, for 10 minutes.

Calories Per Serving: 215
Fat: 2 g
Cholesterol: 0 mg
Protein: 10 g

Carbohydrates: 45 g
Dietary Fiber: 10 g
Sodium: 222 mg

Lemon-Chicken-Barley Soup with Lentils

Lentil-chicken soup is accented with lemon and parsley and thickened with yogurt.

YIELD: 10 servings • *PREPARATION TIME: 20 minutes* • *COOKING TIME: 1 hour*

1 tablespoon olive oil	2 cups dried lentils
1 cup chopped onion	¼ teaspoon ground black pepper
2 cloves garlic, minced	2 cups plain nonfat yogurt
8 cups nonfat chicken broth	1 tablespoon fresh lemon juice
½ cup uncooked pearl barley	½ cup finely chopped fresh parsley

1. Heat oil in skillet over medium flame and sauté onions and garlic until tender, about 3 minutes.
2. Pour broth into a large soup pot and add barley, sautéed onion and garlic, lentils, and pepper. Bring mixture to a boil. Reduce heat and simmer for 50 minutes. Add more stock or water if needed.
3. Add 1 cup of soup to the yogurt and mix until smooth. Add the yogurt mixture to the soup and mix well.
4. Add the lemon juice and parsley; mix, and serve.

Calories Per Serving: 155	Carbohydrates: 22 g
Fat: 3 g	Dietary Fiber: 4 g
Cholesterol: 1 mg	Sodium: 306 mg
Protein: 14 g	

Jalapeño-Barley Salad

This barley-vegetable salad is given a Southwestern twist with the addition of jalapeño and lime juice.

YIELD: 6 servings • *PREPARATION TIME: 20 minutes* •
COOKING TIME: 40 minutes plus barley cooling time

3 cups water	1 cup fresh, frozen, or canned corn
1 cup uncooked pearl barley	kernels, cooked
1 tablespoon minced jalapeño pepper	½ cup diced cucumber
¼ cup fresh lime juice	½ cup diced tomato
1 tablespoon olive oil	½ cup diced green bell pepper
⅛ teaspoon ground black pepper	½ cup chopped red onion

1. In a large saucepan, bring water to a boil and stir in barley. Reduce heat, cover, and simmer until barley is tender, about 40 minutes. Remove from heat and allow to cool. Drain any excess liquid.
2. Combine jalapeño pepper, lime juice, olive oil, and black pepper. Whisk vigorously.
3. In a large serving bowl, mix barley with corn, cucumber, tomato, green bell pepper, and onion. Add jalapeño dressing, toss to coat all ingredients, and serve.

Calories Per Serving: 111
Fat: 3 g
Cholesterol: 0 mg
Protein: 3 g

Carbohydrates: 21 g
Dietary Fiber: 4 g
Sodium: 30 mg

Sun-Dried Tomato–Barley Salad

Sun-dried tomatoes are the special ingredient in this lemon- and dill-accented barley salad.

YIELD: *6 servings* • PREPARATION TIME: *15 minutes* •
COOKING TIME: *50 minutes plus 30 minutes cooling time*

2 cups nonfat chicken broth
1 cup water
1 cup uncooked pearl barley
½ ounce sun-dried tomatoes, chopped
1 tablespoon olive oil
6 scallions, chopped

1 cup chopped fresh parsley
1 clove garlic, minced
¼ cup lemon juice
¼ teaspoon ground black pepper
1 teaspoon dried dill

1. Bring the broth and 1 cup water to a boil in a large saucepan. Stir in the barley and return to a boil; reduce heat, cover, and simmer until the barley is just tender, about 35 minutes.
2. Meanwhile, soak the sun-dried tomatoes in the olive oil.
3. When the barley is tender, add the oil and tomatoes, scallions, parsley, garlic, lemon juice, black pepper, and dill. Toss to mix thoroughly; cool in refrigerator for 30 minutes before serving.

Calories Per Serving: 151
Fat: 3 g
Cholesterol: 0 mg
Protein: 6 g

Carbohydrates: 26 g
Dietary Fiber: 5 g
Sodium: 125 mg

Red Pepper–Broccoli–Barley Salad

Fresh broccoli and red bell pepper are combined with tomatoes, carrot, scallions, and Italian dressing in this chilled barley salad.

YIELD: 8 servings • PREPARATION TIME: 15 minutes •
COOKING TIME: 40 minutes plus 30 minutes chilling time

2 cups water
1 cup uncooked pearl barley
2 cups chopped fresh broccoli
⅔ cup nonfat Italian dressing

2½ cups chopped fresh or low-sodium
*   canned tomatoes*
½ cup shredded carrot
4 scallions, chopped
½ cup chopped red bell pepper

1. Bring water to a boil in a large saucepan. Stir in barley. Reduce heat, cover, and simmer until barley is tender, about 40 minutes.
2. Meanwhile, in a large bowl, combine broccoli and Italian dressing.
3. Add barley, tomato, carrot, scallions, and red bell pepper; toss, and chill for 30 minutes.

Calories Per Serving: 124
Fat: 1 g
Cholesterol: 0 mg
Protein: 4 g

Carbohydrates: 26 g
Dietary Fiber: 6 g
Sodium: 475 mg

Artichoke-Barley Salad

Canned artichoke hearts are tossed with barley, scallions, yellow bell pepper, and cucumber and served with a yogurt dressing.

YIELD: 4 servings • PREPARATION TIME: 30 minutes • COOKING TIME: 1 hour
and 25 minutes plus 30 minutes cooling and 30 minutes chilling time

4 cups water
1 cup uncooked pearl barley
4 scallions, chopped
1 yellow bell pepper, chopped
1 cucumber, chopped

⅓ cup nonfat mayonnaise
⅓ cup nonfat plain yogurt
2 cups canned artichoke hearts, drained
  and chopped

1. Bring 4 cups of water to a boil in a large saucepan. Stir in the barley. Return to a boil, cover, and simmer until barley is just tender, about 40 minutes. Add more water if necessary.
2. When barley is tender, drain any remaining liquid. Set barley aside and allow to cool to room temperature.
3. In a large bowl, combine the barley, scallions, yellow bell pepper, cucumber, mayonnaise, and yogurt. Mix well. Add the artichoke hearts. Refrigerate for 30 minutes.

Calories Per Serving: 164
Fat: 1 g
Cholesterol: 0 mg
Protein: 7 g

Carbohydrates: 35 g
Dietary Fiber: 8 g
Sodium: 241 mg

Black Bean–Barley Salad

Black beans and barley are tossed with a honey-garlic dressing.

YIELD: 8 servings • *PREPARATION TIME: 15 minutes* • *COOKING TIME: 15 minutes*

1 cup water
½ cup quick-cooking barley
2 cloves garlic, minced
¼ teaspoon ground black pepper
2 tablespoons cider vinegar
1 tablespoon honey

1 tablespoon olive oil
2 cups cooked or canned low-sodium
  black beans, rinsed and drained
1 cup chopped tomato
½ cup chopped green bell pepper
⅓ cup chopped onion

1. Bring water to a boil in a medium saucepan. Stir in barley. Return to a boil, cover, and cook, stirring frequently, for 35 minutes, or until barley is just tender. Remove from heat and let stand.
2. In a large serving bowl whisk together the garlic, black pepper, vinegar, honey, and olive oil.
3. Combine barley, beans, tomato, green bell pepper, and onion and toss with dressing to coat all ingredients.

Calories Per Serving: 137
Fat: 2 g
Cholesterol: 0 mg
Protein: 5 g

Carbohydrates: 25 g
Dietary Fiber: 6 g
Sodium: 7 mg

Barley–Kidney Bean Salad

Barley and kidney beans are tossed in an oil-lemon dressing with tomatoes, parsley, and scallions.

YIELD: 6 servings • *PREPARATION TIME: 20 minutes plus barley cooking time*

1 tablespoon olive oil
¼ cup lemon juice
¼ teaspoon ground black pepper
2 cups cooked barley (see p. 362)

2 cups canned low-sodium red kidney
 beans, rinsed and drained
12 cherry tomatoes, quartered
½ cup chopped fresh parsley
¼ cup sliced scallions

1. In a large serving bowl, whisk together the olive oil, lemon juice, and black pepper.
2. Combine the barley, beans, tomatoes, parsley, and scallions and toss with dressing.

Calories Per Serving: 230
Fat: 3 g
Cholesterol: 0 mg
Protein: 9 g

Carbohydrates: 44 g
Dietary Fiber: 10 g
Sodium: 14 mg

Barley Pilaf

This simple pilaf is made with chicken broth, mushrooms, and onion.

YIELD: 8 servings • *PREPARATION TIME: 20 minutes* • *COOKING TIME: 42 minutes*

8¼ cups nonfat chicken broth
½ pound fresh white mushrooms,
 coarsely chopped

½ medium onion, thinly sliced
2 cups uncooked pearl barley
¼ teaspoon ground black pepper

1. Heat ¼ cup broth in a large saucepan over medium heat. Add the mushrooms and onion and sauté until the onion becomes transparent, about 3 minutes.
2. Add barley and sauté until lightly browned, about 3 minutes.
3. Add remaining 8 cups broth and bring to a boil. Reduce heat, cover, and cook, adding more liquid if necessary, until barley is tender, about 35 minutes. Season with black pepper.

Calories Per Serving: 211
Fat: 2 g
Cholesterol: 0 mg
Protein: 10 g

Carbohydrates: 42 g
Dietary Fiber: 8 g
Sodium: 352 mg

Curried Vegetable-Barley Pilaf

Carrots, zucchini, and onion augment this curried pilaf.

YIELD: 5 servings • PREPARATION TIME: 20 minutes • COOKING TIME: 50 minutes

2½ cups nonfat chicken broth
½ cup chopped onion
1 teaspoon curry powder

1 cup uncooked pearl barley
2 carrots, shredded
1 medium zucchini, shredded

1. Heat ¼ cup chicken broth in a large pan over medium heat. Add onion and curry powder. Sauté until onion turns light golden, about 4 minutes.
2. Add remaining chicken broth and bring to a boil. Stir in barley. Return to a boil; reduce heat, cover, and simmer until barley is just tender, about 35 minutes.
3. Add carrots and zucchini; cover and cook for an additional 5 minutes.

Calories Per Serving: 174
Fat: 1 g
Cholesterol: 0 mg
Protein: 7 g

Carbohydrates: 37 g
Dietary Fiber: 8 g
Sodium: 166 mg

Barley—Green Pepper Salad

Barley, green pepper, and onion are served with a dilled vinegar dressing.

YIELD: 8 servings • *PREPARATION TIME: 15 minutes* •
COOKING TIME: 40 minutes plus cooling time and 2 hours chilling time

4 cups water
1½ cups uncooked pearl barley
½ cup cider vinegar
3 tablespoons sugar
1 teaspoon dried dill

1 tablespoon olive oil
1½ cups chopped red, green, or yellow
    bell peppers
¼ cup chopped onion

1. Bring water to a boil in a large saucepan. Stir in barley. Return to a boil; reduce heat, cover, and simmer until barley begins to become tender, about 35
   minutes.
2. While barley is warm, add vinegar, sugar, dill, and olive oil. Mix well.
3. Cool mixture to room temperature. Stir in bell peppers and onion. Refrigerate, covered, for 2 hours before serving.

Calories Per Serving: 179
Fat: 2 g
Cholesterol: 0 mg
Protein: 4 g

Carbohydrates: 37 g
Dietary Fiber: 7 g
Sodium: 8 mg

Cranberry Barley

Cranberries are mixed with barley, wild rice, and a lemon-thyme dressing.

YIELD: 6 servings • *PREPARATION TIME: 20 minutes* • *COOKING TIME: 50 minutes*

5 cups water
½ cup uncooked wild rice
1 cup uncooked pearl barley
½ cup dried cranberries, drained

1 teaspoon olive oil
2 tablespoons lemon juice
1 teaspoon dried thyme
¼ teaspoon ground black pepper

1. Bring 2 cups of water to a boil in a large saucepan. Stir in wild rice. Return
   to a boil; reduce heat, cover, and cook until rice is tender, about 40 minutes.

2. Meanwhile, bring remaining water to a boil in another large pan. Stir in barley. Return to a boil; reduce heat, cover, and cook until barley is tender, about 40 minutes.
3. Combine rice, barley, cranberries, olive oil, lemon juice, thyme, and pepper.

Calories Per Serving: 205	Carbohydrates: 40 g
Fat: 3 g	Dietary Fiber: 6 g
Cholesterol: 0 mg	Sodium: 101 mg
Protein: 7 g	

Toasted Barley Pilaf

Barley is browned in a skillet and simmered in broth with sautéed vegetables.

Yield: 2 servings • *Preparation Time: 20 minutes* • *Cooking Time: 1 hour*

½ cup uncooked pearl barley	*3 tablespoons minced celery*
2½ cups nonfat chicken broth	*¼ teaspoon dried rosemary*
3 tablespoons minced carrots	*1 bay leaf*
3 tablespoons minced onions	*¼ teaspoon ground black pepper*

1. Toast the barley in a nonstick skillet over low heat, shaking frequently, until the barley begins to brown, about 20 minutes. Set aside.
2. Heat ¼ cup chicken broth in a large saucepan. Add the carrots, onions, and celery and sauté until the onions become translucent.
3. Stir in the barley. Add the rosemary, bay leaf, black pepper, and remaining chicken broth. Cover and simmer until the barley is just tender, about 35 minutes.

Calories Per Serving: 207	Carbohydrates: 39 g
Fat: 2 g	Dietary Fiber: 8 g
Cholesterol: 0 mg	Sodium: 400 mg
Protein: 11 g	

Barley with Capers

Barley is sautéed with onion and garlic, simmered with chicken broth, tomato, and parsley, and tossed with capers.

YIELD: 6 servings • *PREPARATION TIME: 15 minutes* • *COOKING TIME: 40 minutes*

1 tablespoon olive oil
¾ cup chopped onion
2 cloves garlic
¾ cup uncooked pearl barley
1½ cups nonfat chicken broth

1 large ripe tomato, chopped
¼ cup chopped fresh parsley
¼ teaspoon ground black pepper
1 tablespoon rinsed, drained capers

1. Heat oil in large saucepan over medium heat. Add onion and sauté until onion begins to turn lightly golden, about 3 minutes. Add garlic and barley and sauté an additional 2 minutes.
2. Add the broth, tomato, 2 tablespoons parsley, and black pepper. Bring to a boil; reduce heat, cover, and simmer until barley is just tender, about 35 minutes.
3. Stir in the capers, sprinkle with remaining parsley, and serve.

Calories Per Serving: 128
Fat: 3 g
Cholesterol: 0 mg
Protein: 4 g

Carbohydrates: 23 g
Dietary Fiber: 5 g
Sodium: 90 mg

Honey-Lemon Barley

Barley is combined with celery, mushrooms, apples, and currants, then seasoned with lemon juice, honey, and parsley.

YIELD: 4 servings • *PREPARATION TIME: 25 minutes* • *COOKING TIME: 50 minutes*

1¾ cups nonfat chicken broth
1 cup water
¾ cup uncooked pearl barley
½ cup chopped onion
¼ cup chopped celery
1 cup sliced fresh white mushrooms

1 cup diced apples
⅓ cup currants
1 tablespoon honey
1 tablespoon lemon juice
2 tablespoons chopped fresh parsley

1. Place 1½ cups of the broth and ¾ cup of the water in large saucepan. Bring to a boil.
2. Add barley and reduce heat. Simmer for 35 minutes, or until barley is tender.
3. Place remaining ¼ cup broth in a skillet over medium heat. Add onion, celery, and mushrooms. Cook, stirring, over medium heat for 5 minutes.
4. Add remaining ¼ cup water, apples, and currants. Simmer for 20 minutes, or until apples are tender.
5. Combine barley and mushroom-apple mixture. Stir in honey, lemon juice, and parsley.

Calories Per Serving: 279
Fat: 1 g
Cholesterol: 0 mg
Protein: 8 g

Carbohydrates: 64 g
Dietary Fiber: 8 g
Sodium: 113 mg

Barley-Mushroom Trio

Shiitake, porcini, and white mushrooms are cooked with barley.

YIELD: 4 servings • PREPARATION TIME: 15 minutes • COOKING TIME: 45 minutes

¼ cup nonfat chicken broth
½ pound fresh shiitake mushrooms, sliced
½ pound fresh porcini mushrooms, or portabello mushrooms, sliced

1½ pounds fresh white mushrooms, coarsely chopped
½ teaspoon ground black pepper
4 cups water
1 cup uncooked pearl barley
2 tablespoons minced fresh parsley

1. Heat the chicken broth in a large, heavy skillet over medium heat. Sauté the shiitake and porcini mushrooms for 10 minutes. Add the white mushrooms and pepper. Reduce heat, cover, and cook for 5 minutes.
2. Add the water and barley; bring to a boil, cover, reduce heat, and simmer until the barley becomes just tender, about 30 minutes.
3. Remove from heat. Stir in parsley and serve.

Calories Per Serving: 285
Fat: 2 g
Cholesterol: 0 mg
Protein: 13 g

Carbohydrates: 61 g
Dietary Fiber: 12 g
Sodium: 48 mg

Butternut-Barley Bake

Barley, onions, squash, and raisins are sautéed, baked, and topped with almonds.

YIELD: 8 servings ・ *PREPARATION TIME: 20 minutes* ・
COOKING TIME: 45 minutes plus 5 minutes standing time

2¾ cups nonfat chicken broth
1½ cups chopped onion
1 clove garlic, minced
1 cup uncooked pearl barley
3 cups diced butternut squash
¼ cup raisins

2 teaspoons minced orange peel
½ teaspoon ground allspice
1 teaspoon ground cinnamon
¼ teaspoon ground black pepper
2 tablespoons chopped toasted almonds

1. Preheat oven to 350 degrees.
2. Heat ¼ cup chicken broth in a large skillet. Add onion and garlic. Sauté until onion turns light gold, about 4 minutes.
3. Stir in the barley and sauté 1 additional minute. Add remaining broth, squash, raisins, orange peel, allspice, cinnamon, and black pepper.
4. Transfer barley mixture to a large ovenproof casserole. Bake for 40 minutes.
5. Remove from oven and let stand, covered, for 5 minutes. Sprinkle with almonds and serve.

Calories Per Serving: 191
Fat: 2 g
Cholesterol: 0 mg
Protein: 6 g

Carbohydrates: 41 g
Dietary Fiber: 6 g
Sodium: 123 mg

Red Pepper–Baked Barley

Barley is simmered in chicken broth and baked with sautéed red bell pepper, mushrooms, and onion.

YIELD: 5 servings ・ *PREPARATION TIME: 25 minutes* ・ *COOKING TIME: 60 minutes*

1 cup uncooked pearl barley
4¼ cups nonfat chicken broth
1 cup minced onion

3 cups chopped fresh mushrooms
½ cup diced red bell pepper
¼ teaspoon ground black pepper

1. Preheat oven to 350 degrees.
2. Spread barley on a shallow baking pan and bake until it begins to brown.
3. Bring 4 cups chicken broth to a boil in a large saucepan. Stir in barley. Return to a boil; reduce heat, cover, and simmer for 25 minutes.
4. Reheat oven to 350 degrees.
5. Heat remaining ¼ cup chicken broth in another large saucepan over medium heat. Add onion, mushrooms, and red bell peppers. Sauté until onion is lightly golden.
6. Combine barley, vegetable mixture, and black pepper and place in a nonstick baking dish. Cover and bake at 350 degrees for 30 minutes.

Calories Per Serving: 183
Fat: 3 g
Cholesterol: 0 mg
Protein: 8 g

Carbohydrates: 34 g
Dietary Fiber: 7 g
Sodium: 142 mg

Chili with Barley

Kidney beans, celery, red bell pepper, tomatoes, corn, and barley are seasoned with jalapeño, chili powder, and cayenne pepper.

YIELD: 10 servings • PREPARATION TIME: 20 minutes •
COOKING TIME: 35 minutes

1¼ cups nonfat chicken broth
1 medium onion, chopped
2 cloves garlic, minced
3 cups chopped celery
1 red bell pepper, chopped
2 cups canned low-sodium kidney
   beans, rinsed and drained
6 cups fresh or canned low-sodium
   tomatoes, chopped, liquid reserved

1 cup fresh or frozen corn kernels,
   cooked
1 cup uncooked pearl barley
2 jalapeño peppers, seeded and minced
¼ cup chopped fresh parsley
1 teaspoon chili powder
⅛ teaspoon cayenne pepper
¼ teaspoon ground black pepper

1. Heat ¼ cup chicken broth in a large, heavy pot or Dutch oven. Add onion and garlic and sauté until onion just turns translucent, about 3 minutes.
2. Add celery and red bell pepper and sauté for 3 additional minutes.
3. Add kidney beans, tomatoes with their liquid, remaining broth, corn, barley, jalapeños, and parsley. Mix thoroughly. Stir in chili powder, cayenne, and black pepper. Bring to boil, reduce heat, and simmer for 30 minutes.

Calories Per Serving: 175 Carbohydrates: 37 g
Fat: 1 g Dietary Fiber: 8 g
Cholesterol: 0 mg Sodium: 284 mg
Protein: 8 g

Chili Loaf

Kidney beans, barley, chili powder, green bell peppers, jalapeño pepper, onion, tomato sauce, and rolled oats are baked in a loaf.

YIELD: *6 servings* ▪ PREPARATION TIME: *30 minutes plus barley cooking time* ▪
COOKING TIME: *50 minutes plus 5 to 7 minutes cooling time*

1½ cups canned low-sodium kidney beans, rinsed and drained
2 cups cooked pearl barley (see p. 362)
1½ teaspoons ground black pepper
2 teaspoons chili powder
¾ cup nonfat chicken broth
2 medium onions, chopped

1 green bell pepper, chopped
1 jalapeño pepper, seeded and minced
2 cloves garlic, minced
½ cup low-sodium tomato sauce
1 cup uncooked rolled oats
3 egg whites

1. Place the beans and barley in a food processor or blender. Blend briefly until chunky. Transfer to large mixing bowl.
2. Combine black pepper and chili powder.
3. Heat ¼ cup chicken broth in a large, heavy skillet. Stir in the onions, green bell pepper, jalapeño, garlic, and black pepper mixture. Sauté until liquid has evaporated, about 5 minutes.
4. Add the tomato sauce and remaining chicken broth. Cook until mixture has thickened, about 10 to 12 minutes.
5. Preheat oven to 350 degrees.
6. Stir the sautéed tomato-vegetable mixture into the beans and barley. Fold in rolled oats and egg whites, and mix well.
7. Place mixture in the center of a nonstick 9-inch-by-13-inch baking dish and form into an oblong loaf. Bake for 30 minutes. Allow to cool for 5 to 7 minutes before serving.

Calories Per Serving: 226
Fat: 1 g
Cholesterol: 0 mg
Protein: 10 g

Carbohydrates: 46 g
Dietary Fiber: 7 g
Sodium: 179 mg

Microwave Barley with Green Peas and Yellow Peppers

Barley is cooked with garlic, green peas, yellow bell peppers, and parsley.

YIELD: 4 servings • *PREPARATION TIME: 10 minutes* •
COOKING TIME: 22 minutes plus 5 minutes standing time

1 cup uncooked pearl barley
1 cup water
2 cloves garlic, minced
1 cup frozen green peas

1 cup chopped yellow bell peppers
¼ cup nonfat chicken broth
2 tablespoons chopped fresh parsley

1. Combine barley, water, and garlic in a microwave-safe casserole and cover with vented plastic wrap. Microwave on HIGH for 5 minutes. Stir. Microwave on HIGH for 7 more minutes. Stir. Microwave on MEDIUM for 5 minutes.
2. Add peas, yellow bell peppers, chicken broth, and parsley. Microwave on HIGH for 5 minutes. Let stand for 5 minutes before serving.

Calories Per Serving: 217
Fat: 1 g
Cholesterol: 0 mg
Protein: 8 g

Carbohydrates: 46 g
Dietary Fiber: 10 g
Sodium: 62 mg

Barley, Wild Rice, and Shiitake Mushrooms

Barley and wild rice are simmered with marjoram and thyme, and combined with carrot, shiitake mushrooms, celery, and onion.

YIELD: 8 servings • *PREPARATION TIME: 20 minutes* •
COOKING TIME: 50 minutes

½ cup uncooked pearl barley
½ cup uncooked wild rice
¾ cup water
2¼ cups nonfat chicken broth
1 teaspoon dried thyme
½ teaspoon dried marjoram

¼ teaspoon ground black pepper
1 medium carrot, thinly sliced
1 cup sliced fresh shiitake mushrooms
1 stalk celery, sliced
1 medium onion, chopped

1. Combine barley, wild rice, water, 2 cups chicken broth, thyme, marjoram, and black pepper. Cover and bring broth to a boil. Reduce heat to low. Cook, covered, for 40 minutes, or until water is absorbed.
2. Heat ¼ cup chicken broth in a skillet over medium heat. Add carrot and stir-fry for 2 minutes. Add mushrooms, celery, and onion. Cook for 2 more minutes.
3. Stir vegetable mixture into rice mixture and serve.

Calories Per Serving: 99
Fat: 1 g
Cholesterol: 0 mg
Protein: 4 g

Carbohydrates: 21 g
Dietary Fiber: 3 g
Sodium: 104 mg

Barley with Chicken and Vegetables

Barley is served with chopped broiled chicken and sautéed zucchini, bell pepper, leeks, and scallions.

YIELD: 4 servings • PREPARATION TIME: 15 minutes • COOKING TIME: 70 minutes

5 cups water
⅔ cup uncooked pearl barley
½ pound skinless chicken breast cutlets
½ cup nonfat chicken broth
¾ cup chopped yellow bell pepper
¾ cup chopped zucchini

¾ cup chopped leek
1½ tablespoons chopped scallion
½ cup chopped fresh parsley
½ teaspoon ground black pepper
4 tablespoons grated nonfat Parmesan

1. Bring water to a boil in a large saucepan. Stir in barley. Return to a boil, reduce heat, cover, and simmer until barley is just tender, about 40 minutes. Drain any excess liquid; transfer barley to a large bowl and set aside.
2. Preheat broiler. Broil chicken cutlets until done, about 3 minutes each side. Allow chicken to cool; chop in small pieces.

3. Heat ¼ cup chicken broth in a large skillet. Add yellow bell pepper, zucchini, leek, and scallion. Sauté until vegetables are just tender, about 5 minutes.

4. Add barley, chopped chicken, parsley, and remaining ¼ cup chicken broth. Cook, stirring, until all ingredients are heated through.

5. Season with black pepper, transfer to serving plates, and sprinkle with cheese.

Calories Per Serving: 234
Fat: 1 g
Cholesterol: 44 mg
Protein: 20 g

Carbohydrates: 38 g
Dietary Fiber: 7 g
Sodium: 176 mg

Curried Barley with Chicken, Lentils, and Spinach

Barley is simmered with green bell pepper, carrots, curry powder, lentils, spinach, and chicken.

YIELD: 4 servings • PREPARATION TIME: 20 minutes • COOKING TIME: 55 minutes

2¼ cups nonfat chicken broth
1 cup chopped onion
2 cups water
¾ cup uncooked pearl barley
1¼ cups chopped green bell pepper
½ cup sliced carrots

1½ teaspoons curry powder
¾ cup dried lentils
2 cups chopped spinach
8 ounces skinless chicken breast cutlets,
    cut into ½-inch cubes

1. Heat ¼ cup chicken broth in a large saucepan over medium heat. Add onion and sauté until lightly browned, about 4 minutes.

2. Add remaining chicken broth and water. Bring to a boil. Stir in barley, green pepper, carrots, and curry powder. Return to a boil; reduce heat, cover, and simmer 10 minutes.

3. Add lentils, cover, and simmer, stirring occasionally, until barley and lentils are tender, about 30 minutes.

4. Stir in spinach and chicken. Cover and simmer until chicken is cooked through, about 10 minutes.

Calories Per Serving: 343
Fat: 3 g
Cholesterol: 37 mg
Protein: 28 g

Carbohydrates: 57 g
Dietary Fiber: 14 g
Sodium: 242 mg

Barley Stuffing

This recipe makes enough stuffing for a 16-pound turkey, but it can also be served as a side dish. It combines barley and bulgur with vegetables, spices, and herbs.

YIELD: 15 servings • PREPARATION TIME: 30 minutes plus bulgur and barley cooking time • COOKING TIME: 5 minutes

¼ cup nonfat chicken broth
3 medium onions, chopped
4 celery stalks, chopped
1 red bell pepper, diced
3 carrots, diced
2 cups cooked barley (see p. 362)

4 cups cooked bulgur (see p. 388)
1 teaspoon dried sage
2 teaspoons ground cumin
1 cup chopped fresh parsley
½ teaspoon ground black pepper

1. Heat chicken broth in a large saucepan over medium heat. Add onions, celery, red bell pepper, and carrots and sauté until vegetables are just tender, about 5 minutes.
2. Combine barley, bulgur, and onion mixture. Add sage, cumin, parsley, and black pepper and mix well.

Calories Per Serving: 134
Fat: 1 g
Cholesterol: 0 mg
Protein: 5 g

Carbohydrates: 29 g
Dietary Fiber: 7 g
Sodium: 28 mg

Chicken-Apple Chowder with Barley

Sautéed chicken chunks, apple, green peas, cabbage, carrots, and leeks are the featured ingredients in this tempting soup.

YIELD: 12 servings • PREPARATION TIME: 35 minutes • COOKING TIME: 50 minutes

4 quarts water
1 tablespoon caraway seeds
¾ teaspoon ground black pepper
2 stalks celery, cut into 2-inch lengths
¼ cup chopped fresh parsley
½ cup uncooked pearl barley
¼ cup nonfat chicken broth

1 pound skinless chicken breast cutlets,
    cut into ¾-inch cubes
2 carrots, sliced
3 leeks, sliced
4 cups shredded cabbage
1 cup skim milk
2 cups frozen green peas
1 large apple, cored and chopped

1. Place water, caraway seeds, ½ teaspoon black pepper, celery, and parsley in a large stockpot. Bring to a boil.
2. Add barley; reduce heat, cover, and simmer for 20 minutes.
3. Heat chicken broth in a large skillet over medium heat. Sauté chicken until it is no longer pink, about 5 minutes. Add carrots and leeks and sauté for 3 minutes. Add cabbage and sauté until it begins to soften, about 5 minutes.
4. Add chicken and vegetables to barley. Stir in milk, peas, apple, and remaining ¼ teaspoon black pepper. Bring to a boil. Reduce heat and simmer until barley is tender, about 30 minutes.

Calories Per Serving: 187
Fat: 2 g
Cholesterol: 25 mg
Protein: 14 g

Carbohydrates: 31 g
Dietary Fiber: 6 g
Sodium: 69 mg

BULGUR

✦

Basic Simmered Bulgur • Basic Soaked Bulgur • Orange-Fig Bulgur
Pilaf • Three-Grain Pilaf • Bulgur with Apples and Raisins • Easy
Microwave Apricot-Bulgur Breakfast • Parsley-Bulgur Salad • Spiced
Tabbouleh • Southwestern Tabbouleh • Asparagus and Yellow Bell
Pepper with Bulgur • Bell Pepper–Bulgur Slaw • Broccoli-Bulgur
Salad • Spinach-Bulgur Salad with Cumin-Yogurt Dressing •
Summer Harvest Bulgur Salad • Warm Shrimp Tabbouleh •
Mandarin-Turkey-Spinach Salad with Bulgur • Bulgur-Stuffed
Tomatoes • Peppers Stuffed with Tabbouleh and Beans • Basic
Bulgur Pilaf • Sage-Bulgur Pilaf • Bulgur Pilaf with Thyme and
Vermicelli • Butternut Bulgur Pilaf • Jalapeño-Apple Bulgur Pilaf •
Lentil-Bulgur Pilaf • Red Lentil–Bulgur Pilaf • Garlic-Chickpea
Bulgur Pilaf • Bulgur-Turkey Meatballs • Mushrooms Stuffed with
Bulgur • Tomatoes Stuffed with Mushrooms and Bulgur • Tomato-
Lentil Stew with Bulgur • Summer Squash–Bulgur Casserole • Chili
with Bulgur • Bulgur and Vegetables • Curried Vegetables with
Bulgur • Bulgur with Baked Chicken • Orange-Cumin Chicken
Breast Cutlets with Bulgur • Turkey-Bulgur Salad • Chicken–Lima
Bean Bulgur • Ginger Chicken with Rice and Bulgur • Black Beans
and Oranges with Bulgur

Basic Simmered Bulgur

This method works well for dishes like stuffed green peppers or cabbage because after simmering the bulgur is easier to work with.

YIELD: 2 servings • *COOKING TIME: 15 minutes*

2 cups cold water   *1 cup uncooked bulgur*

1. Bring the water to a boil and simmer the bulgur for 15 minutes, or until the water is absorbed.

Calories Per Serving: 240   Carbohydrates: 53 g
Fat: 1 g   Dietary Fiber: 16 g
Cholesterol: 0 mg   Sodium: 12 mg
Protein: 9 g

Basic Soaked Bulgur

This method works well for dishes like tabbouleh. Soak bulgur overnight and enjoy its nutty, chewy texture the next day.

YIELD: 2 servings • *PREPARATION TIME: 8 hours*

1 cup uncooked bulgur   *2 cups cold water*

1. Soak the bulgur in the water for 8 hours.

Calories Per Serving: 240   Carbohydrates: 53 g
Fat: 1 g   Dietary Fiber: 16 g
Cholesterol: 0 mg   Sodium: 12 mg
Protein: 9 g

Orange-Fig Bulgur Pilaf

A fruity pilaf of bulgur simmered in orange juice and sherry and accented with figs and orange peel.

YIELD: 4 servings • *PREPARATION TIME: 15 minutes* • *COOKING TIME: 45 minutes*

2 tablespoons nonfat chicken broth
½ cup chopped onion
1 cup uncooked bulgur
2 cups water

¼ cup orange juice
¼ cup sherry
½ cup chopped figs
1 teaspoon finely grated orange peel

1. Heat chicken broth in a skillet over medium heat. Sauté onion for 3 minutes, or until lightly golden.
2. Stir in bulgur.
3. Add water, orange juice, and sherry to skillet. Cover and simmer over low heat for 15 minutes.
4. Add figs and orange peel to skillet. Cook for 5 more minutes.

Calories Per Serving: 192
Fat: 1 g
Cholesterol: 0 mg
Protein: 5 g

Carbohydrates: 41 g
Dietary Fiber: 12 g
Sodium: 18 mg

Three-Grain Pilaf

Brown rice, bulgur, and barley are combined with onion, garlic, and hot pepper sauce.

YIELD: 3 servings • *PREPARATION TIME: 10 minutes* • *COOKING TIME: 35 minutes*

1¼ cups nonfat chicken broth
1 small onion, minced
1 clove garlic, minced
¼ cup uncooked bulgur

¼ cup uncooked brown rice
¼ cup uncooked pearl barley
⅛ teaspoon hot pepper sauce
¼ cup chopped fresh parsley

1. Heat ¼ cup chicken broth in a skillet over medium heat. Add onion and garlic and sauté for 5 minutes.

2. Add remaining broth, bulgur, brown rice, barley, and hot pepper sauce. Bring to a boil. Reduce heat and simmer for 30 minutes, or until liquid is absorbed.
3. Stir in parsley.

Calories Per Serving: 193	Carbohydrates: 39 g
Fat: 2 g	Dietary Fiber: 6 g
Cholesterol: 0 mg	Sodium: 205 mg
Protein: 8 g	

Bulgur with Apples and Raisins

Bulgur is paired with apple, raisins, cinnamon, and skim milk for a delicious and different breakfast.

YIELD: 2 servings ▪ PREPARATION TIME: 5 minutes ▪ COOKING TIME: 15 minutes

1½ cups water	*¼ cup raisins*
¾ cup uncooked bulgur	*⅛ teaspoon ground cinnamon*
1 apple, unpeeled, chopped	*1 cup skim milk (optional)*

1. Bring water to a boil in a saucepan. Add bulgur, apple, raisins, and cinnamon.
2. Return to a boil; reduce heat, cover, and simmer, stirring occasionally, for 15 minutes.
3. Serve immediately, as is or with ½ cup skim milk per serving.

Calories Per Serving: 310	Carbohydrates: 68 g
Fat: 1 g	Dietary Fiber: 14 g
Cholesterol: 2 mg	Sodium: 79 mg
Protein: 11 g	

Easy Microwave Apricot-Bulgur Breakfast

Bulgur, dried apricots, rolled oats, wheat bran, and molasses are combined and chilled overnight, then heated and served with skim milk.

YIELD: 4 servings ▪ PREPARATION TIME: 6 minutes plus overnight chilling time ▪
COOKING TIME: 8 minutes

½ cup uncooked bulgur
⅓ cup chopped dried apricots
2 tablespoons rolled oats
1 tablespoon toasted wheat bran

1 tablespoon molasses
1½ cups water
2 cups skim milk

1. Combine bulgur, apricots, oats, wheat bran, and molasses. Stir in water, cover, and chill overnight in a microwave-safe casserole.
2. Microwave, covered, at 100% HIGH for 6 minutes or until liquid is absorbed. Stir twice during cooking.
3. Transfer to individual bowls and serve with ½ cup skim milk per serving.

Calories Per Serving: 171
Fat: 1 g
Cholesterol: 2 mg
Protein: 7 g

Carbohydrates: 36 g
Dietary Fiber: 5 g
Sodium: 71 mg

Parsley-Bulgur Salad

Chopped parsley, tomatoes, onion, and bulgur are dressed with lime juice.

YIELD: 6 servings • *PREPARATION TIME: 10 minutes plus 15 minutes standing time*

1 cup water
½ cup uncooked bulgur
3 cups chopped parsley
¼ cup minced onion

3 large ripe tomatoes, chopped
¼ cup lime juice
¼ teaspoon ground black pepper

1. Bring water to a boil. Stir in bulgur. Remove from heat and allow to stand until liquid is absorbed, about 15 minutes. Drain any excess liquid.
2. Combine bulgur, parsley, and onion. Add the tomatoes, lime juice, and pepper and toss to coat ingredients.

Calories Per Serving: 59
Fat: 1 g
Cholesterol: 0 mg
Protein: 3 g

Carbohydrates: 13 g
Dietary Fiber: 2 g
Sodium: 30 mg

Spiced Tabbouleh

This version of tabbouleh is flavored with white wine, allspice, and cinnamon.

YIELD: 8 servings　•　PREPARATION TIME: 10 minutes plus 15 minutes standing time and 2 hours chilling time

1 cup water	⅛ teaspoon ground allspice
½ cup uncooked bulgur	⅛ teaspoon ground cinnamon
5 tablespoons lemon juice	6 scallions, chopped
1 tablespoon olive oil	1 cup chopped fresh parsley
2 tablespoons white wine	½ teaspoon dried mint
¼ teaspoon ground black pepper	3 ripe tomatoes, chopped

1. Bring water to a boil and stir in bulgur. Set aside until liquid is absorbed and bulgur is just tender, about 15 minutes. Drain any excess liquid.
2. Whisk together lemon juice, olive oil, wine, black pepper, allspice, and cinnamon.
3. Combine scallions, parsley, mint, and tomatoes in a large serving bowl. Add bulgur and lemon juice dressing. Chill for 2 hours.

Calories Per Serving: 66	Carbohydrates: 11 g
Fat: 2 g	Dietary Fiber: 3 g
Cholesterol: 0 mg	Sodium: 16 mg
Protein: 2 g	

Southwestern Tabbouleh

Serve this combination of bulgur, green bell pepper, onion, tomatoes, and jalapeños with nonfat baked corn chips.

YIELD: 20 servings, 2 chips each　•　PREPARATION TIME: 15 minutes　•
COOKING TIME: 10 minutes plus 15 minutes standing time and 2 hours chilling time

2 cups water	¼ teaspoon ground black pepper
¾ cup uncooked bulgur	3 pitted black olives, chopped
½ cup chopped green bell pepper	2 tablespoons dried cilantro
⅓ cup chopped onion	3 cloves garlic, minced
2 cups fresh or low-sodium canned tomatoes, chopped	3 tablespoons lime juice
1 jalapeño pepper, seeded and minced	1 tablespoon olive oil

1. Bring water to a boil. Stir in the bulgur and allow to stand until bulgur is just tender, about 15 minutes. Drain any excess liquid.
2. Transfer to a serving bowl. Add green bell pepper, onion, tomatoes, jalapeño pepper, black pepper, black olives, cilantro, garlic, lime juice, and olive oil. Mix thoroughly and refrigerate for 2 hours.

Calories Per Serving: 61

Fat: 2 g

Cholesterol: 0 mg

Protein: 2 g

Carbohydrates: 11 g

Dietary Fiber: 2 g

Sodium: 73 mg

Asparagus and Yellow Bell Pepper with Bulgur

Fresh asparagus mingles with yellow bell pepper, scallions, and bulgur.

YIELD: 6 servings ▪ *PREPARATION TIME: 10 minutes* ▪
COOKING TIME: 20 minutes plus 30 minutes chilling time

1½ cups water

⅔ cup uncooked bulgur

1 cup fresh asparagus, cut into 1-inch pieces

¼ cup minced scallions

¼ cup chopped yellow bell pepper

1 teaspoon dried basil

1 teaspoon white wine vinegar

1½ teaspoons olive oil

1. Bring water to a boil in a saucepan. Stir in bulgur. Return to a boil, reduce heat, cover, and simmer for 15 minutes. Drain any excess liquid.
2. Meanwhile, steam asparagus pieces until just tender-crisp, about 4 minutes.
3. Mix asparagus, bulgur, scallions, yellow bell pepper, and basil and set aside.
4. Combine vinegar and oil. Whisk briskly to blend, add to bulgur, and toss gently.
5. Cover and refrigerate for 30 minutes.

Calories Per Serving: 76

Fat: 2 g

Cholesterol: 0 mg

Protein: 3 g

Carbohydrates: 13 g

Dietary Fiber: 4 g

Sodium: 10 mg

Bell Pepper–Bulgur Slaw

A surprising variation on an old tradition.

YIELD: 4 servings • *PREPARATION TIME: 15 minutes, plus overnight bulgur soaking time*

4 cups shredded cabbage
1 green bell pepper, chopped
1 small onion, chopped
1 carrot, shredded
½ cup uncooked bulgur, soaked
   overnight in water (see p. 388)

1 cup nonfat plain yogurt
1 tablespoon lemon juice
¼ teaspoon ground black pepper
½ teaspoon celery seeds

1. Combine cabbage, green bell pepper, onion, carrot, and bulgur.
2. Mix yogurt, lemon juice, black pepper, and celery seeds.
3. Add dressing to vegetables and toss to coat.

Calories Per Serving: 142
Fat: 1 g
Cholesterol: 1 mg
Protein: 7 g

Carbohydrates: 29 g
Dietary Fiber: 7 g
Sodium: 70 mg

Broccoli-Bulgur Salad

Broccoli, carrot, and onion are teamed with bulgur

YIELD: 4 servings • *PREPARATION TIME: 25 minutes* •
COOKING TIME: 6 minutes plus 15 minutes standing time

1½ cups plus 1 tablespoon water
¼ cup uncooked bulgur
2 cups chopped broccoli
½ cup chopped carrot
¼ cup chopped purple onion
½ teaspoon sugar

½ teaspoon grated lemon rind
⅛ teaspoon ground black pepper
3 tablespoons lemon juice
1 teaspoon olive oil
1 clove garlic, minced

1. Bring 1½ cups water to a boil in a saucepan. Stir in bulgur; remove from heat and let stand until liquid is absorbed and bulgur is tender, about 15 minutes. Drain any excess liquid.

2. Steam broccoli until tender-crisp, about 3 minutes.
3. Combine bulgur, broccoli, carrot, and onion and stir well.
4. Whisk together sugar, lemon rind, black pepper, lemon juice, olive oil, garlic, and remaining 1 tablespoon water.
5. Toss with bulgur-vegetable mixture.

Calories Per Serving: 124	Carbohydrates: 25 g
Fat: 2 g	Dietary Fiber: 8 g
Cholesterol: 0 mg	Sodium: 24 mg
Protein: 5 g	

Spinach-Bulgur Salad
with Cumin-Yogurt Dressing

Spinach, red onion, and olive are mixed with bulgur.

YIELD: *4 servings* • PREPARATION TIME: *10 minutes* •
COOKING TIME: *10 minutes plus 20 minutes standing and cooling time*

½ cup water
½ cup uncooked bulgur
8 cups fresh spinach leaves torn into
    pieces
½ red onion, sliced
5 pitted black olives, sliced
3 tablespoons grated nonfat Parmesan

1 cup nonfat plain yogurt
1 tablespoon olive oil
2 tablespoons red wine vinegar
2 cloves garlic, minced
1 teaspoon ground cumin
¼ teaspoon ground black pepper

1. Bring water to a boil in a saucepan. Stir in bulgur. Allow to stand about 15 minutes, until liquid is absorbed. Drain any excess liquid. Allow to cool.
2. Mix together bulgur, spinach, onion, olives, and Parmesan.
3. Combine yogurt, olive oil, vinegar, garlic, cumin, and black pepper.
4. Toss bulgur-spinach mixture with yogurt dressing.

Calories Per Serving: 117	Carbohydrates: 17 g
Fat: 3 g	Dietary Fiber: 5 g
Cholesterol: 3 mg	Sodium: 130 mg
Protein: 7 g	

Summer Harvest Bulgur Salad

This combination of bulgur, balsamic vinegar, tomato juice, tomatoes, cucumber, and green bell pepper is as refreshing as a bowl of gazpacho.

YIELD: 6 servings • PREPARATION TIME: 15 minutes plus 15 minutes standing time and 1 hour chilling time

1 cup water
¾ cup low-sodium tomato juice
¾ cup uncooked bulgur
1 tablespoon olive oil
3 tablespoons balsamic vinegar
1 clove garlic, minced
½ teaspoon ground cumin

¼ teaspoon ground black pepper
⅛ teaspoon hot pepper sauce
3 scallions, minced
2 large ripe tomatoes, chopped
1 cucumber, diced
1 green bell pepper, diced

1. Bring water and ½ cup tomato juice to a boil. Stir in bulgur; remove from heat, cover, and allow to stand for 15 minutes, until bulgur is just tender. Drain any excess liquid.
2. Mix the remaining tomato juice, olive oil, vinegar, garlic, cumin, black pepper, and hot pepper sauce in a small bowl. Add to the bulgur and mix well.
3. Add the scallions, tomatoes, cucumber, and green bell pepper and toss gently.
4. Refrigerate for at least 1 hour before serving.

Calories Per Serving: 133
Fat: 3 g
Cholesterol: 0 mg
Protein: 4 g

Carbohydrates: 29 g
Dietary Fiber: 6 g
Sodium: 22 mg

Warm Shrimp Tabbouleh

Small shrimp, cucumber, onion, parsley, and bulgur are the featured ingredients in this tabbouleh.

YIELD: 4 servings • PREPARATION TIME: 15 minutes plus 15 minutes standing time

1½ cups water
¾ cup uncooked bulgur
1 teaspoon olive oil

½ pound small cooked shrimp, peeled and deveined
1 cucumber, diced

1 cup minced onion   3 tablespoons lemon juice
½ cup chopped fresh parsley

1. Bring water to a boil. Stir in bulgur; remove from heat, cover, and allow to stand for 15 minutes, until bulgur is tender. Drain any excess liquid.
2. Combine olive oil, shrimp, cucumber, onion, parsley, and lemon juice. Mix with bulgur. Serve warm.

Calories Per Serving: 177   Carbohydrates: 27 g
Fat: 2 g   Dietary Fiber: 7 g
Cholesterol: 85 mg   Sodium: 409 mg
Protein: 16 g

Mandarin-Turkey-Spinach Salad with Bulgur

Mandarin oranges, smoked turkey, mushrooms, purple onion, and bulgur are tossed with lemon-flavored dressing.

YIELD: 4 servings • *PREPARATION TIME: 10 minutes plus 20 minutes standing time*

1 cup water   2 ounces smoked turkey, cut into ¼-inch
1 cup uncooked bulgur   strips
2 cups chopped spinach   3 tablespoons fresh lemon juice
1 cup sliced fresh white mushrooms 1½ tablespoons olive oil
1 cup drained juice-packed mandarin 1 tablespoon water
   oranges, halved   ¼ teaspoon ground black pepper
¼ cup chopped purple onion   1 clove garlic, minced

1. Bring water to a boil. Stir in bulgur. Let stand until water is absorbed.
2. Combine bulgur, spinach, mushrooms, mandarin oranges, onion, and turkey in a large serving bowl. Mix well.
3. Whisk together lemon juice, olive oil, water, black pepper, and garlic. Add to bulgur-spinach mixture.

Calories Per Serving: 182   Carbohydrates: 35 g
Fat: 2 g   Dietary Fiber: 10 g
Cholesterol: 8 mg   Sodium: 201 mg
Protein: 9 g

Bulgur-Stuffed Tomatoes

Ripe tomatoes are stuffed with a mélange of bulgur, cucumber, red bell pepper, celery, and parsley.

YIELD: *8 servings* • PREPARATION TIME: *25 minutes plus 15 minutes standing time*

2½ cups nonfat chicken broth
1½ cups uncooked bulgur
8 large ripe tomatoes
1 tablespoon olive oil
1 cucumber, seeded and chopped fine
1 red bell pepper, chopped fine

½ cup chopped celery
½ cup chopped fresh parsley
1 tablespoon dried mint
¼ teaspoon ground black pepper
¼ cup lemon juice

1. Bring broth to a boil. Stir in bulgur. Remove from heat and allow to stand until bulgur is just tender, about 15 minutes. Drain any excess liquid.
2. Cut off the stem end of the tomatoes and discard. Remove the pulp from each tomato, leaving a wall about ¼ inch thick. Discard pulp.
3. Combine the bulgur, olive oil, cucumber, red bell pepper, celery, parsley, mint, black pepper, and lemon juice. Mix thoroughly.
4. Stuff the tomato shells with the bulgur mixture.

Calories Per Serving: 185
Fat: 3 g
Cholesterol: 0 mg
Protein: 7 g

Carbohydrates: 38 g
Dietary Fiber: 8 g
Sodium: 104 mg

Peppers Stuffed with Tabbouleh and Beans

Crisp green bell pepper halves are stuffed with pinto beans, plum tomatoes, and bulgur seasoned with lime juice and cumin.

YIELD: *8 servings* • PREPARATION TIME: *25 minutes plus 20 minutes standing time*

3 cups water
½ cup nonfat chicken broth
1½ cups uncooked bulgur
1 tablespoon olive oil
½ cup lime juice

1 teaspoon minced lime peel
2 cloves garlic, minced
2 cups cooked or canned low-sodium
    pinto beans, rinsed and drained
6 plum tomatoes, chopped

¼ *cup finely chopped radish*
1 *medium onion, chopped*
½ *cup chopped fresh parsley*
1 *teaspoon ground cumin*

4 *green bell peppers, cut in half hori-*
  zontally, seeds discarded
parsley sprigs for garnish

1. Combine water and broth, and bring to a boil. Stir in bulgur, remove from heat, and let stand for 20 minutes, until bulgur is tender.
2. Drain bulgur and transfer to a large bowl.
3. Combine olive oil, lime juice, lime peel, and garlic. Stir into the bulgur.
4. Add beans, tomatoes, radish, onion, parsley, and cumin. Toss gently.
5. Stuff the hollowed peppers with the bulgur mixture, garnish with parsley, and serve.

Calories Per Serving: 219
Fat: 3 g
Cholesterol: 0 mg
Protein: 9 g

Carbohydrates: 44 g
Dietary Fiber: 12 g
Sodium: 21 mg

Basic Bulgur Pilaf

Sautéed scallion and bulgur are simmered in chicken broth.

YIELD: 4 servings ▪ *PREPARATION TIME: 5 minutes* ▪
COOKING TIME: 20 minutes plus 20 minutes standing time

2¼ *cups nonfat chicken broth*
¼ *cup minced scallion*

¼ *teaspoon ground black pepper*
1 *cup uncooked bulgur*

1. Heat ¼ cup chicken broth in a saucepan over medium heat. Sauté scallion until it begins to soften, about 4 minutes.
2. Add remaining chicken broth and black pepper. Bring to a boil. Stir in bulgur. Reduce heat, cover, and simmer until liquid is absorbed, about 15 minutes.

Calories Per Serving: 150
Fat: 1 g
Cholesterol: 0 mg
Protein: 8 g

Carbohydrates: 31 g
Dietary Fiber: 9 g
Sodium: 217 mg

Sage-Bulgur Pilaf

The pungent taste of sage enhances this traditional pilaf.

YIELD: 4 servings • PREPARATION TIME: 15 minutes • COOKING TIME: 18 minutes

1½ cups nonfat chicken broth
3 tablespoons chopped onion
1 clove garlic, minced

⅔ cup uncooked bulgur
½ teaspoon dried sage
1 tablespoon minced fresh parsley

1. Heat ¼ cup chicken broth in a saucepan. Add onion and garlic and sauté until onion is lightly golden, about 3 minutes.
2. Add remaining chicken broth and bring to a boil. Stir in bulgur and sage. Return to a boil, reduce heat, and simmer, covered, until bulgur is tender, about 15 minutes. Drain excess liquid. Stir in parsley and serve.

Calories Per Serving: 93
Fat: 1 g
Cholesterol: 0 mg
Protein: 5 g

Carbohydrates: 19 g
Dietary Fiber: 6 g
Sodium: 131 mg

Bulgur Pilaf with Thyme and Vermicelli

Bulgur and vermicelli are simmered in thyme-seasoned chicken broth.

YIELD: 6 servings • PREPARATION TIME: 15 minutes • COOKING TIME: 20 minutes

2¼ cups nonfat chicken broth
4 scallions, chopped
1 green bell pepper, chopped
3 ounces vermicelli, broken into small
    pieces

1 cup uncooked bulgur
1 teaspoon dried thyme
¼ teaspoon ground black pepper
¼ cup chopped fresh parsley

1. Heat ¼ cup chicken broth in a saucepan. Add scallions and green bell pepper. Sauté until pepper begins to soften, about 4 minutes.
2. Add vermicelli and sauté 3 additional minutes. Add bulgur and cook, stirring, 1 minute.
3. Add the remaining chicken broth, thyme, and black pepper. Bring to a boil. Reduce heat; simmer until bulgur is tender, about 12 minutes.
4. Drain any remaining liquid. Sprinkle with parsley and serve.

Calories Per Serving: 147
Fat: 1 g
Cholesterol: 0 mg
Protein: 7 g

Carbohydrates: 30 g
Dietary Fiber: 6 g
Sodium: 133 mg

Butternut Bulgur Pilaf

Sautéed cubed winter squash and onion are simmered with bulgur and basil.

YIELD: 4 servings • PREPARATION TIME: 10 minutes • COOKING TIME: 20 minutes

1¼ cups nonfat chicken broth
1 cup peeled butternut squash, cut into
    ½-inch cubes
¼ cup chopped onion

½ cup uncooked bulgur
½ teaspoon dried basil
⅛ teaspoon ground black pepper

1. Heat ¼ cup chicken broth in a saucepan over medium heat. Add squash and onion and sauté until onion becomes lightly golden.
2. Add remaining chicken broth and bring to a boil. Stir in bulgur, basil, and pepper. Return to a boil; reduce heat, cover, and simmer until bulgur is just tender.

Calories Per Serving: 100
Fat: 1 g
Cholesterol: 0 mg
Protein: 4 g

Carbohydrates: 22 g
Dietary Fiber: 5 g
Sodium: 110 mg

Jalapeño-Apple Bulgur Pilaf

Chopped apple, jalapeños, and sautéed scallion are simmered with bulgur in chicken broth.

YIELD: 4 servings • PREPARATION TIME: 10 minutes • COOKING TIME: 17 minutes

2 cups nonfat chicken broth
⅓ cup chopped scallion
1 cup uncooked bulgur

2 jalapeño chile peppers, seeded and
    minced
1 apple, peeled and finely chopped
1 tablespoon chopped fresh parsley

1. Heat ¼ cup chicken broth in a saucepan. Add scallion and sauté until pieces begin to soften, about 2 minutes.
2. Add remaining chicken broth and bring to a boil. Stir in bulgur and jalapeño. Return to boil; reduce heat, cover, and simmer until bulgur is just tender.
3. Stir in apple and parsley. Serve hot.

Calories Per Serving: 159
Fat: 1 g
Cholesterol: 0 mg
Protein: 7 g

Carbohydrates: 34 g
Dietary Fiber: 9 g
Sodium: 382 mg

Lentil-Bulgur Pilaf

Lentils and bulgur are spiced with cayenne pepper and cumin.

YIELD: 6 servings ▪ PREPARATION TIME: 20 minutes ▪
COOKING TIME: 20 minutes plus 20 minutes standing time

1 cup lentils
2½ cups water
1 cup uncooked bulgur
3 tablespoons nonfat chicken broth

1 medium onion, minced
½ cup minced fresh parsley
⅛ teaspoon cayenne pepper
½ teaspoon ground cumin

1. Place lentils in a large saucepan. Add water and bring to a boil. Reduce heat, cover, and simmer for 15 minutes. Remove from heat; stir in bulgur, cover, and set aside for 20 minutes, until bulgur is tender. Drain any excess liquid.
2. Heat chicken broth in a skillet over medium heat. Add onion and sauté until it turns lightly golden, about 3 minutes.
3. Combine lentil-bulgur mixture, onion, parsley, cayenne pepper, and cumin in a large bowl and mix well.

Calories Per Serving: 175
Fat: 1 g
Cholesterol: 0 mg
Protein: 10 g

Carbohydrates: 34 g
Dietary Fiber: 9 g
Sodium: 33 mg

Red Lentil–Bulgur Pilaf

Small round red lentils are combined with bulgur and garnished with sautéed onion and minced green pepper and scallion.

YIELD: 6 servings • *PREPARATION TIME: 10 minutes* •
COOKING TIME: 20 minutes plus 20 minutes standing time

1 cup red lentils
2½ cups water
½ cup uncooked bulgur
¼ cup nonfat chicken broth

1 medium onion, chopped
½ teaspoon ground black pepper
1 scallion, minced
¼ cup minced green bell pepper

1. Place the lentils in a large saucepan. Add water and bring to a boil. Reduce heat, cover, and simmer for 15 minutes. Remove from heat, stir in bulgur, cover, and let stand for 20 minutes, until bulgur is tender. Drain any excess liquid.
2. Heat chicken broth in a skillet and sauté the onion until the onion is golden.
3. Season lentil-bulgur mixture with black pepper, pour onion over it, garnish with scallion and green pepper, and serve.

Calories Per Serving: 131
Fat: 1 g
Cholesterol: 0 mg
Protein: 8 g

Carbohydrates: 25 g
Dietary Fiber: 7 g
Sodium: 18 g

Garlic-Chickpea Bulgur Pilaf

Chickpeas, garlic, and cumin are the featured players in this bulgur pilaf.

YIELD: 4 servings • *PREPARATION TIME: 15 minutes* •
COOKING TIME: 15 minutes plus 15 minutes standing time

1½ cups water
1 cup uncooked bulgur
1½ teaspoons olive oil
1 small onion, chopped
1 clove garlic, minced

1½ cups cooked or low-sodium canned
*   chickpeas, rinsed and drained*
1 teaspoon ground cumin
1 cup nonfat chicken broth
¼ teaspoon ground black pepper

1. Bring water to a boil. Remove from heat; stir in bulgur, cover, and let stand for 15 minutes, until bulgur is tender. Drain any excess liquid.
2. Heat olive oil in a large, heavy skillet. Add onion and garlic; sauté until they are golden. Stir in chickpeas; add cumin, bulgur and chicken broth. Bring to a boil; reduce heat, cover, and simmer until liquid is absorbed, about 10 minutes. Season with black pepper and serve.

Calories Per Serving: 243
Fat: 3 g
Cholesterol: 5 mg
Protein: 10 g

Carbohydrates: 46 g
Dietary Fiber: 14 g
Sodium: 395 mg

Bulgur-Turkey Meatballs

Ground turkey, onion, bulgur, and parsley are shaped into appetizer-size meatballs.

YIELD: *40 meatballs (8 servings, 5 meatballs each)* • PREPARATION TIME: *20 minutes*
• COOKING TIME: *15 minutes plus 15 minutes standing time*

1 cup water
½ cup bulgur
1 pound ground turkey breast
1 medium onion, minced

2 tablespoons minced fresh parsley
½ teaspoon dried mint
⅛ teaspoon ground black pepper

1. Bring water to a boil. Stir in bulgur, cover, and let stand 15 minutes, until bulgur is just tender.
2. Preheat oven to 375 degrees.
3. Drain any excess liquid from bulgur, and add turkey, onion, parsley, mint, and black pepper. Mix well. Form balls 1¼ inches in diameter.
4. Place meatballs in a nonstick baking dish and bake until lightly browned, about 15 minutes.

Calories Per Serving: 101
Fat: 1 g
Cholesterol: 31 mg
Protein: 16 g

Carbohydrates: 8 g
Dietary Fiber: 2 g
Sodium: 32 mg

Mushrooms Stuffed with Bulgur

Large mushroom caps are stuffed with a mixture of mushroom stems, bulgur, and scallion, then baked.

YIELD: 12 servings, 2 mushrooms each ▪ *PREPARATION TIME: 25 minutes* ▪
COOKING TIME: 30 minutes

¼ cup nonfat chicken broth	¼ teaspoon ground black pepper
3 cloves garlic, minced	1 scallion, minced
½ cup uncooked bulgur	2 egg whites
1 cup water	3 tablespoons grated nonfat Parmesan
½ cup mushroom stems, chopped	2 tablespoons chopped fresh parsley
½ teaspoon dried oregano	24 large, fresh white mushroom caps

1. Heat chicken broth in a large saucepan over medium heat. Add garlic; sauté 1 minute. Stir in bulgur and mix to coat.
2. Add water, mushroom stems, oregano, black pepper, and scallion. Cook, stirring occasionally, until mixture comes to a boil, about 3 minutes.
3. Reduce heat, cover, and simmer until bulgur is just tender, about 10 minutes.
4. Preheat oven to 400 degrees.
5. Beat egg whites. Combine with 2 tablespoons Parmesan and parsley. Add to bulgur mixture.
6. Arrange mushroom caps on a nonstick baking sheet. Place a spoonful of bulgur on each mushroom cap. Bake for 12 minutes. Sprinkle with remaining Parmesan and serve.

Calories Per Serving: 34	Carbohydrates: 6 g
Fat: 0 g	Dietary Fiber: 2 g
Cholesterol: 1 mg	Sodium: 27 mg
Protein: 2 g	

Tomatoes Stuffed with Mushrooms and Bulgur

Grilled tomatoes are filled with a mushroom–bulgur stuffing.

YIELD: 6 servings ▪ *PREPARATION TIME: 25 minutes* ▪
COOKING TIME: 12 minutes plus 20 minutes standing time

1 cup water
½ cup uncooked bulgur
2 tablespoons nonfat chicken broth
1½ cups thinly sliced scallions
1 pound fresh white mushrooms,
    quartered
¾ teaspoon hot pepper sauce
⅓ cup chopped fresh parsley

½ teaspoon dried basil
2 tablespoons lemon juice
3 tablespoons grated nonfat Parmesan
6 tomatoes, halved lengthwise, pulp re-
    moved
1 tablespoon olive oil
¼ teaspoon ground black pepper

1. Bring water to a boil. Stir in bulgur. Remove from heat and allow to stand until bulgur just turns tender, about 20 minutes. Drain any excess liquid.
2. Preheat broiler.
3. Heat chicken broth in a large skillet over medium heat. Add scallions and sauté until they begin to soften. Add mushrooms and hot pepper sauce, and sauté until the mushrooms begin to brown. Add parsley and basil.
4. Add bulgur, lemon juice, and 2 tablespoons Parmesan. Stir well.
5. Brush the cut edges of the tomato halves with olive oil. Arrange them in a single layer in a large, shallow, nonstick baking dish and sprinkle with black pepper.
6. Fill the tomato halves with the bulgur-mushroom mixture. Broil for 15 minutes. Remove from broiler and sprinkle with remaining cheese.

Calories Per Serving: 216
Fat: 2 g
Cholesterol: 3 mg
Protein: 8 g

Carbohydrates: 46 g
Dietary Fiber: 9 g
Sodium: 46 mg

Tomato-Lentil Stew with Bulgur

Lentils, onion, and celery are simmered with carrots and tomatoes and served over bulgur.

YIELD: 8 servings • PREPARATION TIME: 20 minutes •
COOKING TIME: 50 minutes plus 15 minutes standing time

1½ cups dried lentils
1 cup low-sodium tomato sauce
½ cup chopped onion
½ cup chopped celery
1 teaspoon dried thyme

1 teaspoon dried oregano
3 cups water
2 carrots, chopped
2 large ripe tomatoes, chopped
½ cup uncooked bulgur

1. Combine lentils, tomato sauce, onion, celery, thyme, oregano, and 2 cups of water in a large pot. Bring to a boil. Reduce heat, cover, and simmer for 30 minutes.
2. Add the carrots and tomatoes. Return to a boil; reduce heat, cover, and simmer for 20 minutes.
3. Meanwhile, bring remaining 1 cup water to a boil. Stir in bulgur. Remove from heat, cover, and let stand for 15 minutes, until bulgur is just tender. Drain any excess liquid.
4. Serve bulgur topped with lentil stew.

Calories Per Serving: 126
Fat: 1 g
Cholesterol: 0 mg
Protein: 7 g

Carbohydrates: 25 g
Dietary Fiber: 6 g
Sodium: 27 mg

Summer Squash–Bulgur Casserole

Bulgur, onion, yellow squash, mushrooms, tomatoes, and cheddar cheese are joined to make this hearty casserole.

YIELD: 6 servings • PREPARATION TIME: 20 minutes •
COOKING TIME: 40 minutes plus 20 minutes standing time

2 cups water
1 cup uncooked bulgur
2 tablespoons lemon juice
2 tablespoons nonfat chicken broth
2 cups chopped onion
1½ cups diced yellow summer squash
2 cloves garlic, minced

1½ cups sliced fresh white mushrooms
1½ cups fresh or low-sodium canned tomatoes, diced
½ cup shredded nonfat cheddar
½ cup skim milk
4 egg whites, beaten

1. Bring water to a boil. Stir in bulgur; remove from heat, add 1 tablespoon lemon juice, cover, and let stand for 20 minutes, or until bulgur is just tender. Drain any excess liquid.
2. Preheat oven to 325 degrees.
3. Heat chicken broth in a large skillet over medium heat. Add onion; sauté for 3 minutes. Add squash and garlic; sauté 3 more minutes. Add mushrooms and tomatoes; sauté 4 additional minutes.
4. Remove vegetables from heat. Add remaining 1 tablespoon lemon juice. Mix well and set aside.

5. Combine cheese, milk, egg whites, and bulgur. Mix well.
6. Spread half the bulgur in a nonstick baking dish. Cover with the vegetable mixture. Top with the remaining half of the bulgur.
7. Cover and bake for 20 minutes. Uncover and bake for an additional 10 minutes. Serve immediately.

Calories Per Serving: 164
Fat: 1 g
Cholesterol: 0 mg
Protein: 10 g

Carbohydrates: 30 g
Dietary Fiber: 7 g
Sodium: 309 mg

Chili with Bulgur

Bulgur is prepared in tomato juice, then combined with chili powder, red bell pepper, celery, carrot, pinto beans, and mushrooms.

YIELD: 8 servings • PREPARATION TIME: 30 minutes plus 5 minutes standing time •
COOKING TIME: 50 minutes

2½ cups low-sodium tomato juice
½ cup uncooked bulgur
2¼ cups nonfat chicken broth
2 medium onions, chopped
1 red bell pepper, chopped
2 cloves garlic
2 stalks celery, chopped
1 carrot, chopped

1 pound fresh white mushrooms, chopped
1 tablespoon low-sodium tomato paste
3 tablespoons chili powder
2 teaspoons ground cumin
2 cups low-sodium canned pinto beans, rinsed and drained
8 tablespoons shredded nonfat cheddar

1. Bring tomato juice to a boil in a saucepan. Stir in bulgur; remove from heat, cover, and let stand for 15 minutes. Drain, reserving the tomato juice, and set the bulgur aside.
2. Heat ¼ cup chicken broth in a large Dutch oven. Add the onions and sauté until they become translucent, about 2 minutes. Add the red bell pepper and garlic and sauté 1 minute. Add the celery and carrot and sauté 1 more minute. Add the mushrooms and sauté 1 additional minute.
3. Add the reserved tomato juice, remaining chicken broth, tomato paste, chili powder, and cumin. Bring to a boil. Reduce heat and simmer for 20 minutes. Add the pinto beans and simmer for 15 minutes. Stir in the bulgur and simmer for 5 minutes.

4. Transfer to serving bowls, sprinkle each with a tablespoon of cheese, and serve.

Calories Per Serving: 169	Carbohydrates: 31 g
Fat: 2 g	Dietary Fiber: 9 g
Cholesterol: 0 mg	Sodium: 305 mg
Protein: 12 g	

Bulgur and Vegetables

Mushrooms, broccoli, carrot, yellow squash, and green peppers are served over cooked bulgur.

YIELD: 8 servings ･ *PREPARATION TIME: 25 minutes* ･ *COOKING TIME: 25 minutes*

2½ cups water	½ cup sliced yellow summer squash
1 cup uncooked bulgur	2 green bell peppers, cut into ¼-inch
¼ cup nonfat chicken broth	strips
½ cup chopped onion	1 teaspoon dried thyme
2½ cups sliced fresh white mushrooms	½ teaspoon dried rosemary
1 cup broccoli florets	½ teaspoon ground black pepper
1 cup chopped carrot	½ cup shredded nonfat cheddar

1. Bring 2 cups water to a boil. Stir in bulgur; remove from heat, cover, and set aside.
2. Heat chicken broth in a large skillet over medium heat. Add onion and sauté until it is lightly golden.
3. Add bulgur. Return to a boil; reduce heat, cover, and simmer until bulgur is tender, about 15 minutes.
4. Combine remaining ½ cup water, mushrooms, broccoli, carrot, squash, and green bell peppers in a large saucepan. Cover and cook over medium heat until broccoli is just tender, about 6 minutes.
5. Sprinkle vegetables with thyme, rosemary, and black pepper. Simmer for 2 additional minutes.
6. Pour vegetables over bulgur, sprinkle with cheddar, and serve.

Calories Per Serving: 91	Carbohydrates: 19 g
Fat: 0 g	Dietary Fiber: 5 g
Cholesterol: 0 mg	Sodium: 120 mg
Protein: 5 g	

Curried Vegetables with Bulgur

Sautéed onion, bulgur, peas, and corn are simmered in curried chicken broth.

YIELD: 4 servings • PREPARATION TIME: 15 minutes • COOKING TIME: 12 minutes

2 teaspoons olive oil
1½ cups chopped onion
½ cup uncooked bulgur
1 teaspoon curry powder

1 cup nonfat chicken broth
½ cup fresh or frozen green peas
½ cup fresh, thawed frozen, or canned
   corn kernels

1. Heat oil in a large skillet. Add onion and sauté until it turns translucent. Stir in bulgur and curry powder and mix well.
2. Add chicken broth. Stir well; simmer for 10 minutes.
3. Add peas and corn and continue to simmer until vegetables are heated through and bulgur is tender, about 5 minutes.

Calories Per Serving: 136
Fat: 3 g
Cholesterol: 0 mg
Protein: 5 g

Carbohydrates: 25 g
Dietary Fiber: 7 g
Sodium: 103 mg

Bulgur with Baked Chicken

Baked chicken is served over bulgur simmered with mushrooms, peas, dill, and thyme.

YIELD: 6 servings • PREPARATION TIME: 15 minutes • COOKING TIME: 55 minutes

6 skinless chicken breast cutlets, about 4
   ounces each
2¼ cups nonfat chicken broth
1 cup sliced fresh white mushrooms
1 cup uncooked bulgur

1 teaspoon dried dill
¼ teaspoon ground black pepper
¼ teaspoon dried thyme
1 9-ounce package frozen peas, thawed
½ cup chopped onion

1. Preheat oven to 350 degrees.
2. Wrap chicken cutlets in foil and bake until tender, about 30 minutes.
3. Heat ¼ cup chicken broth in a large saucepan over medium heat. Add mushrooms and sauté until they become lightly golden, about 2 minutes.

4. Stir in bulgur, remaining 2 cups chicken broth, dill, black pepper, and thyme. Bring to a boil; reduce heat, cover, and cook for 10 minutes.
5. Stir in peas and onion. Continue to cook for 6 minutes.
6. Serve baked chicken on the bulgur-mushroom mixture.

Calories Per Serving: 280   Carbohydrates: 24 g
Fat: 3 g   Dietary Fiber: 7 g
Cholesterol: 110 mg   Sodium: 179 mg
Protein: 42 g

Orange-Cumin Chicken Breast Cutlets with Bulgur

Bulgur is flavored with garlic, cumin, and orange juice and baked with chicken cutlets.

YIELD: 6 servings ∙ *PREPARATION TIME: 20 minutes* ∙ *COOKING TIME: 70 minutes*

3¼ cups nonfat chicken broth
6 skinless chicken breast cutlets, about 4 ounces each
3 small onions, chopped
2 cloves garlic, minced

1½ cups uncooked bulgur
½ teaspoon ground cumin
¼ cup minced green bell pepper
¼ cup orange juice

1. Preheat oven to 350 degrees.
2. Heat ¼ cup chicken broth in a large skillet over medium heat. Add chicken and sauté until browned, about 6 minutes. Transfer the chicken to a large nonstick baking dish.
3. Add the onions and garlic to the skillet and sauté until onions turn golden.
4. Add the bulgur to the onions and stir. Add the cumin, green pepper, and orange juice. Mix thoroughly and spoon over the chicken.
5. Bring the remaining 3 cups broth to a boil and pour over the chicken. Cover and bake until the meat is tender, about 20 minutes.

Calories Per Serving: 314   Carbohydrates: 36 g
Fat: 3 g   Dietary Fiber: 10 g
Cholesterol: 98 mg   Sodium: 267 mg
Protein: 40 g

Turkey-Bulgur Salad

Turkey breast, peas, and scallion are joined with bulgur in a mustard-vinaigrette dressing.

YIELD: 4 servings ▪ PREPARATION TIME: 15 minutes plus 20 minutes standing time

2 cups water
⅔ cup uncooked bulgur
1 cup frozen peas, cooked and cooled
8 ounces turkey breast cutlets, cooked
   and cut into ½-inch cubes
1 scallion, minced

1 tablespoon Dijon mustard
2 tablespoons white wine vinegar
1 teaspoon olive oil
¼ teaspoon ground black pepper
1 teaspoon dried dill

1. Bring water to a boil. Stir in bulgur; remove from heat, cover, and allow to stand for 20 minutes, until bulgur is tender. Drain any excess liquid.
2. Add peas and turkey cubes and toss gently.
3. Combine the scallion, mustard, vinegar, olive oil, pepper, and dill and whisk until all ingredients are blended.
4. Toss the salad with the dressing.

Calories Per Serving: 173
Fat: 2 g
Cholesterol: 28 mg
Protein: 14 g

Carbohydrates: 25 g
Dietary Fiber: 8 g
Sodium: 184 mg

Chicken—Lima Bean Bulgur

Chicken breast, yellow bell pepper, and lima beans are combined with bulgur and topped with yogurt dressing.

YIELD: 6 servings ▪ PREPARATION TIME: 20 minutes ▪
COOKING TIME: 10 minutes plus 15 minutes standing time and 1 hour chilling time

1½ cups water
1 cup uncooked bulgur
¼ cup nonfat chicken broth
3 skinned chicken breast cutlets, about 3
   ounces each, cut into ½-inch cubes
1 cup plain nonfat yogurt

1 teaspoon dried dill
3 tablespoons lemon juice
1 yellow bell pepper, chopped
1 cup frozen baby lima beans, cooked
   and cooled
6 large leaves romaine lettuce

1. Bring water to a boil in a saucepan. Stir in bulgur, remove from heat, and allow to stand for 15 minutes, until bulgur is tender. Drain any excess liquid.
2. Heat chicken broth in a large skillet over medium heat. Add chicken and sauté until cooked through and lightly brown, about 10 minutes. Transfer chicken to a large bowl.
3. Combine yogurt, dill, and lemon juice. Mix well, cover, and refrigerate until ready to serve.
4. Combine bulgur and cooked chicken with yellow bell pepper and lima beans. Mix well, cover, and refrigerate for 1 hour.
5. Serve salad on lettuce leaves and top with yogurt dressing.

Calories Per Serving: 186
Fat: 1 g
Cholesterol: 28 mg
Protein: 16 g

Carbohydrates: 29 g
Dietary Fiber: 7 g
Sodium: 65 mg

Ginger Chicken with Rice and Bulgur

Chicken breast, fresh gingerroot, sun-dried tomatoes, and mushrooms are baked with bulgur and rice.

YIELD: 6 servings • *PREPARATION TIME: 25 minutes plus 10 minutes standing time* • *COOKING TIME: 25 minutes*

1 ounce sun-dried tomatoes
¼ cup boiling water
3¼ cups nonfat chicken broth
1 medium onion, chopped
3 cups sliced fresh white mushrooms
2 cloves garlic, minced
½ cup uncooked bulgur
4 teaspoons ground cumin

1 teaspoon minced fresh gingerroot
1 cup uncooked white rice
1 teaspoon dried thyme
¼ teaspoon ground black pepper
1½ pounds skinless chicken breast cutlets
¼ cup chopped fresh parsley

1. Cover sun-dried tomatoes with boiling water and let soak for 10 minutes, or until tomatoes begin to soften. Drain the tomatoes, reserving the liquid. Slice very thin.
2. Meanwhile, heat ¼ cup chicken broth in a large oven-safe pot over medium heat. Add the onion, mushrooms, and garlic, and sauté until onion is translucent, about 3 minutes. Add bulgur, cumin, and gingerroot and cook for 1 minute. Add the rice and cook, stirring constantly, for 2 additional minutes.

3. Preheat oven to 325 degrees.
4. Add remaining 3 cups broth, tomato soaking liquid, soaked tomato slices, thyme, and black pepper to the pot. Bring to a boil. Remove from heat.
5. Add chicken to pot; cover and bake until it is thoroughly cooked, about 20 minutes. Drain.
6. Serve chicken over bulgur and rice. Garnish with parsley.

Calories Per Serving: 288
Fat: 3 g
Cholesterol: 55 mg
Protein: 26 g

Carbohydrates: 43 g
Dietary Fiber: 4 g
Sodium: 234 mg

Black Beans and Oranges with Bulgur

Bulgur, black beans, and fresh orange sections are tossed with lemon juice.

YIELD: *8 servings* ▪ PREPARATION TIME: *15 minutes plus 15 minutes standing time*

1 cup water
½ cup uncooked bulgur
3 large oranges
⅓ cup lemon juice
2 cloves garlic, minced

½ teaspoon ground black pepper
2 cups low-sodium canned black beans,
   rinsed and drained
¼ cup chopped onion

1. Bring water to a boil. Stir in bulgur. Remove from heat and allow to stand until bulgur is just tender, about 15 minutes. Drain any excess liquid.
2. Separate oranges into whole sections and mix into the bulgur.
3. Whisk together the lemon juice, garlic, and black pepper.
4. Mix beans and onion with the bulgur. Add the lemon juice dressing and toss to coat.

Calories Per Serving: 149
Fat: 1 g
Cholesterol: 0 mg
Protein: 7 g

Carbohydrates: 32 g
Dietary Fiber: 11 g
Sodium: 7 g

OTHER GRAINS

❖

Basic Cooked Wheat Berries ▪ Basic Hominy Grits ▪ Basic Cooked Millet ▪ Wheat Berry Salad Italia ▪ Zucchini Stuffed with Millet and Mushrooms ▪ Vegetable–Wheat Berry Salad ▪ Raisin–Apricot–Three Grain Salad ▪ Millet-Vegetable Medley ▪ Acorn Squash–Hominy Toss ▪ Dilled Kasha with Orzo ▪ Lemon Millet ▪ Parsleyed Kasha and Penne ▪ Zucchini-Kasha Boats

Basic Cooked Wheat Berries

This delightful, nutritious basic grain dish is made with wheat berries.

YIELD: 3 servings • COOKING TIME: 65 minutes plus 10 minutes standing time

¾ cup wheat berries   3 cups water or nonfat chicken broth

1. Combine the wheat berries and water, and bring to a rolling boil.
2. Cover, reduce heat, and simmer for 35 minutes, or until most of the liquid is absorbed.
3. Uncover and cook for 10 minutes longer to separate the grains.
4. Reduce heat, cover, and cook until wheat berries are tender and all liquid has been absorbed, about 20 minutes.
5. Remove pan from heat and let wheat berries stand, covered, 10 minutes.
6. Fluff with a fork.

Calories Per Serving: 104   Carbohydrates: 15 g
Fat: 3 g   Dietary Fiber: 3 g
Cholesterol: 0 mg   Sodium: 11 mg
Protein: 7 g

Basic Hominy Grits

A long-time favorite in the South, hominy grits are made from corn with the hull and germ removed.

YIELD: 3 servings • COOKING TIME: 20 minutes plus 5 minutes standing time

5 cups water or nonfat chicken broth   1 cup hominy grits

1. Bring water to a boil over high heat in a saucepan.
2. Slowly add hominy and cook, covered, over low heat for 20 minutes.
3. Remove from heat and let stand for 5 minutes.
4. Fluff with a fork and serve.

Calories Per Serving: 290   Carbohydrates: 62 g
Fat: 1 g   Dietary Fiber: 9 g
Cholesterol: 0 mg   Sodium: 18 mg
Protein: 7 g

Basic Cooked Millet

Tiny yellow whole kernels of millet can be stored in the refrigerator for 5 months.

YIELD: 3 servings • *COOKING TIME: 20 minutes plus 10 minutes standing time*

1 cup hulled millet seeds   *3 cups water or nonfat chicken broth*

1. Place millet in a large skillet and stir over medium-high heat until the seeds turn light gold. Remove from heat.
2. Pour water or broth into a large saucepan, add millet, and bring to a boil over high heat.
3. Cover and cook over medium-low heat until millet is tender and all liquid has been absorbed, about 20 minutes.
4. Remove from heat and let stand, covered, 10 minutes.
5. Fluff with a fork.

Calories Per Serving: 252   Carbohydrates: 49 g
Fat: 3 g   Dietary Fiber: 10 g
Cholesterol: 0 mg   Sodium: 10 mg
Protein: 7 g

Wheat Berry Salad Italia

Eggplant, tomato, white rice, and mozzarella are tossed with nutty-tasting wheat berries in this Mediterranean salad.

YIELD: 6 servings • *PREPARATION TIME: 20 minutes* •
COOKING TIME: 1 hour 15 minutes plus rice cooking time

2 cups water
½ cup wheat berries
1 medium eggplant, about 1 pound, peeled and cut into ½-inch slices
2 teaspoons olive oil
2½ cups cooked long-grain white rice (see p. 190)
2 cups fresh or low-sodium canned tomatoes, chopped

¼ cup chopped fresh parsley
½ teaspoon dried basil
⅛ teaspoon ground black pepper
1 clove garlic, minced
1¼ cups nonfat mozzarella cut into small cubes
1½ tablespoons red wine vinegar

1. Preheat oven to 400 degrees.
2. Bring water to a boil. Stir in wheat berries and return to a boil. Reduce heat, cover, and simmer until wheat berries are tender, about 45 minutes.
3. Meanwhile, place eggplant slices in a single layer on a nonstick baking sheet. Lightly brush the tops with half the olive oil. Bake for 15 minutes. Turn eggplant slices over, brush with remaining oil, and bake for 15 additional minutes.
4. Cool eggplant for 5 minutes, then dice.
5. Toss wheat berries with eggplant, rice, tomatoes, parsley, basil, black pepper, garlic, mozzarella, and wine vinegar.

Calories Per Serving: 213
Fat: 2 g
Cholesterol: 5 mg
Protein: 13 g

Carbohydrates: 36 g
Dietary Fiber: 2 g
Sodium: 211 mg

Zucchini Stuffed with Millet and Mushrooms

A delightful and different treatment for an old favorite.

YIELD: 4 servings • PREPARATION TIME: 20 minutes • COOKING TIME: 26 minutes

¼ cup nonfat chicken broth
1 small onion, chopped
2 cloves garlic, minced
1 cup sliced fresh white mushrooms
2 cups cooked millet (see p. 417)
¼ cup chopped fresh parsley

2 teaspoons dried oregano
2 teaspoons dried basil
2 large zucchini, halved lengthwise, seeds and ½ of flesh removed
4 egg whites, beaten

1. Heat broth in a large skillet. Add onion, garlic, and mushrooms and sauté for 3 minutes. Stir in millet, parsley, oregano, and basil and cook for 3 more minutes. Set aside.
2. Preheat oven to 350 degrees.
3. Arrange zucchini halves in a shallow nonstick baking dish.
4. Stir beaten egg whites into onion-millet mixture and fill the zucchini halves.
5. Pour ½ inch of water in the baking dish and bake the zucchini for 30 minutes.

Calories Per Serving: 189
Fat: 2 g
Cholesterol: 0 mg
Protein: 9 g

Carbohydrates: 35 g
Dietary Fiber: 7 g
Sodium: 83 mg

Vegetable–Wheat Berry Salad

Wheat berries, snow peas, bean sprouts, carrot, cucumber, and water chestnuts are served with a flavorful ginger-sesame dressing.

Yield: 6 servings ▪ *Preparation Time: 20 minutes* ▪
Cooking Time: 50 minutes plus 45 minutes chilling time

4 cups water
1½ cups wheat berries
¼ pound snow peas, trimmed and cut
   into julienne strips
1½ cup bean sprouts, rinsed and drained
1 carrot, grated
1 cucumber, chopped
½ cup thinly sliced water chestnuts
¼ cup rice wine vinegar
2 tablespoons low-sodium soy sauce

1 tablespoon sesame oil
1 tablespoon sugar
⅛ teaspoon chili sauce
½ teaspoon ground black pepper
¼ cup minced scallion
1 teaspoon dried cilantro
2 tablespoons minced fresh gingerroot
1 teaspoon minced orange peel
1 clove garlic, minced

1. Bring water to a boil in a large saucepan.
2. Stir in wheat berries; reduce heat and simmer until tender, about 45 minutes. Drain thoroughly.
3. In a large bowl, evenly mix wheat berries, snow peas, bean sprouts, carrot, cucumber, and water chestnuts.
4. Whisk together vinegar, soy sauce, sesame oil, sugar, chili sauce, black pepper, scallion, cilantro, gingerroot, orange peel, and garlic.
5. Toss wheat berry mixture with dressing. Chill for 45 minutes before serving.

Calories Per Serving: 128
Fat: 3 g
Cholesterol: 0 mg
Protein: 5 g

Carbohydrates: 23 g
Dietary Fiber: 3 g
Sodium: 200 mg

Raisin–Apricot–Three Grain Salad

Wheat berries, brown rice, and protein-rich millet are combined with raisins, apricots, and an orange juice dressing.

YIELD: 15 servings • PREPARATION TIME: 15 minutes •
COOKING TIME: 50 minutes

2 quarts water
1½ cups wheat berries
1¼ cups uncooked long-grain brown rice
1 cup uncooked millet
1 cup raisins
1 cup chopped dried apricots

1 tablespoon olive oil
1 cup orange juice
½ teaspoon ground cumin
½ cup chopped fresh parsley
3 tablespoons slivered toasted almonds

1. Bring 2 quarts water to a boil in a large pot. Stir in wheat berries; reduce heat and simmer for 10 minutes.
2. Stir in rice and simmer for 25 minutes more.
3. Stir in millet and continue to simmer for 15 minutes.
4. Drain grains and rinse them under cold running water to chill them.
5. Toss wheat berries, rice, millet, raisins, and apricots with olive oil, orange juice, and cumin. Garnish with parsley and almonds before serving.

Calories Per Serving: 187
Fat: 3 g
Cholesterol: 0 mg
Protein: 5 g

Carbohydrates: 38 g
Dietary Fiber: 5 g
Sodium: 5 mg

Millet-Vegetable Medley

Lima beans and tomatoes are features of this quick and easy dish.

YIELD: 6 servings • PREPARATION TIME: 5 minutes plus overnight millet soaking time
• COOKING TIME: 1 hour

2 cups uncooked millet
4 cups water
1 medium onion, chopped
2 cloves garlic, minced
2 cups fresh or canned Italian plum
tomatoes, with juice, chopped

1 cup fresh or frozen, thawed lima
beans
2 teaspoons dried basil
¼ teaspoon ground black pepper
2 tablespoons chopped fresh parsley

1. Soak millet overnight in 4 cups water.
2. Preheat oven to 350 degrees.
3. Combine millet with onion, garlic, tomatoes, beans, basil, black pepper, and parsley in a nonstick baking dish and bake for 1 hour.

Calories Per Serving: 309

Fat: 3 g

Cholesterol: 0 mg

Protein: 10 g

Carbohydrates: 60 g

Dietary Fiber: 13 g

Sodium: 14 mg

Acorn Squash–Hominy Toss

Other winter squash, such as butternut, can be substituted for the acorn squash in this salad, which includes hominy, red bell pepper, and scallions.

YIELD: 6 servings ▪ *PREPARATION TIME: 30 minutes* ▪
COOKING TIME: 12 minutes

2 cups water

4 cups acorn squash, peeled and cut into
   ½-inch cubes

2 cups canned hominy, drained

1 red bell pepper, chopped

½ teaspoon chili powder

¼ teaspoon hot pepper sauce

¼ cup chopped fresh parsley

1 tablespoon olive oil

¼ teaspoon dried cilantro

¼ cup chopped scallions

1. Bring water to a boil in a steamer.
2. Steam squash for 12 minutes, or until it is just tender.
3. Combine the squash, hominy, red bell pepper, chili powder, and hot pepper sauce. Chill for 45 minutes.
4. Combine parsley, olive oil, cilantro, and scallions. Toss with squash mixture and serve.

Calories Per Serving: 118

Fat: 3 g

Cholesterol: 0 mg

Protein: 2 g

Carbohydrates: 23 g

Dietary Fiber: 3 g

Sodium: 123 mg

Dilled Kasha with Orzo

Orzo and kasha are joined with celery, scallions, and a dill-accented dressing.

YIELD: 4 servings ▪ *PREPARATION TIME: 10 minutes* ▪ *COOKING TIME: 23 minutes*

4 cups water
¾ cup orzo
1½ cups nonfat chicken broth
¾ cup kasha
¾ cup sliced celery

1 teaspoon olive oil
½ teaspoon dried dill
½ teaspoon ground black pepper
¼ cup chopped fresh parsley
2 scallions, chopped

1. Bring water to a boil in a saucepan. Stir in orzo, reduce heat, and simmer for 8 minutes.
2. Bring chicken broth to a slow boil.
3. Meanwhile, stir kasha in a nonstick skillet over low heat until lightly toasted, about 3 minutes.
4. Add hot broth to skillet and stir into kasha. Add celery, olive oil, dill, and black pepper. Cover and cook for 12 minutes. Drain.
5. Toss orzo into kasha mixture with parsley and scallions.

Calories Per Serving: 225
Fat: 3 g
Cholesterol: 0 mg
Protein: 10 g

Carbohydrates: 40 g
Dietary Fiber: 5 g
Sodium: 148 mg

Lemon Millet

Lemon juice and lemon peel add tang to basic millet.

YIELD: 3 servings ▪ *COOKING TIME: 20 minutes plus 10 minutes standing time*

1 cup uncooked millet
4 cups water
2 tablespoons lemon juice

1 tablespoon minced lemon peel
¼ cup honey

1. Place millet in a large skillet and stir over medium-high heat until the seeds turn light gold. Remove from heat.
2. Combine water, lemon juice, lemon peel, and honey in a saucepan. Bring to a boil. Stir in millet.

3. Cover, reduce heat to medium-low, and cook until millet is tender and all liquid has been absorbed, about 20 minutes.
4. Remove pan from heat and allow millet to stand, covered, for 10 minutes.
5. Fluff with a fork.

Calories Per Serving: 341
Fat: 3 g
Cholesterol: 0 mg
Protein: 7 g

Carbohydrates: 73 g
Dietary Fiber: 10 g
Sodium: 14 mg

Parsleyed Kasha and Penne

Pasta is paired with sautéed kasha and fresh parsley.

YIELD: 7 servings • PREPARATION TIME: 15 minutes plus pasta cooking time • COOKING TIME: 16 minutes

2¼ cups nonfat chicken broth
¼ cup chopped onion
1 clove garlic, minced
1 cup kasha

1 egg white, beaten
⅛ teaspoon ground black pepper
4 cups hot cooked penne
2 tablespoons minced fresh parsley

1. Heat ¼ cup chicken broth in a skillet over medium heat. Add onion and garlic. Sauté until onion is golden.
2. Combine kasha and beaten egg white. Mix well. Add kasha mixture to skillet.
3. Cook, stirring, over medium heat for 3 minutes. Reduce heat.
4. Bring remaining 2 cups broth to a boil in a saucepan. Slowly stir in kasha mixture. Add black pepper. Reduce heat, cover, and simmer until liquid is absorbed, about 10 minutes.
5. Combine kasha-onion mixture, penne, and parsley. Toss and serve.

Calories Per Serving: 190
Fat: 1 g
Cholesterol: 0 mg
Protein: 8 g

Carbohydrates: 38 g
Dietary Fiber: 4 g
Sodium: 118 mg

Zucchini-Kasha Boats

When gardens and produce departments overflow with zucchini, try baking them with this kasha stuffing.

YIELD: 6 servings • *PREPARATION TIME: 20 minutes* • *COOKING TIME: 35 minutes*

8 cups water
3 medium zucchini, halved lengthwise
2 egg whites
½ cup kasha
1 tablespoon olive oil
1 medium onion, chopped

3 cloves garlic, minced
1 cup nonfat chicken broth
½ teaspoon dried basil
⅛ teaspoon ground black pepper
2 tablespoons grated nonfat Parmesan

1. Preheat oven to 350 degrees.
2. Bring water to a boil in a large pot; add zucchini. Reduce heat, cover, and cook until just tender, about 5 minutes.
3. Drain zucchini and rinse with cold water. Scoop out pulp, leaving a ¼-inch shell. Reserve pulp.
4. Measure ¾ cup of zucchini pulp and chop. Save the rest for another use.
5. Place zucchini halves in a shallow, nonstick baking pan and set aside.
6. Beat egg whites; stir in kasha and mix until well coated.
7. Heat olive oil in a large skillet. Add onion and garlic and sauté until onion is light brown, about 3 minutes. Add kasha and cook, stirring, for 1 minute.
8. Stir the chopped zucchini pulp into the kasha mixture. Add broth, basil, and black pepper. Cover and cook until kasha is just tender, about 8 minutes.
9. Remove from heat. Fill the zucchini shells with the kasha and bake for 15 minutes. Sprinkle with Parmesan and serve.

Calories Per Serving: 111
Fat: 3 g
Cholesterol: 2 mg
Protein: 6 g

Carbohydrates: 17 g
Dietary Fiber: 2 g
Sodium: 250 mg

INDEX

✦